The Nebraska hardcover edition includes:

The Journals of the Lewis and Clark Expedition, Volume 1
Atlas of the Lewis and Clark Expedition

The Journals of the Lewis and Clark Expedition, Volume 2
August 30, 1803–August 24, 1804

The Journals of the Lewis and Clark Expedition, Volume 3
August 25, 1804–April 6, 1805

The Journals of the Lewis and Clark Expedition, Volume 4
April 7–July 27, 1805

The Journals of the Lewis and Clark Expedition, Volume 5
July 28–November 1, 1805

The Journals of the Lewis and Clark Expedition, Volume 6
November 2, 1805–March 22, 1806

The Journals of the Lewis and Clark Expedition, Volume 7
March 23–June 9, 1806

The Journals of the Lewis and Clark Expedition, Volume 8
June 10–September 26, 1806

**The Journals of the Lewis and Clark Expedition, Volume 9
The Journals of John Ordway, May 14, 1804–September 23, 1806, and Charles Floyd, May 14–August 18, 1804**

The Journals of the Lewis and Clark Expedition, Volume 10
The Journal of Patrick Gass, May 14, 1804–September 23, 1806

The Journals of the Lewis and Clark Expedition, Volume 11
The Journals of Joseph Whitehouse, May 14, 1804–April 2, 1806

The Journals of the Lewis and Clark Expedition, Volume 12
Herbarium of the Lewis and Clark Expedition

The Journals of the Lewis and Clark Expedition, Volume 13
Comprehensive Index

BISON BOOKS

Sponsored by the Center for
Great Plains Studies,
University of Nebraska–Lincoln
and the American
Philosophical Society, Philadelphia

A Project of the Center for Great Plains Studies, University of Nebraska–Lincoln

GARY E. MOULTON, EDITOR

The Definitive Journals of Lewis & Clark

John Ordway and Charles Floyd

VOLUME 9 of the Nebraska Edition

University of Nebraska Press

Lincoln and London

Manufactured in the United States of America. First paperback printing: 2003

∞

LIBRARY OF CONGRESS CATALOGING-IN-PUBLICATION DATA
Journals of the Lewis and Clark Expedition. Volume 2–8
The definitive journals of Lewis and Clark / Gary E. Moulton, editor ; Thomas W. Dunlay, assistant editor.
p. cm.
Vols. 7–8: Gary E. Moulton, editor.
"A project of the Center for Great Plains Studies, University of Nebraska–Lincoln."
Paperback edition of v. 2–8 of the Journals of the Lewis and Clark Expedition, originally published in 13 v. by the University of Nebraska Press, c1983–2001.
Includes bibliographical references and index.
Contents – v.2. From the Ohio to the Vermillion – v.3. Up the Missouri to Fort Mandan – v.4. From Fort Mandan to Three Forks – v.5. Through the Rockies to the Cascades – v.6. Down the Columbia to Fort Clatsop – v.7. From the Pacific to the Rockies – v.8. Over the Rockies to St. Louis.
ISBN 0-8032-8009-2 (v.2: alk. paper) – ISBN 0-8032-8010-6 (v.3: alk. paper) – ISBN 0-8032-8011-4 (v.4: alk. paper) – ISBN 0-8032-8012-2 (v.5: alk. paper) – ISBN 0-8032-8013-0 (v.6: alk. paper) – ISBN 0-8032-8014-9 (v.7: alk. paper) – ISBN 0-8032-8015-7 (v.8: alk. paper)
1. Lewis and Clark Expedition (1804–1806). 2. West (U.S.) – Description and travel. 3. Lewis, Meriwether, 1774–1809 – Diaries. 4. Clark, William, 1770–1838 – Diaries. 5. Explorers – West (U.S.)–Diaries. I. Lewis, Meriwether, 1774–1809. II. Clark, William, 1770–1838. III. Moulton, Gary E. IV. Dunlay, Thomas W., 1944– . V. University of Nebraska–Lincoln. Center for Great Plains Studies. VI. Title.
F 592.4 2002 917.804'2–dc21 2002018113

ISBN 0-8032-8021-1 (vol.9: alk. paper)

Contents

Preface

This volume and the two to follow rely largely on the editorial work of previous books in this edition. Therefore, the editorial notes and supporting material in these three books owe a debt to former consultants and friends of the project. Here again we extend our great appreciation to the unselfish work of these generous people.

Nevertheless, we have several persons to thank specifically for help with this volume. The journal of Sergeant John Ordway is located at the American Philosophical Society, Philadelphia, where the project received the able assistance of Beth Carroll-Horrocks, Martin L. Levitt, Martha Harrison, Roy E. Goodman, and Edward C. Carter II. At the State Historical Society of Wisconsin, Madison, we were aided with the journal of Sergeant Charles Floyd by Josephine L. Harper and Harry Miller. Closer to home, help came from John R. Wunder, Linda J. Ratcliffe, and Sharon Bays of the Center for Great Plains Studies, University of Nebraska–Lincoln, and Thomas W. Dunlay and Doris VanSchooten of the project.

Scholars again provided advice in their respective disciplines. BOTANY: A. T. Harrison, Westminster College, Salt Lake City, and Robert B. Kaul, University of Nebraska–Lincoln. ETHNOLOGY: John Ludwickson, Nebraska State Historical Society, Lincoln. LINGUISTICS: American Indian linguistic data in the notes were collected by Raymond J. DeMallie, Indiana University, and were provided by himself and by the following persons: *Shoshone.* Wick R. Miller, University of Utah, and Christopher Loether, Idaho State University. TOOLS: Michael E. Dotson, Brookston, Indiana.

The project received financial support from Samuel H. Douglas III (Whittier, California), Nelson S. Weller (Piedmont, California), the Lewis and Clark Trail Heritage Foundation, and the National Endowment for the Humanities, an independent federal agency.

We extend our sincerest appreciation to all these individuals but must ourselves carry blame for any deficiencies in the present work.

Editorial Procedures

For volumes 9, 10, and 11, the final journal-volumes in this edition of the journals of the Lewis and Clark expedition, the principal editorial goal remains that stated in volume 2, that is, to present users with a reliable text largely uncluttered with editorial interference. Readers can find a fuller statement of editing principles in the Editorial Procedures in volume 2. The following paragraphs explain the purpose and extent of editorial annotation included in the present volumes, since the approach to annotation here differs from the method followed with the journals of Lewis and Clark.

Believing that the annotation to Lewis's and Clark's journals in the previous volumes furnished the essential information to understand the events, persons, and inquiries of the expedition, we deemed it unnecessary to reproduce those notes in their entirety in these enlisted men's volumes. We assume that most users turn to Lewis's and Clark's journals as their primary source of information on the expedition and use the enlisted men's journals as supplements. Where the enlisted men provide new or substantially different material in their journals, however, we have commented on that fact and explained the matter as extensively as we did in the captains' journals.

The annotation for the present three volumes falls under four large categories: people, places, animals, and plants. These have been the fields of greatest interest to users of the journals and were the areas most often noticed by the enlisted men. These were also the points on which these men were most likely to provide information not found in the captains' journals. Our aim was to establish a method that was not unnecessarily redundant to previous volumes but that provided readers with essential information so they did not need to refer constantly to other books.

In these volumes the notes have been abbreviated considerably. For example, authoritative sources are not listed in most notes since that information was provided in previous volumes. We do not provide geographic locations for every point mentioned in the enlisted men's journals, nor do we necessarily locate each day's campsite: these locales were discussed in detailed notes to the captains' journals. In the present volumes we try to give a sense of place from day to day by locating the major physical features passed each day. In this way readers should have no trouble determining the party's location at any given time. For natural history matters we provide both the popular and scientific names for flora and fauna. Occasionally we direct readers to notes for the captains' journals for extended discussions of difficult identifications. For the most part, the enlisted men were observing and commenting on the same plants and animals as the captains. In fact, there appears to be only one instance in which a biological specimen was mentioned by an enlisted journalist but was not also identified in the captains' journals.

Wherever possible we recognize every Indian tribe noted by the journalists, no matter how indirectly, and name all Indian individuals who we are able to identify. We also transliterate and translate native terms that have not previously been addressed or direct readers to fuller explication in earlier volumes. Sergeant John Ordway seems to have been the only enlisted man to mention Indian terms not noted by Lewis or Clark. It is in fact likely that the enlisted men copied the scant scientific information they have in their diaries from the journals of Lewis and Clark. Because of this we try not to add repetition in the notes to necessary redundancies in the text. Our hope is to give readers sufficient annotation to understand the text without reporting the obvious.

EDITORIAL SYMBOLS

[roman]	Word or phrase supplied or corrected.
[roman?]	Conjectural reading of the original.
[*italics*]	Editor's remarks within a document.
[*WC: italics*]	William Clark's emendations or interlineations.
[*X: italics*]	Emendations or interlineations of the unknown or an unidentified person.
⟨roman⟩	Word or phrase deleted by the writer and restored by the editor.

Introduction to Volume 9

The essential, definitive record of the Lewis and Clark expedition is contained in the journals and observations of the two captains, "the writingest explorers of their time," in the words of Donald Jackson.[1] If no one else associated with the enterprise had written a word we would still have a marvelous narrative replete with geographic, zoological, botanical, and ethnographic information. In fact, however, at least four other members of the party did set down their own daily accounts. This edition brings them together with those of their commanders for the first time.

President Thomas Jefferson did not order the actual keeping of separate journals by anyone other than the captains. In his final instructions to Lewis, however, he did suggest that "several copies of these as well as of your other notes should be made at leisure times, & put into the care of the most trust-worthy of your attendants, to guard, by multiplying them, against the accidental losses to which they will be exposed."[2] All this would seem to require is that some of the "attendants" copy the captains' journals verbatim. Apparently Lewis and Clark, at an early stage, decided to do something else. On May 26, 1804, less than two weeks out from River Dubois, the captains noted that "The sergts . . . are directed each to keep a separate journal from day to day of all passing accurences, and such other observations on the country &c. as shall appear to them worthy of notice.—"[3]

In his last communication to Jefferson from Fort Mandan in April 1805, Lewis wrote: "We have encouraged our men to keep journals, and seven of them do so, to whom in this respect we give every assistance in our power."[4] Lewis had a sense of history; in departing westward from the Mandan villages he compared his little fleet of pirogues and canoes to the vessels of Captain Cook.[5] The significance of his enterprise warranted as complete a record as possible. It might be too much to ask any enlisted men to copy their officers' voluminous journals, but those so inclined could be encouraged to add their bit to the record.

At least some of the men who went with Lewis and Clark seem to have shared that sense of history. They were volunteers, after all, and although some of them no doubt simply hoped to escape from irksome military discipline or to find good beaver streams, others evidently knew very well that this was the chance of a lifetime, that they were involved in something that would survive them, something greater than their individual contribution. The combination of that sense of history with a degree of literacy and considerable diligence made a few of them journal keepers.

To appreciate the work of these men, let us remember the conditions under which they wrote. Most days of the voyage involved hard physical labor, working canoes upstream, loading and unloading bulky equipment, hunting and butchering, tanning leather, making moccasins, cooking, chopping and shaping wood, caring for horses and searching for strays, mounting guard, portaging around falls and rapids, all of it while exposed to every kind of weather and to the attacks of insects and grizzly bears, with the constant danger of physical injury from accidents. At the end of such a day, perhaps while others were dancing to Pierre Cruzatte's fiddle, a journal keeper would have to write by the light of a campfire in notebooks somehow kept safe from the elements. According to Lewis, seven of the thirty-odd men had the perseverance and the sense of the destiny to try.

They wrote under the same conditions as the captains, and like them wrote not only for themselves. It seems probable that they examined each other's journals, and perhaps Lewis and Clark read them, too. We know that on July 14, 1804, having lost his notes for the previous day, Clark had "to refur to the . . . Journals of Serjeants." The enlisted men's journals were intended as part of the record; they were public documents and we cannot expect any deep psychological revelations. No one recorded explicitly, for example, his opinion of Lewis or Clark or Sacagawea.

Literacy was the first requirement. It is probable that some of the men could not even write their own names. Historians have expressed considerable humor over Clark's awkward grammar and his versatility as a speller, but he was little worse than many contemporaries who like him were men of affairs, government officials, and army officers. Comparison of Clark's journal with those of the enlisted men should keep us from laughing too much at Clark. Nor should we be overly amused at the enlisted men, for none of their journals suggests stupidity or dullness. They tried to the best of their ability to record an extraordinary experience.

Sergeants in the army had to be literate, since they kept records for their companies, and it is not too surprising that three of the four enlisted men's journals that we now have are those of sergeants. John Ordway and Charles Floyd held that rank from the start of the trip, and Patrick Gass was promoted some three months out to fill the place of the deceased Floyd. Joseph Whitehouse is the only private whose journal we now have. Ordway's spelling and grammar are, if anything, better than Clark's. We cannot judge Gass's performance for we do not have his original writing. Floyd and Whitehouse apparently struggled with writing, but there is rarely doubt about what they meant.

We have four enlisted men's journals, in one form or another. Lewis indicated that seven men were keeping journals, and the discrepancy requires some notice, although few hard conclusions can be made. Since the other sergeants were expected to keep journals, one would assume that Sergeant Nathaniel Pryor would also do so, but no document demonstrating this has come to light. Pryor served later on as an army officer and an Indian agent, but other men filled those posts on the frontier who could barely sign their names. On August 12, 1806, Clark noted that Pryor had left behind saddlebags containing his "papers," but Pryor had just returned from being separated from the main party, and the papers could have consisted only of letters he was supposed to deliver to a Canadian trader, and perhaps a journal of his separate trip, which began barely three weeks before. In any case, Pryor went back and recovered the saddlebags, so the papers, whatever they were, were not then lost. There is simply no clear evidence to show that Pryor was one of the seven journal keepers mentioned by Lewis.

It is fairly certain that one private besides Whitehouse kept some sort of journal, because Robert Frazer announced his intention to publish by issuing a prospectus soliciting subscribers barely a month after the party returned to St. Louis, promising "An accurate description of the Missouri and its several branches; of the mountains separating the Eastern from the Western waters; of the Columbia river and the Bay it forms on the Pacific Ocean; of the face of the Country in general; of the several Tribes of Indians on the Missouri and Columbia rivers . . . ," and with all this "a variety of Curious and interesting occurrences during a voyage of two years four months and nine days." The account, Frazer made clear, was "Published by Permission of Captn. Meriwether Lewis."[6] If the journal was anything like what Frazer promised, that it was never published is a great pity. Given the importance of the expedition this is surprising, especially since Patrick Gass was able to secure publication of his work the next year and since there were six further editions of his book in six years. Clearly it was not lack of public interest in Lewis and Clark's discoveries that held Frazer's work back. Whatever the problem was, Frazer passed from view and so did his journal; we have no clue as to its fate.

In April 1805, when Lewis wrote that seven men were keeping journals, Floyd was already dead. If we accept Pryor and Frazer as journal keepers, along with Gass, Ordway, and Whitehouse, we still have two others to account for. It is possible that Lewis counted Floyd, whose journal was sent back from Fort Mandan, even though his record had ceased the previous August. There is a possibility that Private Alexander Willard kept a journal, and with Willard and Floyd we would have Lewis's seven journal keepers.[7] One way or another a considerable part of the record appears to be lost, perhaps forever.

The journals that remain belong with those of Lewis and Clark, supporting them to the best of their ability as they did during the voyage. After the return Lewis evaluated his men, each according to his individual merits, and then wrote of them all: "the Ample support which they gave me under every difficulty; the manly firmness which they evinced on every necessary occasion; and the patience and fortitude with which they submitted to, and bore, the fatigues and painful sufferings incident to my late tour to the Pacific Ocean, entitles them to my warmest approbation and thanks."[8]

JOHN ORDWAY

Sergeant John Ordway clearly made an important contribution to the success of the expedition, and he has left us in many ways the fullest of the enlisted men's records. Yet we know frustratingly little about him. Virtually every mention of him in the captains' journals refers simply to his performance of some duty, with no other comment. There could be no better evidence that he did his job well. Born in New Hampshire in about 1775, apparently he had some of the qualities often attributed to New Englanders, including steadiness, diligence, and dependability. He was serving in Captain Russell Bissell's company of the First Infantry Regiment when he joined Lewis and Clark, and the captains apparently made him a sergeant before any of the others who held that rank with the Corps of Discovery. He was left in charge at Camp Dubois on various occasions when the two officers had to be absent.[9] In other words, he was the "top sergeant" of the outfit, expected to preserve discipline and see that things ran smoothly. He probably had a regular army way of doing things that pleased Lewis and Clark but perhaps did not sit too well with some of the newly enlisted frontiersmen. At any rate, on returning to Camp Dubois on one occasion, the captains reprimanded Reubin Field and John Shields for disobeying Ordway who, Lewis noted, "has during their necessary absence been charged with the execution of their orders; acting from those orders expressly, and not from his own capriece, and who, is in all respects accountable to us for the faithfull observance of the same."[10] That Ordway continued as a sergeant indicates that his performance was satisfactory.

Since Ordway, like the other members of the Corps, was a volunteer, we might assume that he had a sense of adventure and wanted to do something more than serve out his enlistment. More insight into his character can be gained from some family letters written before he left on the voyage of discovery. In September 1803 he wrote to his brother Stephen of his homesickness, denying a rumor that he had become engaged, and asking his brother to present his compliments to a young lady named Betsey Crosby, saying, "the probability is, that if She remains in a State of celibacy till my return I may perhaps join hands with hir yet."[11] Miss Crosby apparently found Ordway's promises too indefinite, or the state of celibacy too irksome, and married someone else. Ordway probably joined the Corps of Discovery when the captains passed Kaskaskia, Illinois, where he was stationed, in November 1803. In April 1804 he wrote to his "Honored Parence" telling them of his new enlistment: "I am now on an expidition to the westward, with Capt. Lewis and Capt. Clark. . . . We are to ascend the Missouri River with a boat as far as it is navigable and then to go by land, to the western ocean, if nothing prevents, &c." He also told them that "I am So happy as to be one of them pick'd men from the armey, and I and all the party are if we live to Return, to Receive our Discharge when ever we return again toe the united States if we chuse it." He expected to be gone eighteen months to two years and to receive a "great Reward," of "15 dollars pr. month and at least 400 ackers of first Rate land, and if we make Great Discoveries as we expect, the united States, has promised to make us Great Rewards more than we are promised, &c."[12]

Ordway was the most faithful of all the party's journal keepers; even Clark missed a few days, but the sergeant has an entry for every day from May 14, 1804, when the Corps left River Dubois, to September 23, 1806, when they returned to St. Louis—863 days in all. He perhaps waited a day or two to fill in entries in especially trying times, but he cannot have waited long. Even during the most difficult periods, such as the journey over the Lolo Trail in September 1805, his entries are fair-sized paragraphs. During the uneventful days at Fort Mandan and Fort Clatsop, he contented himself with a few lines. His grammar, spelling, and vocabulary are at least as good as Clark's.

Ordway did not record the detailed courses and distances of each day's journey, as the captains did, nor the wealth of scientific data; the events of each day were his primary concern, yet he shows evidence of curiosity and an interest in the things and people around him. On May 5, 1805, he noted that the grizzly "bair" killed that day was one "which the natives and the french tradors call white but all of the kind that we have seen is of a light brown only owing to the climate as we suppose." The captains have no such thoughts about the animal's color that day, although they give a more detailed description. While among the Flathead Indians on September 5, 1805, Ordway observed, "these natives have the Stranges language of any we have ever yet seen. they appear to us as though they had an Impedement in their Speech or brogue on their tongue. we think perhaps that they are the welch Indians, &. C." Clark, the only one of the officers keeping a journal at this point, said only that the Flathead (Salish) tongue "is a gugling kind of language Spoken much thro the Throught." Ordway also reconsidered the old legend of the elusive Welsh Indians when he was among the Flatheads.

On July 16, 1805, Lewis and Clark both tell us that they sent a man back for an axe forgotten at their previous night's camp, their standard procedure when such a lapse occurred. They do not mention the man's name, and it is to Ordway's honesty that we owe the knowledge that he was the culprit. On the return journey, when Clark and Lewis made separate explorations, Clark sent Ordway with nine other men in canoes down the Missouri from the Three Forks to the Great Falls. The sergeant was on his own and provides the only record of this part of the expedition from July 13 to July 19, 1806, when he joined the party under Sergeant Gass that Lewis had left at the Great Falls. Ordway then promptly recorded the events of Lewis's party when they were separated from Clark, and after meeting Lewis on July 28 he described the tragic events of the captain's party. Describing Reubin Field's killing of a Blackfeet Indian on July 27 he became almost poetic: "he drew but one breath the wind of his breath followed the knife & he fell dead."

Ordway did not choose any more than did the other journal keepers to provide much information about the day-to-day personal relationships within the party. The nature of his office surely caused special strains and frustrations, but he said nothing of this; there is no hint of the incidents of disobedience at Camp Dubois, which occurred before he began his journal. We would like to know how the top sergeant of the Corps of Discovery evaluated the men who served with him, and the two men who commanded him, but the New Hampshireman maintained his discretion. Like the captains he was writing a public document, not a private record of emotions. Even the desertion of Moses Reed, which aroused Floyd's indignation, is reported by Ordway in the most matter-of-fact way, on August 6, 1804.

Ordway's life following the return to St. Louis is nearly as obscure as it was before. He accompanied Lewis and a party of Indians to Washington, D.C., in late 1806, took his discharge from the army, and returned to New Hampshire. In 1809 he settled in Missouri, where he married and became prosperous, acquiring "two plantations under good cultivation peach and apple orchards, good buildings &c &c." He did not enjoy them for long, however, for both he and his wife were dead by 1817.[13]

Ordway's journal is in three notebooks. The first, handstitched sheets covered by loose boards, apparently started out as the Orderly Book of the Corps, which the sergeant would have kept as part of his duties, and became his journal on May 14, 1804, when the expedition set out. This book lasted him until the end of September 1805. The next day, October 1, at the Canoe Camp on the Clearwater River in Idaho, he commenced writing in a notebook bound in stiff boards and covered with marbled paper that lasted until May 15, 1806, when he was back on the Clearwater some miles upstream at Camp Chopunnish. A collection of uncovered sheets then served him until September 23, 1806, when he closed: "the party all considerable much rejoiced that we have the Expedition Completed and now we look for boarding in Town and wait for our Settlement an then we entend to return to our native homes to See our parents once more as we have been so long from them.— finis."

Ordway turned his journal over to the captains in return for $300. It was among the papers that Clark provided Nicholas Biddle for use in preparing his history of the expedition. Biddle found it very useful and judged it much better than Gass's journal, which he also examined, probably in its printed form. Indeed he was so fond of it that he never returned it to Clark, as he was supposed to, nor did he turn it over to the American Philosophical Society with other expedition documents in 1816, as Jefferson wished. His grandsons found it among his papers in 1913, and it was edited by Milo Milton Quaife for publication with Lewis and Clark's Eastern Journal by the State Historical Society of Wisconsin.[14] It now appears together with the other expedition journals for the first time.

CHARLES FLOYD

Sergeant Charles Floyd, according to Lewis, was "a young man of much merit."[15] We do not know a great deal more about him. He has the tragic fame of being the only man of the party to die on the expedition, and an impressive monument rises over his remains at Sioux City, Iowa, near the place where he died. Born in 1782, he was one of the "nine young men from Kentucky" who joined Lewis at the Falls of the Ohio. He may have been a relative of Clark; at any rate, on hearing of his death his brother Nathaniel wrote to their sister Nancy that "he was well cared for as Clark was there." We do know that he was a cousin of Sergeant Pryor. Although he enlisted from civilian life, the captains made him a sergeant over men who were older, had much more frontier experience, and had served in the regular army. This elevation must have reflected his education, his character, and perhaps his family connections. Writing shortly after the sergeant's death, Clark said that Floyd "had at All times given us proofs of his impatiality Sincurity to ourselves and good will to Serve his Countrey."[16] There is little mention of Floyd in the captains' journals, which is probably an indication that he did his duty efficiently and caused no trouble. Starting with the official beginning of the expedition on May 14, 1804, he kept his journal faithfully until two days before his death on August 20, 1804, although he must have been feeling the effects of his illness well before then.[17]

Floyd kept his journal in a small notebook with marbled paper over the covers, in which there are also a few notes by Clark. He had filled most of it by the time of his death. The captains of course preserved it during the winter at Fort Mandan and apparently sent it back to his relatives in Kentucky with the returning party in the spring of 1805. In 1893 Reuben Gold Thwaites discovered it among the papers of Lyman Draper, former head of the State Historical Society of Wisconsin. Draper, an assiduous collector of historical documents, had acquired a large number of Clark's papers from the captain's nephew, John Croghan, and had also corresponded with Floyd's sister, Mary Lee Walton. He kept no records of his own acquisitions, and the exact source of this find is unknown. It remains in the Draper Collection in the State Historical Society of Wisconsin, Madison.

Floyd's entries are generally brief and factual; they resemble Clark's at his most laconic. His spelling and grammar are also reminiscent of Clark, and like the captain his vocabulary and phrasing suggest a man who had done some reading. In some cases it is clear that he had copied passages verbatim from Clark, in the spirit of Jefferson's instructions. It may be that much of his writing was simply a condensation of Clark's field notes, but occasionally he provides information that Clark does not. On July 9, 1804, Clark notes a spot in Doniphan County, Kansas, "where Several french men camped two years ago to hunt.—" Floyd describes it as "a prarie on the South Side whare Seveal French famileys had Setled and made Corn Some Years ago Stayed two years." The next day Clark tells us that "R. *Pape*" (present Cedar Creek in Doniphan County) was "called after a Spanierd who killed himself at th[e] mouth." Floyd clarifies this somewhat by noting that "it is Called after a man who by drawning his Gun out of the Boat Shot him Self."

In reporting the desertion of Private Moses Reed, Clark is entirely matter-of-fact; Floyd records details not found elsewhere and expresses the indignation that perhaps they all felt: "pon examining his nap-Sack we found that he had taken his Cloas and all His powder and Balles, and had hid them out that night and had made that an excuse to Desarte from us with out aney Jest Case." Floyd apparently had an eye for such details, which makes us regret all the more that he did not live to complete a record of the whole journey. As it is, the two captains have made it clear that he did his duty as long as he could.

Notes

1. Donald Jackson, ed., *Letters of the Lewis and Clark Expedition with Related Documents, 1783–1854* (2d ed., 2 vols. Urbana: University of Illinois Press, 1978), 1:vii.

2. Jefferson's Instructions to Lewis [June 20, 1803], ibid., 1:62.

3. See the Orderly Book entry for May 26, 1804.

4. Lewis to Jefferson, April 7, 1805, Jackson, ed., *Letters,* 1:232.

5. See Lewis's journal entry for April 7, 1805.

6. The Robert Frazer Prospectus [October 1806], Jackson, ed., *Letters,* 1:345–46.

7. On Willard's journal, see Olin D. Wheeler, *The Trail of Lewis and Clark, 1804–1806* (2 vols. New York: G. P. Putnam's Sons, 1904), 1:124; and Robert B. Betts, "'The writingest explorers of their time': New Estimates of the Number of Words in the Published Journals of the Lewis and Clark Expedition," *We Proceeded On* 7 (August 1981): 7–8, 8 n.34.

8. Lewis to Henry Dearborn, January 15, 1807, Jackson, ed., *Letters,* 1:369.

9. See Lewis's Detachment Orders for February 20, 1804.

10. See the Detachment Orders for March 3, 1804.

11. John Ordway to Stephen Ordway, September 5, 1803, Jackson, ed., *Letters,* 1:120–21.

12. John Ordway to His Parents, April 8, 1804, ibid., 1:176–77.

13. Milo Milton Quaife, ed., *The Journals of Captain Meriwether Lewis and Sergeant John Ord-*

way Kept on the Expedition of Western Exploration, 1803–1806 (Madison: State Historical Society of Wisconsin, 1916), 28; Charles G. Clarke, *The Men of the Lewis and Clark Expedition: A Biographical Roster of the Fifty-one Members and a Composite Diary of Their Activities from All Known Sources* (Glendale, Calif.: Arthur H. Clark, 1970), 40–41.

14. Paul Russell Cutright, *A History of the Lewis and Clark Journals* (Norman: University of Oklahoma Press, 1976), 128–29; Nicholas Biddle to Clark, July 7, 1810, Jackson, ed., *Letters,* 2:551; Quaife, *Journals of Lewis and Ordway,* 25–26.

15. Jackson, ed., *Letters,* 1:366. See also Clarke, *The Men of the Lewis and Clark Expedition,* 39.

16. See Clark's first entry for August 20, 1804, in the Field Notes. The Codex B entry, perhaps written some time later, says much the same.

17. On the nature of Floyd's illness see Eldon G. Chuinard, *Only One Man Died: The Medical Aspects of the Lewis and Clark Expedition* (Glendale, Calif.: Arthur H. Clark, 1979), 238–39.

The Journals of the Lewis and Clark Expedition, Volume 9

The Journals of John Ordway and Charles Floyd

Part 1: The Journal of John Ordway

Chapter Forty-Two

Up the Missouri

May 14–September 24, 1804

A Journal commenced at River Dubois[1]

Monday May the 14th 1804. Showery day. Capt Clark Set out at 3 oClock P. M. for the western expedition. one Gun fired. a nomber of Citizens see us Start. the party consisted of 3 Sergeants & 38 Good hands,[2] which maned the Batteaux and two pearogues.[3] we Sailed up the Missouri 6 miles & encamped[4] on the N. Side of the River.

1. This is the first of three notebooks that comprise Ordway's journal. The first notebook contains handstitched sheets covered with loose boards, 322 pages (erratically paged) in length, divided into four parts, and of varying size, from about 8½ by 6½ inches to about 7¾ by 6¼ inches. This notebook covers the period from May 14, 1804, to September 30, 1805 (see Appendix C, vol. 2). Random writing appears on the front and back of the outside cover, too faint and blurred to read. On the inside front cover are several random words, "Silas," "John Munsell," "[H]udon," "J Howard," "Wife," and others too faint to decipher. On the inside back cover is the following: "No. II. Orderly Book commencing 26th February 1793 Thomas Hughes Major 1st S L"; and a column of numbers too faint to read. Hughes was a major in the first sublegion of the U.S. Army from November 1792 until he resigned from the service in October 1794; it is not known how Ordway came to have his notebook. On the first page, preceding the page which begins the expedition entries, is the following: "John Ordways Journal Book Detachment Orders, Camp River Dubois Lat at Dubois 38d 19m N. Lon[gitude at Dubois] 90[m] N. W—"; and several words crowded in above this, including, "Silas [Delash?]," "Said Silas," and "7000 miles to Mandan." The remainder of the page is blank.

2. The composition of the party at this time is discussed in Appendix A, vol. 2.

3. The keelboat (batteaux) is discussed at Lewis's entry for August 30, 1803, and the pirogues are considered at entries for September 4, 1803, and May 13, 1804.

4. Near the mouth of Coldwater Creek, St. Charles County, Missouri, a little above the town of Fort Bellefontaine.

Map of Expedition's Route, May 14, 1804–September 23, 1806

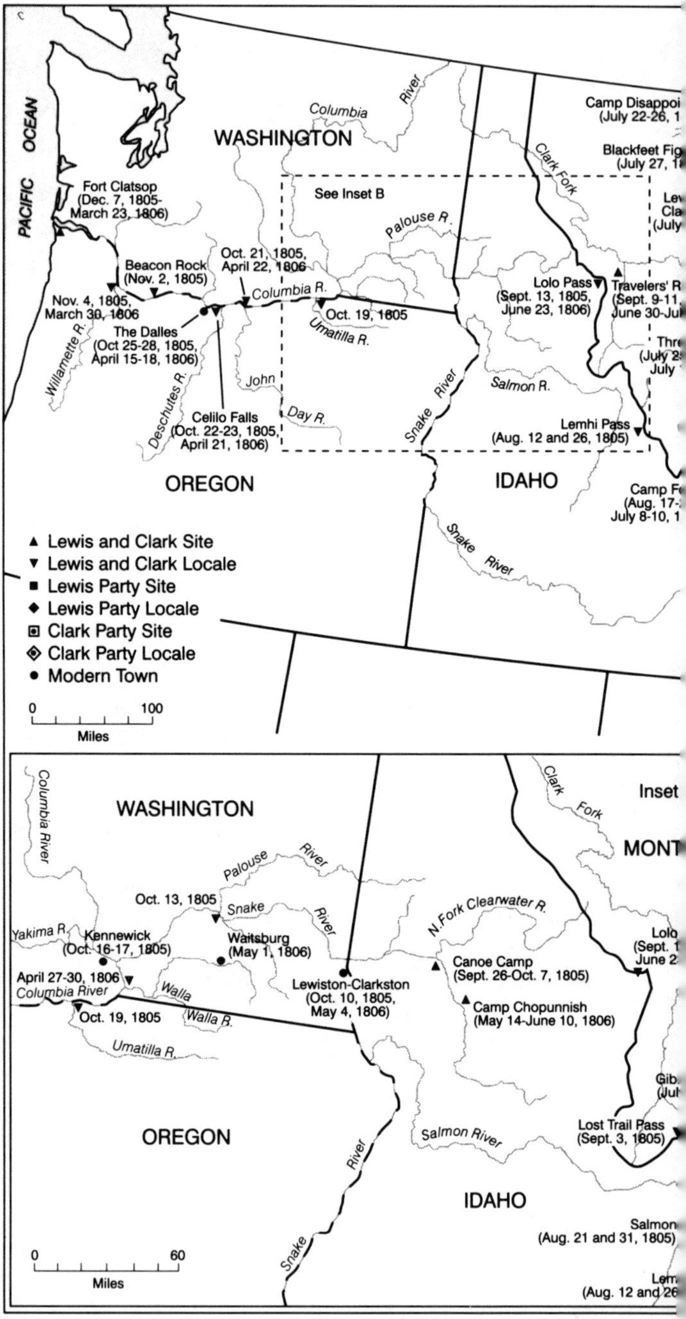

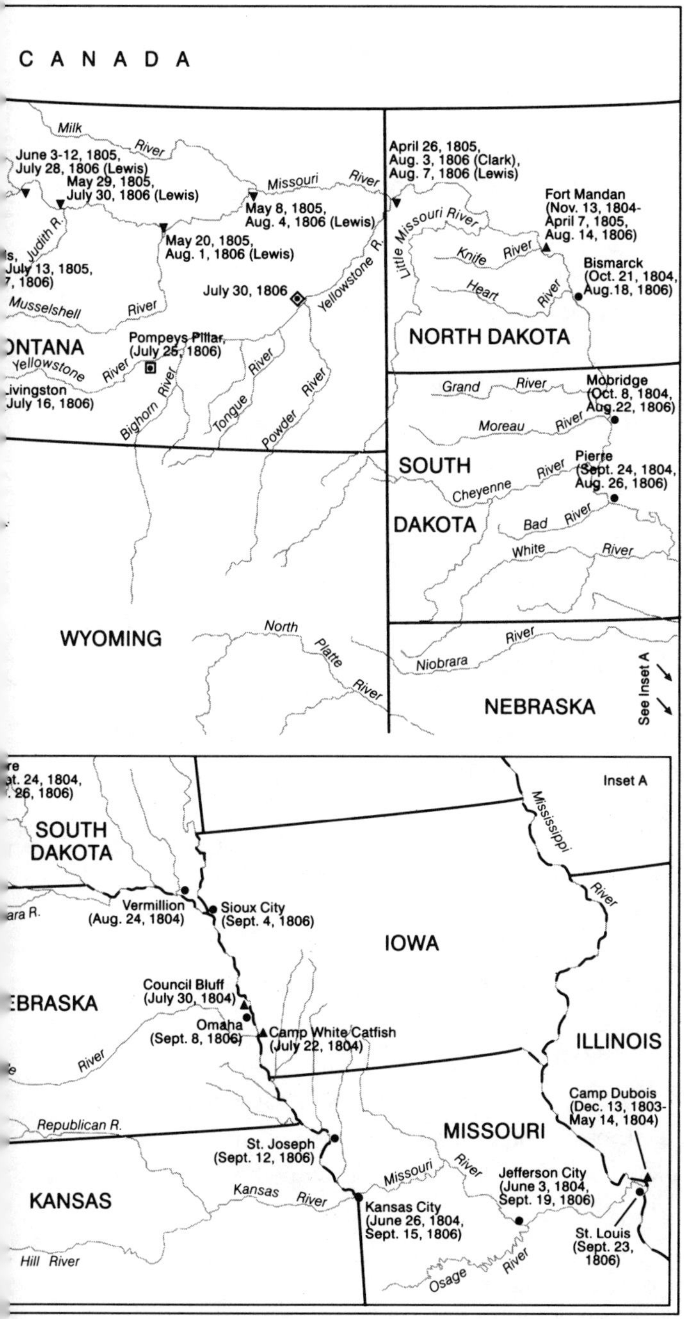

CANADA
Milk River
June 3-12, 1805,
July 28, 1806 (Lewis)
May 29, 1805,
July 30, 1806 (Lewis)
Missouri River
May 8, 1805,
Aug. 4, 1806 (Lewis)
May 20, 1805,
Aug. 1, 1806 (Lewis)
Judith R.
July 13, 1805,
Musselshell River
July 30, 1806
Yellowstone R.
Pompeys Pillar
(July 25, 1806)
Yellowstone River
Livingston
July 16, 1806)
Bighorn River
Tongue River
Powder River
April 26, 1805,
Aug. 3, 1806 (Clark),
Aug. 7, 1806 (Lewis)
Little Missouri River
Fort Mandan
(Nov. 13, 1804-
April 7, 1805,
Aug. 14, 1806)
Knife River
Heart River
Bismarck
(Oct. 21, 1804,
Aug.18, 1806)
NORTH DAKOTA
Grand River
Mobridge
(Oct. 8, 1804,
Aug.22, 1806)
Moreau River
SOUTH DAKOTA
Cheyenne River
Pierre
(Sept. 24, 1804,
Aug. 26, 1806)
Bad River
White River
WYOMING
North Platte River
Niobrara River
NEBRASKA
See Inset A
Inset A
SOUTH DAKOTA
Mississippi River
Vermillion
(Aug. 24, 1804)
Sioux City
(Sept. 4, 1806)
IOWA
Council Bluff
(July 30, 1804)
Omaha
(Sept. 8, 1806)
Camp White Catfish
(July 22, 1804)
River
ILLINOIS
Camp Dubois
(Dec. 13, 1803-
May 14, 1804)
Republican R.
MISSOURI
St. Joseph
(Sept. 12, 1806)
Missouri River
Jefferson City
(June 3, 1804,
Sept. 19, 1806)
KANSAS
Kansas River
Kansas City
(June 26, 1804,
Sept. 15, 1806)
St. Louis
(Sept. 23,
1806)
Hill River
Osage River

Tuesday May 15th 1804. rainy morning. fair wind later part of the day. Sailed Some. encamped[1] on N. Side Some land cleared, the Soil verry Rich, &c.

1. About five miles downstream from St. Charles, St. Charles County, Missouri.

Wensday May 16th 1804. Set out eairly, this morning pleasant. arrived at St. Charles[1] at 2 oClock P. M. one gun fired, a great nomber of French people Come to See the Boat &C— this place is an old French Settlement & Roman Catholick. Some Americans Settled in the country around,

1. St. Charles, St. Charles County, Missouri.

Thursday May 17th 1804, a fair day, but Rainy night, nothing occured worthy of notice this day

Friday May 18th 1804. we lay at St Charles—

Saturday May 19th 1804. a Rainy day Capt Lewis arived, Capt Stoddard & Lieut. Worrell came with him[1]

1. Amos Stoddard, captain of artillery and military commandant of Upper Louisiana (see Clark's entry, January 2, 1804), and Stephen Worrell, a junior officer serving with Stoddard (see Lewis's entry, May 20, 1804).

Sunday May 20th 1804. I and a nomber of the party went to the Mass, & Saw them perform &C

Monday May 21st 1804,

left St. Charles at 4 oClock P. m. Showery, the men all in high Spirits. George Drewyer & willard[1] Stayed on business Encamped[2] on the N. Side of the River

1. George Drouillard and Alexander Willard.
2. About three miles southwest of St. Charles, St. Charles County, Missouri.

Tuesday May 22d 1804. passed Bonom Creek[1] on the South Side of the River. came 15 miles encamped on N. [*over* S] Side of the River, at clifts ⟨our arms inspected⟩ Some Indians came to us &C

1. Bonhomme Creek, St. Louis County, Missouri.

Wendsday May the 23d 1804. we Set out at 6 oC. A. M. pleasant. passed the wife or faim of the Hoozaw River,[1] 1 mile & half to we passed the Corn tavern a noted place on the S Side of the River, 120 feet long 40 abt. high & 20 perpenticular high clifts, 1 mile to Tavern Creek.[2] encamped on S Side of the River. our arms & amunition Inspected,

1. Femme Osage River, St. Charles County, Missouri.
2. Tavern Creek, Franklin County, Missouri.

Thursday May the 24th 1804. nothing remarkable as recollected encamped[1] on S Side

1. About four or five miles below Washington, Franklin County, Missouri.

Friday May 25th 1804, came 3 miles passed a Creek called wood River[1] on S Side land handsome the Soil Rich &C— high Banks, encamped at a French village N. S. called St John,[2] this is the last Settlement of whites on this River,

1. Dubois Creek, Franklin County, Missouri.
2. La Charette, Warren County, Missouri; St. John is an alternate name.

Saturday May the 26th 1804. we Set out at 7 oC. A. M. hard thunder & rain this morning passed a Creek called otter creek,[1] encamped on N. Side

1. Loutre River, Montgomery County, Missouri, across from Hermann, passed on the next day, according to Clark but to none of the other journal keepers.

Sunday May the 27th 1804

passed Ash Creek[1] high Clifts on S. Side Arrived at the Mouth of the Gasganade River[2] at 5 o. C. P. M. on S Side Shannon killed a Deer[3] encamped on an Island opposite to the Mouth of the River, which is a handsome place, the Soil is good, the Country pleasant &C. arms & ammunition Inspected—

1. Probably Frame, or Frene, Creek, at Hermann, Gasconade County, Missouri.
2. Gasconade River at Gasconade, Gasconade County.
3. White-tailed deer, *Odocoileus virginianus.*

Monday May the 28th 1804. the provisions & cloths put out to air Several men out hunting &C. Reuben Fields killed a Deer. the Mouth of the Gasganade River is 157 yards wide—

Tuesday May the 29th 1804, rain last night Several men out hunting, &C— we Set out from the Gasgonade River at 5 O.C. P. M. Come 3 miles passed Deer Creek[1] on the S. Side encamped all night Jest above on the S Side ⟨Some rain this night⟩ one man Whitehouse lost hunting Frenchman's pearogue[2] Std. for him

1. Probably Bailey Creek, Gasconade County, Missouri.
2. Otherwise called the red pirogue.

Wednesday May the 30th 1804. we Set out at 7 oClock A. M. after a hard rain, rained all last night. a little after dark last night Several Guns were fired below we expect the Frenchmen were firing for whitehouse who was lost in the woods on N. Side oppisite an Island above Clifts Called Monbrans Tavern[1] at 12 oClock a hard Shower of rain & hail passed a Creek called rush Creek[2] on the N. Side of the River Came 4 miles passed Mud creek[3] on River on N. Side of the River, the Soil is good the timber is Cotton-wood Secamore hickery & white walnut &.C. Some Grape vines Rushes &.C—.[4] came about 14 miles encamped at Grind Stone Creek or Panther Cr.[5]

1. At Little Tavern Creek, Callaway County, Missouri
2. Actually on the south side, also called Rest Creek by Clark in his Field Notes; it is Greasy Creek, at the town of Chamois, Osage County, Missouri.

3. Evidently Muddy Creek, Callaway County.

4. Ordway and Patrick Gass call attention to the vegetation this day. The trees are cottonwood, *Populus deltoides* Marsh., sycamore, *Platanus occidentalis* L., some unknown hickory, *Carya* sp., and white walnut, butternut, *Juglans cinerea* L. The grape is probably river-bank grape, *Vitis riparia* Michx., and the rush is unknown, *Equisetum* sp.

5. "Grinestone Creek" to Clark and Gass, "Panther River" to Joseph Whitehouse; probably Deer Creek, Osage County.

Thursday May 31st 1804, we lay at panther creek on acct. of a hard wind from N. West Several of the party out hunting in the later part of the day Reuben Fields killed a Deer. Several Frenchman Stayed with us last night, came down the R. with Peltry &C

Friday June 1st 1804. we Set out from Panther or Grind stone Creek at 5 oC a fair day. came 1½ miles passed Big Muddy Creek[1] on N. Side R. high Banks on S. Side came 2½ miles passed Bear Creek.[2] arrived at the Osage River[3] at 4 oC. P. M We Encamped & fell a nomber of Trees in the Point for the ⟨purpose of⟩ Captains Takeing observations, &.C—

1. Probably Auxvasse River, Callaway County, Missouri.
2. Perhaps Loose Creek, Osage County, Missouri.
3. Osage River, at the Osage-Cole county line.

Saturday June 2d 1804, we Stayed all day at the Osage R. the width of the Missouri at this place is 875 yds wide, the Osage River 397 yds. wi[de] the pearogue Arived with the lost man &c—

Sunday June 3d 1804. we lay at the osage R. the four part of the Day. the Hunters[1] killed five Deer while we delayed at this place. we Set out at 5 oC. in the afternoon and proceeded along the Clifts. we encamped at Morow Creek[2] on S. Side.

1. Including Lewis and Drouillard, according to Clark.
2. Moreau River, Cole County, Missouri, east of Jefferson City.

Monday June 4th 1804. a fair day 3 hunters went out. our mast broke by my Stearing the Boat ⟨alon⟩ near the Shore the Rope or Stay to the mast got fast in a limb of a Secamore tree & it broke verry Easy. passed a Creek on the South Side about 15 yds wide which we name nightingale Creek,[1] this Bird Sung all last night & is the first we heard below on the River we passed Seeder Creek on S Side line fine land above & below the Creek. Rising land, Delightfull Timber of oak ash, Black walnut hickery &C &C—[2] passed a Creek called on car[3] on the S Side ⟨3 miles to⟩ we encamped on S Side of the River at the Lead mines our hunters killed 8 Deers it was Jerked this evening &C

1. Either Wears Creek or Coon Creek, both at Jefferson City, Cole County, Missouri. The disputed identity of the bird is discussed at Clark's entry for this day.

2. Only Ordway notes that the walnut is black walnut, *Juglans nigra* L., otherwise the trees cannot be identified specifically, oak is *Quercus* sp., ash, *Fraxinus* sp., and hickory, *Carya* sp.

3. Clark's "Zoncar," Charles Floyd's "Zon cer." Perhaps Meadow Creek, Cole County.

Tuesday June 5th 1804. a fair ⟨day⟩ passed Lead Creek[1] on South Side of the River & Little Good woman Creek[2] on the N. Side, came 9 miles. passed the Creek of the Big Rock[3] 15 yds. wide, at a 11 oClock we met 2 Frenchmen in 2 canoes locked together Loaded with Peltry &C. they came from 80 Leagues up the Kansias River,[4] where they wintered, then we passed a high Clifts of Rocks on which was painted the pickture of the Devil on South Side of the River. we Encamped[5] on the N. Side of the River at the upper point of an Island. the land is Rich well watered &.C. the hunters killed 2 Deer this day—

1. Rock Creek or Mud Creek, Cole County, Missouri.

2. Bonne Femme Creek, Boone County, Missouri.

3. Rock Creek or Mud Creek, again.

4. Kansas River.

5. In Boone County, across from the later town of Sandy Hook, Moniteau County, Missouri.

Wednesday June 6th 1804. we mended our mast this morning and Set out at 7 o.C. with a gentle wind up the River. we passed a place in the projecting Rock the hole of the Split Rock River. a little above we passed Split Rock Creek.[1] the Country around is Delightful Good Timber. I Saw one handsome Run from under the Clifts of Rocks, passed Saleen Creek[2] on South Side of the River. Salt has been made their &.C. we encamped on North Side of the River, [*words erased and crossed out, illegible*]

1. Contrary to Ordway's wording, there seems to be only one stream here, Perchee Creek, Boone County, Missouri.
2. Petite Saline Creek, Moniteau County, Missouri.

Thursday June 7th 1804. we Set out at 5 OClock fair day & f. wind passed high Clifts & a fine large Spring which Run from under the clifts of Rocks, about 2 miles further we Come to a Creek Called the Big Devil.[1] we Stayed to Breakfast. Capt. Lewis & Several men went with him out to a lick, up the Creek. high Bluffs on N. Side. this Maneteau Creek is 30 yds. wide at the mouth. we passed a pointed part of a projecting Rock we found this to be a den of rattle Snakes,[2] we killed three. high Land on South Side of the River. we Encamped at the mouth of good womans River[3] on Right the hunters came in with 3 Bears[4] this evening & informed us that the Country between these Rivers is Rich

1. Moniteau Creek, at Rocheport on the Howard-Boone county line, Missouri.
2. Probably the timber rattlesnake, *Crotalus horridus.*
3. Bonne Femme Creek, Howard County.
4. Black bear, *Ursus americanus.*

Friday June 8th 1804. we Set out at 4. OC. proceeded on passed a run[1] on left Side above a point of rocks on 3 miles on which their is a nomber of Deer licks, 3 miles to the mo. of mine River,[2] this River is navagable for Perogues— we met 3 Frenchman in 2 canoes from R. des Soud[3] above this Nation loaded with fur. we encamped[4] on the Lower point of an Island called mills Island. our hunters killed 5 Deer. Some rain the Country on the right is verry fine—

1. Perhaps Loupes Branch, at Booneville, Cooper County, Missouri.
2. Lamine River, Cooper County, a few miles above Booneville.
3. Probably Big Sioux River, which forms the boundary between Iowa and South Dakota.
4. Perhaps on island later called Arrow Rock Island, near the Saline-Cooper county line.

Saturday June 9th 1804. we Set out eairly we got fast on a log Detained us half an hour, Rain last night ⟨oppisite⟩ we passed prarie & arrow Creek on South Side of the River.[1] the land is high & verry good towards evening we passed a prarie & a Small Lake below. we Camped[2] on an Island at left Side.

1. The prairie is in the vicinity of the town of Arrow Rock, Saline County, Missouri, and the creek is probably Pierre Fresne Creek, Saline County.

2. Somewhat above Richland Creek (called Blackbird Creek by Clark and other journalists), Howard County, Missouri.

Sunday June 10th 1804. we Set eairly after Some rain, a fair day, we passed hilley land on Right hand of the River. On the left the land is level plenty of Mulbery Trees.[1] the mulberys Ripe on them. The timber is walnut hickery ash &c. Grape vines Run over the trees &C.—[2] at 10 oC we passed Deer Creek[3] on the Right we passed the 2 Charlitons River[4] on the North Side, those Rivers are navigable Some Distance up & the Mouths are near together Capt Lewis killed a ⟨Deer⟩ Buck little above We Camped on South Side of the River Capts went hunting, Several men with them. Drewyer killed a Deer. the land is excelent, large praries along the South Side of the River. the Timber on the bank is white walnut hickery Some Cotton wood &C—

1. The mulberry is probably red mulberry, *Morus rubra.*

2. Ordway is the only one to mention the vegetation this day, other than Clark, who notes the discovery of a plum.

3. Perhaps Hurricane Creek, Howard County, Missouri; not mentioned by Clark but noted by other enlisted men.

4. Little Chariton and Chariton rivers, Chariton County, Missouri.

Monday June 11th 1804. we lay by on acct. of the wind Blowing hard from the N. W. Drewyer & Several more went out in the Praries a hunting, & Drewyer killed two Bear & one Deer. R Fields killed one Deer

Tuesday June 12th 1804. we Set out eairley this morning. a fair ⟨day⟩ morning. we passed plumb Creek[1] on South Side of the River. the plumbs[2] are plenty up sd. Creek. near below Sd. Creek the land is high well Timbered & well Situated for a plantation. The Timber Soil &C. is verry excelent, we Camped on N. Side of the River. Several Frenchmen Stayed with us all night comming down the River in Several pearogues Loaded with peltry Bound to St. Louis. came from the Shew nation.[3] they passed the last winter their & had an amence Side of Bufloe Green Skins &C we Got an old Frenchman[4] to go with us which could Speak Sevral languages, among the indians for a long distance.—

1. Perhaps Bear Creek, Saline County, Missouri.
2. Any number of possibilities of *Prunus* sp.; see Clark's entry for June 10.
3. Meaning the Sioux Indians, probably the Yankton Sioux.
4. Pierre Dorion, Sr.

Wednesday June 13th 1804. fair morning we set out eairly. passed the Creek of the praries,[1] large praries above the Creek. verry excellent land we passed a Creek Called Round bend Creek on N. Side passd. prarie on the South Side of the River. we arrived at Grand River[2] in good Season to encamp. Beautiful prarie across ⟨from⟩ in the point Between the Missouri & Grand River high Land Back from the River, it being on the N. Side of River

1. This may be the first of the "round bend Creeks." See Clark's and Floyd's entries of this day.
2. Grand River forms the boundary between Carroll and Chariton counties, Missouri.

Thursday June 14th 1804. we Set out eairly from the Grand River, foggy but fair day we passed a handsome Small prarie on North Side of the River. verry hard water, about noon we met 2 canoes loadd with peltry. four Frenchman bound to St. Charles, came from the Pawnie nation,[1] where they had been hunting for 2 years. they came to us about 11 oClock A. M. left us at 3 O.C. P. M. we proceeded on passed high Land on the N. Side called Snake hills of the River, then we passed Snake Creek[2] on the N. Side of Missouri. we camped on N. Side.

1. Pawnee Indians.
2. Probably Wakenda Creek, Carroll County, Missouri.

Friday June 15th 1804. we Set out eairly a fair day. we passed high Land on South Side of the River we passed Indian Creek[1] little above we stopped at 12 O.C. to eat dinner & for Capt. Lewis to take the Meridan altitude &C— We camped on the N. Side of the R. their is Beautiful high Good praries on the South Side &C— pleasantest place I have ever Seen. their is five Islands & a nomber of Sand bars in the River about this place.— and the Current is exceedingly Reapid all this day.— the aforesaid prarie is called village La pero, formerly Ind. Town.[2]

1. Perhaps Van Meter Ditch, Saline County, Missouri; mentioned only by Ordway and Floyd.

2. Only Ordway applies this name to what is apparently the Gumbo Point site, Saline County, where the party camped. Its meaning is unknown. See entries of Floyd and Clark for this day and also Clark for June 13.

Saturday June 16th 1804. we Set out Eairly. we passed some handsome praries on the North Side of the River. the Current is verry Strong all this day, So that we were obledged to waid & Toe the boat over sand bars, &.C— we encamped[1] on the North Side of the River, Jest above a verry bad Sand bar

1. Near Waverly, but on the opposite side in Carroll County, Missouri.

Sunday June 17th 1804. we set out eairly Came one mile[1] and Stoped on N. Side to make Some oars. Some men went out hunting the hunters came in towards Evening with one bear— we got out Timber for 20 oars this day.

1. Carroll County, Missouri, about one mile above the previous day's camp.

Monday June 18th 1804. hard Rain this morning we remained here to finish the oars. Several men went out hunting, killed & brought in 4 Deer & one bear, they Inform us that their is handsome praries & very good land on the South Side of the River,

Tuesday June 19th 1804. we Set out at 9 o.C. with a fair wind. we passed a beautiful large prarie on the North Side, high Rich Bottom on

South Side we passed Tabbo Creek[1] on South Side we Saw pleanty of goos Berries & Ras Berries[2] on the banks, we passed a bad place of Rocks. the water So Swift that we were obledged to hole the Boat by a Rope, we Camped[3] on South Side opposite a pond, which was near to where we camped The Musquetoes[4] are verry troublesome. we Got Musquetoes bears[5] from Capt Lewis to sleep in,

1. Tabo Creek, Lafayette County, Missouri.
2. Perhaps Missouri gooseberry, *Ribes missouriense* Nutt., and black raspberry, *Rubus occidentalis* L.
3. A few miles below Lexington, Lafayette County.
4. Probably *Aedes vexans*.
5. A bier or mosquito netting.

Wednesday June 20th 1804, we Set out at 5 oC and after some rain passed Tiger Creek[1] on the N. Side passed Some high land on the South Side. we passed a large Beutiful prarie called Sauke prarie, we had verry hard water all this day. we passed Some high land on the South Side, Saw Some Crabb apple Trees[2] on the bank &C.[3]

1. Apparently Crooked River, Ray County, Missouri. Clark indicates that the party passed this stream on June 19; see his entry for this day for a discussion of this matter.
2. Mentioned only by Ordway this day, it is probably wild crab, *Pyrus ioensis* (Wood) Bailey.
3. The camp was apparently on Wolf Island, below Wellington, Lafayette County, Missouri.

Thursday June 21st 1804. we Set out at 7 oC. passed a Creek on the south side called or Eue bow Creek[1] peulaur the Land high on South, on the N. fine Rich Bottom. I went on Shore with Drewyer all day & I never Saw as fine Timbered land in my life nor Such Rich handsome bottom land, Drewyer killed one Deer & him & me brought it to the River, one Turkey[2] likewise, we encamped on the South Side of the River, low land on S. Side high land on the N. Side.

1. Clark has it "Eue-beux" and "Eue-bert" while Floyd gives it as "Deubau"; now the several creeks called Little Sni a Bar Creek, Sni Creek, and Big Sni a Bar Creek, in western Lafayette County, Missouri.
2. The wild turkey, *Meleagris gallopavo*.

Friday June 22d 1804. we Set out at 7 oC after a hard Shower of rain & high wind from N. E. Thunder and lightning &.C— the day fair proceeded on 2½ miles one of the men[1] killed a goose. we passed a handsome prarie on the South Side & a Creek Called little fire Creek.[2] passed a Creek on the N. Side called Big fire Creek where our hunters were waiting for us. we Camped opst. on South Side

1. Perhaps Ordway himself; see Clark's entry for this day.

2. See Clark's entry for this day for a discussion of the difficulties in identifying the two creeks mentioned in this entry and in locating the camp for this day.

23d June Saturday Some wind this morning from the N. W. we Set out at 7 O.C. the wind Raised. Capt. Clark went out hunting, by 11 OC. we were obledged to Camp[1] it being too windy for to See the Sand bars &.C. The Hunters killed 2 Deer & got them to camp they went out again. Capt. Clark Remained on Shore all day & all night. we lay Camped on the upper point of an Island, our arms Inspected &.C— we lay all night on this Island. Jurked our meat &.C—

1. The main party camped on an island in the vicinity of Sibley, Jackson County, Missouri.

Sunday June 24th 1804. we set out at 6 O.C. a fair day passed a Creek on the South Side Called the Creek of the Hay Cabbins.[1] Capt. Clark Came to the Boat this morning with a fat Bear. we Delayed at noon a Short time ⟨long⟩ [*one word illegible, crossed out*] to Jurk & take care of it. high hills on the South Side of the River near Sd. Creek. the land is Rich & well Timbered on both Sides of the River. Gege Drewyer killed 2 Deer [*several words illegible, crossed out*] and R. Fields killed one Deer while we Stoped. we passed a Creek on the North Side little above Some Rocks. Called Sharriton Cartie Creek.[2] a prarie on the South Side. Capt Lewis killed a Deer & Turkey we Camped on the South Side of the River. Collins killed 3 Deer in the course of this Day.

1. Little Blue River, Jackson County, Missouri.

2. Perhaps Big Shoal Creek, Clay County, Missouri; see Clark's entry for this day.

Monday June 25th 1804. a foggy morning. it Detained us about an hour. we Set out, passed a Coal Bank on the North Side which appears to have Great quantity of Coal in it. we passed a Small Creek Called Coal[1] or (Chaboned) on the Same Side. we passed a Creek on the South Side called *Labeenie.*[2] we Saw a great nomber of Deer feeding on the Sand Beachs they feed on young willow[3] & are verry numerious. we passed Some handsom high praries on the South Side of the River. passed Some high hills on the South Side. Some rocks, &.C. Signs of Springs on the N. Side of Sd. hills. R. Fields killed a Deer. we Came 11½ Miles & Camped on an ⟨the⟩ Isd. lower point of an Island Near the North side of the River. Capt Lewis killed a Rabit.[4] R. Fields kille a Deer this evening. our flanking party did not git to us this evening,

1. Perhaps Sleepy Branch, Jackson County, Missouri.

2. Evidently Sugar Creek, Jackson County, and perhaps named for François M. Benoit (see Clark's entry for this day). Only Floyd (or a writer in his journal) adds the words "um batteur," probably meaning "a bateau."

3. An unknown willow, *Salix* sp.

4. Only Ordway and Floyd (or a writer in his journal) report Lewis getting an eastern cottontail, *Sylvilagus floridanus,* on this day.

Tuesday June 26th 1804. we Set out eairly proceeded on passed an Island on the South Side back of this Island a large Creek Comes in called Blue water Creek.[1] hills & high land along the River, Swift water this afternoon the Rope Broak & the Boat Swong But Took no Injury. at Sunset we arrived at the Kanses River,[2] our flanking party joined us. we camped on the fork between the Two Rivers. on South Side of the Missouris, Several nations of Indians up this River,

1. Big Blue, or Blue, River, at Kansas City, Jackson County, Missouri.

2. Kansas, or Kaw, River, at Kansas City.

Wednesday June 27th 1804. all the party out eairly this morning cutting the Timber off a cross the point & made a Hadge a cross of the Timber & bushes to answer as defence & made Room for Capts to take obser. The black pearogue[1] unloaded & Turned up to mend &C. The Captains were Taking observations &C. peter Crusat killed a Deer, The Kansas River is 230 yds.

wide at the mouth & [wider?] further up, a high bank 1 mile up, fine place for a fort &.C.

1. Probably the larger of the two pirogues, the red pirogue.

Thursday June 28th 1804. pleasant. the loading put out to air. I went out hunting 2½ miles & passed a fine Spring Running from under the hills I drank hearty of the water & found it the best & coolest I have seen in the country. Several of the party went hunting & 4 Deer, R. & J. Fields killed a young woolf[1] & brought one home to camp for to Tame. one man Saw Several buffelow[2] up the Kansas River. this is 366 Miles from mouth of Missouri. The Latidude 38d 31m 13s North, the width of M. here is 500 yd. wide

1. Presumably a gray wolf, *Canis lupus*.
2. *Bison bison*.

Friday June 29th 1804, Several large Cat fish[1] was Cought last night, the Captains engaged taking observations &C. a Court martial held &.C.[2] we set out from the Kansas River at half past 4 O.Clock P. M. proceeded on passed a small creek[3] on the South Side of the Missouris Swift waters one mile & half came to hills on the South Side, proceeded on passed Some Small Islands, camped[4] on the North Side of Missouris, excelent bottom land. the Rushes are So thick that it is verry troublesome to walk through them,

1. Either the channel catfish, *Ictalurus punctatus*, or the blue catfish, *I. furcatus*.
2. Ordway is the only enlisted man to call attention to the court-martial proceedings against John Collins and Hugh Hall. See the Orderly Book entry for this day.
3. Perhaps Jersey Creek, Wyandotte County, Kansas.
4. In the vicinity of Riverside, Platte County, Missouri.

Saturday June 30th 1804, we Set out eairly proceeded on Saw a verry large woolf on the sand beach this morning at 10 miles from or above the Kansis passed the mouth of a Small River called *Petete platt* R. or little Shole river,[1] this river is about 50 yd. wide and has Several Rapids & falls, well calculated for mills, the Land on this River is Said to be roaling the men killed 2 Deer Swimming the River. The hunters killed 7 Deer the most of them were bucks. we broke our mast comming to Shore against a Small Tree which hung over the River. came about 10 miles this day camped[2] on the South Side of the Missouris,

1. Platte, or Little Platte, River, Platte County, Missouri, not to be confused with the Platte River in Nebraska.
2. In the vicinity of the village of Wolcott, Wyandotte County, Kansas.

Sunday July 1st 1804. we Set out at Sun rise passed a Small Creek which we call Bisquet Creek[1] on the South Side of the Missouris, we passed a Sand barr in the river which was covered for a mile with Drift wood, the Day is exceding hot. So we Stoped at 12 oClock & Delayed about 3 hours to rest in the heat of the day, high land on the South Side fine Bottom on the North Side of Missouris, we came to a high prarie on the South Side. we Camped[2] after Comming about 10 or 12 miles, on the North Side of the Missouris. passed Several Islands in course of the Day

1. Probably Island Creek, near the Wyandotte-Leavenworth county line, Kansas.
2. Opposite Leavenworth, Leavenworth County.

Monday July 2nd 1804. we Set out verry early this morning passed a High beautiful Situation on the South Side of the river, a Creek Comes in on the North Side called parques or fence Creek or River,[1] we passed a Creek on the South Side called *Turquie* or Turkey Creek,[2] we Delayed at 12 o.C. for to put up a Temperary mast as the wind was fair, we passed a prarie on the South Side of the River called the old Village of the Kansars &C.[3] we passed Several Islands. Several Deer killed this day, we camped[4] on the North Side of the River Our flanking party did not Join us at night

1. Probably Bee Creek, Platte County, Missouri.
2. Perhaps Corral Creek, Leavenworth County, Kansas.
3. The Kansa, or Kaw, Indians lived in this locale in the 1740s and 1750s.
4. Near Weston, Platte County,.

Tuesday July 3rd 1804. we Set out eairly & proceeded on under a gentle Breese from the South. passed a long Island[1] & Several Small ones we found a white horse on the bank of the river near whare their was an old Trading house built by a French merchant from St. Louis to Trade with the kansars Indians. The land is Good high bottom pine Timber & black wallnut honey locas oak &C. &C— I Saw waat they call bucks Eye with the nuts on them[2] we passed a high prarie oposite to the Trading house & Camped[3] at a point on the South Side of the Missouris

1. Cow Island was still on maps in the 1890s, a short distance above the Atchison-Leavenworth county line, Kansas, on the opposite side in Platte County, Missouri.

2. Ordway is the only one to call attention to the vegetation this day. The trees are an unknown pine, black walnut, honey locust, *Gleditsia triancanthos* L., an unknown oak, and western buckeye, *Aesculus glabra* Willd.

3. In Atchison County, Kansas, somewhat above Oak Mills.

Wednesday July 4th 1804, we Set out Eairly & passed the mouth of the out let of a large lake which comes in on the north Side. this pond or lake is large & their has been a Great many bever[1] found in it, high land on the South Side & praries, we Delayed a Short time at noon to dine. a Snake bit Jo. Fields on the out Side of his foot, this was under the hills near the praries on the South Side, we passed a Creek on the South Side about 15 yards wide. comes out of the large prarie, and as it has no name & as it is the 4 of July, Capts. name it Independence Creek[2] we fired our Bow piece this morning & one in the evening for Independance of the U. S. we saw a nomber of Goslins half grown to day. we camped in the plans one of the most beautiful places I ever Saw in my life, open and beautifully Diversified with hills & vallies all presenting themselves to the River,

1. American beaver, *Castor canadensis*.

2. Probably Independence Creek on the Atchison-Doniphan county line, Kansas. See Clark's entry for this day for a discussion of the confusion between this creek and the one the party called Fourth of July Creek.

Thursday July 5th 1804 we Set out verry eairly. we Swam the white horse a cross this River, proceeded on for two miles under the bank where the old Kansas Town formerly Stood (Say in 1724) the cause of those people moveing from this place we cannot learn, but naturly conclude that war has reduced their nation and compelled them to retire further into the plains with a view of Defending themselves. I did not mention on yesterday that the Lake on the north side was large say ¾ of a Mile wide & 7 or 8 miles long one Creek & several Creeks running in to it from the hills it contains a great quantity of fish and Goslings from which it takes its name, we passed Some verry bad Sand bars the Boat turned three times once on a Drift wood, but recived no procevable Damage, we came too at a beaver house for Dinner. the high land on the South Side is open a fiew trees Scattering, we passed a Small creek on the left named yallow Oakey Creek,[1] we Camped[2] on the South Side under a high bank. the land on the opposite Side is well timbered Good bottom, fine place for a Range verry thick high Rushes for common,

1. Any of several small streams in Doniphan County, Kansas, at this point; see Clark's entry. Ordway seems to borrow heavily from Clark's Field Notes for this day's entry, and also for the next.
2. In Doniphan County, some miles northeast of Doniphan.

Friday July 6th 1804, we Set out eairly this morning proceeded on (the river falls Slowly) the weather is verry warm, Several day's, the Sweet pores off the men in Streams, opposite the 3d point we passed a handsome Prarie on the north side called Reeveys or St. Michele prarie,[1] from a man of that name being killed in it we passed Round the Grand Bend which is 2 miles out in the River. we Camped[2] on the South Side of the River a whiper will perched on the Boat for a short time,

1. In Buchanan County, Missouri; see additional information in notes at Clark's entry.
2. Perhaps at Peter's Creek, Doniphan County, Kansas, near St. Joseph, Buchanan County, Missouri, on the opposite side. Clark called it Whip-poor-will Creek after the bird, *Caprimulgus vociferus,* that perched on their boat.

Saturday July 7th 1804. we Set our eairly passed Swirt waters on the South Side, verry warm morning, passed a beautiful prarie on the North Side which extends back, those praries called St. Michel has much the appearance from the river of farms Divided by narrow Strips of woods those Strips of timber grows along the runs which rise on the hills, & pass to the River, I went on Shore with the Horses in the afternoon In the North Side crossed a Creek 2 miles up in the evening followed down to the mouth, and Camped it being too late to find the boat, the Musquitoes troubled me So that I Could not Sleep, as this Creek is without name & my Describeing it to my Capt. he named it Ordway Creek.[1] Some of the men in the Boat killed a wolf to day they Camped[2] on the South Side of the Missouris. one man taken Sick (Frasier).

1. Clark does not mention the creek in his entries for the day, nor does he show it on any of his maps. It may be Mace Creek, north of the Andrew-Buchanan county line, Missouri, where the party met Ordway the next day; see Clark's entry of July 8.
2. The main party camped a little upstream of St. Joseph, Buchanan County, Missouri.

Sunday July 8th 1804. we Set out eairly this morning I came on board about 8 oClock proceeded on along the North Side of an Island called Nodaway Island. high well timbered land on the North Side, passed a Creek near the upper end of this long Island called Nodaway Creek or River[1] we Camped on the North Side of the Missouris, the Hunters killed one Deer to day but did not Join us at night,

1. Nodaway River forms the boundary between Holt and Andrew counties, Missouri.

Monday July the 9th 1804, we Set out eairly Sent Bratton Back to the Creek to blaze some trees, So the Hunters might See we had passed. proceeded on passed a Creek or leading from a big pond called the Creek of the big pond.[1] this pond is near the River, and about 3 miles long & handsom a great many beaver, & fish, fine land and well timbered about this place, Rainy. the wind changed from the N. E. to the S. W. at 6 miles passed the mouth of a Small Creek on the South Side called Monters or wolf Creek,[2] passed a place on the South Side about 2 miles above the Creek where Several Frenchman Camped 2 years for to hunt & raise corn &c— high land on the South Side we passed a Creek on the South Side called River DeLoup,[3] the wind Shifted to the N. W. in the evening. Camped on the South Side of the Missouris, a Gun fired on the opposite Side Supposed to be our hunters the pearogue went over for them but did not find them nor any body else. we fired our bow peace.

1. Probably Little Tarkio Creek, Holt County, Missouri, which seems to have had various beds over the years.

2. Either Charleston Creek or Mosquito Creek, Doniphan County, Kansas; Ordway is in error to add the name "wolf" (see the next note).

3. Wolf Creek to Floyd and the stream's present name in Doniphan County. *Loup* is French for "wolf."

Tuesday July 10th 1804. we Set out this morning with a view to land near where we Saw the Seen last night & to reconortre but Soon Discovered that our men were at the fire, they were a Sleep eairly last night and did not know that we Sent for them by the pearogue, proceeded on passed a prarie on the upper side of woolf Creek or River at 4 miles passed a Small called River pake[1] this Creek is about 15 yd. wide, and called after a Spaniard who killed himself at the mouth, at noon we dined on an Island called De Selamen[2] and Delayed 3 hours. proceeded on opposite this Island on the South Side is a beuautiful Bottom prarie which will contain about 2000 acres of Land covered with wild rye and wild potatoes.[3] Great numbers of Goslins on the Banks and on the Ponds near the River. Capt M. Lewis killed 2 this evening we came too & Camped[4] for the night on the north Side opposite a Yellow Clay Clifts.— the Bottoms on the north Side is verry extensive & thick the hills or high Land is near the River on South Side & are but thinly timbered back of those hills is open prarie.

1. "Pape" Creek to Clark and Floyd; it is probably later Cedar Creek, Doniphan County, Kansas.

2. See Clark's entry of this day for the possible identity of this island.

3. Probably Canada wildrye, *Elymus canadensis* L., and Indian potato, ground nut, *Apios americana* Medic.

4. In Holt County, Missouri, near the Nebraska-Kansas boundary on the opposite shore.

July 11th *Wednesday,* 1804. we Set out eairly Drewyer & Jo. Fields went out to hunt, proceeded on passed a Creek which comes in behind a willow Island on the North Side called by the Indians Little *Tar-ci-o* Creek,[1] we proceeded on 6 miles camped on the North Side of a willow Island opposite a Creek which came in on the South Side of the Missouris Called the Grate Nahhau.[2] Several men went out hunting to day 2 came in with five Deer (Drewyer killed 6 Deer to day) and brought them in. 2 men Stayed out all night, Capt. Clark found a grey horse on the beach Supposed to be left by hunters.

1. Perhaps Little Tarkio Creek, Holt County, Missouri.
2. Big Nemaha River, Richardson County, Nebraska, just above the Nebraska-Kansas line.

Thursday July 12th 1804. we lay by for to Rest and wash our Cloaths, &.C—, the Capts take observations. Several hunters went out this morning the hunters which went out yesterday on the South Side went up the Ne Mahas River this River is about 80 yds. wide and navigable for pearogues Some distance up. this prarie comes to its mouth and continues both Sides. A long distance in the Country, one Sentinel a Sleep on his post last night, and tried by court martial this day.[1] Drewyer killed 2 Deer to day.

1. Ordway is the only enlisted man to mention the court-martial of Willard, found guilty of sleeping while on guard duty. Ordway was the one who discovered him asleep. Willard was sentenced to receive one hundred lashes on his back. See the Orderly Book entry for this day.

Friday July 13th 1804. we Set out at Sun rise, proceeded on passed the Mouth of the Big *Tar ki o* River.[1] last night at 10 oClock a violent Storm from the N. N. E. which lasted for one hour. a small Shower succeded the wind. the Latidude of yesterday 39d 55″ 56′ Long. [*blank*] passed a prarie level and beautiful below Some high hills, containing an amence Site of Grapes, wild Rye &.C— Capt. Clark killed 2 Goslins, Drewyer 2 also— the wind favourable from the South, the men Caught 2 Geese on a Sand barr one an old one (the old Geese have pin feathers yet cannot fly.) Since passing the *Nodaway* River the hills could only be Seen in a fiew places at a great Distance from the River on the North Side of the Missauris. But on the South Side their is high Land, & handsome praries the most of the way from the old Village of the Kansars, we Camped on a large Sand bar in the mi. of the River opposite a high & extensive prarie, on the North Side, (came about 20 miles today)

1. Tarkio, or Big Tarkio, River reaches the Missouri River in Holt County, Missouri.

Saturday July 14th 1804, Some hard Showers of rain accompanied with some wind which detained us untill about 7 oClock, we then Set out and proceeded on about a mile then their came up a violent Storm from the N. E. of wind & rain which passed through an open prarie, it came So Suddenly by a black cloud & dismal looking. we were in a Situation near the upper point of a Sand Island & on the opposite Shore falling in, the boat nearly quartering & blowing down the current. the Boat was in danger of being thrown up of the Sand but the men were all out in an Instant holding hir out Stemming the wind the anchor was immediately carried out. So by all exertion we could make we kept the boat from filling or takeing injury. the 2 pearogues ware about a quarter of a mile ahead the men on board were much put to it to keep them Safe. this Storm Suddenly Seased, and in one minute the River was as Smooth as it was before, the wind Shifted to the S. E. and we Set Sail & proceeded on passed small Island on the north Side & dined. R. Field who had charge of the horses on Shore did not join us last night.— passed an old fort on the north Side, Where Roe Bennet[1] of St. Louis wintered 2 years & traded with the Zotteaus & paunies. proceeded on passed a handsome Sand beach on the South Side, where we Saw three large Elk[2] the first wild ones I ever Saw. Capt. Clark & drewyer Shot at them, but the distance was too long, they Ran or trotted in to the River and Seamon[3] ⟨cross⟩ Swam across after them, we proceeded on passed a large Creek behind the lower point of an Island on the North Side called *Neash-na-Batto-na*,[4] this Creek is as large as the Mine River & runs parrelel with the Missouris for Some considerable distance, the men who were with the horses joined us this evening. Capt. Clarks notes & Remarks of 2 days blew Overboard this morning in the Storm, and he was much put to it to Recolect the courses &.C.— we Camped on the South Side opposite an Island.

1. Probably Benoit again, who traded with Oto and Pawnee Indians.
2. *Cervus elaphus.*
3. Lewis's Newfoundland dog Seaman.
4. Nishnabotna River, Atchison County, Missouri; today it mouths farther upstream.

Sunday July 15th 1804. a foggy morning which Detained us untill 7 oClock, Drewyer & Sgt. Floyd went on Shore. we proceeded on till Breakfast af[ter] I went on Shore with Capt. Clark on the South Side we Saw fresh Sign on bank of Elk. crossed a creek named faun Creek[1] which came in on the South Side of Missouris. we walked on over a Ridge came to high large praries & hills. we walked on found Some cherries near a handsome Spring River named cherry Run, at which we drank at the forks then followed it or one branch to the head which came out of a ridige which joined the praries, and went up on a high R. Ridge of prarie where we could See all around for a long distance in the open praries or as far as our eyes could behold, and on the opposite Side of the Missouris we Saw a large & extensive prarie which looked verry handsome, we walked along the hill prarie came to a large Creek called ne-ma-haw Creek[2] whic is about 30 yds. wide we delayed their till the boat came in Site then crosed & went on to a point where the Boat came & Camped, the flanking party who were with the horses did not join us this night, Jo. Fields went out on the North Side & killed a Deer.— we found plenty of ripe grapes along the Bottoms.

1. Clark mentions but does not name Ordway's two creeks; Floyd calls one (perhaps Ordway's second) "Plumb Run," which may be either Beadow or Deroin creeks, in southeastern Nemaha County, Nebraska.

2. Little Nemaha River, Nemaha County.

Monday July 16th 1804. we Set out verry eairly this morning proceeded on the side of a prarie above the prarie the hills make near the River passed Several Small Islands one large one called fair Sun[1] the Boat Ran fast on a Sawyer. the wind from the South, we delayed at 12 oClock for the Captains to take the Meridian altidude & Set their watches &-C— we then Sailed along & Stoped to Dine little above where the hills came close to the R. on South Side we passed a high Sand Bank which appeared to be Sliding in at times. little above a Bank of Sand Stone which was high & many Birds nests in the holes we proceded on to a large handsome prarie on the North Side where we camped.[2] the party who were with the horses joined us with 2 Deer. The River *neesh-nah-ba-to-na* Runs along back of the Bottom prarie under the Ball hill[3] along this River is plenty of Timbers every fiew miles which Stands in Handsome Groves. these hills are in Some places from 3 to 6 miles from the Missouris

1. The island, later called Sun Island and then perhaps Sonora Island, a few miles upstream from Brownville, Nemaha County, Nebraska, has disappeared.

2. Atchison County, Missouri, a few miles northeast of Peru, Nebraska.

3. The area Clark called the bald-pated prairie, the term Ordway applied the next day, now within Wabonsie State Park, Fremont County, Iowa.

Tuesday July 17th 1804. a pleasant warm day. we delay at this place for to hunt & take observations &-C— Several men out hunting eairly this morning—through the aforesaid Ball pated prarie. Capt Lewis Rhode out hunting also, the hunters killed 4 Deer to day Lat. 40 29′ 54″ North—

Wednesday July 18th 1804. we Set out at Sun rise under a gentle Breeze from the S. E. by S. a fair morning, we proceded on along this prarie passed Several Islands, the current of the River Runs 50′ fathom in 41 Seconds, their is but little timber on either Side of the River, except the Islands and points which are low wet & covered with lofty trees Cotton wood Mulbery Elm[1] &C.—&C.— we passed hill praries, and a place in a high bank where Some appearance of Iron oar where the Bank Sliped in to the River about 200 feet high. we camped[2] on the South Side of the Missouris. towards night we Saw an Indian dog on the Bank of the River, which appeared to have been lost. Drewyer joined us with 2 Deer this evening late.

1. American elm, *Ulmus americana* L.

2. Probably in Otoe County, Nebraska, a little south of Nebraska City.

Thursday July 19th 1804. we Set out eairly. between 2 Islands passed a place called Bakers oven & an Island called Bakers Island.[1] we passed the mouth of a Small creek[2] in a bend above high clifts on the South Side passed high land along the South Side forming clifts to the river of yallow earth. praries on the top. we Saw Some Signs of Elk. we gethered a quantity of cherries[3] at noon time & put in to the Whisky barrel we proceded on passed Several Sand bars & Islands and we camped on the north Side of an a willow Island which is in a round bend of the river. G. Drewyer Joined us with 2 Deer this evening. Bratton also. he found Callimous[4] opposite where we camped & a large quantity. (Sweet flag we call it)

1. In the vicinity of Nebraska City, Otoe County, Nebraska; see Clark's entry for July 18.

2. Either North Table Creek or South Table Creek, both of which reach the Missouri River at Nebraska City.

3. The enlisted men all mention the cherries, perhaps because they added them to their whiskey barrel. It is probably choke cherry, *Prunus virginiana* L., as Gass indicates.

4. Ordway is the only writer to mention William Bratton's observation of sweet flag, *Acorus calamus* L. The final, parenthetical phrase may not be in Ordway's hand.

Friday July 20th 1804. a heavy Deaw last night. Some foggy this morning. we Set out at Sun rise. Sergt. Pryor & Jo Fields went on Shore with the Horses. George Drewyer Sick, we passed a fine Spring runing out of a high clift of Rocks consisting of lime Stone and Iron oar. little above we passed weeping water Creek or the creek which Cryes.[1] Capt. Clark & R. Fields went on Shore after Breakfast, passed praries on both Sides of the Missouris, passed handsome high praries all along the east Side. passed Several runs Capt. Clark found an excelent Spring on the South Side, near a Small pond in Site of the River we passed Several Islands & Sand bars and camped[2] on the South Side nearly under a high hill prarie which appeared beautiful. Jo. Fields killed 2 Deer to Day & brought them in

1. Weeping Water Creek, Otoe County, Nebraska.
2. Cass County, Nebraska, a little above Spring Creek.

Saturday July 21st 1804. Some Rain this morning We Set out at Sun rise under a gentle Breese from the South or S. E. we proceded on verry well, passed Several Islands &C— Some high lands covered with Timber. in this hill is Semented rock & Limestone Some fine Springs &C— we arived at the mouth of the *platte River*[1] S. S. about 1 oClock this River Runs out and forms Several large Sand bars thrown out by the Platte River.— their is Some high handsome praries about this River, the Rapidity of the River Platt which is much greater than that of the Missouris, its width at the mouth across the bars is about ¾ of a mile, higher up we are told by one of our French Bowman[2] that he was 2 ⟨years winters⟩ years up or on this River and that it does not rise four feet but Spreads open 3 miles at Some places, we proceeded on round a large Sand bar S. S. a hard ⟨head⟩ wind from N. W. we put Below [past?] the last mentioned Sand Bar we passed a creek on S. S. called pappeo R.[3] praries in pt between the Missouris & the Great R. Platt but flat Subject to overflow. Some large cotten wood Timber but thin on the point. we Camped on the South Side of the River, a prarie on the N. Side of the Missouris the party who were with the Horses joined us with four Deer,

1. The Platte River enters the Missouri between Cass and Sarpy counties, Nebraska.
2. Either François Labiche or Pierre Cruzatte, more likely the latter.
3. Papillion, or Big Papillion, Creek, Sarpy County, just north of the entrance of the Platte River.

Sunday July 22nd 1804. we Set out eairly to find Some Good Timbered land and a good place to encamp we proceeded on along a high bank S. S. hand some praries along this bank to the hills, which commenced about 10 miles above G. R. Plat. we passed m of a Creek on the N. called Marringua (French) Musquetoe (English) Creek[1] which comes in behind a willow Island. we proceeded on 12 miles from G. R. Plate and encamped[2] at 11 [10?] oClock on the N. Side of the Missouris at a point convenient for observations & we cleared away the willows & pitched our Tents and built boweries &C.

1. Still Mosquito Creek, Pottawattamie County, Iowa, but perhaps its mouth was farther south at this time. Ordway's French word is *maringouin,* "mosquito."
2. At the party's Camp White Catfish, near the Mills-Pottawattamie county line, Iowa.

Monday July 23rd 1804. clear morning. G. Drewyer and [St?][1] Peter went to the Zottoas & Panies village (45 miles to nations) to invite them to come to our Encampment to treat. we hoisted the american Collours on the Bank the loading of the Boat put out to air &C—. The Latd. at this place is 41D 3m 19¾s North, one of the hunters killed 2 Deer,

1. Whitehouse also uses this designation for Cruzatte.

Tuesday 24th July 1804. Some rain wind blew from N. E. 4 men went to making ores for the Boat. we found a Great quantity of Ripe Grapes at this place.

Wednesday July 25th 1804. a pleasant morning Some men out hunting. G. Drewyer & peter Returned from the Zottoes village found no Indians it is Supposed by the Signs they Saw that they were all out in the praries hunting buffelow. Collins killed 2 Deer Jo Feilds killed 1 Turkey to day—

Thursday July 26th 1804. pleasant morning Some men out hunting. G. Drewyer killed 2 Deer & one Turkey. the Party Generally bussey dressing Skins &C— all the latter part of the day the wind blew hard from the S. a nomber of beaver has been caught here Since we arived at this place they appear to be verry pleanty on this River.

Friday July 27th 1804. cloudy morning. the Boat loaded. The Horses Swam over the River. we Set out under Sail ⟨pr⟩ about one oClock proceeded on verry well passed along high wood land on the South Side & praries on the N. Side hills 2 miles back of those low bottom praries. Shannon killed one Deer to day. towards evening we Saw Sign of Elk on the South Side Capt. Clark went out to hunt on Shore little above we passed along a prarie on S. S. we passed many Sand bars. the River verry crooked. we came about 15 miles & and Camped[1] on the bank of a high handsome prarie on the S. S. Some lofty Cotton wood in Groves along this bank the 2 men which were with the Horses did not join us to Night

1. Within the limits of Omaha, Douglas County, Nebraska, and in the vicinity of the Douglas Street Bridge (Interstate 480).

Saturday July 28th 1804. Cloudy morning we Set out eairly proceeded on past a h. bottom prarie on N. S. back of these praries a high Ridge with Some Timbers on it & in the vallies near the prarie above these praries the hills made in close & Steep to the River. a nomber of high round knobs on those hills which are bare from Timber. Some Timber in the vallies we passed the mouth of a Small Creek which comes in behind an Island from among those Ridges which is named Round Knob Creek.[1] the land opt. on the S. S. is low, the Timber mostly Cotton wood. G. Drewyer came to the bank with the horses, brought in a Deer which he killed The wind hard from the N. E. Detained us Some time we proceeded on passt a high bank on S. S. thin Timbers on the N. S. G. Drewyer found three of the Zotaus Indians Dressing an *Elk.* they were friendly and Gave him a part of it and one of them came with him in order to find the Boat. Drewyer killed one Deer & joined us brought the Indian with him, where we was Camped on the north Side of the River in Timbered land below an Isld. & prarie.—

1. Or Indian Knob Creek, apparently Pigeon Creek, Pottawattamie County, Iowa.

Sunday July 29th 1804. Rain all last night. Cloudy morning. we Set out Eairly. Jo. Barter[1] a Frenchman who could Speak the Zoteau language went with the Indian, in order to Git as many of them together as possable & bring them to the River above this ⟨where⟩ place So that we may See & treat with them &C.— we proceded on along a large bottom prarie on N. S. passed a Small Creek on N. S. called Boyer Creek, about noon we came to high land on the S. S. where we Stoped to Dine & jerk our meat which Drewyer brought to us. Willard Sent back to last nights Camp for his Tommahawk, which he left we Delayed about 2 hours, Caught Several of the largest cat fish we have ever caught in this River.— (one Swallowed a hook bit of the line, caught the Same G. hook) the Missouri is much more crooked since we passed the Great River Platte than before but not So Rapid in general; & more praries, the Timber Scarser &C— The Timber mostly Cottonwood except on the hills: which is oak Black Walnut hickery Elm Bass wood[2] &C— Willard lost his rifle in a ⟨Small⟩ large Creek Called Boyer[3] N. S. came back for help to find it. the white pearogue went back with him & got out his Rifle, which was sunk deep in the mud, we proceded on along a round bend & prarie on N. S. We Camped on the North Side in a thin Grove of cottonwood.—

1. La Liberté, who would abandon the expedition. See Appendix A, vol. 2, and Clark's entry for this day.
2. Perhaps linden, basswood, *Tilia americana* L., called "lynn" the next day.
3. Boyer River, or Creek, in northwest Pottawattamie County, Iowa.

Monday July 30th 1804. we Set out very eairly this morning in order to find a Good place to Camp & wait for the Zottaus Indians; to come in &C we proceded on passd. where G. Drewyer camped last night. The white Horse dyed last night. fell down the Bank being weak by gitting filled with water Swimming the Missouri on 28th ult.— G. Drewyer killed one

Deer.— we proceeded on past a high bank & bottom prarie. arived at high blufs on S. S. we camped about 7 oClock close under the foot of the bluffs in a Strip of woods which make along under the Ridge to the River the Timber is coffee nut[1] white oak Black walnut Elm bass wood or lynn hickery &C— below this handsome bottom prarie, above the Timber and bluffs is a beautiful high prarie, I think it is the Smothest, & prittyset place for a Town I ever Saw. back of this high Large prarie, their is uneven praris Some Timber in the vallies & on the branches &C— Jo. Fields & Reuben went hunting Jo killed & brought in an animel which the French call a brarow[2] (we hoisted the american Flag &C— expect the Zottous &c—[)] ⟨after which we name this place Camp Brarow⟩[3] this animal Resembles our Ground hogs in colour & Shape—nearly but the head like a dogs. four feet like a bear especially the claws. Inside like a hog long teeth. they live on flyes & bugs &.C. and dig in the Ground like a G. Hog they Say they growl like a possom, Capt. Lewis had this animal Skined the Skin Stuffed in order to Send back to St. Louis; the 2 hunters killed 3 deer took out the horses to bring them in. This place is named Counsel Bluffs. Latd. 41° 17m 00 North—

1. Kentucky coffee tree, *Gymnocladus dioica* (L.) K. Koch.

2. A badger, *Taxidea taxus*, the French word being *blaireau*. The groundhog used for comparison is the woodchuck, *Marmota monax*.

3. Ordway and Whitehouse note what may have been the initial name for the party's Council Bluff. It is in Washington County, Nebraska, near the town of Fort Calhoun and within Fort Atkinson State Historical Park.

Tuesday July 31st 1804. pleasant & Cool this morning. Jo Fields did not Return with the horses last night. they returned this morning with out them & Set out with 2 more men to hunt them George Drewyer killed a fat Buck this morning, & caught a young Beaver in a trap last night which he keeps in order to tame (which is easy to doe—[)] a nomber traps Set in the evening on the opposite Side on a point, where their is a verry large Sand Bar back of the bar is a young Groth of Cotten wood and back of that a bottom prarie which extends back to the Ridge which appears to be about 4 or 5 miles back from this River.— the Missouri is verry crooked couses on one Side or the other all the way from the Great River Platte, but the current not So Swift as below.— Sergeant Floyd has been Sick Several days but now is Gitting Some better.—[1] we expected the Zotteau nation of Indians to day & the man which went for them but they did not come. The reason is as we expect that they were So much Scatred hunting that it takes Some time for them to Git ready but we wait for them.

1. Clark noted Floyd's illness the previous day. Clark's mention was perhaps the first indication of the illness that would result in the sergeant's death the next month.

August 1st 1804 Wednesday. a fair morning. 2 men out hunting the Horses not found. 1 large bever caught last night in G. Drewyers trap. Drewyer went to hunt for the Horses. Shields went out a short time and killed & brought in a Deer; the wind from S. E. Jo. Fields killed & brought in a Deer. George Gibson killed a fat Buck brought in the Skin & Tallow & Some of the meat &C.—

Thursday 2nd Cool & pleasant this morning. 2 beaver caught in the traps last night. one of them gnawed of his leg he being large & got away. G. Drewyer returned found the Horses & killed a fine Elk & brought it all in; Labuche went out and killed & brought in one Deer. Collins killed a verry fat Buck weighed 134 pounds willard & he brot in only the quarters R. Fields killed a faun. the afternoon Cloudy. The wind Southerly. appearence of rain, Peter Cruset killed one fine Buck & brought it in about 14 of the Zottous Indians[1] arived here at Dusk. 2 Guns fired from our Bow peace, we Gave them Some provisions. they appear to be friendly &C—

1. Oto and also Missouri Indians, according to Clark.

Friday 3rd a foggy morning. no Diew last night. This morning the two Captains held a Counsel With the ⟨13⟩ Zottous Indians & made 6 Chiefs under the american government, they all Recd their medel[1] & other presents With Great kindness & thankfulness they all appeared to be Glad that they had Got freed from all other powers &C— they made Some verry Sensable Speeches Smoaked and drank with us. Shook hands and parted. Jos. Barter the man who went for those Indians Set out from their camp a day before them & has not returned. we Set out about 3 oClock P. M. proceeded on Round a large Sand bar & Camped[2] on the S. S. the Musquetos verry bad. Some place near Councile Bluff is arround the most proper place for a tradeing house as their are these three or four nations, the ottoes Ponies & mahar &C.

1. Presenting medals to Indian dignitaries was a longstanding custom. Lewis and Clark carried medals of various sizes and inscriptions. The most common displayed the profile of President Jefferson on one side, with clasped hands and crossed tomahawk and pipe on the reverse.

2. Some miles south of Blair, Washington County, Nebraska, but perhaps on the Iowa side, in Harrison County.

Saturday 4th at 7 oClock last night, a violent wind from the N. W. & thunder & rain which lasted about an hour then ceased blowing but hard rain followed, all Set out eairly this morning proceeded on through a narrow part of the River which is filled with Snags & logs the River in many places is confined within 200 yards. (Reed went back for knife) we passed an Old Tradeing house where one of our party passd. 2 years *P. C.*[1] trading with the Mahar, & ponies.— above that we passd. a Small Creek[2] which comes in behind a large Sand bar this Creek is the outelet of 3 ponds which make in from towards the hills.— the Bottom and high praries extends along Both Sides of the River the most of this days march, Some young Groves of cotton wood on the points we Road 10½ miles and Camped[3] on the S. S. on a high bank of willows.

1. Apparently Cruzatte, at a spot south of Blair, Washington County, Nebraska.

2. Apparently Fish Creek, near Blair.

3. In either Washington County, Nebraska, or Harrison County, Iowa, northeast of Blair.

Sunday 5th 1804. we Set out eairly proceeded on till about 7 oClock. a Shower came up from N. W. Some wind attending it. which Detained us about 2 hours. we then proceded on Round Sand bars. Delayed a Short time at 12 o.C. for Capt Lewis to take m. observation, proceded on along the Bank of a large prarie one of the men kild a large spoted bull Snake[1] under the bank a nomber of birds[2] which live in the bank flying about this Snake it is supposed the Snake charm them.[3] a head wind.— we proceded on round a long bend. Capt. Clark went on Shore towards evening in the point of Cottonwood & Grape Vines the Grape plenty C. Clark was at the River below this point which is only 370 yards across, & 12 miles round. C. Clark killed a Turkey & came to the Boat at dark, where we Led Roed abot 18 miles. Camped[4] on the N. S. of the Missouri below an Island.—

1. The bullsnake is *Pituophis melanoleucus sayi.*
2. Probably the bank swallow, *Riparia riparia.*
3. Ordway is the only journal keeper to relate the folk belief that snakes could somehow charm birds. Clark recorded other snake stories on June 14 and 24, 1804.
4. In Harrison County, Iowa, across the river and not far from the Burt-Washington county line in Nebraska.

Monday 6th a violent storm came up about 12 oClock last night of wind & rain from N. W. we Set out eairly this morning. passed a large Isld. on N. S. back of this Isld. comes in a Creek Called the *Soldiers* R.[1] on N. S. as big as the Nardaway R. at the mouth passed round bends & Sand bars & a prarie on S. S. & Groves of cottenwood on the bank, on N. S. near the River is a Spit of cottenwood timber but praries back of that Generally.— M. B. Reed who went back on 4th ult has not returned yet nor La Liberty who went for the Indians has not returned we expect he got lost attempting to come to us from the nation but we have all reason to think that Reed has deserted. we came 20½ miles this day & camped[2] on the S. S. of the River, George Drewyer Joined us this afternoon & fetched 2 Deer & one faun &.C.—

1. Soldier River, Harrison County, Iowa.
2. In Harrison County, roughly halfway between Soldier and Little Sioux rivers.

Tuesday 7th last night about 8 oClock a Storm from N. W. of wind and rain which lasted about ¾ of an hour. the Musquetoes verry troublesome last night we set out late this morning. the wind N. we proceeded on round bends & Sand bars &C— til about 12 oClock we then sent G. Drewyer W. Bratton R. Fields & W. Labuche Back to the ottaus village after M. B. Reed who had deserted from us with orders to fetch him Dead or alive, and to look for La Liberty who was lost as we expect with a publick horse.

they have orders to bring them all if they can find them to the mahar village where we are to wait their arrival; we Roed on about 18 miles & Camped[1] on the N. S. of the Missouri.

1. Probably in northwest Harrison County, a few miles below the mouth of the Little Sioux River.

Wednesday 8th we Set out at the usal time this morning at about 2 miles passd a part of the River Choked up with logs & Snags. So that we found it difficult to pass through with Safety. the wind from N. W. one of the Soldiers Dame[1] killed a pillican[2] on a Sand Island, we passed the mouth of little River *Des Cueoux* or Stone R.[3] on N. S. this River is about 80 yds wide & navagable for perogues for a considerable distance it contains a Great quantity of fish common to the country. this Stone R. as we are told runs through or from a large lake a long distance from the Mouth 20 L. in S. in the afternoon Capt Clark & Collins went out hunting on a point S. S. Collins killed an Elk. the Capt. Shot Several times at one but his rifle carried a Small Ball, took 2 men went to hunt it and he did not Git it, we Saw the Sand bars covered with white pillicans this afternoon Capt. Lewis Shot one which had a bag under his neck & bill which held 5 Gallons of water. we Roed about 16 mils. and Camped on N. S. of the Missouri River at a willow bank

1. John Dame; apparently his only mention in the journals comes on this day, in Clark's and in Ordway's journals.
2. American white pelican, *Pelecanus erythrorhynchos*.
3. Little Sioux River, Harrison County, Iowa.

Thursday 9th[1] a foggy morning, which detained us till past 7 oClock at which time we Set out under a gentle Breeze from S. E. we passed Round Several points of high wood land Capt. Clark & Sgt. Floyd went out hunting on S. S. came 11 miles by 12 o.C. where the River had formerly Cut across a bend Said to be 15 mes. Round & a very Short distance a cross where it had Broke through a narrow Stripe of woods on each side of the River, the old Channel in the above mentiond bend is ponds & Islands. the hills are a Great distance from the River this Several days. the land on the River is low chiefly covered with Cottenwood & Grape vines &.C. the Grapes are verry pleanty on the River for this Several days. Capt. Clark killed a Turkey & Joined us towards evening. we camped[2] on S. S. of the River The Musquetoes more troublesome than ever.—

1. What is apparently a pointing hand precedes this entry.
2. Probably at a spot now in Harrison County, Iowa, a mile or so south of Onawa.

Friday 10th we Set off eairly a fair day. Some fish & one Beaver caught last night. we passed a place where the River had cut through & Shortened the river Several miles, we passed high Ridge of prarie land on S. S. Smooth plains back from the river, the Timber Scarse, a Great nomber of Elk Sign on the Sand beaches &.C. we passed high clifts on S. S. about 60 feet from the Surface of the of Sand Stone. the ridge on the top is covered with Short Grass Some bushes &.C. the wind hard from the S. W. (Sailed Some.) we came 22½ miles this day & camped[1] on a Sand bar N. S. of the Missouri River.

1. In Monona County, Iowa, across the river and a few miles above the Thurston-Burt county line in Nebraska.

Saturday 11th hard Showers this morning comenced at day break & lasted & detained us about an hour, hard wind from S. W. Succeeded it we passed a Round knob on a high Ridge 300 feet high— near the River S. S. Where we See a Grave where an Indian chief was buried 4 years ago called the *Black bird* of the *Mahar* Nation.[1] this Black bird was a great king among his people. they carry him provision at certain times &.C. Capt. Lewis & Clark went up to the grave & carried a white flag & put up on the pole which Stood over the grave, which was a round heap, (9 miles by land from below Nation) we proceeded on the wind hard Some Thunder, the river verrey crooked, after we passed this hill we passed a bend of cottonwood Timber on N. S. we came abot. 18 Miles & camped[2] on the N. S. in a bend of the River,

1. Blackbird, chief of the Omahas, was buried on Blackbird Hill, Thurston County, Nebraska.
2. Due to changes in the course of the Missouri River, the campsite would be in the vicinity of Badger Lake, Monona County, Iowa.

Sunday 12th a fair morning. we Set off eairly this morning. proceeded on round a bend which was 18 miles Round by water & only little better than half a mile a cross by land, S. S. we Sailed on with a S. E. wind. passed a Red Ceeder[1] Bluff on S. S. abot. 200 feet high the course bearing North,— the land on the N. S. is low the Timber cottenwood & large willows, & Subject to overflow, (Grapes &.C. in abundance[)] we heard a prarie woolf[2] bark on the bank N. S. it resembled our Indian dogs.— we Camped[3] on a Sand bar S. Side of the Missourie River,—

1. Eastern red cedar, *Juniperus virginiana* L.
2. A coyote, *Canis latrans.*
3. In either Monona or Woodbury County, Iowa, near the county line.

Monday 13th we Set out eairly. proceeded on under a gentle Breese from Souhard we passed the mouth of the Mahar Creek[1] below an Island S. Side of the Missouri R. we proceeded on to the lower point of another Island N. S. opposite to which we Camped on S. Side Near the Mahar Village,[2] I and 3[3] more of the party went out to the Village or to the place where it formely Stood.[4] we passed through high Grass in the low prarie & came to the Mahar Creek on our way. proceeded along Creek till we came to 3 forks which came in near together below the Village. we crossed the North branch and proceded along the South branch which was verry fatigueing for the high Grass Sunflowers & thistles[5] &C all of which were above 10 feet high, a great quantity of wild peas[6] among those weeds, we broke our way through them till we came to where their had been a village of about 300 Cabbins called the Mahar village. it was burned about 4 years ago immediately after near half the Nation died with the Small pox, which was as I was informed about 400, we found none of the natives about the place they were out hunting the Buffelow, we ascended the hill above the village on which was all the Graves of the former, I Saw the grave also where the Grand chief of the Punckhas[7] was buried about the Same time the Mahars were &.C. &.C— we Camped on the hill about 5 miles from the Boats. we Struck up a fire the Musquetoes verry troublesome, we were in Great want of warter but found none,

1. Omaha Creek, north of the Dakota-Thurston county line, Nebraska.

2. The Omaha village called Tonwontonga or Big Village, Dakota County, Nebraska, about one mile north of Homer.

3. Cruzatte, George Shannon, and "E. Cann." See Clark's entry for this day.

4. Ordway's route this day cannot be determined with great accuracy, but he seems to have gone up Omaha Creek and then crossed it to what he conceived to be forks of the creek, perhaps Fiddlers, Wigle, and South Omaha creeks. He then apparently camped on a hill near the Omaha village for the night. The village he discusses in this entry is Tonwontonga (see Clark's entry for this day). The rest of his discussion about the village, its surroundings, and the Omaha people is apparently taken from Clark's entry of August 14 (see notes there).

5. Probaby the common sunflower, *Helianthus annuus* L., and an unknown thistle, *Cirsium* sp.

6. An unidentified legume with pea-like characteristics.

7. No information seems to be available to identify a chief of the Poncas buried here. The statement may be unreliable or inaccurate.

Tuesday 14th we Set out at light, & walked along down the hills past the Graves. we Saw also a nomber of large holes in the Ground where they used to hide their peltry &C. in, when they went out hunting and when they returned they would dig it out again, I put up a paper on a pole Stuck in a round hill, as a Signal for G. Drewyer &.C— then we crossed the Small run which came in to the bottom from behind the hills, we then crossed this bottom prarie which is high & verry rich & formed a handsom vallie for a long distance back between the hills which is nearly half a mile wide across above the village the Mahar Creek makes down along the South Side next to the hills, we crossed the creek about 10 yds. wide, and ascended the hill below the creek we See a nomber of beaten pathes leading in different directtions, but no Signs of any being their lately. we walked along the ridge which is high prarie all back as far as my [eye?] could behold. we expected to have found Some corn or Something growing Some where in the bottom but we could not see any appearence of anythig being planted this year, we walked along the Ridge about 1½ miles then decended the hill & passed along, Round S. S. of a long pond[1] which lay between the hills & the Missouri, we crossed the out let of the pond which is verry mirry along the edge of the pond. we came to the Missouri and went up. crossed the mouth of the Mahar creek, & Returned to the Boats about 10 oClock A. M. the Grapes are verry pleanty near the Missouri R,—

1. The pond appears on *Atlas* map 16.

Wednesday 15th a pleasant morning, Capt. Clark and 10 of the party[1] went out to the Mahar Creek in order to catch Some fish & they caught & brought in upwards of 300 different Sorts of fine fish. Some Salmon Some bass pike[2] &.C—&.C— we Saw a Smoke arise on the N. Side of the Missouri River ⟨3⟩ 4 men[3] went over to See if their was any Indians, they Returned without finding any Indians; hard wind F. N. w. A niew mast made for the Batteaux to day.—

1. Including Floyd, according to himself.
2. Since no species of salmon are native to the region, the fish may be mooneye, *Hiodon tergisus,* or goldeye, *H. alosoides.* The bass is either smallmouth bass, *Micropterus dolomieui,* or largemouth bass, *M. salmoides.* The pike is probably northern pike, *Esox lucius.*
3. One of the men was Dorion.

Thursday 16th a pleasant morning. the party in high Spirits fiddleing & danceing last night. I was up all night on duty, the latter part of the night verry cold, for the month of august. Capt. Lewis & 12 of the party went out to the Mahar Creek a fishing they returned in the afternoon with more than a barrell or in nombers 709. 167 of them pike, of a Tolrable Size, of excelent fish of different Sorts & Sizes. one beaver caught to day, hoisted our mast &.C,—

Friday 17th of August 1804, a clear morning, the wind from S. E. we are yet waiting here for G. Drewyer & the 3 men who were with him, the men remained in camp reparing the arms & Cloathing &C. Labuche who was one of the Messengers arivd towards evening Informed us that Drewyer & the Zottaus Chiefs was comming near with the Deserter &.C—

Saturday 18th pleasant, G. Drewyer & the other 2 men Returned. brought with them Reed the deserter, likewise a the Big chief of the Zottaus called the Big horse, and another chief called petevaliar, of Missouri, & a Frenchman & 7 of the wariers came for the purpose of treating with the Mahas &C—[1] Reed tried & punished towards evening; the Chiefs verry Sorrey &.C— an Liberty (had been at the village) has not returned with Drewyer

1. Actually, Big Horse was a Missouri Indian, and Little Thief ("petevaliar" for the French *petit voleur,* "little thief"), an Oto. Also in the group was apparently the Frenchman the party had met on August 2; see Clark's entry for that day and for the next.

Augt. *Sunday 19th* pleasant, S wind, the Indians got up their horses to water them, all the Indians appear to be friendly.— at about the hour of 9 o.C. Capt. Lewis & Capt. Clark read a Speech to the Indians & counseled with them. Gave one a medel & the rest they gave commissions & made them all chiefs &C. they appeared to be willing to make peace with the Mahars & all other Nations. the Captains Gave them Some Small articles of Goods &.C—& gave them provisions while they remained with us. the most of this day taken up in giving the Indians Good counsel &.C., Sgt. Floyd taken verry Sudenly Ill this morning with a collick. Capt. M. Lewis invited the above petevaliar the Big Chief to go to See the presidant &C. &C.

Augt. *Monday 20th* pleasant, we Set of under a gentle Breeze from S. E. the Indians chiefs Set out to return to their village. Sgt. Floyd worse than he was yesterday we Sailed on verry well till noon when we came too on S. S. Sergt. Charles Floyd Expired directly after we halted a little past the middle of the day. he was laid out in the Best Manner possable. we proceeded on to the first hills N. S. there we dug the Grave on a handsome Sightly Round knob close to the Bank.[1] we buried him with the honours of war. the usal Serrymony performed (by Capt. Lewis[)] as custommary in a Settlement, we put a red ceeder post, hughn & branded his name date &.C— we named those Bluffs Sergeant Charles Floyds Bluff. Distant from the Mouth of the Missouri 949½ miles by water, we then proceeded on a Short distance to a creek which we Call Floyds Creek.[2] (came 15 or 18 mil. to day.[)] where we Camped N. S.

1. At Sioux City, Woodbury County, Iowa; see the Introduction in this volume.
2. Floyd River, Woodbury County.

Tuesday Augt. 21st we Set off eairly this morning under a hard Breeze from the S. we proceded on verry well passed a large Sand bar on N. S. the wind blew so hard that we were oblidged to take a reefe in our Sail & the Sand blew So thick from the Sand bars that we could not see the channel far ahead & it filled the air before us about a mile. we Saw Several woolves on Sd. Sand beach we passed the Mouth of the Grand River de Souix[1] close above a high clay Bluff below Sd. Sand bar on the N. S. the white pearogue could hardly Sail for want of Ballass, we put in Several kegs of pork &.C. Shannon went out to hunt on N. S. we proceeded on 20 odd miles to day & Camped on S. S. Shannon joined us late. But killed nothing. the man with the horses did not join us yet,

1. The Big Sioux River forms the South Dakota–Iowa boundary.

Wednesday 22d August 1804. we Set off eairly the current verry Swift. the wind hard from the South, we proceded on round a bend & Sand bar N. S. the hills make to the River on S. S. below the hills their is Some large Timber of cottonwood Elm maple[1] &.C. Some oak & ceeder on the Bluffs. we halted under the Bluff & found different kinds of oar which has the appearence of brass, copperas alum &.C. &C all of which has a Sulpheras Smell, Broken praries Back. The 2 men who had been with the horses from the Mahars village, joined us below Sd. Bluffs. had killed 2 Deer, 2 other men went on with the horses hunting; G. Drewyer caught one Beaver last night.— a Small creek comes in close above Sd. Bluffs which we call Roloje Cr.[2] on S. S. we proceeded on under a fine Breeze from the South. passed a Red ceeder Bluff on the South Side & little above on the Same Side we passed an Alum Stone clift about 50 feet high & a great nomber of birds nests, near the top of the clift. we Sailed on to a prarie where we Camped on N. S. after Sailing 19 Miles. back of Sd. prarie is a large pond. we See a great deal of Elk Sign,

1. An unknown species of maple, *Acer* sp.
2. Probably Aowa, or Ayowa, Creek, Dixon County, Nebrasaka, near Ponca.

Thursday 23rd we Set off eairly. 2 men went out hunting, the wind favourable from the South. G. Drewyer and Jo. Fields went out hunting on N. S. passt. on round a bend Capt. Clark walked on Shore a Short time & killed a fine Buck, we halted to Breakfast, 2 Elk Swam the River close by the Boat both of them we wounded. at the same time Jo. Fields came to the Boat informed us that he had killed a Bull Buffelow, Capt. Lewis & myself & 10 more of the party went out Bucherd & Brought it to the Boat, Collins killed a faun Deer. the 2 hunters on the South Side came to the Boat with 2 Deer which they had killed, we then proceeded on past a Butiful bottom prarie N. S. which is verry large & wide I walked about 1 mile & ½ in it when I went for the abo. ment. Buffelow, I Saw the beds & Signs of a great many more Buffelow But this was the first I ever Saw & as great a curiousity to me. we halted in a bend opposite a Sand Isd. ⟨in Sd prarie⟩ the wind blew So hard that it detained us the most of the afternoon, So we pickled down our Buffelow meat, & jerked the venison, the Sand blew So thick from the Sand Island that we could not see across the River for a long time, towards evening the wind abated & we proceeded on to the head of sd. Sand Isd. & camped on S. S.[1] one of the party wounded an Elk after we landed.—

1. In either Dixon County, Nebraska, or Clay County, South Dakota, a mile or so southeast of Vermillion, Clay County. The shifting of the Missouri River over time makes the campsite difficult to determine.

Friday 24th Some Small Showers of rain the latter part of last night. rainy morning. we Set off about Sunrise, proceeded on past a high Bottom of wood land large Cottonwood, Elms &.C. Some Small Sized timber on N. S: near the river.— Smooth praries back from the River. we halted took Breakfast at high Ragged Bluffs on S. S. a nomber of round knobs on Sd. Bluffs covered with verry Short Grass. Some ceeder on the edge of the Bluff along under those Bluffs we found a great quantity of red berries[1] which grows on a handsome bush about as high as I could reach. these Berries are a little Sour (& are called Rabbit berries) (English) But pleasant to the taste we found also a burning bank or Bluff which was verry high & had fire in it. it had a Sulpheras Smell, we found in it a great quantity of asney & a great quantity of different kinds of mineral Substance, &.c. Capt. Clark went out hunting on S. S. we proceeded on passed the upper end of the Butiful Bottom prarie. there the high butiful prarie commenced which is extensive & Smooth. Back about 2 miles we are informed that their is a verry high hill called The Hills of the little ⟨Christian⟩ Devils[2] by the natives & they amagan that it is inhabited by little people with Big heads &

they are afraid to go up to them for fear they will shoot them with their Bows & arrows, we passed the mouth of White Stone River,[3] which came in above the high prarie their is large points of land covered with Timber on boath sides of the river Such as cottenwood ash Elm &.C—. Capt. Clark joined us towards evening had killed 2 Buck Elk & 1 faun. Capt. Clark & Capt. Lewis & 10 more of the party in order to fetch the meat in, they returned with the meat, which was jurked at the Same time we had a fine Shower of Rain which lasted abt. half an hour, at which place we Camped on South Side. the Musquetoes Troublesome.

1. Probably the buffaloberry, *Shepherdia argentea* (Pursh) Nutt., mentioned also by Clark this day, but not with Ordway's colloquial name.
2. Spirit Mound, Clay County, South Dakota, about eight miles north of Vermillion.
3. Vermillion River, Clay County.

Saturday 25th 2 men of the party caught 9 cat fish last night 5 of them verry large. a fair & pleasant morning. Capt. Lewis & Clark & 10 more of the party I was with them.[1] we went back to the mouth of white Stone or little peoples Rivers in the white pearogue and walked out to the hill of the little people we walked hard 3 hours from the Missouri to git to the hill, we crossed white Stone River on our way, when we came near the hill we Saw a great flock of Birds flying about the top of it we ascended the hill found none of the little people ther we Saw Several holes in the ground. Some Stone piss ants[2] &.C. we could See a Great distance in everry direction which the land is verry Rich. high Smooth praries & Some fine Bottom. when we was on the Top of the hill of the little Devils (which is 60 feet high) we Saw Several gangs of Buffelow at a considerable distance from us. we was allmost famished for the want of warter. the Sun beat down verry hot the air Sultry. we went the nighest course to the River of little children, from hence after we took a little refreshment. we proceded on down that R. & Struck our old track & returned back to the pearogue, about Sunset, we walked the whole day in the Beautiful prarie found Some plums & grapes, but little Timber. we returned back to the old Camp of last night & camped. the Big Boat had Set off about 11 A. M. oClock & proceeded on,[3] we had a little rain this evening, we killed one duck & Several Birds only,

1. According to Clark, the men were Drouillard, Ordway, John Shields, Joseph Field,

John Colter, Bratton, "Cane" (perhaps *engagé* Cann), Labiche, Richard Warfington, Robert Frazer, and perhaps York.

2. Perhaps the harvester ant, *Pogonomyrmex* sp., mentioned by Clark this day.

3. The main party camped on the Nebraska side, near the Cedar-Dixon county line.

Sunday 26th we Set off eairly in order to overtake the Boat. we came to the Boat abt. 9 o.C. A M they had not left their last nights Camp. G. Shannon had killed an Elk the evening before, they delayed to jurk it &.C; one of the horses lost Drewyer & one man hunting them we then proceeded on passed a white clay Bluff on S. S. found a fine place of plumbs in a prarie N. S. we proceeded on to the mo. of little *petark (French)* [(] *little Bow)*[1] *English* S. S. abo. the hill opposite to which we camped on N. S. at petite wave formerly an old Indian village,

1. Bow Creek, Cedar County, Nebraska. Ordway is attempting the French *petit arc,* "little bow."

Monday 27th we heard G. Drewyer hollow before day this morning. the pearogue went over eairly for him he had not found the horses. 2 other men went out to hunt them, 2 of the party caught 12 fine cat fish last night, we Set off at Sun rise under a gentle Breeze from the S. E. we Saw a mink[1] under the bank we Sailed on passed a Chalk Bluff on S. S. in the Same Bluff their is a vane of Black Sulpheras clay which has the appearance of Slate or Stone coal & Some kinds of mineral Substance, we proceeded on the Sand blew thick till abt. 3 o.C. P. M. passed the Mouth of a large creek called River [pt.?] *Shark* Jaque[2] on N. S. here we See a likely young Indian of the Mahar nation. he told us that their camp was near; their is considerable of cottonwood Timber about this place, while we were halted here 2 more young Indians came to us. one a Mahar the other a Siowee. Sergt. pryor & 2 more[3] went from the Boat with 2 of the Indians out to their Camp to invite them in to See us especially the Chiefs, the other Indian came along and went with us, we proceeded on till dark and Camped on a large Sand beach on the N. S.

1. Ordway is the only writer who mentions seeing a mink, *Mustela vison.*

2. James River, Yankton County, South Dakota.

3. Dorion and another Frenchman with him.

Tuesday 28th a pleasant morning we Set off eairly under a fine Breeze from S. E. we proceeded on till Breakfast time we then halted at a large prarie N. S. the Indian left us in order to go to his camp; we proceeded on passed handsome Groves of cottonwood Timber on boath Sides of the Missouri River. passed high banks high prarie on N. S. handsom & ascending graddually from the river, at 2 oClock P. M. the wind Blew hard from S. W. the large pearogue drove against the Shore on N. S. & a hole got knocked in her So that it let the water in verry rapid they began to unload. Capt. Clark went with Some men from the Big Boat to their assistance. they Soped in a Cappoe &.C. & made it Safe to cross. we then crossed the river on S. S. & Camped[1] to wait the arival of the men who went for the Indians & the Indians in order to counsel with them Some of the party went out hunting we hoisted a flag pole, the 2 men who had been out to hunt for the horses returned to the Boat informed us that the horses & ⟨the⟩ Shannon was gone a head, we Saw Several large Bucks run at a distance from our Camp, this place is below a large Island & Sand bar a hill & Bluff on the Same Side little above. Our Camp was in the handsome Bottom & Groves of oak Timber &.C— appearance of rain.—

1. Below Gavins Point Dam, Cedar County, Nebraska.

Wednesday 29th a hard Storm arose from the N W. of wind & rain about 8 o.C. last night rained considerable part of the Night. the men who went for the Indians did not return last night Cloudy morning. Some Thunder, Colter Sent on for to find the man that went on with the horses the pearogue repaired. the lading put in the white pearogue; the men engaged making a Towing line out of our Green Elk hides, we have plenty of fine fat Cat fish the most of the Time. Several large ones caught last night.— The Misouri river affords us pleanty of fish, & the Country pleanty of all kinds of Game. in the afternoon Sergt. pryor & the 2 men who went with him returned to our Camp & brought with them 60 Indians of the Souix nation. they Camped on the opposite Shore & did not incline to cross this evening. our Captains Sent them over Some lyed Corn & Tobacco &.C— Sargt. pryor informed me that their Town is about 9 miles from the Missouris up the R. Jacque. their Town consisted of abt. [*blank*] lodges which was made of painted red & white dressed Buffelow & Elk Skins & is verry handsome; the Women homley the most of them old, but the young men handsome. G. Drewyer killed one Deer to day.

Thursday 30th A foggy morning, a heavy diew last night. Shannon nor Colter did not come to us last night. the fog remained on the River late this morning & So thick that we could not See the Indians camp on the opposite Shore.— at about 8 oClock the fog went away. Some of the Indians Swam across the river to git Some breakfast with us, at the hour of 9 oClock the commanding officers had all things in readiness to hold a counsel with the chiefs and warries of the Souix nation, they Sent a pearogue across for them, they all [c]ame into our Camp in the most friendly manner &C their was four of them which were always a Singing & playing on their curious Instruments which were as follows, viz. they had each of them a Thrapple[1] made of a fresh buffelow hide dressed white with Some Small Shot in it and a little bunch of hair tied on it, the head man of the[m] was painted white, the rest of them were painted different colours. when they arived at our Camp & took the Commanding officers by the hand 2 Guns was fired from our bow peace. the colours displaying &-C— Each man of our party Gave the 4 men of Band a peace of Tobacco, they Sang around our camp during the time of the counsel. Each man of those Musicians had War hoop it was made of thickest buffelow hides dressed white covered with thin Goat Skin dressd. white & ornamented with porcupine quills & feathers &.C. and in Such a defensive manner that a M. Ball could not penetrate through it they wore them on their Backs when at practice, But when in attack at war they wear them on their right arm tied fast, the talk was finished by our Comdg. officers about 4 oClock, they made five Chiefs & Gave Each a Medel & Gave the whole Some preasants, they Gave the Grand Chief which they call in Indian weucha,[2] La librator in french, a red laced coat & a fine cocked hat & red feather & an american flag & a white Shirt &.C. all of which he was much pleased with, they recd. all their presents verry thankfully, & divided them among one another &c— the captains Gave the young Boys Some beeds to Shoot for with their Bows & arrows, their was one in particular that beat all the rest. Stuck his arrow everry time in the mark &.C—. after dark we Made a large fire for the Indians to have a war dance, all the young men prepared themselves for the dance. Some of them painted themselves in curious manner Some of the Boys had their faces & foreheads all painted white &C a drum was prepared, the Band began to play on their little Instruments, & the drum beat & they Sang. the young men commenced dancing around the fire. it always began with a houp & hollow & ended with the Same, and in the intervales, one of the warries at a time would rise with his weapen & Speak of what he had done in his day, & what warlike actions he had done &.c. this they call merrit &.C they would confess how many they had killed & of what nation they were off & how many horses they had Stole &-C—they Camped along Side of us & behaved honestly & cleaver &C. &C—

N. B. The Chiefs had time untill next morning to give answers to the questions which had been asked them by Capt. Lewis & Capt. Clark—

1st that they Should make peace with their neighbours the Zottous, & Missouris, as for the Mahars and them are at peace with each other.

2nd that the head Chief We-ucha and four or five more of their nation Should go to visit the Seat of Government in the ensuing Spring, that they might See their Great Father the presidant & receive his Counsel &C to which they agreed to and expresed a wish to see their G. father.

1. Referring to the windpipe and perhaps to the Jew's harp as noted by Whitehouse this day, but Ordway seems to describe a rattle or tambourine.

2. Clark identifies the principal chief as "Shake Hand," a name that bears no apparent relation to Ordway's rendition of the Dakota or French. See Ordway's next entry for a discussion of the identity of the Indian chiefs.

Friday 31st August 1804. pleasant morning the Chiefs not ready to Speak till half past 7 o.C. at which time the talk of the chiefs[1] beginning at the oldest the we-u-che—head chief, of the Bob Brulee[2] tribe my great father, his 2 sons I See before me this day. You See me, and the rest of the Chiefs & warries we are verry poor, we have neither powder, Ball or knifves, nor the women at the village has no Cloaths nor our children to war [wear] and wishes that my fathers Sons would be charitable enofe to Give them Some things, as his Brothers gave him a fine Suit of cloaths with a flag, and a Meaddel, or Gave him permission to Stop the first trading boat or pearogue that would come up the river to trade with them &-c— & he Said he would make peace with or between the paunies and Mahars, as his nation, and he would bring chiefs from each nation to the Seat of Government next Spring with him & his chiefs, and that his Situation was Such that he could not leave his nation to go before Spring; and he Said if he Spoke to them it would be better than it would for his Great fathers Sons, for they would hear him better, he Said likewise that he went to the English & they gave him a Meddal & cloaths & but when he went to the Spanish they never Gave him any thing to keep the meddal from his Skin, he Says that now you gave me a meddal & cloaths but we are poor as the trader did not come to bring us goods for Some time I wish you would consider & give me Something for our Squaws at home my Brothers,— the Captains told them that they were not traders, that they had only come to make the road open for the traders to come & that in a Short time their would be pleanty of traders on with Goods and would Supply their wants on better terms than ever they had got them before.

2nd Chief Speaks Mot, thouge, the white *Crain* my fathers word I have listened to yesterday, and to day it pleases me to See how you have dressed our old Chief. I am a young man, I do not want to take much, my father has made me a chief. I had much Sence But now I think I have more than ever, But what the old chief Said I will agree to & Say & doe as he & you have told me &c &C and I wish you to take pity on us for we are poor—

3rd Chief Speaks His name if *pan-dan-apappy*— I am a young man and know but little, & cannot Speak well, But what you have told the old chief I will hear to & will hear him &c.

4th Chief Speaks Ane, a, wish, a Shaddie La, dom, my fathers I cannot Speak Much to you, but little, you make our old chief higher than all of us; I am Glad to See him So finely dressed by you & will agree to what you told him, and will doe Every thing you & he Says &

5th Chief Speaks his name is Mede, thunk, a pertizon— my father the Meddel you gave me gives me a heart to go with my old Chief to See my Great Father

4th Chief began again, I am not rich, but poor, I wish you would have pitty on me, I was chief when I was a boy, now I am a man you See before you (my 2 fathers) you made my old chief So fine that I will not go to war but take his advice, and burry the tomahawk and knife in the ground and go with my old chief to See my Great father, when I was a young man I went to the Spanish; and did not like their Sayings So well as yours &.C. I am glad you Come to See my fathers land and all his red children, and the flag you Gave us it is So large as to Cover our children, from the heat of the Sun, he Says also that he is willing to make peace with his neighbours, the Zottous and Missouries &c. &c. but the fine meddels that you gave us we will Give or Show them, So that they need not take our horses &.c. we have got our horses & bows & arrows here but we want a little powder & lead to kill the Buffelows for our horses are poor at this Season & cannot run after them as they can in the Spring &C— their is one tribe of red men my fathers that have not their Ears open, but the old chief & us will do the best we can for you, with regard to the punkaws nation & all others as far as in our power lies &.C—

51y— a worrier Speakes my father I am glad to See how fine you have made the old chief, before now I could not Spare him but now I am willing to let him Go to See my Great father;—my father as you gave us a fine flag we wish you would give a little powder and a little of our Great fathers milk (or whiskey) that we may rejoice under our Great fathers Collours &.C. &.C. when all was over the most of the warries went across the river, the Chiefs remained till dusk the Commanding officers Shewed them the air gun and a great many other curiousityes, which pleased them verry much, our Intreperter old Mr Dunienoir left us & went with his Son in to this nation, the Comdg. Officers Gave the Indians com [*commission?*], more Tobacco & corn to take them to their lodges, &.C— at dark a blue crain fly[3] over attempted to lite on the mast of the B. Boat missed it and fill on the Boat one of the men caught and Gave it to one of the Indians, the pearogue crossed with the chiefs and all landed Safe on the opposite Shore, where they camped, directly after a hard Storm arose of the wind and rain from the N. W. which lasted 2 hours. rained considerable part of the night, a considerable quantity of fish caught at this place, gave the Indians Some of them &.c George Shannon & Colter has not joined us yet,—

The names of the chiefs above mentioned ⟨&.C⟩ in Indian

1st Weu-cha
2nd Mathuga
3rd pandan, a pappya,

4th Anckas, week, a chappa,
5th Mead, a, tuncka;—

N. B. The above place where the last Counsel was held with the Souix nation, as named by Capt. Clark. *Calamel Bluff,*[4] Minral

N. B. their was Several of the Indians which had Strings of White Bears[5] claws around their necks, which was 3 inches in length, & Strung as close as possable to each other on the String all around their necks.— ⟨the⟩ all those nations have one language for considerable part of their words &C.

1. Ordway's names for the chiefs differs from Clark's and he is the only enlisted man to provide such detail. Ordway's "we-u-che" or "Weu-cha" (or "weucha, La librator" in the previous entry), called the head chief, is apparently not the same as Clark's head chief, Shake Hand. It is the Yankton term *wic'á,* "male," and thus may not signify an actual person. "Mot, thouge" or "Mathuga," White Crane, is Clark's "Mar to Se ree," with the translation probably a mistake for "white bear," that is, the grizzly bear. But Ordway's term may be Yankton *mağát'aŋka,* "big goose" (for the swan). "Pan-dan-apappy" or "Pandan, a pappya," is probably Clark's "Par nar ne Ar par be" (*p'anani ap'api*), "Struck by the Ree (Arikara)." Ordway's "Ane, a, wish, a Shaddie La, dom" or "Anckas, week, a chappa," is Clark's "Ar ca we char chi" (*haŋké wic'áša*), "The Half Man." "Mede, thunk a pertizon" or "Mead, a, tuncka" is a name not given by Clark, nor does the captain list a fifth chief. He may have been a leading warrior who spoke at the council, as indicated by the term "pertizon" (partisan). The Yankton term may be *mdotáhuŋka,* "war leader."

2. Ordway means to write Bois Brulé, the name for a group of Sioux, or Dakota, Indians; these were actually Yankton Sioux.

3. Probably the great blue heron, *Ardea herodias.*

4. The captains called the area Calumet Bluff; see Clark's entry of August 28.

5. The grizzly bear, *Ursus horribilis,* not encountered until October 20.

Saturday 1st September 1804, we Set off eairly the frenchman called from the other Shore that they had forgot their tin kittle last evening. the pearogue crossed Brought him to the Boat for his kittle we found it & gave it to him, & 2 fish with it, we proceeded on under an unsteady Breeze from S. W. passed a chalk Bluff on N. S. where we found pleanty of fine plumbs, little above is a white clift called the den of the White Bear, we See large holes in the clift which appeared to go Deep into the clift; this clift is about 70 feet high on the top is ragged round knobs & praries all praries on Boath Sides of the river, Some Timber in the vallies, Cottonwood Elm oak &.C. & on the Islands which is covered with Small Cottonwood Timber

&.C. & on the Islands which is covered with Small cottonwood Timber &.C— G. Drewyer went out hunting on N. S. he returned in a Short time had killed a fine Buck Elk; it was all put on board the pearague, we then proceeded on past Bottom praries to the lower point of a large & well Timbered Island where we Camped[1] on N. S. & jurked our Elk, Capt. Lewis and Capt. Clark went across the river where they was Informed that their was a Deep pond where their is a large Beaver house & about 3 hundred Beaver or more, as they amagine in the pond. The Captains had a curiousity to See the pond & Beaver house; or Cabbin; they returned in the evening, but did not See the pond nor did not Go to it for we had passed it some distance, N.B. we passed in the course of this day a large Island between the two Bluffs covered with timber. above the White Bear clift we passed two Islands in Sight of each other the last of which is verry large, from the Calumet Bluffs covered with young Timber also, the high lands approach the river & in Some places touch on each Side of the Missouri.—

1. Bon Homme Island, Bon Homme County, South Dakota, is now inundated by Lewis and Clark Lake.

Sunday 2nd Sept. 1804. a hard Storm arose the latter part of last night ½ past 1 oC. of wind & rain from N. W. which lasted abt. 2 hours. Cloudy this morning we Set off eairly. Sailed a Short distance with a S. E. wind & in less than 2 hours the wind Shifted in to the N. W. which Blew hard a head, G. Drewyer R. Fields & Collins out hunting this morning on N. S. as we passed or passing a prarie on S. S. we heard Several guns fire which we Supposed to be our hunters. directly we heard them hollow from the Island for help to bring in their Game, R. Fields killed one Buck Elk, and Drewyer killed 2 Elk & Newman & Howard killed one on the opposite Shore; we halted to take Breakfast at 8 o.C. at the Bottom prarie, where their was an ancient fort.[1] the Entrenchment which formed a Circle from the river in the form of a half moon, at the lower pt. End Capt. Clark went on Shore with the compass in order to find the angles &.C. the Boats went on to the head of Elk or Bon hommen Isd. Island, the wind Shifted into the North & Blew So heard that we were obledged to lay by at ⟨the⟩ a high Bluff, abo. Elk or Bon hommen[2] Isl. handsome high praries back from the river, we found plumb orchads on a Spring run & an amence Site of Grapes as before, we Scarcely passed a day as yet on the Missouri, in the time or Season of them but what we found them in great abundance &.C. the weather is Cool & rainy to day Capt. Clark returned to the Boat, & Informed us that had been a large ancient fortification made their. Some places remains yet 5 feet high & on one Side of it is nearly Strait across the point & strikes the river, & is more than a mile & half in length & So ancient that Some Trees Stands on the works &.C. considerable of cottonwood Timber on the Upper part of this point back from the river is Broken Barron hills which are verry high & Sandy &.C.

1. Clark conducted a survey of the supposed fortifications across from Bon Homme Island in Knox County, Nebraska. The formations are actually the result of natural sand ridges.
2. "Bon hommen" appears to be a later addition in both instances of its use in this entry.

Monday 3rd Sept 1804. a Cool & pleasant morning we Set off at Sun rise, the wind blew from the west, passed yallow Bluff, Some Stone under the bank near the water. passed round a large sand point N. Side, the Timber Scarce on both Sides of the River.— N.B. a great many Beaver Sign & Cabbins on the river today. We proceeded on a Swift current passed a white Chalk Bluff close above we passed plumb Creek[1] on N. S. which formed a vallie between or in the bluff, we Camped on S.S. in a Grove of cottonwood Timber,

1. Probably Emanuel Creek, Bon Homme County, South Dakota.

Tuesday 4th Sept. 1804. Cold wind from S. W. we Set off eairly, proceeded on passed a Small Creek[1] on S. S. where we took breakfast found some plumbs & hack burrys[2] &.C. passed a high yallow red ceeder Clift on the S. S. & above the clift we passed the mo of a creek called white paint C. the wind Shifted to the South & blew verry hard we hoisted Sail ran verry fast a Short time. Broke our mast, we [the] Sand flew from the Sand bars verry thick we landed at 12 o.C. to dine at a large bottom prarie on S. S. opposite to a yallow & blew Clift N. S. we passed the Mouth of the Big *Rapid* River[3] & ponkias village on S. S. the water Shoots in to the Missiouri verry

Swift, & has thrown the Sand out, which makes a Sand bar & Sholes from the mouth a considerable distance we Saw 2 Deer, & large flocks of geese up the mo of this river; we proceeded on passt a handsom Bottom covered with different kinds of Timber Such as red Ceder, honey locas, oak arrow-wood Elm, Coffee nut &.C. we Saw an Indian raft where they had crossed not long before; Drewyer killed one Turkey & one duck; we Camped on the South Side in a Ceeder Bottom back of which are Steep Clifts covered with ceeder. N. B. a Smoke was made to find where Shannon had passed, but no tracks found

1. The two creeks on the same side, this one and "white paint" creek, are probably Lost and Bazile creeks, Knox County, Nebraska. See the discussion of their identification at Clark's entry for this day.

2. Hackberry, *Celtis occidentalis* L., not mentioned by Clark.

3. Niobrara River, Knox County, with a Ponca village nearby; see Clark's entry for September 5.

Wednesday 5th Sept. 1804. we took a niew mast on board, Set off eairly. the wind Blew hard from the South we passed a large Island, Reuben Fields Jo Fields & Drewyer went on the Isd. hunting; we Sailed on, halted at ½ past 7 took breakfast at a Small creek called Goat Creek[1] N. S. the Beaver had made a curious dam across near the mouth which made considerable of a pond above, found plumbs; 2 men Sent across on the S. S. to hunt on Shore N. B. at ponca River[2] which we passed for the 2 men with the horses &.C. passed Some handsome Mineral Springs on N. S. under a clift. the 2 men who crossed to hunt the horses come to the Boat in a Short time at a fine Bottom prarie had killed a Deer, we Saw Several Goats[3] on the Side hill on N. S. we proceeded on till 4 oClock & Camped on an Island. made a niew ceeder mast. the hunters out hunting returned to the Boat & R. Fields killed a fat Buck. Dreuwyer killed an Elk & Newman killed a faun Elk & a faun Deer.— tracks of the horses Seen where the 2 men passd. &.C.—

1. Chouteau Creek, the boundary between Bon Homme and Charles Mix counties, South Dakota.

2. Ponca Creek, Knox County, Nebraska.

3. Pronghorn, *Antilocapra americana.*

Thursday 6th a cloudy morning the wind from N. W. We Set off eairly, got fast Several times on the Sand bars. could not make Much headway with the oars nor poles & were oblidged to cross over on N. S. & make use of the Towing line.— the current Swift & Shallow. we came to verry long Strait high Raged yallow L S. clifts S. S. Colter Came to the Boat *N. B. the Boat got fast on the Sand bar the L S. Swung the men all out Got* [whiskey?] had not found Shannon nor the horses But had killed one Buffelow, one Elk 3 Deer one wolf 5 Turkies & one Goose— one Beaver also rainy & cold weather.— Reuben Fields killed 1 Deer & 1 faun.— we Camped[1] at a handsome Bottom prarie on N. S. above a fine Grove of C. wood Timber.—

1. In Charles Mix County, South Dakota, probably a little below the Knox-Boyd county line, Nebraska, on the opposite side.

Friday 7th a fair, cool morning. *N. B.* a verry large cat fish caugt. by Goodrich last night. we Set off verry eairly. the wind from N. W. we proceeded on. took breakfast at one of Colters Camps where he had a scaffal of jurk &.C.— passed a Bottom prarie Back of which is a round naked high round knob[1] the Captains went out to look at it.— they returned in a Short time & informed us that it was a curious place as if it had been made with hands of man. Shields killed a prarie dog,[2] which was cooked for the Capts dinner.— the Captains went out with Some men of the party to See the Ground where those little dogs make their villages & they found more than an acre of Ground covered with their holes, they attempted to drown Several of them out of their holes, but they caught but one which they brought in alive, they are a curious annimal about the Size of a little dog, & of a grayish coulour resembles them nearly except the tail which is like a Ground Squirrel. They will Stand on their hind feet & look &.C.— we Camped on the South Side near the Steeple of the round knob

1. Old Baldy, eastern Boyd County, Nebraska.
2. Prairie dog, *Cynomys ludovicianus;* the squirrel used for comparison is the gray squirrel, *Sciurus carolinensis.*

Saturday 8th Sept 1804. a pleasant morning. we Set off eairly the wind from the S. E. we proceeded on under a gentle breeze passed the mouth of a Small creek on S. S. Some thin Timber close along each Side of the river. the hills are near the river on boath Sides & are verry Broken &.C.— we passed an Island N. S. halted on S. S. to dine. G. Drewyer joined us who went the evening before, had killed a Buck Elk & a faun Elk & a faun Deer & caught 2 large Beaver,— likewise one prarie dog. Capt. Clark went out this morning to walk on N. S. we passed a Trading house[1] piched in on the Same Side abo. where the capt. went out in a handsome Timbered Bottom,— which had been built in 1796.— we proceeded on past Several Islands, late in the afternoon we Saw Several Buffelow Swimming the river. Capt. Lewis went out with Some of the party on S. S. in a grove of Timber & killed 2 Buffelow Shot at one of them Several times in the river he being wounded Swam a Shore again & they Shot him down at the edge of the water.— we proceeded on about 1½ miles & camped on the lower point of a handsome Timbered Island.[2] on which we Saw large gangue of Buffalow.— Capt. Clark joined us after dark. had killed 1 faun Deer 3 turkies & a Squirril.—[3] he informed us that he Travelled over a riged and mountanious Country without water & riseing 5 or 600 feet, where these hills had been lately burned over by the natives.—

1. Jean Baptiste Truteau evidently wintered here in 1794–95, some thirty-plus miles above the mouth of the Niobrara River, Charles Mix County, South Dakota.

2. Evidently later called Chicot, or Strehlow, Island, on the Gregory-Charles Mix county line.

3. Clark says it was a fox squirrel, *Sciurus niger.*

Sunday 9th Sept. 1804. we Set out at Sun rise & proceeded on passed the Island. Several gangues of Buffalow on the Sides of the hills on the South Side.— we halted took breakfast on the South Side opposite to the upper end of the Island. we heared the prarie woolves bark on the hills Capt. Clark went on Shore in order to kill or See Some of them &.C. we passed Several creeks & 2 Islands before dinner we passed a high Bluff on S. S. & a Small creek at which place we took dinner. G. Drewyer killed 1 Buck & 2 fauns. R. Fields came to the Boat had killed one Buffalow. passed red ceder on the in Several places along the Bluffs & Several creeks Capt. Clark joined us at dusk had killed a Buffalow near where we camped[1] on a Sand beach S. S. Capt. Clark informed us that the plains were allmost covered with Buffalow the most of this days walk. I saw Several on the bank.

1. In Gregory County, South Dakota, opposite Stony Point on the opposite shore.

Monday 10th a foggy morning. we Set off eairly. proceeded on. passed a run & a Bluff on N. S. which is of a hard blue clay & verry rough on the top (a Small crk on L. Side) we Sailed on verry well halted at 12 oClock took dinner. Newman went out on the hills & killed a Deer South Side we Saw the rack of Bones of a verry large fish[1] the Back bone 45 feet long. passed a high Black Bluff S. S. See 8 Elk Swimming the River. See a nomber of Buffalow. passed Several Islands & Several Creeks & Sand bars little Timber in the course of the day. and camped on an Island S. S.[2] Sergt. Pryor who walked on Shore to day joined us informed us that he Saw a large Salt Spring S S 1½ miles from the river, & killed one Buffalow, Corpl. Worvington of the pearogue walked the afternoon on S. S joined us also killed 2 Buffalow

1. A plesiosaur, an aquatic dinosaur of the Mesozoic era.
2. On Pocahontas, or Toehead, Island, between Gregory and Charles Mix counties, South Dakota.

Tuesday 11th Sept. 1804. we Set off eairly Sailed on to the head of the Isl. Capt. Clark myself and 2 more[1] walked on Shore S. S. I killed a verry large porkapine[2] put it on board the pearogue. Capt. Clark killed a Buck Elk a deer & a deer faun. G. Gibson killed Buck Elk a deer & faun also.— Saved the Skins & the best of the meat &.C. the Boat Sailed on passed Several Islands & Small runs, at each side.— I walked a long the S Shore See a high red hill. I climbed up to the top which is verry Seep on 2 Sides & about 150 feet high. I Saw 16 Bull Buffalow in the vally to the W. Side, rained hard. I amed to keep my rifle dry. I went around the gang of Buffaloe, crept near them as they were feeding, with their heads towards me as I was a watching them to get one side ways one of them discovered me I kept Still had on a red Shirt he looked at me, & walked up near to me. I was obledged to Shoot, at his head. as I shot him in the head among the long hair he turned & run off. the gang ran a Short distance & went to feeding, rained So hard my gun got wet loading, & I returned over mountains & rough hills & Gullies &.C. &.C. George Shannon who had been absent with the horses 16 days joined the boat about one oclock. he informed us that the reason of his keeping on so long was that he see some tracks which must have been Indians. he to[ok] it to [be] us and kept on, his bullets he Shot all away & he was with out any thing to eat for about 12 days except a fiew Grapes, he had left one of the horses behind, as he Gave out, only one horse with him he had gave up the idea of finding our boat & was returning down the river in hopes to meet Some other Boat, he was near killing the horse to Satisfy hunger, &C. &.C— he Shot a rabit with Sticks which he cut & put in his gun after his Balls were gone. he had been 2 days walk abov this &.C. See a village of little Dogs in the four part of the day We passed Some Timber on the Islands and points. none at all back on the mountains.— rained hard till late in the evening we Camped[3] on S. S. near a line of dark Bluffs.

1. One of them was Nathaniel Pryor, according to Whitehouse; George Gibson may have been the other one, as Ordway seems to indicate.

2. The porcupine is *Erethizon dorsatum.*

3. Apparently a short distance south of the Lyman-Gregory county line, South Dakota.

Wednesday 12th Sept. 1804. the wind shifted Since last night in to the North. Set off as usual proceeded on Slowly. the current Swift & wind a head.— Capt. Clark walked on Shore S. S. Sergt. Gass & Newman with him.— we had Some difficulty owing to the river being Shallow. the Boat wheeled Several times and creened on hir Side So that we were obledged to Spring out and hold hir from oversetting. we hunted for the channel & were forced to turn back some distance & take another channel.— We Camped on S. S.[1] Capt. Lewis went out found another village of little Dogs in a Bottom prarie above the Island we called Troublesome Isd.

1. Apparently a short distance north of the Lyman-Gregory county line, South Dakota.

Thursday 13th Sept. 1804. we Set off eairly proceeded on passed high hills on N. S. & a Bottom prarie. Some part covered with Timber Grape vines covered with ripe grapes.— pasd. a black Bluff on S. S. & Broken hills & a run of allum & copperass water.— Some Musquetoes, rainy.— G. Drewyer caught 4 Beaver in his Traps last night. myself Sergt. Pryor & Shannon walked on Shore S. S. in order to get Some plumbs in a bottom prarie. we found pleanty but they were not quite ripe. Shannon killed a porcupine. we could not git to the Boat for a willow Island which was between & Sand bars &.C. *N. B. the Boat passd. Several Isds. & camped on N. S*— we Camped[1] in a grove of cottonwood Timber. Eat one porcupine for Supper. the Musquetoes Troubled us verry much.— passd. a range of black Bluffs on S. S. &.c.

1. Ordway and his group camped in Lyman County, South Dakota, while the main party stayed on the opposite shore in Brule County.

Friday 14th Sept. 1804. we Set off eairly. a foggy morning. Cloudy. George Drewyer caught 3 Beaver last night. I Sergt. Pryor & Shannon returned to the Boat at 8 o.C. where they were at breakfast, near a grove of Timber N. S. the water Shallow. all hands out in water Several times to drag the Boat over the Sand bars &.C. passd a black Bluff on S. S. Capt. Clark &.C. one man went out hunting on S. S. John Shields who went on Shore with the horse killed a verry large white rabbit or haire[1] it was as big as a Ureopian hare.— nearly all white—& of a different discription of any one ever yet Seen in the States.— passed a creek on S. S. & a grove of Timber Some rain we Camped[2] on the South Side in a Stripe of woods. Capt. Clark joined us had killed a curious annamil resembling a Goat Willard brought it on board. it was 3 feet high resembles a Deer in some parts. the legs like a Deer. feet like a Goat. horns like a Goat only forked Turn back picked hair thick & of a white a dark redish coullour. Such an anamil was never yet known in U. S. States.— The Capt had the Skins of the hair & Goat Stuffed in order to Send back to the city of Washington. the bones and all.—

1. White-tailed jackrabbit, *Lepus townsendii.*
2. Near the mouth of Bull Creek, Lyman County, South Dakota.

Saturday 15th Sept. 1804. hard rain the greater part of last night. we Set of eairly this morning. passed a creek on s. s. where George Shannon

Camped Six days in a Timbered bottom we call this creek Shannons Creek[1] which Shoots in to the Missouri verry rapid.— proceeded on passed a black Bluff on the N. S. passed the mouth of white River[2] on the South Side. Several Sand bars opposite the mouth So that we could not land at its mouth ⟨Capt⟩ the Capts. went out in the pearogue for to look of the white River &.C.— the Boat went on above the Sand bars.— where Capt Clark came to us had killed an Elk. Capt Lewis came on board little above a black Bluff. we proceeded on Capt. Clark went on an Island S. S. covered with Timber red Ceeder & cottonwood and covered all over with fine Grapes. Capt. Clark killed a Rabbit named the Isl. Rabit Island.— we proceeded on till night with a head wind. Camped on the North Side at a Bluff.—

1. Bull Creek, Lyman County, South Dakota.

2. Retaining this name, White River reaches the Missouri in Lyman County.

Sunday 16th Sept. 1804. we Set out verry eairly this morning.— Cool & Clear, proceeded on in order to find a good place to Camp & dry & arange all afairs on board & refresh the party &.C. passed a large Creek on S. S. called [*blank*] we Camped[1] on S. S. in a handsome bottom of thin Timbered land, lately burned over by the natives, it had grown up again with Green Grass which looked beautiful. we Saw Several Deer in this Grove. Capt. Clark killed one Capt. Lewis one G. Drewyer one. Collins who had been with the Horse joined us had killed two Deer, one yesterday 1 this morning We found a large plumb orchad back of this Bottom of fine large ripe plumbs. Capt. Lewis went on an Island little above the camp to hunt. Battest Decamps killed one Bufalow, Roie killed a faun Deer.[2] Capt. Lewis killed a buffalow. Saved the Skins to cover the loading in the pearogue.— Greater part of the loading taken out of the Boat and aired to day— the large red pearogue loaded out of the Batteaux & are to continue on with us to the Mandan Nation of Indians—

1. Near Oacoma, Lyman County, South Dakota, where the party remained for a couple of days.

2. Jean Baptiste Deschamps and Peter Roi, French *engagés*.

Monday 17th Sept. 1804. Capt Lewis & Several of the party went out hunting. Drewyer caught 1 Beaver to day a pleasant day. The Boat loaded— we remained here all day.— towards evening Capt Lewis & party retarned they had killed 13 common Deer. Some of them were handsome fauns— 2 Black tailed Deer[1] which differ from the other Deer. verry large ears Scarce any hair on their tail only the bunch of black hair on the end of a grayish colour they are pleanty in this Country but not discribed in any other parts— they killed another kind of Deer[2] with Small horns & long tail. Gibson killed 1 its tail is 18 Inches long & differ also from any yet seen by the party. they killed 3 Buffalow. one Goat which differs also (plenty[)] & one curious Bird[3] of a blackish & greenish coullour Black Bill & a verry long tail— resembling a bird that we call a magpy— the hunters inform us that the Country back of the hills and on the hills are level & Smooth but the Timber verry Scarce &.C.—

1. Mule deer, *Odocoileus hemionus.*

2. Western white-tailed deer, *Odocoileus virginianus dacotensis*; see Clark's entry for September 16.

3. Black-billed magpie, *Pica pica.*

Tuesday 18th Sept. a fair morning. we Set off at ½ past 5 o.C. proceeded on, passed an Island at our wright Some Timber along the S. S. Elm, ash, Scrubby oak &.C— George Drewyer killed a prarie woolf Some larger than a fox. long teeth & of a different discription from any in the States &.C. we proceeded on to a Bottom prarie covered with thin cottonwood Timber where Jo Fields with the horse had killed a Buck Deer— took on board the meat killed yesterday— Capt. Clark & G. Drewyer walked on Short on S. S. no Timber seen by the hunters back from the river— Capt. Clark & G. Drewyer returned towards evening. had killed 10 Deer & one prarie woolf We Camped on the South Side in a Small Grove of Timbers,[1] 2 hours eairlier than usal the wind being a head, in order to jurk our meat &.C the Bones of the woolf was taken apart and Saved as well as the Skins of them boath in order to Send back to the States next Spring, with the other curiousities we have or may have &.C.—

1. A few miles northeast of Oacoma, Lyman County, South Dakota.

Wednesday 19th Sept. 1804. a pleasant morning. we Set off eairly. proceeded on passed a Steep clay Bluff on S. S. Some ceeder on the edge of the Bluffs— a fine Timbered Bottom opposite on N. Side. Jo. Fields who was with the horse killed a black tailed Deer & hung it on the Bank. we took it on board. we landed for Breakfast on N. S. Capt. Clark & 3 men went out hunting. we proceeded on passed a Timbered Bottom on S. S. about 11 oC. Capt. Clark Shot a fat Brown Buffalow cow opposite to us on the N. S. a large Gang of them Swam the river near the Boats we Shot a fat Cow likewise & a Small Bull. took the meat & hides on bord the pearogues. we proceeded on under a fine Sailing Breeze from E. S. E. passed 3 large Creeks (called the Sioux 3 river pass)[1] on N. S. which came in behind an Island (along a Bluff), passed a long Timbered bottom on N. S. passd a large Creek on S. S. & Camped[2] after Sailing 24 miles on S. S. above Sd. Creek. Capt. Clark joined us late in the evening had killed an Elk & a Deer, the men who went with him returned also much fatigued &.C.— Drewyer killed 2 Black taild Deer on S S near a range of Bluffs &.C—

1. Probably Crow, Elm, and Campbell creeks, Buffalo County, South Dakota.

2. The difficulty in identifying this creek is discussed with Clark's entry for this day; likewise, the problem in establishing the day's campsite, which was in Lyman County, South Dakota.

Thursday 20th Sept. a fair morning Drewyer & Shields went on with the horse across a bend in order to hunt— we Set off eairly proceeded on under a gentle Breeze from the E. passed an Isl. on N. S. passd. the mo of a creek on S. S. named prickly pair creek[1] passd. a bottom (& long bend point) covered with thin Timber. Capt. Clark walked on Shore across the point— we proceeded on passed a handsom Bottom covered with Timber on S. S. where we halted took dinner. Capt. Lewis & R. Fields walked out to hunt we Sailed along Round the Big Bend about 27 miles[2] passd. 2 Islands & Several Sand bars & a Saltish Sand run on N. S. & camped[3] on a Sand bar on N. S. the Captains & the men who had been with them returned to the Boat had killed 1 he Goat one She Goat & 1 long tailed Deer— We Saved the Skins of the Goats and the Bones in order to Send back to the States next Spring— The She Goats have verry little horns but are a handsome animal— about 1 OClock at night the Sand bar where we lay was falling verry fast. the current Swift. we ware obledged to git on board as Soon as possable & proceed on about a mile & made over to S. S. where we Camped again. the moon Shined pleasant all night.— we passed a black Bluff on S. S. where their is Some Salt peter on the Stones &.C.

1. The identification of this creek is related to problems with the previous day's streams; see Clark's entry of September 19.

2. Big Bend of the Missouri River, enclosing land in Lyman County, South Dakota.

3. In Hughes County, South Dakota.

Friday 21st Sept. 1804. a clear & pleasant morning we Set off eairly. proceeded on. passed a beautiful high prarie or plains on N. S. passed on round the point of the Big Bend a handsome place & high prarie grad-dually ascending from the river on N. S. & a ceeder Bluff— and ceeder Bottom on S. S. passd. Tylors River[1] on S. S. we found 2 Deer at the mouth of this R. that the hunters had killed & hung up for us. they had gone on— here we Saw the Sand bars covered with [green?] W. head ⟨leged⟩ plovvers.[2] Capt. Lewis Shot Some of them for his dinner.— we passed Some Timber on S. S. But verry little on the N. S. passd. Several Small runs & Camped on the N. S. little below a mock Island at a handsome Bottom prarie— we have now passed round the Big Bend which is 30 miles round and only 1¼ m. across in the nearest place.—

1. Medicine River, Lyman County, South Dakota.

2. Probably the bird Clark called the "green leged plove" in his weather remarks for September 22; perhaps either the stilt sandpiper, *Calidris himantopus,* or the pectoral sandpiper, *C. melanotos.*

Saturday 22nd Sept. 1804. a foggy morning. we Set out at Sun rise. we passed Some Timber on S. S. high handsome plains on N: S. (See large gangs of Buffalow on N. S) about 3 OClock we passed a handsom Ceeder Island on N. S. (one of the 3 Sisters) where Mr. Louisells built a fort and Tradeing house in the winter 1803.[1] it was all built of Ceeder and picketed in with ceeder about 65 or 70 feet Square with a Sentery Box in 2 angles corners the pickets is 13½ feet high above Ground. the Tradeing house is 45½ by 32½ feet. divided into four equal apartments one for Merchantise one for a common hall. one for peltery &C. 2 peltery presses. this Tradeing house is built all of ceeder high and covered with hughn guttered ceeder, in the winter they cover them over with Buffaloe hides which answer a Good purpose. the chimneys built with Stone Clay & wood— their is Indian camps for a large distance about this place where the Souix Indians came to Trade with Mr Louisell, opposite to this Island on S. S. G. Drewyer & Shields joined us had killed 2 Deer & one white woolf— Colter went ⟨out⟩ on with the horse— we passed a creek & islands of the 3 Sisters. proceded on passd. an Indian camp on S. S. where we found Some of their ceeder dog poles, they answer us for Setting poles. we are informed that the Indians tie theirs dogs to these poles and they have to dragg them from one camp to another loaded with their Baggage &.C—[2] Captain Clark walked a Short time on Shore on S. S. & killed a large Doe Deer. we Camped[3] on N. S. at the mouth of a Small Creek where he joined us—

1. Régis Loisel built *Fort aux Cedres* about 1800, or perhaps two years later, to trade with the Sioux. The exact location of the fort, on later Dorion Island No. 2, Lyman County, South Dakota, was not discovered before the area was inundated by Big Bend Reservoir. See Clark's entries, May 25 and September 22, 1804.

2. A dog travois, used extensively by Plains Indians before the introduction of the horse.

3. Nearly opposite the mouth of Loiselle Creek, in Hughes County, South Dakota (see Clark's entry for this day).

Sunday 23rd Sept 1804. a fair pleasant morning. we Set off eairly— proceeded on. passed a large Bottom on N. S. covered with Timber and Grapes &.C. R. Fields out to hunt Capt. Clark returned had Spied a large fire in the praries a fiew miles back on S. Side— we Saw large Gangs of Buffalow on the hills N. S. the wind favourable from S. E. we passed a Creek on N. S. called Smoke Creek.[1] we passd. Elk Island at the lower end of the long reach. passd. a Timbered bottom on N. S. & barron hills on S. S. &.C— towards evening we Saw 4 Indians on the Sand beach S. S. we

Camped on the N. S. & 3 of them Swam over to our Camp. they belonged to the Souix Nation. they Informed us that their Camp was near where their was a Grand chief and a nomber of their nation, the Capts. Gave them Some Tobacco & we Set them across. they return to their Camp R. Fields joined us. had killed a female Goat—

1. Chapelle Creek, Hughes County, South Dakota.

Monday 24th Sept. 1804. a Clear and pleasant morning. we Set off eairly. proceeded on passed a handsome prarie on N.S. where we found large plumb orcheds covered with ripe plumbs.— passd. the mo. of a high water creek on S. S.[1] proceeded on under a gentle breeze from S. E.— about 1 oClock we Saw Colter who had been with the horse on an Island S. S. he called for the pearogue to take in the Game he had killed which was 2 Elk & a Deer. while they were a Dressing and gitting the meat on board the Indians Stole the horse & Some Salt out of his bag &.C. we Saw 5 Indians on Shore. Colter came running along the Shore Informed us that the Indians had Stole the horse & bridle &.C. took Colter on bord. Sailed up opposite to the 5 Indians, halted, ankered out 100 yds. from Shore. One of our frenchman Spoke to them in Nemaha language[2] and asked them who their chief is. they could not understand but little. they informed us that the Grand chiefs name is the Black Buffalow. the Captains told them that they or Some of the young men had Stole our horse and if they would bring the horse We would Speak to them, and if they did not we would not Speak to them. they Said they knew nothing of the horse but if their young men had Stole him they must find him & return him again. the Capts. told them it was well & we would Speak to their chiefs Tomorrow. we then proceeded on to the mouth of Teton River where we Encamped[3] on S. S.— we ankered out 100 yds. from Shore, all remained on bord except the Guard Cooks & frenchman who remained on Shore with one pearogue. the 5 Indians Stayed with the Guard all night verry peaceable. we had an old frenchman with us who could speak a little of the Souix language he found that one of them was a chief. the Capts Gave them Some Tobacco Shook hands and Smoked with them &.C—. This chiefs name is Buff the Medicine[4] he told us that all their lodge would come tomorrow.— they Eat and Slept with us friendly.— a flag pole hoisted

1. Antelope Creek, Stanley County, South Dakota.

2. Probably Labiche or Cruzatte speaking Omaha.

3. Bad River, Stanley County, opposite Pierre.

4. Buffalo Medicine, perhaps a third chief of this group of Teton Sioux (see the next day's entry for the other chiefs).

Chapter Forty-Three

Winter at the Knife River

September 25, 1804–April 6, 1805

Tuesday 25th Sept. 1804. a clear and pleasant morning.— all things made ready to receive the Band of the Souix nation of Indians, Called the Tribe of Tetons. about 10 o.C. A. M. they Came flocking in from boath Sides of the River. when 30 odd was selected under the american Collours Capt. Lewis & Capt Clark went out to Speak and treat with them. Gave the 3 Chiefs 3 niew meddals & 1 american flag Some knives & other Small articles of Goods— & Gave the head chief the Black Buffalow[1] a red coat & a cocked hat & feather &.C— likewise Some Tobacco.— We had no good interpreter but the old frenchman[2] could make them understand tollarable well. but they did not appear to talk much untill they had got the goods, and then they wanted more, and Said we must Stop with them or leave one of the pearogues with them, as that was what they expected. Capt. Lewis Shewed them the air Gun. Shot it Several times. then the Captains brought the 3 chiefs[3] and one warrier they had with them. Gave the warrier a Sertifficate. then Shewed the chiefs Some curioussities. Gave them a draghm. they brought a quantity of fat Buffaloe meat and offered us the Captains accepted of Some of it & Gave them pork in return— then the Captains told them that we had a great ways to Goe & that we did not wish to be detained any longer,— they then began to act as if they were Intoxicated. with Some difficulty Capt. Clark got them to Shore. they then began to Show Some Signs of Stopping or attempting to Stop us. one of them Stayed on board the pearogue when Capt. Clark & the chiefs went out of it. the head chief the Black Buffaloe, Seized hold of the cable of the pearogue and Set down. Capt. Clark Spoke to all the party to Stand to their arms Capt. Lewis who was on board ordered every man to his arms. the large Swivel loaded immediately with 16 Musquet Ball in it the 2 other Swivels loaded well with Buck Shot, Each of them manned. Capt. Clark used moderation with them told them that we must and would go on and would go. that we were not Squaws, but warriers. the chief Sayed he had warriers too and if we were to go on they would follow us and kill and take the whole of us by degrees or that he had another party or lodge above this and that they were able to destroy us. then Capt. Clark told them that we were Sent by their great father the presidant of the U. S. and that if they misused us that he or Capt. Lewis could by writing to him have them all distroyed as it were in a moment. they then requested that we would Stay all night; they wished to have their women and children See the Boat as they never Saw Such an one, the Capt. told them that we could not go far as the day was far Spent, but we would let them see that they Should not Stop us and that we Should go a Short distance and Camp for the night. the chief then let go the Cable, and Sayed that he was Sorry to have us Go for his women and children were naked and poor and wished to Git Some Goods, but he did not think we were Marchants, nor that we were loaded with Goods, but he was Sorry to have us leave them So Soon— they wished to come on board. Capt. Clark took the chief and warriers on bord to Stay all night with them— we then Set off and proceeded on about 1 mile and Camped[4] ankered out. the Guard and cooks on Shore &.C— the Indians Camped on S. S. our Camp was on a willow Isl. in the middle of the river, at our Starbord Side.—

1. Black Buffalo, also known as Black Bull.

2. Probably Cruzatte.

3. In addition to Black Buffalo were Buffalo Medicine (of previous day's entry) and Partisan.

4. On the expedition's Bad Humored Island, probably later Marion Island, Stanley County, South Dakota, opposite Pierre.

Wednesday 26th Sept 1804. a clear and pleasant morning, we Set off eairly. proceeded on 4 or 5 miles the Indians Strung along the Shore the most of the way.— We then halted ankered out 100 yards from Shore.[1] Capt.

Lewis went out with the chiefs to where they had fixed their lodge in the neatest manner near the river. and their whole lodge had assembled. brought with them their horses, women & children. Some of their women are verry handsome, & friendly the nomber of Indians at this lodge of the Teton tribe is between 2 & 300 they had been lately at war with the Mahars. we [they] have Sixty five of the Sculps and 25 prisonrs Squaws of the Mahars nation which they had with them. they told us that they had 23 Squaws prisoners more at a lodge above this.— their lodge is verry handsome in a circle and about 100 cabbins[2] in nomber and all white, made of Buffalow hides dressed white one large one in the center, the lodge for the war dances.— they Gave Capt. Lewis Some fine Soup made of what they call white apples.[3] they Sent all the party Some fat Bufaloe meat cooked and Some dryed and pounnded fine.[4] the marrow of the Buffalow Bones, mixed together, which Eat verry well.— Capt Clark went out with some of them, and they made Great preperations for a dance this evening. they Sent for Capt. Lewis to come and See them he went over to the Shore they Spread a Buffaloe robe dressed white on the Ground for him to Git on as Soon as he landed he Set on it 8 of the Savages carried him to the lodge which is a Great Mark of friendship. they killed Several dogs and cooked them in a decent manner to treat our people with. in the evening the 2 Captains myself and a nomber more of the party went to their village to See them dance. they had a fire in the center of their lodge. the Band formed a line which were the men. the Squaws formed on each Side of the fire & danced and Sang as the drumm and other ratles &.C. were playing. they danced to the center untill they met, then the rattles Shook and the houp was Given. then the Squaws all fell back to their places. when the [other?] mens music Seaced the womens voice Sounded one part of the tune delightful. then the other Music would commence again, our Captains Gave them some Tobacco to Smoke during the dance. one of the warries thought he had not received a Small peace of the last tobacco they had he Got mad and broke one of their drumms, hove 2 in the fire and left the line. Some of the rest took them out, they then took a Buffaloe Robe & held up in their hands and beat on it and continued on their dance till late in night.— The chiefs came on & Selept with us in a friendly manner—

1. In Stanley County, South Dakota, about four miles north of Fort Pierre.

2. Probably tipis.

3. Prairie turnip (and other common names), *Psoralea esculenta* Pursh.

4. Probably pemmican—pulverized, dried meat mixed with melted fat and various kinds of berries.

Thursday 27th Sept. 1804. a clear and pleasant morning. the most of the party went to the village in the course of the day 5 or 6 at a time, as the chiefs desired us to Stay this day as they Sayd that another lodge would came to day (600 men) (& 7 chiefs) the chiefs and chiefs Sons came on board Several times in the course of the day and dined with the officers &.C. Sergt. Gass informed me as he was at the village to day that he counted 80 Lodges (of the Teton Tribe) which contain ten persons each, which were built round with poles about 15 or 20 feet high & covered with dressed Buffalo hides painted Some of them red &.C. they draw them from one place to another with their dogs. they tackled one to day which carried about 80 weight with ease— about 2 thirds are women and children. the women are employed in dressing Buffaloe Skins for cloathes and lodges &.C. they appear to be verry friendly. But will Steel & pilfer if they have an oppertunity— the vessells they carry their worter in are Deers ponches & other kinds. Some wooden Bows which they make.— the chiefs promised our Captains that they would Send the prisoners back to their nation again.— towards evening they made prepparations for another dance this evening, at dark the officers and 7 or 8 of the party went over to the dance and See them dance and carry on nearly as the evening before only the men danced and made Speaches after the women had danced a while &.C.— the dance lasted till about 12 oClock at night, at which time the Captains returned to the boat brought with them 2 Chiefs. the men all returned also. an accident happened as they came on board by the neglect of the men at the helm of the pearogue, who Steared hir above the big boat. She Swung round with the current and She came full force down against the Bow of the Barge Broke the cable of hir. we found we were all on float. roused all hands and got Safe to Shore on S. S. the Indians hearing us, and expected that the Mahars Indians had come to attack us. they all ran to our assistance on the bank of the river & fired Several guns for an alarm only. we informed them the cause &.C. Some of them remained with us the remainder part of the night. we examined the pearogue that met with the Stroke found that She had Sprang a leak at one place. we corked it and bailed the pearogue. found her not verry much damaged, but if the cable of the Boat had not Gave way the pearogue must have broke in too or turned over. I being on duty Set up the remainder part of the night, and had all the party on their Guard's—

Friday 28th Sept. 1804. a clear and pleasant morning. Capt. Clark went with the pearogues eairly. this morning to hunt for the anker. Searched Some time with the Boat hook & poles, could not find it. they took a chord and put Sinkers to the middle and took each end to the 2 pearogues and dragged the river diligently along time but could not find it. took breakfast about 10 O.Clock. the whole lodge of Indians were waiting on the bank to See us Start as we intended if the excident had not of happened last night. we gave up the Idea of finding our anker.— We then were about to Set off. Some of the chiefs were on bord insisting on our Staying untill the others came. We told them we could not wait any longer.— they then did not incline to let us go on they Sayed we might return back with what we had or remain with them, but we could not go up the Missouri any further, about 200 Indians were then on the bank. Some had fire arms. Some had Spears. Some had a kind of cutlashes, and all the rest had Bows and Steel or Iron pointed arrows. Several of the warries Set by the chord where our boat the big Barge was tied the 2 pearogues were tied on the outside of the Barge. Capt. Clark was Speaking to the chiefs in the cabbin. Capt. Lewis asked the chiefs if they were going out of the boat. they did not incline to. then Capt. Lewis came out. ordered every man to his place ordered the Sail hoisted, then one man went out untied the chord, which the warrier had in his hand, then 2 or 3 more of their warries caught hold of the chord and tyed it faster than before. Capt. Lewis then appeared to be angerry, and told to Go out of the Boat and the chief then went out and Sayd we are Sorry to have you go. But if you will Give us one carret of tobacco we will be willing for you to go on & will not try to Stop you. Capt. Lewis Gave it to them. the head chief Sayd then that we must Give him one more carrit of tobacco more for his warries who held the chord and then we might go, boath of our Captains told him that we did not mean to be trifled with. nor would not humer them any more, but would Give him 1 carrit more for the warriers, if he would be a man of his word and Stand to his word like a man. the chief Sayd he was mad too, to See us S[t]and Som much for 1 carrit of tobacco. if we would Give it we might go on. Capt. Lewis Gave it to him. he then took the chord in his hand & Gave it to us. we then Set off under a gentle Breeze which happened to be favourable. we proceeded on passd bottom prarie on S. S. high land on N. S. went 4 miles and halted. we fixed 2 large Stone to our boats to answer as ankers, as we did not intend to Camp on Shore again untill we Got to an other Nation. We Saw one of the fourmentioned chiefs comming up the river S. S. we took him on board. he informed us that their was 300 Indians around which was the other lodge.—they wished to have us Stop. we told his Son to tell them that we Should not Stop. this old chief Sayd he was our friend and wished to go with us for a while. the Capts. alowed him to Stay on board. we then proceeded on. at Sunset we cast anker near a small Sand bar in the middle of the river, where we Stayed all night.[1] heared Some Indians on boath Sides of the river. corn cooked on the little Sand bar for the next day all but the cooks Slept on board.—

1. About three miles above Oahe Dam, Hughes and Stanley counties, South Dakota; the area is now inundated by the reservoir.

Saturday 29th Sept. 1804. we Set off eairly. the weather fair. proceeded on passed a handsome Bottom covered with Timber on N. S. bluffs on S. S. We Saw Several Indians on S. S. walking up the Shore we Spoke to them, found they were Some of those we left yesterday 1 or 2 of them chiefs. they Sayed that they would be Glad if we would give one carrit of tobacco for the chiefs of the other band to Smoak. we sent them 2 carrits to a Sand bar but told them we Should not land any more untill we got to the Rick Rea Nation[1] of Indians. the Missouri is verry Shallow. a great nomber of Sand bars. We passed an old village[2] on S. S. where the Rick Rias lived 5 years ago & Raised corn on the Bottom Round the village. we Saw a verry large flock of Elk on the Bottom S. Side. Some Indians Shot at them.— we crossed 2 Indians in the pearogue to N S of the River. Came 15 Miles today and Camped[3] at a large Sand beach S. S. the Guard only on Shore.

1. Arikara Indians.

2. At Chantier Creek, Stanley County, South Dakota. The village is believed to have been abandoned by 1794.

3. About three miles above Chantier Creek, between Sully and Stanley counties.

Sunday 30th Sept. 1804. we Set off eairly under a fine Breeze of wind from the E. passed a willow Island N. S. passd. a large Bottom covered with Timber on N. S. Barron hills on S. S. See an Indian on S. S. Spoke to him. found it was one of those we Saw at village below. he told us that the other band was comming on, and wished us to Stop. we told him we could not Stop neither did we wish to See them. passed handsom Bottom prarie on N. S. a bottom covered with Timber on S. S. proceeded on 10 miles at 10 oClock we discovered a large nomber of Indians on a hill S. Side comming down towards the river a head of. we halted on a Sand bar, took breakfast. the Indians assembled on S. Shore hoisted a white flag. we then took down our red flag. directly after they hoisted another. We then took them to be our friends. the weather being cool, cloudy a mist of rain ⟨the⟩ our officers Gave Each man of the party a draghm. we then hoisted our Sails & Sailed up to where the Indians was assembled about 200 of them on the Bank of the River S. S. had put up one or 2 lodges which was white. we ankered out opposite to them about 100 yards. Spoke to them to know what they wanted. they Sayed they wanted us to come on Shore and eat with them & Smoak, for they were our friends &.C. our Capts. told them our reason was that we had been ill treated by the band below, and that we would not Stop but we were friends to them & would Send them Some tobacco for a token that he had taken them by the hand. And then we Should go on to the Rick Rees where we Should halt again. we then Sent them Some tobacco &.C. hoisted Sail proceeded on passed a Creek on S. S.[1] passd. a bottom covered with Timber on N. S. passd an Island & large Sand bars on S. Side. the old Teton chief remained with us in order to go to the R. Rees nation.— We passed a large quantity of Grapes in the Bottom of

Small Timber on N. Side.— proceeded on till about 4 oClock put to Shore in order to take Some fire wood on board. when we put off the Stern of our Barge got fast. She Swang round in the Stream the wind being So hard from E. that caused the waves to run high the Boat got in the trough & She rocked verry much before we could git hir Strait we hoisted Sail and came Strait. Sailed verry fast. the Indian chief we had on board was verry fraid. he Said he thought our Boat was a medicine & he would go no further with us. we then put him to Shore our Captains Gave him a Blanket, Some tobacco a knife and Some other Small articles. he then Set of to return to his Band. We Sailed on verry fast. came 24 miles this day. Camped on a Sand bar on N. S.[2]

1. Not mentioned by Clark or other journalists, nor shown on expedition maps. It may be Agency Creek, Stanley County, South Dakota.

2. Perhaps on or near later Cheyenne Island, just below the mouth of the Cheyenne River. The "north side" would be in Sully County.

Monday 1st October 1804. we Set of as usal under a hard Breeze from E. Sailed on verry well past an Island. passed an old village of the Rick Rees nation on S. S.[1] passed the Mouth of a large River on the South Side called ashea or dog River,[2] which is about [*blank*] yards wide a Great nomber of Sand bars at & near the Mouth (we had Some difficulty to pass) Some Scattering Timber on the Bottoms about the mouth of this River. passd. a bottom on N. S. Some thin timber near the River on Sd. Bottoms. Barren hills back from the River on boath Sides, & little or no Timber back from the River except on creeks & Streams, this Side of the River Platte The wind blew So hard that it was difficult to find the channel. we halted about 9 oClock took breakfast. dilayed about 2 hours then dragged our Boat over a verry Shallow channel. hoisted Sail proceeded on to a bend in the river at 2 oC. where the wind came a head. took dinner. then proceeded on passed a Bottom covered with Small Timber on ⟨S.⟩ N. S. a cool day. came 14 miles & Camped on a large Sand beach N. S. we Saw a man on the South Shore he called to us in french. Some of our frenchman answered him & knew him, ⟨he⟩ found he wished to See us. we desired him to come he came in a pearogue over to us. it was a young french man who lived with Mr. [Roi?] Valley[3] a trader from little Coat.

1. This area below the mouth of the Cheyenne River, Stanley County, South Dakota, is the site of a series of late prehistoric and early historic Indian villages.

2. Cheyenne River, mistakenly thought to have derived from the French word for dog, *chien*.

3. Jean Vallé, a trader from Ste. Genevieve, Missouri. By "little Coat" Ordway means *Côte Noir,* or Black Hills, where Vallé had been trading.

Tuesday 2nd Oct. 1804 (we Set off as usal) a frenchman came over to us this morning, we found him to be Mr. Valley, the Trador among the Souix nation he could talk English. he informed us that we Should not See many more of the Souix to Trouble us. he came with us a Short distance & returned. we proceeded on passed a large Bottom on S. S. Some Timber on the edge of the river. about 2 o.Clock we came round a bend where we had come 20 miles round, & it was only 2 miles across by land. we discovered Some Indians on the hills N. S. one of them came down to the River. we asked him what he wanted he Said (their was 20 lodges) or so in the Yanktown Souise language that he wanted us to come to Shore. we told him we had Spoke to his chief &.C. & proceeded on. the wind Shifted to N. W. passed an Island[1] on N. S. & a creek on the S. Side. Camped on a Sand bar in the middle of the River.— no hunting for Indians Troublesom.—

1. The expedition's Caution Island, later Plum Island, Dewey County, South Dakota, now probably inundated.

Wednesday 3rd Oct. 1804. the wind raised at 1 oClock last night & blew hard from N. W. & continues to blow this morning. So that it detained us untill ½ past 7 oClock. Cloudy. Some Thunder last night. a little rain this morning. we Set out ½ past [seven] proceeded on 7 miles. the wind So hard a head that we halted about noon at a black Bluff S. S. delayed about 3 hours & proceeded on 3 miles found we had the rong channel. the water Shallow, we Camped[1] at high Bluffs on S. S. we Saw Several Indians opposite on the N. S.

1. Probably near the Potter-Sully county line, South Dakota, and near Pascal Island of later times; see Clark's entry for a more detailed discussion of determining the day's campsite.

Thursday 4th Oct. 1804. we Set off eairly. returned Back 3 miles took the channel & proceeded on. passed Several Indians on N. S. at 9 oCock halted took breakfast on S. S. an Indian Swam the River to See us. he asked for powder &.C. proceeded on passed an Island N. S. passed a Creek on S. S. called Teed creek.[1] we Camped on a Sand beach at the upper point of an Island on N. S.

1. Or "Teel" Creek, Stove (perhaps actually Stone), or Cherry, Creek, Dewey County, South Dakota.

Friday 5th Oct. 1804. a white frost this morning. Clear & Cool. we Set off eairly. passed Some wood in a bottom S. S. See Several Indians on the Shore on N. S. at 11 oClock we Saw a flock of Goats Swimming the River towards the South Shore. one of our hunters ran up the Shore & killed 4 of them we took them on board the Boat & pearogues. passed a Creek on N. S. called white Goat Creek.[1] passd black Bluffs on S. S. we halted took dinner at a Timbered bottom S. S. below an Island. dressed & took care of our Goat meat as we had no other fresh meat on hand. found it to be verry Sweet Good meat. proceeded on passing the Island we killed a Small prarie woolf Swimming the River. passed high Black Bluff on N. S. & a large Bottom covered with Timber. Capt. Clark & 2 of the hunters went out hunting— we passed the Bottom & Camped on N. S. Capt Clark & the rest of the hunters returned. had killed & brought in a Deer.— had killed or wounded 2 more but did not get them.

1. Clark's White Brant Creek; it is today's Swift Bird Creek, Dewey County, South Dakota.

Saturday 6th Oct. 1804. we Set off eairly proceeded on passed Black Bluffs on S. S. high land, hilley & plains on boath Sides of the River no Timber only in the Bottoms on the River.— passd a Timbered Bottom on S. S. 2 men went out hunting— at 1 oClock we halted at an old Rickree Village on S. S. took dinner. our hunters came to us had killed a fat Elk. we found at this village Some Squashes. the Rick Rees left it last

Spring. their village was built verry close compact, & covered each Sepperate house with Earth. we Saw Several canoes made of Buffalow hides[1] which would carry 2 men & considerable baggage, also Some baskets we took Several of them & Some of the Squashes &.C—&.C— we proceeded on Capt. Lewis & one hunter went out hunting in a handsome Bottom covered with Timber on N. S. passed a creek on the South Side[2] we Camped on a large Sand beach on N. S. Capt. Lewis & the hunter joined us. brought no Game with them.— the 2 Capt. & 2 more knockd for bow pack[3]

1. Probably bullboats, buffalo skins stretched over a hemispherical frame.

2. Perhaps Four Bears Creek, Dewey County, South Dakota, mentioned by other enlisted men but not by Clark.

3. This final sentence does not make sense. The words "knockd," "bow," and "pack" may not be correct. The other journals are no help.

Sunday 7th Oct. 1804. a clear & pleasant morning. We Set off at day light. proceeded on passed a creek[1] on N. S. called [*blank*] halted took breakfast at a River[2] named [*blank*] where their was an old Rickree village built in the Same Manner as that we passd yesterday on S. S. passd a timbered Bottom on S. S. abo. mo. of this River a Small Shower of rain the wind more from the S. Sailed on Saw 2 of the Souix Indians on N. S. Spoke to them they Sd. they wanted Something to eat & that their band was a going up to the Rickrees, we Gave them Some Venison & proceeded on to an Island about 4 oC. I went out with Capt. Clark & 2 men hunters on Sd. Island to hunt. we killed a Black tailed Deer which was verry large especially the Ears & a handsome Brarow which Capts. had the Bones & skin Saved in order to Send back to the States. we Camped on N. S. abo. the head of Sd. Isl. where I came on board

1. Probably Clark's Otter Creek, now Swan Creek, Walworth County, South Dakota.

2. Moreau River, Dewey County.

Monday 8th Oct. 1804. a pleasant morning. We Set off eairly. proceeded on passd. high land on S. S. passd. a run on S. S. named Slate run.[1] Some hunters out on Shore N. S. hunting in a bottom covered with Timber on N. S. passd an Island we halted at 12 oC. took dinner at the Mouth of a River which came in on S. S. a large Timber Bottom at the Mouth of this River. we named this River Marappa—.[2] the hunters came on board. they Saw a large flock of goats, wounded an Elk, but killed nothing. the wind from the North. Capt. Lewis took the Medrian altd. & made the Lat. [*blank*] we proceeded on passd. a Timbered Bottom land on S. S. Barron hills on N. S. [movd?] on one mile passd another creek on S. S.[3] proceeded on passed an Island[4] on S. S. where we found a large Rickor Ree village on S. S. a nomber of the Indians assembled on the Sand bar opposite the village to See us. a frenchman[5] with them. we took the frenchman on board he Informed us that they were all friendly & Glad to See us. we Camped about one mile abo. the first Ricka Ree village. Capt. Lewis went to the village. carried Some tobacco & Smoaked with the chiefs of thee Nation. thier is 2 more villages of the Rickarees a Short Distance abo. this place &.C.

1. Deadman Creek, Corson County, South Dakota.

2. Oak Creek, Corson County, according to Ordway's name, but perhaps Grand River according to his position.

3. Probably the actual Oak Creek.

4. Ashley Island, with its Arikara Indian village.

5. Joseph Gravelines.

Tuesday 9th Oct. blustering cold wind this morning. Some Showers of rain. Some chiefs & other Indians came to See us; but it being So cold & windy that they did not assemble to counsel. this day we raised a flag pole &.C. Some men went to the village. nothing further particular—

Wednesday 10th Oct. a pleasant morning. I went down to the village which was built on the Island. found their lodges in this village about 60 in nomber and verry close compact. in a round form large & warm covered first after the wood is willows and Grass. Then a thick coat of Earth &.C— except the chimney hole which Goes out at center & top—[1] they Raise considerable of Indian corn, beans pumkins Squasshes water millons a kind of

Tobacco &.C. &.C.[2] they Supply Several nations around them in corn as we are told. their is a 2 frenchman who trade here, Mr. Tabbo[3] livees here now. has Some Goods & trades with them for their peltry &.C. we left one of our frenchman with Mr. Tabbow & took his Soon in his place.[4] all things made ready to hold a counsel with the nation. they have used us in the most friendly manner. Gave us corn & beans dryed pumkins & Squasshes &.C. &.C— Some of their women are verry handsome & clean &.C. &.C.

Wednesday October 10th 1804.[5]

A Journal continued from 90th page[6] at R. Ree villge. 10th Oct. About 2 oClock P. M. the chiefs & Warrirs of the Rick a Rees Nation assembled at our Camp under the american flag to Counsel with our Officers. Capt. Lewis read a Speech to them Giving them Good counsel &.C. after the talk was inded to them three Guns was fired from our Bow peace. then our officers Gave the three Chiefs Some presents & ⟨a⟩ 3 flags & each Chief a meddel. their is 3 villages of this nation & three chiefs one at each village.[7] our officers Gave Each an equal proportion of the Goods. Each an american flag, a red coat (& cocked hat & feathers) & Meddels as abo. mn. [mentioned] Some Paint they divided the Goods & paint among themselves & tobacco &.C. &.C after all was over our Capts. Shot the air Gun. they appeared to be astonished at the Site of it & the execution it would doe. they were verry thankful to us for what they had Recd. from us, & Sd. that we were So Good that we must go where we pleased after they would have a talk tomorrow & Give us Some Corn &.C. the chiefs Shook hands with [our?] officers in the most friendly manner, & returned to their villages. I & one man went to the 2nd village with them in the evening which is about 4 miles from the lower village. the chief took us into his lodge which was verry large & their village is built nearly in the Same form as the lower village. the chiefs wife Brought us a bowl full of Beans & corn. we Eat Some of it. She then brought 3 more one after another of different kinds of victuls. we Eat Some of each & found it verry Good. we Smoaked a while with them. they were verry friendly to us & Seemed to be desirous to talk with us & Scarcely kept their Eyes off us (we returned to camp late) [*undated, after October 10, 1804*][8]

Latitudes of the Different remarkable places on the Missouri River—

	D	M.	S.	
" of St. Charles ⟨Village⟩	38	54	39	N.
Mouth Gasconade River	38	44	35	"
Mouth of the osage river	38	31	6	"
Mouth of Grand River	38	47	54 9/10	"
Do of Kanzas River	39	5	25	N.
" 1½ miles above dimond Island	39	9	38	N.
" 3 miles below the 2nd old village of the Kansas	39	25	42	"
" of Nordway River	39	39	22	"
at good Island	40	20	12	N.
Mouth of Nemahar river	39	55	56	N.
" Bald pated prairie	40	27	6	N
" White Cat fish Camp 10 mil abo. R. platte	41	3	19	N
" Counsel Bluff	41	17	0	"
Mo. of Stone River or little Souix R.	41	42	34	"
" on the South Side where the king of the Mahas was buried 4 years ago	42	1	3	N.
	D.	M.	S.	
" at Fish Camp near the Mahars Village abov. mo. of the Creek Augt. 14th 1804	42	13	41	N.
" at the Chalk Bluff, (Calumet)	42	53	13	
" at Louisells Fort	44	11	13	
" at Dog River	44	19	36	
" at the mouth of Wa-ter-hoo, River	45	39	5	
the mouth of River Bullette	46	29	00	
Fort Mandans on N. E. Side	47	21	00	

July 24th 1804[9]

The estimated Distance of the Missouri River from the mouth as taken by Capt. William Clark in May June & July 1804 of remarkable places as follows. viz.—

21	miles	from the mouth to the Village of St. Charles N. S.	
104¾	miles	do	to the Gasconnade River S. S.
138¾	miles	do	to the Great Osage River, S. S.
201	miles	do	to the Mine River— S. S.
226¾	miles	Do	to the Two Rivers of Charlton, N. S.
245	do	do	to the old village of the Missourie N. S.
255	miles		to the Grand River on the— S. S.
366	miles	do	to the Kansas River— S. S.
433	miles	do	to the 2nd old village of the Kansas S. S.
481	miles	do	to the Nordaway River— N. S.
511¼	do	do	to the Grand Ne-ma-har River S. S.
570¾	do	do	to the Bald pated prairie N. S.
632	miles		to the Great River plate or Shoal S. S.
644	miles		to the point of observations on N. S. at W. Camp 10 miles N. 15 W. from the plate River

above equal to 213 Leagues & ⅔

	D	M	S	
Latitude	41	3	19¾	N. as Taken 12 miles abv. River Platte

Augt. 1804

682	miles to the Counsel Bluff on the S. Side
766	miles to the Little River Souix on N. Side
870	miles to the Mahars Village S. Side
1235	mls to Isl. of Ceders Louisells Fort on North Side
1275	ml. to the Teton River on the S W. Side
1320	ml. to the mo. of Chien or Shehor c. dog R. S. W. S.
1400	ml. to the mo. of Sur-war-har-na River S. W. Side
1425	ml. to the mo. of We-tor-hoo River S. W. Side
1430	ml. to the *Ricaree Village* on the S. W. Side
1505	ml. to the River Bullette on the S W. Side
1550	ml. to the River Clifs abo. old vill. of Mandans S. W. S.
1600½	ml. to Fort Mandens on the N. E. Side

1. A good, brief description of a typical earth lodge of the village Indians of the Missouri River and adjacent regions.

2. Corn, beans, pumpkins, and squashes were the principal crops of the village Indians of the Great Plains. The watermelon is probably not the familiar watermelon, an African species (see Clark's entry for August 2, 1804). Indian tobacco is *Nicotiana quadrivalvis* Pursh.

3. Pierre-Antoine Tabeau.

4. It is unclear whether this is the son of Tabeau (who is not known to have had a son) or the son of an unnamed *engagé*. The identity of the person who remained behind is also not known. See Clark's entry for this day.

5. The entry for October 10 is divided above this dateline, separated by several pages of miscellaneous notes, reading backwards to the journal entries. Four pages separating the entry have latitude readings along the Missouri River, a blank page, and two pages of estimated distances from the mouth of the Missouri to Fort Mandan. These notes are printed next, and the October 10 entry is brought together here. Following those tables in the journal is one page that has the following: "S 76 W 3½" and "S. 60 W. 3 a pt."; then the following words crossed out, "Orderly Book For the Detachment Kept by Sert. Ordway—Commenceing on the 1st day of April 1804." The word "Silas" appears in this title, but upside down to the rest of the text. Four sheets, eight pages, have been cut out at this point and only the stubs remain.

6. Ordway's pages are numbered in the upper corners, but the numbers are not always visible now.

7. Kakawissassa or Lighting Crow, Pocasse or Hay, and Piaheto or Eagle's Feather are the Arikara chiefs. See Clark's entries for October 8–11 for a discussion of the meeting with the Arikaras and notes on the Indian villages.

8. The undated portion of the material that interrupts the entry, apparently completed some time after October 10 since it gives the distance to Fort Mandan. Ordway's "Wa-ter-hoo" River is Grand River, Corson County, South Dakota, which the sergeant apparently missed naming on October 8. His "Bullette" River is the Cannonball River, dividing Morton and Sioux counties, North Dakota, which the party passed on October 18.

9. Another portion of the interrupting material. Although it carries a date of July 24, the entry must have been completed later and even after October 10 since it gives the distance to Fort Mandan. At the top of one page of the table, between entries for miles 570¾ and 632, is the heading, "Sgt. John Ordways Journal Book. Detachment Orders."

Thursday 11th Oct. 1804. a clear & cool morning. the wind from the N. W. Some of the party down at the village below this last night they informed us that one of the chiefs lost all the good he Recd. from us in the River, Going home. the Skin cannoe got over Set turned everry thing out of it he Grieved himself considerable about his loss &.C. at 11 oClock the Indians assembled at our camp Brought us Some corn & Beans dryed Squasshes &.C. we Gave them a Steel Mill which they were verry much pleased with. the chiefs made a Short Speech & told us that he was verry Glad to See us & that we must pass where we pleased & none of his nation would attempt to hold our cable &.C. he also desired that we Would Speak a good word for them to the Mandan nation for they wished to make pease with them about 1 oClock we Set off. proceeded on passed a Creek[1] on S. S. & a Timbred Bottom. Sailed on at 4 oC. arived at the 2nd R. Ree village on the Bank of the River S. Side a handsome place a high Smoth prarie. a Timbred Bottom of the opposite Shore a large Sand beach makes out from the vill. they had their coulours or flags hoisted that we Gave them, & all assd. on the bank of the river to See us. we camped on a Sand bar below the ville. Capt. Lewis & Clark took an observation which made them amazed at the instrument went up to the ville. took Several of the party with them— they all returned in the evening. found that the two upper villages were near each other & built nearly alike. their is no wood near these 2 villages. they cross the River for the Greater part of their wood to a Timbred Bottom on N. S. opisite their villages &.C— in the evening our cooks took the Best axe we had on Shore for to cut Some wood & it was Stole by Some of those Indians.

1. Possibly Clark's Kakawissassa Creek, later Cathead Creek, now Fisher Creek, Corson County, South Dakota.

Friday 12th Oct 1804. a Clear & pleasant morning. the Indians assembled on the bank near us for to Trade with us. they wanted red paint mostly, but would Give whatever they had to Spare for any kind of Goods one of the men Gave an Indian a pin hook & the Indian Gave him in return a pair of Moggisins we Gave them Some Small articles of Goods for Buffalow Robes & Moggn. &.C. the officers went to the villages in order to hear what the chiefs had to Say. They Gave us 10 or 12 bushels of corn & beans &.C. &.C. the officers came on board about 12 oClock took a Good Indian with us who had been to the head of the Missouri River. about 1 oClock we Set off the fiddle playing & the horns Sounding &.C. little abo. the Towns we Saw a great nomber of Squaws employed in toteing wood across the River in their Buffalow hide cannoes proceeded on. passd. a timbred bottom on S. S. also one on the N. S. where we Camped[1] at the upper end of the Bottom on N. S. Newman & Reed confined.[2] 3 Indians came to Camp

1. In Campbell County, South Dakota, in an area now inundated by the Oahe Reservoir.

2. John Newman was tried the next day for "having uttered repeated expressions of a highly criminal and mutinous nature," was found guilty, and sentenced to receive seventy-five lashes on his back. He was also dismissed from the permanent party and had to return with other non-permanent members from Fort Mandan in the spring of 1805. Clark does not mention the incident until the next day and no one mentions Moses B. Reed's connection with the incident.

Saturday 13th Oct. Cloudy. proceeded on passed Pond River[1] on N. S. about 50 yds. wide at the Mouth. about 12 oClock it rained Some. we halted a court Martial was held which detained us 2 hours. we then proceedd on. passed Several Bottoms covered with C. W. Timber the River Gits narrower & deeper than below the hills make near the River on each Side. at dark we Camped[2] on N. S. jest abo. a Bottom of fine Timber,—

1. Clark's Stone Idol Creek, now Spring, or Hermaphrodite, Creek, Campbell County, South Dakota. Ordway's name reflects its supposed origin in a nearby small lake.

2. In Campbell County, a mile or so south of the North Dakota state line, the last camp in South Dakota on the outbound journey.

Sunday 14th Oct. Cloudy & rain. we Set off eairly. passed a bottom covered with Timber on S. S. passd a creek[1] & Black Bluffs on S. S. we halted at 12 oClock on a Sand bar. the proceedings of the Court martial was read & put in to Exicution. it [rained] Slowly the greater part of the Day. Camped on N. S. below a Timbred Bottom.—

1. Clark's Piaheto, or Eagle's Feather, Creek, probably Baldhead Creek, Corson County, South Dakota, about a mile south of the North Dakota state line.

Monday 15th Oct. Some rain last night. Cloudy morning we Set off eairly. passd. a Timbred bottom where we Saw Some Indians. at 7 oC. we met a hunting party of the Rickarees comming down the river returning to their village, they had 12 Cannoes made of Bufflow hides loaded with excelent fat meat. we halted with them about 2 hours. they Gave us Some of their fat meat to carry with us & Gave us Some that they cooked to eat. we Smoaked with them. their party consisted of men women & children. our officers Gave them in return Some fish hooks Beeds &.C. we proceeded on passed Barron hills on the South Side of the River. at 10 oC. we passed another hunting party who were Encamped in a timbred bottom on S. S. passed a handsome Bottom prarie & the Mouth of a creek[1] where their was an old village Some years ago of the Chien Nation[2] on S. S. we proceeded on. passed timbred bottoms on each Side of the River we Saw a nomber of Indians on the Shore on N. S. passd. a creek on S. S.[3] at Sunset we Camped on N. S. at a hunting Camp of the R. Ree nation. their was abt.30 men & a nomber of women & children at this Camp. they treated us in the Same manner as the rest of their nation did. the Greatest Curiousity to them was York Capt. Clarks Black Man. all the nation made a Great deal of him. the children would follow after him, & if he turned towards them they would run from him & hollow as if they were terreyfied, & afraid of him.

1. Probably Four Mile Creek, Sioux County, North Dakota.

2. Meaning the Cheyenne Indians, which Ordway gave as "Shian" in his next entry. See Clark's entries for this day and the next.

3. Perhaps Clark's Sharhá Creek, either Long Soldier or Porcupine Creek, Sioux County.

Tuesday 16th Oct. 1804. a clear & pleasant morning. we Set off at day light. passed an old Shian fort on the S. S. where the Chian nation of Indians lived Some years ago. proceeded on passed a creek on S. S. called [*blank*][1] passed a Bottom covered with Timbers on N. S. at half past 7 oC. we halted took breakfast on a willow Island S. S. passd. the Mouth of a River on S. S. called [*blank*][2] high naked hills back from the River. we proceeded on under a gentle breeze from the S. W. towards evening Capt. Lewis & one hunter went out hunting on S. S. of the River. directly after we passed a hunting Camp of the R. Ree nation on N. S. abo. the camp we Saw a Great nomber of Indians on each side of the River. they were Shooting a flock of Goats which they had drove into the River. They Shot upwards of 40 of them & Got them to Shore. they had Shot them all with their Bows & arrows. we Saw Some of the Goats floating down with the arrows Sticking up in them. we Saw a large flock of Goats back on the hills, which we Suppose they had Scared from the River. our hunter killed 3 Goats out of the same flock. the Indians killed theirs when the Indians killed the Goats in the River they Swam in & drew them out to each Shore we Saw them all lying along the Shore & Some Indians on horse back to keep them or the flock in the River. So that they might kill as many as they pleased. we Camped on the S. S. where Capt. Lewis & our hunter joined us.

1. Probably Clark's Girl Creek, either Porcupine or Battle Creek, Sioux County, North Dakota.

2. Ordway may mean on the north (actually east) side, thus Clark's Warreconne River, today's Beaver Creek, Emmons County.

Wednesday 17th Oct. Eight Indians came on from their Camp last night & brought us Some meat. they remained with us all night & Sang the most of the night in the morning our officers gave them Some fancy goods in return for the meat. the weather clear. the wind from N. W. we Set off eairly. proceeded on. passed a Bottom covered with Small timber on S. S. Barron hill on N. S. which make in close to the River,— abt. 10 oC. Capt. Clark our Indian & one hunter went out hunting on S. S. & at 11 oC. the [wind?] arose & blew So hard a head that we were obledged to lay by. we halted on N. S. 2 men went out hunting. towards evening the wind abated So that we proceeded on untill some time after dark before we found a good place to camp the moon Shined pleasant. we Camped on South Side in a timbred bottom.[1] Capt. Clark & all the hunters except one who camped on the opposite Shore, joined us they had killed Six Deer. Some of them verry fat. we took care of all the meat & Skins &.C.

1. A mile or two south of the entrance of Cannonball River, Sioux County, North Dakota.

Thursday 18th Oct. a clear & pleasant morning white frost & froze Some last night. we Set off eairly. one man out hunting on ech Side of the River. we proceeded on 2 miles met a cannoe coming down the River which belonged to the frenchman we had on board Mr. Gravelleen. their was 2 frenchman[1] in the cannoe who had been a hunting up to the Manden nation and was Robed by a hunting party of the Mandens. they took their Guns & amunition &.C. axe, & 30 beaver Skins & all they had So they were obledged to turn back but when they met us they turned about in hopes we Should See them & make them Give up all they had taken from them. we proceeded on ⟨passed a Sand Stone Bluff on the S. S. one of [men?] came on board had killed an Elk & a pillican⟩ men went out hunting on N. S. the man who Stayed out last night joined us. had killed 2 fat Goats. we proceeded on passed the mouth of Cannon Ball River[2] on S. S. about 100 yds. wide passed Sand Stone Bluff on the Same Side abo. the River where we found round Stone in the form of cannon balls. Some of them verry large we took one of them on Board to answer for an anker. one of our hunters joined us here had killed an Elk & a pillican. we Saw large flocks of Goats & Buffaloe on N. S. proceeded on passed a creek on N. S.[3] Timbred Bottoms the most of the day on Each Side of the River. Roed & poled about 16 Miles & Camped on a large Sand beach on the S. S. our hunters all joined us had killed Six Deer 4 Goats & 3 Elk we Got all the Meat except 2 of the Elk which was too late to find them. the most of the Meat was verry fat. the Game is verry pleanty here the man that killed the 3 Elk Said he counted 150 in the Same flock. (handsome plains back f.[rom?] R.[iver?])

1. The identification of these men is rather involved and not completely sure. Some persons conjecture that they are François Rivet and Phillippe Degie, but that seems doubtful. One of them may have been Francis Fleury *dit* Grenier, but there are other possibilities. See Clark's entry for this day.
2. Cannonball River, Morton and Sioux counties, North Dakota.
3. Badger Creek, Emmons County.

Friday 19th Oct. a clear & pleasant morning. we Set off eairly. 2 men out hunting on S. S. a gentle breeze from the South we proceeded on passed a Timbred bottom on N. S. 2 men went out hunting on N. S. & in a fiew minutes killed an Elk. we took it on board & proceeded on untill abt. 1 o.C. when we halted for dinner on S. S. one of the hunters that went out this morning joined us had killed 2 Elk. Capt. Clark & 2 more hunters went out hunting on S. S. Sailed on. Saw an abundance of droves of Buffaloe on

N. S. passd. a Bottom on N. S. where we took on board 2 of the hunters who had killed 3 deer— towards evening our hunters all joined us. had killed 4 more Deer. the Skins were all Given out to the party &.C.[1]

1. The camp for the day, not entirely certain, would be a few miles upstream from Huff, Morton County, North Dakota.

Saturday 20th Oct. Set off eairly a pleasant morning. Several hunters out hunting on each Side of the River. we passed a creek[1] on N. S. 20 yds. wide. passed Bottoms covered with Timber on Boath Sides of the River. passd. a creek[2] on S. S. opposite the lower point of an Island. towards evening we passed the 1st old village of the Mandens[3] on the S. S. (Saw Buffalow Swimming the River) we Camped at a Stone coal Bluff on S. S. our hunters joined us. Brought in the Game which they had killed this day which was 12 Deer one Goat & a woolf, one of the hunters wounded a White Bare.[4]

1. Probably Clark's Shepherd's Creek, modern Apple Creek, Burleigh County, North Dakota.
2. Little Heart River, Morton County.
3. Now called On-a-Slant (or Slant) Village, below the mouth of Heart River.
4. Cruzatte made the party's first encounter with the grizzly bear.

Sunday 21st Oct. Some frozen rain last night Snow this morning. the wind from N. E. we Set off as usal. proceeded on the current Swift. we passed the mo. of a River called Chifschetar River[1] on S. S. Snowed Slowly untill 12 oClock. passd Bottom on S. S. barron hills on the N. S. on the River & back from the [river] is Smoth handsom plains. about 3 o.C. Capt Clark & one hunter went out hunting on N. S. & in a Short time they Shot a Bull buffaloe which was Tollorable fat. one of the hunters Shot an otter.[2] a cool & chilley day We Camped on the S. S. at a high prarie.—

1. Heart River, Morton County, North Dakota.
2. River otter, *Lutra canadensis.*

Monday 22nd Oct. Some Snow last night. the frenchman in the cannoe who are in company with us have Caught Several large Beaver every night for Several nights back. we Set off eairly Cloudy & cool this morning. we proceeded on at 9 oClock we met a 11 Indians of the Souix nation yankton tribe. they were naked & Sd. they were on their way down the River Gave them Some meat and proceeded on. at 11 oC. I went out hunting. the after part of the day pleasant. I Saw on the hills flocks of Goats & Buffaloes. Several Salt Runs in the vallies. I killed a Buffalow and Returned to the Boat in the evening. Camped on the South Side.[1]

1. Probably in southeast Oliver County, North Dakota, just above the Morton County line.

Tuesday 23 Oct. a little Snow last night a cloudy morning. we Set off eairly. about 9 o.C. we passed the Indian Camp N. S. where the 2 frenchman was Robed a fiew days ago, they had left their Camp. their was 3 of their lodges Standing on N. S. which was built in the Same manner as those in their villages. proceeded on passed Several Timbred bottoms where we Saw pleanty of Grasses Rushes &.C. Camped[1] on S. S. at a Bottom covered with timber where we found a large quantity of Graze the Buff. or Rabit Berryes of which we eat freely off. they are a Small red berry, Sower & Good to the taste. we have Seen them pleanty in this Country.

1. Near Sanger, Oliver County, North Dakota.

Wednesday 24th Oct. Cloudy. we Set off eairly. proceeded on passed a Bottom on N. S. covered with fine Timber Such as oak & large cottonwood &.C. at 12 o.C. we halted at an Isl.[1] on N. S. where we found a hunting camp of the Mandan Nation of Indians. the chief we had on board Spoke to the chief of this party told them our business &.C. they had Some handsome women with them. at 2 oC. we proceeded on passed the Isl where the River cut th[rough?] [*paper worn, several words illegible*][2] which formerly used to be 10 miles Round by its cutting across forms the Isl. Camped on the N. S.[3] 4 of the natives came to our Camp but did not remain with us but a Short time.

1. Now probably part of Painted Woods Lake, McLean County, North Dakota.
2. The bottom of this page, and several pages following, are so badly curled and worn that some of the text is lost or illegible.
3. About two miles below Washburn, McLean County.

Thursday 25th Oct. a clear morning. we Set off eairly under a fine breeze from the S. Sailed on passed a handsom high prarie on S. S. where their was formerly a village of the Rickarrees nation.[1] we Saw a nomber of the natives Strung along the Shore on horse back looking at us. at 2 o.C we halted for to dine on S. S. our chief went over to Speak to the natives on N. S. in a cannoe as we could not land on that Shore with our boat for the Sand beaches &.C. proceeded on round a Bend passed a handsome Timbred bottom on N. S. Camped on the N. S.[2] one of the natives came to our Camp with our chief & remd. all night &C

1. Probably either the Bagnell site or Greenshield site, which were occupied by Mandan, Hidatsa, and Arikara Indians, in Oliver County, across from and somewhat south of Washburn, McLean County, North Dakota.

2. In the vicinity of historic Fort Clark, in either Oliver County or McLean County, depending on shifts in the river.

Friday 26th Oct. a clear morning. we Set off eairly. passed a large willow Bottom on S. S. high land on N. S. we proceeded on at 10 oClock we halted at a hunting camp of the Mandens, consisting of men women and children. here we found an Irishman[1] who was here tradeing with them from the N. W. Company of Traders. we delayd about an hour with them, & proceedd on. took 2 of the natives on board with their Baggage in order to go to their Village. the Greater part of that Camp kept along Shore Going up to the villages. we Camped on the S. S. below the 1st village[2] at an old field where the manden nation had raised corn the last Summer, & Sun flowers &.C. of which they eat with corn. Capt. Lewis walked up to the village this evening. found the nation verry friendly,—&.C.

1. Hugh McCracken, apparently an independent trader. See Clark's entry for this day.

2. The camp was below the Mandan village Mitutanka, also known as the Deapolis site, and due to river shifts the campsite is perhaps in McLean County, North Dakota, on the opposite side of the river from where they located.

Saturday 27th Oct. a clear & pleasant morning. we Set off eairly. proceeded on. at 7 oC. we arived at the 1st village of the Mandens on S. S. their is about 40 houses or lodges in this village which are built much in the manner of the Rekarees. we found two or 3 frenchmen[1] one of them kept a Squaw & had a child by hir which was tollorable white. we delayed about 2 hours with them. they were assembled on the bank, especially the children, who are verry numerous. the men mostly a hunting. we proceeded on passed a Bluff on the S. S. with a black Stripe through the center of it resembling Stone coal, a bottom opposite on N. S. on which is the 2d village of the Mandens.[2] we Camped on N. S. little above the 2 village. the 3rd village nearly opposite on S. S.[3] this is the most conveneint place to hold a counsel with the whole nation. we hoisted a flag pole &.C. from the mouth of the Missouri to this place is 1610 miles.

1. One of them was René Jusseaume, or Jessaume, a free trader. See Clark's entry for this day.

2. The Mandan village Ruptáre, McLean County, North Dakota, called the Black Cat site after the village chief. It has been destroyed by river changes.

3. The Hidatsa village Mahawha, in Stanton, Mercer County, called the Amahami site after their band designation, a group also designated as the Awaxawi.

Sunday 28th Oct. a clear morning all things made ready to hold a counsel the wind blew verry high from the N. W. So the Indians did not assemble, but the prinsible men of the tribe called the Big Belleys[1] came down to this village in order to be at the counsel. the form of these Savvages burrying their dead is after they have disceased they fix a Scaffel on & raised 4 forks abt 8 or 10 feet from the Ground. they lye the dead body on the Sd. Scaffel Raped up in a Buffalow Robe a little distance from their villages—their villages are close compact & picketed in. when any of them loose a partickulor friend or relation they morn and cry for Some time after.

1. A designation for the Hidatsa Indians. See Clark's entry for October 27.

Monday 29th Oct. a clear & pleasant morning. we expect the Indians to assemble to day for to hold a Council with our officers.— especially the chiefs & warries of 3 nats. at 11 oClock the counsel commenced a Gun was fired from our Bow peace when our officers took the chiefs by the hand Capt. Lewis delivered a Speech to them through Intreperters, & counseled with the Manden Grovantrs & Weta Soaux[1] nations, the counsel was ended about 4 oC. P. M. another Gun was fired, & then our officers Gave the or each head chief a meddel & a flag and made a 1st & 2nd chief to each village & Gave the head chiefs a Suit of cloaths and a quantity of Small Goods for their nations, cocked hats & feathers &.C. &.C Gave also a Steel corn mill to the Manden nation which pleased them verry much the captains requested them to assemble again tomorrow if possable to Give us answer to what we had Sd. to them respecting makeing peace with the Rickarees and all other nations & whether they mean to Go to See their Great father &.C. Capt. Lewis Shot the air Gun which pleased them much they returned home to their village. hoisted the flag we Gave them as well as the officers Gave an american flag for each village &.C. &.C.—

1. *Gros Ventres,* "big bellies," is the French term for the Hidatsas, who were also called Watersoons (variously spelled, as Ordway demonstrates) as well as other designations. Again, see Clark's entry for October 27.

Tuesday 30th Oct. a clear and pleasant morning. we delayed in order to Give the Savvages time to consider & Give an answer to the counsel &.C. at 10 o.C. A. M. Capt. Clark and 8 of the party went in a pearogue Six miles up the River to look on an Isl. for a place for our winter quarters. one or 2 of the natives went with them at 5 oC. P. M. they returned and enformed us that it the place was not Suitable for us to winter &.C. the natives were a nomber of the men & women about our camp with Some corn & Bread made of the corn meal parched & mixed with fat &.C. which eats verry well, they expect us to give them Some Small article in return for their produce, Such as corn Beans Squasshes &C of which they raise pleanty off for themselves & to trade with other nations &.C.—

Wednesday 31st Oct. a Clear & pleasant morning. the wind Blew high from the South. the Savvages has not Gave us an answer yet. about 12 oClock Capt. Clark & Some of the men went down to the 2nd village. the chiefs Gave them 9 or 10 Bushels of corn & 1 or 2 Buffalow Robes &C

Thursday 1st November 1804. a clear & [*illegible*] morning the wind high from the N. W., cool at 3 oClock P. M. we Set off to return a Short distance down the River in order to find a Good place for winters quarters. the wind abated. But the River So Shallow the we Struck the Sand bars. Capt. Lewis myself and Several more of the party halted at the 1st village of the Mandens in order to git Some corn. the head chief told us that they had not Got the corn ready. But if we would come tomorrow they [w]ould have it ready. they Gave us 3 kinds of victuls to eat which was verry Good. they were verry friendly Gave the pipe round everry fiew minutes &.C. they live verry well. have pleanty of corn Beans Squashes meat &.C. Capt. Lewis told the chief that he would come again tomorrow. then we went on abt. 2 miles down to a Bottom covered with Timber, where we Camped on the N. Side of the Missouris River.

Friday 2nd Nov. a cloudy morning. Capt. Clark went with Some men down the Bottom to look for a place to Build our huts. they Returned Shortly had found a Good place a Short distance down where their was an Indian camp in a Grove of large cottonwood Timber.[1] Sevral Indians at Sd. camp Capt. Lewis & Several of the party[2] went in a pearogue up to the lst village of the Mandans in order to Git corn. we droped down a Short distance farther to a body & Bottom of large Timber where we commenced falling Timber, and fixing a camp close by the place where we intend for to build. picthed our tents & laid the foundation of one line of our huts, which consisted of 4 Rooms 14 feet Square. the other line will be the Same Capt. Lewis returned. brought us 10 or 12 bushels of Good corn. we find the cottonwood Timber will Split Tollorable well, and as their is no other building timber in this bottom we expect to Split punchin to cover the huts with. one of our french hands is discharged & gone down the river.

1. Fort Mandan, McLean County, North Dakota, about fourteen miles west of Washburn, where the party would remain until April 1805. The actual site has been washed away by the Missouri River.

2. Including Gass, according to Gass.

Saturday 3rd Nov. 1804. a clear and pleasant morning. Six hunters Set out to Go 20 or 30 miles down the River in a pearogue to good hunting Ground in order to kill meat for the party. we continued building. layed the foundation of the other line of huts 4 by 14 feet also. the timber large and heavy. Mr [*blank*][1] our Intreperter moved down from village with his famialy to Stay with us. a frenchman[2] came from the village also who has engaged to join us for the expedition &.C— Some of the Squaws came from the vil. brot. Capt. meat &C.

1. Jusseaume.
2. Jean Baptiste Lepage took the place of the discharged Newman and went to the Pacific and back with the permanent party (see Clark's entry for this day).

Sunday 4th Nov. 1804. cold last night & white frost this morning. clear and pleasant. we continued raiseing our huts. Several more of our french hands is discharged and one makeing a pearogue in order to descend the Missourie & Several of the natives come to our Camp to See us build our huts, and to See our boats &.C— we got one line of our huts raised So that we got the Eve Beames on & all of large Timber So that it took all the men hard lifting to put the 16 foot eve Beames.

Monday 5th Nov. 1804. a clear & pleasant morning. all hands to work eairly raiseing the other line of our huts & Splitting out punchiens for to lay the loft which we intend covering over with earth in order to make the huts more warm and comfortable. we dug a vault[1] 100 yds abo. the huts to make or keep the place healthy.

1. A latrine.

Tuesday 6th Nov. it was uncommon light in the north the Greater part of last night[1] a clear morning. about 9 oC it clouded up cold look likely for Snow at 11 o.C. our french man[2] who came with us from the R. a. Rees as an Intreperter and Several of our french hands Set off to descend the River in a pearogue [*one line illegible at bottom of page*]

1. The aurora borealis.
2. Including at least Gravelines, Paul Primeau, and Jean Baptiste La Jeunesse.

Wednesday 7th Nov. a Cloudy morning. we continued building. the Capts. Room being hughn down the inside, we layed the loft over with hughn punchien then Stoped the craks with Some old tarpolin & Grass Some morter then a thick coat of earth over all, which will make it verry warm. commenced building the chimneys &.C.

Thursday 8th Nov. Cloudy. we continued building with as much haste as possable in order to Git in them before winter Sets in. we found that the C. W. [cottonwood] will rive well So that we are in hopes to make enofe to cover our buildings. but afterwards found it difficult and Gave up the Idea.

Friday 9th Nov. a hard white frost last night. a clear & pleasant morning. we continued building as usal. we expect our hunters Soon as we are in Great want of fresh meat.— a nomber of the natives visits us everry day.

Saturday 10th Nov. Cloudy & cold. the 2nd Chief[1] & a Squaw came from the 1st village down in a buffaloe hide cannoe. brought us Som fat buffalow meat we finished raising one line of our huts. commenced hughing & Guttering the punchien for the purpose of covering the huts.

1. Probably Sho-ta-harro-ra, The Coal, the second chief of the Mandans and apparently an Arikara by birth, from Mitutanka.

Sunday 11th Nov. a clear and pleasant morning. we commenced dobbing our huts & covering them &.C. a frenchmans Squaw[1] came to our camp who belonged to the Snake nation. She came with our Intreperters wife & brought with them 4 buffalow Robes and Gave them to our officers. they Gave them out to the party. I Got one fine one myself. chilly this evening &.c.

1. Clark has both Shoshone Indian wives of Toussaint Charbonneau arriving, one of whom would be Sacagawea. It could be that two Indian women came, only one of whom was the wife of Charbonneau and not necessarily Sacagawea (see also Ordway's entry of November 20).

Monday 12th Nov Clear & cold this morning. a verry hard frost. froze Some last night. we continued our buildings as usal. the chief of the lower village of the Mandens[1] brought us Some buffalow meat which we were in want as our hunters has not arived yet. we unloaded the pearogue in order to fetch Stone.

1. Big White or Sheheke; see Clark's entry of October 29.

Tuesday 13th Nov. Snowey morning the Ice run considerable fast in the river. we unlaoded the boat for fear the Ice would take it off. we put the loading in the Store house, all though it was not finished, but we continued the work Capt. Lewis & 6 men went in the pearogue up the River through the Ice to the first village of the Mandens after Stone for the backs of our Chimneys. Some of the Souix Indians[1] came here with a chief of the Mandens. they asked for whiskey &.C. but we Gave them none. Capt. Lewis returned with his party towards evening much fatigued. they got fast on a Sand bar & had to be out in the water abto. 2 hours. the Ice running against their legs. their close frooze on them. one of them got 1 of his feet frost bit. it hapned that they had Some whiskey with them to revive their Spirits.

1. According to Clark, they were Assiniboine Indians.

Wednesday 14th Nov. a Snowey morning. one man Sent down the River in order to meet the pearogue & h. See what was the cause of their delaying So long. abto. 3 o.C. P. M. we Saw a cannoe comming up the River with 2 men on board which we Supposed to be the frenchmen who went down the River Some days ago traping. at dark the 2 frenchman ari. had caught 22 beaver. they did not See our hunting party.

Thursday 15th Nov. Cloudy. George Drewyer arived with the frenchman who went after them. he Informed us that the pearogue was abt. 18 mls. below loaded with meat. the frenchman Sent back to the pearogue with a kittle to put on the Bow of the pearogue was cut with the Ice &.C

Friday 16th Nov. a cold frosty night. the Trees were covered with frost which was verry course white & thick even on the Bows of the trees all this day. Such a frost I never Saw in the States. we continued building. raised a provision & Smoak house 24 feet by 14 f. the air verry thick with fogg from the R.

Saturday 17th Nov. a cold clear morning. the frost fell from the trees by the Sun Shineing upon them. at 11 o.C. the frenchman arived with a fat Elk from our pearogue. we have worked Several evenings back to make our Sevels comfotable. the party all moved in to the huts

Sunday 18th Nov. clear & cold. we raised the roof of the meat & Smoak house bringing it up with Timber cross drawing in, So as to answer with chinking & dobbing & covering with earth & ashes for the covering without plank, as it is Troublesom to Git any more than to cover our huts. abt. noon a chief[1] came down from the villages. his Squaw brought a back load of corn in ears for us.—

1. Black Cat, according to Clark.

Monday 19th Nov. the River Riseing the wind from S. W. the weather moderates as the day is pleasant. we dobbed the Store & Smoak house. all hands employed at different Sort of work. abt. 3 o.C. P. M. our hunters arived with the pearogue loaded with meat consisting of 5 buffalow 11 Elk & 30 Deer also Several kinds of Small Game of which they brought the Skins, all the meat we put up on poles in the Roofs of our meat & Smoak houses.—

Tuesday 20th Nov. clear & pleasant at 11 oC. a frenchman[1] who is to be our Inter. for Grovantaur arived with 4 horses loaded with peltry meat &.C. brought another of his wifes with him. the day warm. the work go on as usal. Captains moved in their Room, &.C. got Stone &.C.

1. Apparently Charbonneau.

Wednesday 21st Nov. cloudy & warm 1 of the pearogues Sent a Short distance down the River for Stone for the Back of our chimneys 4 backs made &.C

Thursday 22nd Nov.[1] pleasant & warm Sgt. Pryor & 5 men Sent with a pearogue to the 2nd village of the mandens for corn we completed building the backs of our chimneys. the pearogue returned towards evening with abt. 12 bushels of mixed coullourd corn in ears traied which the natives took out of the Ground where they burry it in holes in their village—

1. Ordway does not mention an episode reported by Clark. It involved the sergeant sleeping with an Indian woman, whose husband was then about to kill her; see Clark's entry for this day.

Friday 23rd Nov pleasant & warm the pearogue Sent for Stone. Rope works fixed. Several hands employed makeing a large Rope for the purpose of drawing the Barge up the Bank &.C.

Saturday 24th Nov. warm & pleasant. the work continued on as usal. the Guard reduced to a Sgt. & 3 men. a nomber of the natives visits us everry day.

Sunday 25th Nov. a pleasant morning. Capt. Lewis the 2 Intrepreters & Six men Set off this morning in order to go 24 miles abo. this place to a nation of Indians called the [*blank*] Capt. Lewis & the Intr. Rode on horseback 5 men went in a pearogue up the the Missourie The men employed compleating the huts &.C

Monday 26th Nov. cold & windy. Some pickets out &C.

Tuesday 27th Nov cold & chilly, the Ice Ran in the River thick. we finished dobbing & covering & compleating the remainder of our huts &.C— Capt Lewis & command brought with them three chiefs from the upper villages of the Grovantaur.[1] they appear to be verry friendly. Gave us a little corn & were Glad to come & see us. they Sd. that the Manden nation told them that we would do them harm, & that was the reason they had not been to see us before. we had a dance this evening. Rivet danced on his head &C

1. According to Clark, they were Hidatsa chiefs Mar-noh-tah or Big Steeler and Man-se-rus-se (Man-nes-surree) or Tail of Calumet Bird, and a prominent, unnamed individual. They

were all from the Hidatsa village Metaharta, called the Sakakawea site after Sacagawea who lived there at the time of Lewis and Clark's arrival.

Wednesday 28th Nov. Snowed hard the Greater part of last night. Snow this morning. the wind from N. E. the River falling. Gealousy between Mr Gisom[1] one of our Intr. and George Drewyer last evening &.C.

1. Jusseaume.

Thursday 29th Nov. the Snow fell yesterday and last night about 12 Inches on a level. a cold Frosty clear morning. 2 or 3 men out hunting. the River fell abt. 2 feet last night So that our Boat lay dry on Shore. we took out the mast & every thing which was in hir & let hir lay as She appeared to be Safe. one of the hunters killed an old Elk brot. in the horns which were verry large, but it being poor we did not go for the meat.

Friday 30th Nov. a clear Sharp frosty morning. froze hard last night. about 9 oClock A. M. an Indian came to the opposite Side of the River and called to come across. our Intrepter Spoke to him found he was come to bring news from the village So we brought him across in a pearogue. he Informed us that a party of the Sauix nation had atcked a party of the Mandans. they killed 1 man on each Side Several more wounded, but the Souix Robbed the party of Manden of their horses 5 or 6 this being done lately our officers thought it best to offer the Mandens Some assistance if they were disposed to fight the Souix. So Captain Clark, myself & 20 more of the party turned out voluntarrely and crossed the River and marched through a bottom covered with Small Timber, willows & all kinds of thick brush for abt. 3 miles. flanking parties out each Side & a rear Guard. I being on the left flank found it difficult Getting through the brush. we raised a Steep bank back of this bottom which brot us on the level prarie, then turned our course & went to the first village of the mandens, Capt Clark told the M. chief what we had come for, and if he would Send a war party from his village & the Black cat another from his village we would go with them & fight the Souix but the chief declined Sending any at present for he Sd. the Snow too deep &.C. So we delayed in the village abt. 2 hours they appeared to be pleased at our comming to their assistance & used us friendly. they would have us to Eat in every lodge we went in &.C. we then Set off from the village & crossed the river on the Ice little abo. above the vil. but the River was Shet up for Some distance below. we then returned down to our Garrison. our officers Gave each man a drink of Taffe,[1] which we Stood in need off,

1. Probably tafia, an inferior grade of rum.

Saturday 1st December 1804. the morning fair. we commenced bringing the pickets & preparing to picket in our Garrison &.C. an Indian came from the Manden village to Inform us that a large nomber Sd. 300 lodge of the Shian or [*blank*] nation had Come to their villages. a Scotsman[1] who is tradeing at the Mandens came to visit us. he belonged to the hudson bay company [*page torn, some words illegible*] he brought over Tobacco Beeds & other kinds of Goods & traded with the Mandens for their furs & buffalow Robes. they bring Some Guns to trade for horses &.C. this hudsons bay compy. lay Garrisoned near the N. W. Compy. on River [*blank*] Eight or 10 days travel by land a North course from this.

1. George Henderson of the Hudson's Bay Company.

Sunday 2nd Decr. a pleasant thoughy [thawing?] morning the work continued on. a nomber of the Shian or dog Indians came from the village to visit us. we Gave them victuels & used them friendly. our officers Gave them Some tobacco & a fiew Small articles of Goods &.C.

Monday 3rd Decr. cold & windy. the work carried on as usal. commenced Setting up the pickets and bring pickets &.C. &.C.

Tuesday 4th Decr. clear & cold. we continued Setting up the pickets & bringing them &.C. the chief of the 2nd vil. the Black cat came to dine with our officers accompanied by Several other Indians &.C.

Wednesday 5th Decr. cloudy & cold. look likely for Snow. we continued the work as usal. we layed a platform upon the meat & Smoak house for a Sentnel to walk.

Thursday 6th Decr. a cold Blustry morning. Some Squalls of Snow & wind high it being So disagreeable weather that we delayed on the work.

Friday 7th Decr. a clear cold frosty morning. 2 or 3 hunters went out early a hunting. about 9 o.C. the head chief of the 1st vill. of the Mandans called the Big White came to our Garrison in Great haste on horse back & Informed us that the Buffalow were comming towards the River in large Gangs and that the praries a little back was covered with Game. Capt. Lewis Immediately Started with 12 men in order to hunt with the natives. they had not been Gone long before we Saw Some buffalow in cite abo. the Garrison near the bank of the River two of our men & Several of the natives were Shooting at them. they Shot three & run one off a Steep bank in to the River which we got out with a chord, and halled it down on the Ice to our landing as the River Shut up last night the Ice had not Got Strong enofe to bear the Buffalow out in the middle of the R. but we dragged Sd. bufo. down near Shore & dressed it. it was a cow with calf our Interpreters Squaws cut the calf. the 2 men who went out this morning came in & Informed us that they had killed Six buffaloe out in the prarie besides those 4 they had killed in part with the natives. the horses were got up & Several men Sent with them out for the meat, but they found that the Savvage had carried off 3 of them. the 4 horses came in loaded with meat also the most of the men they Said that the Savvages had killed upwards of 20 buffalow & our men killed abt. 12 one of them very fat Som of them cows & Some calfs or yearlins. they Saw also large flocks of Goats in the praries & could See the prarie black with buffaloe at a distance aiming to come into the bottoms on the River. the prarie being covered with Snow and extreamly cold 2 of our men Got their feet frost Bitten & one Got his Ear frost bitten this day by being exposed in the praries. a half Gill of Taffee gave to the men by our officers this evening.

Saturday 8th Decr. the weather is 12 degrees colder this morning than I ever new it to be in the States.[1] clear the wind N. W. about 9 oC Capt. Clark and 14 of the party set off a hunting [*page torn, several words illegible*] The prarie we Shortly came in cite of a large gang of Buffalow. we Saw a nomber of the Savvages on horse back running after them. we proceeded on Capt. Clark & myself Saw 2 or 3 Buffalow by themselves we got near them & fires at them wounded one. the men all Scattered So that we missed oppertuntities of Surrounding the gangs of Buffalow. But we saw the praries Black at a distance down the River & in a Bottom which is abt. 5 miles from our fort we then went in to the Bottom and killed 2 cow Buffalow out of a large gang & wounded Several more. one of our men came to us who had killed a calf Buff. we left 2 men to take care of the meat. we then Set off to return to our fort walked a short distance to where calf was and carried it with us. walked fast. Saw a Deer 2 men met us with horses. we got to the fort a little after dark the hunters all come in had killed in all 6 Buffalow & one Deer. the men who went with Capt. Clark he gave a drink of Taffee the air thick with Ice all this day, like a fog.—

1. The captains recorded the temperature as -12° F.

Sunday 9th Decr. the morning pleasant but not So cold as it was yesterday. about 10 o.C. Capt. Lewis & 12 men went out a hunting and concluded to leave a fiew men down in a Bottom abt. 5 mls. below in order to hunt & take care of the meat. a nomber of the Savvages came to our Garrison. Some of them brought Some fat meat and Gave to our officers. Some of the hunting party returned in the evening with our horses loaded with fine meat Capt. Lewis camped with Several hunters in a Bottom 5 or 6 ml. from the Fort and took care of the meat which they had killed in the course of the day which was about Six buffalow in all.

Monday 10th Decr 1804. a Cloudy cold morning. Capt. Lewis & Several of the hunters returned to the fort. the horses were Sent eairly this morning down to their last nights camp for meat. they returned with large loads of meat. the weather Gits colder verry fast So that the Sentinel had to be relieved every hour. one of the Mandan Indians who had been wounded by the Souix came to our officers to be cured. G. Drewyer killed ⟨a buffalow⟩ two Buffalow and a deer & brought in the Deer this eving. the weather is [*blank*] degrees colder this evening than it was this morning. Blanket cappoes[1] provided for each man who Stood in need of them &.C.

1. A capote, or blanket coat, a long, hooded coat of heavy blanket material.

Tuesday 11th Decr. a clear cold morning. three men Started eairly for the horses in order to go down to the camp for the meat and for the men to all return to the Fort. the men returned in the afternoon with the horses loaded with meat. one of the hunters who came from the camp had killed a Buffaloe. the rest of the hunters all returned. had killed 5 Buffalow but the weather was so cold that they did not dress but one of them.

Wednesday 12th Decr. clear and cold. the frost was white in the Guard chimney where their was a fire kept all last night. it is Several degrees colder this morning than it has been before, so that we did nothing but git wood for our fires. our Rooms are verry close and warm So we can keep ourselves warm and comfortable, but the Sentinel who Stood out in the open weather had to be relieved every hour all this day.—

Thursday 13th Decr. clear frosty morning but not So cold as it was yesterday. we had 2 Sleds ready provided for the purpose of halling in the meat. 2 men[1] went out a Short time and killed 2 buffaloe one of them came in and 5 men were Sent out with him took a Sled with them and brought in the 2 buffaloe. they Saw a nomber of the Savvages returning from the prarie with their horses loaded with meat one of killed a Goat & brought it in to the fort & Gave it to our officers. 2 of my mess went up to the 1st village of the Mandans to day and bought Some corn and beans with a little paint and a fiew rings &.C. one of the men belonging to the N. W. Compy. came down from the Grovantares upper village to See us.

1. One of the two was Joseph Field.

Friday 14th Decr. Cloudy & moderate this morning. Capt. Clark Set out with 14 men to Go down the River a hunting. directly after it Set in to Snowing verry fast. a nomber of the Mandans came to See us. 14 of them eat in my Room at one time. the Big White dined with Capt Lewis. towards evening Several of the hunters came in & informed us that the Buffalow had left the river. they Saw but 2 they had killed 2 Deer. Capt. Clark & 8 men camped in a Bottom of wood 8 or 10 ml. down the river from our Fort.

Saturday 15th Decr. 1804. Cloudy cold and Snowey. I & 2 more of the party went up to the 1st & 2 villages of the Mandans. traded for a little corn &.C. they had all their corn in holes made in the Ground close in front of their lodges. although the day was cold & Stormy we Saw Several of the chiefs and warries were out at a play which they call [*blank*][1] they had flattish rings made out of clay Stone & two men had Sticks abt. 4 feet long with 2 Short peaces across the fore end of it, and neathing on the other end, in Such a manner that they would Slide Some distance they had a place fixed across their green from the head chiefs house across abt. 50 yds. to the 2 chiefs lodge, which was Smothe as a house flour they had a Battery fixed for the rings to Stop against. two men would run at a time with ⟨stick⟩ Each a Stick & one carried a ring. they run abt. half way and then Slide their Sticks after the ring. they had marks made for the Game but I do not understand how they count the game. they gave us different kinds of victules & made us eat in everry lodge that we went in. they were verry friendly we returned to the fort. Capt. Clark had returned with the hunters. had not killed any Buffaloe for they are all back in the praries.

1. The Mandan hoop and pole game, not mentioned by Lewis or Clark. Stewart Culin, *Games of the North American Indians* (1907. Reprint. 2 vols. Lincoln: University of Nebraska Press, 1992), 2:511–13. Biddle places a paraphrase of this material under December 19. See Jackson, ed., *Letters*, 2:553.

Sunday 16th Decr. Clear & cold. Some of our men went up to the Mandan Village[1] 4 men[2] came here which belonged to the N W. Compy. of Traders, which are now at the Mandans & Grovantiaus. came for the purpose of tradeing for their Robes & furs, &.C. Some of our men got Some Tobacco from them. they remained with all night.

1. Including Gass, according to Gass.
2. Including Hugh Heney, François-Antoine Larocque, and George Budge. Only these three are mentioned by Clark; Gass counts only three, as well.

Monday 17th Decr. a clear & cold morning. the Thurmometer Stood at about 35 fat. it has been Several degrees lower Some days past. towards evening the chiefs Son came from 1st vill. of the Mandans & Informed us that the Buffalow were comming in towards the River, & that their was a large

Gang near the Fort So that our men Scared them back by cutting fire wood for the night.—

Tuesday 18th Decr. verry cold last night So that the Sentinel had to be relieved everry half hour dureing all last night. the Tradiors from the N. W. Compy. remained with us yesterday and last night.— a clear Sharp morning. the Thurm. S. at 42 ds. abt. 12 hunters Got ready eairly to hunt the buffalow. Some of them went out on the hills but found it So cold that they would not follow the Buffo in the praries So they returned to the Fort. the Tradors left us eairly this morning. we accomodatd them with a Sled which they draw by a horse their Robes & furs over to their Forts.

Wednesday 19th Decr. the weather has moderated Some Since yesterday morning. So that we went about Setting up our pickets. half the men out at a time & relieved every hour, it being too cold to be out all the time.

Thursday 20th Decr Some cloudy & Warm this morning, but a pleasant day. we continued Setting up the pickets &.C.

Friday 21st Decr. the morning clear & warm we continued bringing & Setting pickets. a nomber of the Savages came Staying about our Garrison espacally Several of the women.

Saturday 22nd Decr. pleasant moderate weather. we continued Setting the Pickets a Great nomber of the Savages visited us brought corn & beans to Trade with us they wanted of us looking Glases Beeds buttens or & other kinds of articles pleasing to the Eye.

Sunday 23rd Decr. a clear & pleasant morning. we continued raiseing our pickets the Savages came in large crouds the Squaws loaded with corn & Beans. we found them troublesome in our huts.

Monday 24th Decr. Some Snow this morning. we finished Setting pickets & arected a blacksmiths Shop. the afternoon pleasant. the Savages came as usal we fired our Swivels as tomorrow is cristmas day &C,

Tuesday 25th Decr. 1804. cloudy. we fired the Swivels at day break & each man fired one round. our officers Gave the party a drink of Taffee. we had the Best to eat that could be had, & continued firing dancing & frolicking dureing the whole day. the Savages did not Trouble us as we had requested them not to come as it was a Great medician day with us. we enjoyed a merry cristmas dureing the day & evening untill nine oClock—all in peace & quietness.

Wednesday 26th Decr. pleasant Seven of our men went up to the Mandan Villages

Thursday 27th Decr. cloudy Some Snow we went about laying a flower [floor] in the Intrepeters room & finishing the blacksmiths Shop &.C.

Friday 28th Decr. clear & cold. high wind Some of the Savages visited us.—

Saturday 29th Decr. clear & cold. we finished laying the Intr. flower [floor] a Great nomber of the natives men women & children visited us the whole day as we Got the Blacksmiths Shop fixed they Brought their Squaw axes[1] & kittle to fix and mend for which they Gave us corn & beans Squasshes &C— one man who went out hunting to day killd a woolf & kept it for the tradors who Give as much for a woolf Skin as a Beever Skin. N. B. *an Indian Stole a drawing nife.*[2] took it again.

1. Otherwise known as a camp or felling ax, usually having a rounded poll and a short handle. Perhaps so named because it was favored by native women.

2. The underlining is in red. In this case, as elsewhere in Ordway's journal, the "N. B." is Ordway's "*nota bene*," not the editorial insertion for "Nicholas Biddle" as in notes for previous volumes.

Sunday 30th Decr. clear & cold this morning. a great nomber of the Mandans came to Trade with us. they Brought us corn & Beans Squasshes, also a Some of their kind of Bread which they make of pearched corn and beans mixed to gether & made in round balls. they have a Sweet kind of corn which they Boil considerable of it when it is in the milk & drys it which they keep through the winter Season.

Monday 31st Decr. a clear & cold morning. three men went up to the 2nd village of mandans in order to look in that bottom for timber to make pearogues.—

Tuesday 1st Jany. 1805. cloudy but moderate. we fired a Swivel & drank a Glass. about 9 o.C. 15 of the party went up to the 1st village of Mandans to dance as it had been their request. carried with us a fiddle & a Tamber-een & a Sounden horn. as we arived at the entrence of the vil. we fired one round then the music played. loaded again. then marched to the center of the vil, fired again. then commenced dancing. a frenchman danced on his head[1] and all danced round him for a Short time then went in to a lodge & danced a while, which pleased them verry much they then brought victules from different lodges & of different kinds of diet, they brought us also a quantity of corn & Some buffalow Robes which they made us a present off. So we danced in different lodges untill late in the afternoon. then a part of the men returned to the fort the remainder Stayed all night in the village— rained a little in the eve.

1. Probably Rivet again, as on November 27.

Wednesday 2nd Jany. Snowed fast this morning. Capt. Lewis and the Greater part of the party went up to the 2nd village of the mandans a frolicking, after the Same manner as yesterday at the 1st village. a nomber of Indians and Squaws came to the fort from the first village. Brought us corn to pay our blacksmiths[1] for repairing their Squaw axes Bridles &.C. the most of the men returned toward evening & Sd. that the Indians were much diverted at seeing them dance. they used them verry friendly &.C.

1. Shields and Willard were the party's blacksmiths.

Thursday 3rd Jany. 1805. Snowed this morning, Several men went out hunting this morning as the Savages Informed us that the Buffalow were comming in towards the River, but they went out first with their horses & Scared them off after killing five of them. one of our party killed a woolf they Sd Saw a nomber of buffalow. & killed one old Bull.—

Friday 4th Jany 1805. Cloudy, warm morning. Several men went down the River a hunting. the afternoon blustry. Some of the hunters returned had killed one buffalow calf & one woolf.

Saturday 5th Jany. 1805. high blustry winds all last night & verry cold three of our hunters Stayed out all night. a cold morning. one of the hunters Set a trap last night & caught a large Grey woolf.

Sunday 6th Jany. 1805. a clear cold morning. the wind high & blustry. Bratton caught a fox in a Steel trap where it had a hole through the pickets. it had freequently come through in to the Garrison after bones where we divided meat.

Monday 7th Jany. a clear cold morning the wind high from N. W. in the evening the three men returned who had been down the River a hunting. had killed one wolf which they eat as they had nothing else with them. they killed also 2 Deer and one buffalo but had Suffered considerable with the cold.

Tuesday 8th Jany. I went up to the village the wind blew cold from N. W.

Wednesday 9th Jany. Some Snow this morning Squally the after part of the day blustry and exceeding cold a nomber of the Savages out hunting the Buffalo & came in towards evening with their horses loaded with meat ⟨and told us that two of their young men was froze to death in the prarie⟩ that Several of the natives were missing. 2 of our party went out a hunting this morning; they got parted from each other & one of them returned in the evening. had Suffered considerable with the cold. we expected nothing else but the other man had froze or would freeze this night. a young

Indian came in the Garrison with his feet frost bit. Several of the Savages Stayed in the fort all night.

Thursday 10th Jany. a clear cold morning. five men got ready to go to hunt for the man who Stayed out all night, but before they Started he came in & Sd. he had a fire & was tollarable comfortable. directly after a young Indian came in to the fort with his feet froze verry bad. it is the Same Boy that the Indians had left last night & expected that he was froze to death in the praries. we kept him in the fort and our officers took the Greatest care of him possable. three men went a hunting to Stay out Several days

Friday 11th Jany. clear cold morning. nothing extroordnary accured.—

Saturday 12th Jany. cloudy 2 of the hunters came in[1] had killed 3 Elk 4 men Sent after the meat & got it—

1. The Field brothers, according to Clark.

Sunday 13th Jany. a clear cold morning. 2 men went last evening a hunting. the Savages visit us as meat is Scarce among them they Intrude on us and we use them as well as possable. Mr Sharbinow[1] arived in the evening with the horses loaded with Grees fat meat &.C.

1. Charbonneau.

Monday 14th Jany. Sergt & 5 men went out hunting this morning to Stay out Several days. G. Shannon came in this evening and informed us that Whitehouse had his feet frost bit & could not come in without a horse Shannon & Collins killed a buffaloe Bull a woolf and 2 porkapines & a white hair.[1]

1. The last a white-tailed jackrabbit.

Tuesday 15th Jany. a warm pleasant day. Shannon Sent with the horses down to the hunters. about 2 oClock Several of the Grovantares chiefs came to See us.   the weather is thoughy [thawing] So that the Snow melts off the huts &.C.

Wednesday 16th Jany.   cloudy & warm. Several of the Savages came to the Fort   their Squaws loaded with corn for to pay us for Blacksmiths work &.C. three men returned from hunting with the horses, but brought no meat. Some of the Snake Indians[1] Stayed with all night.—

1. If these were Shoshone Indians, they would probably have been slaves captured in Hidatsa raids.

Thursday 17th Jany.   a clear cold morning.   the wind high from the N. W.

Friday 18th Jany.   moderate weather.   in the afternoon 2 of the Tradors[1] from the N. W. Compy. came to the Garrison from the Grossvanters villages in the evening two of the hunters came in   brought with them 4 wolf Skins which they had caught in Steel traps   they killed a braro also.   a large woolf took off one of their traps.   they tracked it Some distance but could not find it.—   they Informed us that Sergt pryors hunting party had killed 3 Elk 4 Deer & 2 porkipines.

1. Larocque and Charles McKenzie (see Clark's entry of November 27).

Saturday 19th Jany   cloudy.   2 men Set off with the horses to Go down the River to Bring home the meat abt. 30 mls. abo. this place.

Sunday 20th Jany.   a pleasant morning   the natives bring us considerable corn.

Monday 21st Jany.   moderate weather   the hunters all came in had killed 3 Elk 4 Deer & one fox two porcupines [*X: two porcupines on 18th*] & a hare.[1]   they Brought in three horse loads of the Meat.   the Savages bring considerable Corn to day, to pay for their Black Smiths work.   2 men went up to the Grossvarntares village to trade Some woolf Skins with the N. W.

Compy Traders for Tobacco. they Got 3 feet of twist tobacco for each Skin.—

1. Again, the white-tailed jackrabbit.

Tuesday 22nd Jany. a pleasant morning. all hands Employed at cutting away the Ice from round the Barge & pearogues. they Soon cut through the Ice in places. the water Gushed over where they had cut so they had to quit cutting with axes.—

Wednesday 23rd Jany. Snowey this morning. 2 men employed makeing hand Sleds for the Savages for which they Gave us corn & beans.—

Thursday 24th Jany. colder this morning than it has ben for Several days past. in the afternoon five men employed cutting coal wood as our coal was jest Gone.

Friday 25th Jany. clear & cold this morning. the men generally employed at cutting and Splitting coal wood & Setting up the pit &.C.

Saturday 26th Jany. Cloudy & warm the Wind from the South. the party at work Same as yesterday. the Savages brought us considerable corn this day.

Sunday 27th Jany. 1805. Cloudy. Some men employed Gitting hay from the prarie for to cover the Coal kill.[1]

1. Meaning the blacksmith's kiln.

Monday 28th Jany. 1805. Clear and cold. all hands employed cutting the Ice from round the Barge. Got large prizes[1] & attempted to Shake hir loose but found that we could not move hir without considerable more cutting or other means.

1. Pries or pry bars.

Tuesday 29th Jany. 1805. Clear & pleasant all hands employed halling Stone on hand Sleds from a bluff below in order to heat a large nomber of Sizeable Stone & put warter in to the pearogues & barge & make the water hot with the Stone So as to git them loose but come to heat the Stone they flew in peaces as soon as they Got hot, So that we could not make use of them at all.

Wednesday 30th Jany. 1805. Some Cloudy. Sergt Gass Sent up the River to an other bluff in order to look for another kind of Stone that would not Split with heat he brought one home & het it found it was the Same kind of the other as soon as it was hot it bursted asunder So we Gave up that plan.—

Thursday 31st Jany. 1805. Snowed the greater part of last night. the wind high from N. W. the Snow flew five men went out a hunting took two horses with them.—

Friday 1st day of Feby. 1805. clear & cold. one man went out a Short distance to hunt and killed a Deer the hunters who went out yesterday returned the weather being bad they killed nothing.—

Saturday 2nd Feby. 1805. a clear morning. my hat got burnt exedantly this morning. the river raiseing one of the hunters went out a Short distance from the Fort and killed a Deer & packed it in.—

Sunday 3rd Feby. 1805. clear & cold. Some men went out a Short distance to hunt. the Game is Scarce. they Shortly returned without killing any thing.—

Monday 4th Feby. 1805. clear and pleasant. Capt. Clark and 14 men of the party & 2 frenchman Set off this morning with 2 horses and 2 Sleds in order to Go a considerable distance down the River a hunting Shields went out a Short time in this bottom and killed two Deer.—

Tuesday 5th Feby. 1805. the morning clear. the River Riseing So that the water Spreads over the Ice in Sundry places near this. the Coal being ready for the blacksmith to work the Savages bring corn to have their war axes made & to get Scrapers to dress their buffaloe Robes with &.C.—

Wednesday 6th Feby. 1805. clear and pleasant the Savages trouble us verry much. Capt Lewis took his observations. Shields went out towards evening to hunt & killed 3 Goats which we brought in and eat the meat.—

Thursday 7 Feby. 1805. pleasant & warm. the Savages continue comming to See us and to get blacksmiths work done &.C.—

Friday 8th Feby. 1805. moderate weather. we hear nothing of our hunting party yet.

Saturday 9th Feby. 1805. Some cloudy, the water which run over the Ice in the River has froze Smoth. the Squaws from the 1st village are cutting their lodge timber on the opposite Side of the River from the Fort, So as to hale it up to the village on the Ice.—

Sunday 10th Feby. 1805. high wind from N. W. Squawlly flights of Snow. an Instance happned last evening a little Singular one of our men returning from the Mandans village 2 or 3 young Indians followed him the Gate being Shut in Stead of calling to the Guard he went round back of the Fort and Scaled over. one of the Indians followed him over. Capt. Lewis ordered the Indian away after Giving him a Scolding at the Same time telling him that he was not So much to blame as the white man Setting the example, & Gave him a piece of tobacco & Started him & confined the man for Setting Such a pernicious example to the Savages. to day at 12 oClock he was tried by a court martial.[1] towards evening Mr Sharboner a frenchman who had been with the hunting party returned to the Fort and Informed us that he left 3 horses loaded with meat about 8 mls. down the River. the Ice being Smoth the horses could not Go on Ice with out Shoes. he Informed us also that the hunting party had killed 13 Elk 33 Deer & 3 buffaloe, one of the hunters killed 2 deer at one Shot, at Sunset the proceedings of The court martial came out the prisoner was Sentenced 50 lashes & laid to the mercy of the commanding officer who was pleased to forgive him the punishment awarded by the court.—

1. Ordway provides the most detail on the proceedings of Thomas P. Howard's court-martial. The trial was not recorded in the Orderly Book. This was the last serious disciplinary problem of the expedition, or at least the last to merit any notice.

Monday 11th Feby. 1805. 6 men Sent down the River with 2 hand Sleds to bring up the 3 horse loads of meat, So that the horses might come by land to be Shod. the day clear but cold.—

Tuesday 12th Feby 1805. a clear morning abt. 2 oClock the 6 men returned with the 3 horse loads of meat. the horses came by way of the praries. the blacksmith employed in Shewing 3 of the horses, So as we might send them down to the hunting camp on the Ice for meat, the lower Camp is about 50 mls. from this place, late in the evening Capt. Clark returned with all the hunting party they informed us that they had built pens & put the meat up Safe from the wolves, they had fleced the Greater part of it & picked the bones.

Wednesday 13th Feby. 1805. 2 men sent 18 mls. down the River to butcher an Elk which the hunters killed yesterday and to hunt, Snow the later part of the day. the 2 men returned had dressed the elk but killed nothing.—

Thursday 14th Feby. 1805. Snowed the Greater part of last night. 4 men Set out eairly with three horses and 2 Sleds in order to bring up a load of meat from the hunting Camp. the day pleasant.

Friday 15th Feby. 1805. about 2 OClock last night the 4 men who dispatched yesterday returned and informed us that they were Stoped about 25 mls. down the River by about 105 of the Souix Savages, they emediately Seized the horses cut of the collars (hooping and yelling) jurked the halters from one to another through Several hands. then they jumped on two of them and rode of uppon the run, our men with much difficulty kept the Gray mare which had a coalt at the Fort. one of the horses which they took was a fine large Gilding which belong to one of the N. W. Compy. tradors by the name of Mackinzie— the other was a publick horse as soon as we was informed of this Capt. Lewis and 20 odd of the party vollunterily to go and fight. Sent word up to the 1st village to See if they would turn out the head chief & a nomber of warries came emediately to the Fort. we Got ready to Start directly but did not set out untill after Sunrise I then Set out with Capt. Lewis and 20 odd more of the party.[1] Several warries of the Mandans Set out with us but their was only 3 or 4 remained with us the whole day. we walked about 18 mls. and halted. Got Some meat that our hunters had left hanging upon a tree & boiled & eat Some then proceeded on to the place where the horses was taken. we found a Sled their which they had cut the horse out of. found also a nomber pair of moccasons at their camp. we took the Sled and proceeded on their trale untill late in the evening. we then arived at 2 old Indian lodges which we Some expected to find them their we sent in a Spy but found none so we went to the lodges and Slept all night Some of the mens feet were sore walking 30 odd mls. on the Ice to day.—

1. Including also Sergeant Gass, according to Gass.

Saturday 16th Feby. 1805. a clear cold morning one of our men got lame and turned back. the Indians all returned also, we proceeded on about 6 mls. to where their was Some lodges where Mr Gravelleens men was Robed last fall by some of the Mandanes. when we came in Site we Saw a Smoak which we expected that they were all their waiting for another oppertunity to Seel more horses or to attach us. we then went up the bank of the river a considerable distance above the place in to the bushes. left the horse, sled & baggage even our blankets. Capt. Lewis Sent a Sergt. with a part of the men a little back from the River with orders to advance immediately after hearing the horn Sound which would be the Signal for us to fire in case of an attack. Capt. Lewis went with the rest of the party down the bank of the River untill we came to the lodges, where we found that they had left place 24 hours before that, & had Set 2 of the largest lodges on fire which caused the Smoak. I then Sounded the horn the other party came up, we found they had tore down the meat pen which our men had built & left 2 Elk in it. they took the meat all away, except a fiew small peaces of buffaloe meat which they left in the small lodge which they broiled. we found that they had left the River here and took up a Steep bluff in to the praries we concluded not to follow them any further, but to turn in to hunting. Some proceeded on down the River. 4 men went down this bottom to hunt. we marched about 10 miles and camped at the upper end of a bottom on S. S. the hunters came up one of them had killed a Deer which he brought in with him 2 or 3 men of the hunters went out towards evening. one of them killed a deer & a wolf.—

Sunday 17th Feby. 1805. all hands able to walk went out to hunt in different directions. aiming to drive the Game in to the bottom of wood as much as possable So that the best hunters who was in the bottom might kill them. they all returned in the evening had killed 10 deer and 4 Elk. packed Some of them in hung up the remainder on trees so as to keep the wolves from it.

Monday 18th Feby. 1805. clear and pleasant. Several of the hunters went out eairly a hunting. the remainder moved the camp about 5 mls. down the River to a bottom where Capt. Clarks party had Some time before been a hunting, and had made a pen and put up 2 Elk and 11 deer which we found Safe as they left it. Several men out packing in the meat which was killed yesterday we fixed our camp at an old Indian cabbin near the meat pen. the hunters came in had killed one Elk & Seven deer we got the meat all packed in, Capt. Lewis concluded that we would Start for the Fort the next morning. we fleased the meat from the bones and eat the marrow out of them.

Tuesday 19th Feby. 1805. a clear pleasant morning. 4 hunters Sent on eairly to hunt through the bottom as we were Going home. we made ready and loaded the two Sleds with meat the Smallest drawn by the Gray horse. the other drawn by 15 of the party on the Ice loaded heavy. about 9 oClock we Set off & proceeded on verry well a fiew miles Saw a Deer hanging up at the edge of the River which the hunters had killed. we took it on the Sled and proceeded on about 8 miles halted took dinner on a broiled Deer, went on about 4 miles further and camped at a timbered bottom S. Side where the hunters joined us had killed in all Six Deer & one Elk which we got them all.

Wednesday 20th Feby. 1805. a clear & pleasant morning. the hunters went on eairly we delayed a Short time to let them Git on a head. we then Set out and proceeded on verry well about 10 miles & halted broiled & eat Some meat & proceeded on a Short distance & took on 3 deer which the hunters had killed and halled on the Ice. we came about 8 miles further which took us above the Mandans Island as we call it.[1] we heard the hunters Shooting on the S. Side. we camped on the South Side the hunters came in had killed five Elk we packed in three of them and night came on so that the hunters could not find the other 2.

1. Now Painted Woods Lake, McLean County, North Dakota, passed on October 24.

Thursday 21st Feby. 1805. clear and pleasant. two hunters Stayed to find and take care of the meat 2 Elk which was left in the woods, and to hunt Some. we Set off eairly and proceeded on verry fast. the Snow and Ice thoughed on the River considerable So that it was wet & Slopy halling the Sled. we pushed on and arived at the Fort before Sunset with all our meat and Skins &.C. the men generally fatigued halling a heavy load 21 miles on the hard Ice & Snow in places which made the Sleds run hard except where the Ice was Smoth under—

Friday 22nd Feby. 1805. rained a Short time and turned to Snow. Snowed a Short time and cleared off, the men came home last night rested today after a hard fatigue but the men who had remained at the Fort was employed clearing away the Snow from round the Barge and perogues.

Saturday 23nd Feby. 1805. a pleasant morning. all the party employed cutting the Ice away from round the 2 perogues. towards evening by hard cutting with the water up within an Inch of filling it. Started it loose with pryzes and pulled it out on the Ice & turned on its Side. loosed the Ice from round the other.

Sunday 24th Feby 1805. a beautiful morning. all hands employed cutting away the Ice from round the Barge. found that the Ice was verry thick clear under hir. we worked hard the water came up in places untill it Got all round hir. towards evening we Got large prizes and put under hir and with much adieu we Got hir started loose and hoisted hir Stern up on the Ice found She had a Small leak where the corking worked out as She came loose. bailed the water out of hir. Got out the perogue also.

Monday 25th Feby. 1805. all hands employed fixing the road and gitting rollers. brought up the peaces for the windless and all things Got ready to hall up the pearogues on the high bank. in the afternoon we halled up the 2 perogues without any difficulty. one of them we halled up without the help of the windless. we then made an attempt at the Barge but our Rope which was made of elk Skin broke Several times. we mended it Got hir cleverly Started. night came on and obledgd. us to leave hir laying on the Skids.—

Tuesday 26th Feby. 1805. a pleasant morning. all hands employed Gitting more Timber to raise the Barge. doubled the Rope & raised up the Barge. Got the windless Going. Got hir Started again and moved hir a little at a time untill with much difficulty Got hir Safe up on the upper bank, and left hir laying beside the pickets, without being Injured as perseveable.—

Wednesday 27th Feby. 1805. a beautiful pleasant Morning. we fixed Skids under the Barge So as to have hir lay Safe without takeing any Injury. moved the 2 perogues along the N. Side of the line of huts So as to keep the Sun from cracking them.— 16 men Got their tools in order to make 4 perogues 4 men destined to make each perogue. the commanding officers mean to leave the Barge here in the Spring, and go on with 5 perogues one old one as they will be much better to Go from this place to the head of the Missouri.

Thursday 28th Feby. 1805.[1] about 3 oClock Mr. Gravelleen and Mr. Roie 2 frenchman came up from the Rickarees[2] 2 of the R. Ree Indians came with them they all Informed us that they Saw the Souix Savvages who Robed our men of the 2 horses, & they said their was 106 in nomber and that they had a mind for to kill our men & that they held a counsel over them whether to kill them and take their arms and all or not. but while they were doing that our men were off and got clear, but they Say if they can catch any more of us they will kill us for they think that we are bad medicine and Say that we must be killed. Mr. Tabbo a frenchman who is among them & Rick a Rees trading, Sent a letter up to the commanding officers & Mandans chiefs to keep a Good lookout for he had heared the Souix Say that they Should Shurely come to war in the Spring against us and Mandanes. in the evening the men returned who had been cutting trees to day for the perogues. they Said they had Several good trees cut, but had Broke Several of their axes.—

1. There is no break between the entries for this day and the previous one. Ordway inserted the date, most of it interlinearly, before the word "about."

2. "Roie" may have been Peter Roi, one of the expedition's *engagés*, who may have gone down to the Arikara villages after being discharged at Fort Mandan in the fall. Or he may have been some other, unknown person; the captains did not use the title "mister" for the French boatmen.

Friday 1st March 1805. cloudy & warm this morning. the perogue men got their axes repaired and drew two days provisions and went up to camp out near their work untill they Git it done or Git the 4 perogues completed.

Friday 1st March 1805.[1] cloudy & warm this morning. the work hands got their axes repaired and drew 2 days provisions and went up to camp by their work untill they have the 4 perogues completed. the after part of the day clear and pleasant.—

1. Ordway here begins a second entry for the day on a new page of his journal. He left part of the preceding page blank following his first entry for the day, then follows a blank page and the stubs of two pages cut off. At the top of the new page are the words, "A journal continued from page (145)."

Saturday 2nd March 1805. a beautiful pleasant morning. the Savages continue to visit us in Order to git their impliments of War made. they bring us in pay corn and beans dryed meat & persimblans[1] &.C.—

1. Persimmon, *Diospyros virginiana* L.

Sunday 3rd March 1805. clear & pleasant. Some men employed making coal, and Some makeing toing lines for the perogues. Some men who are makeing perogues came to the Fort for provisions. The 1st and 2nd chief of the 2nd village[1] Came to visit our officers. A nomber others came with corn &.C.

1. Black Cat and Raven Man Chief (Car-gar-no-mok-she) of Ruptáre Village.

Monday 4th March 1805. the wind high from the N. W. a nomber of the Savages bring us dryed meat and corn. The day pleasant.

Tuesday 5th March 1805. clear and pleasant. the men at work making coal &.C. a light Squawl of Snow fell about 4 oClock this morning. *nothing* extroardinary.

Wednesday 6th March 1805. moderate weather. the wind from N. E. Several of the Grossvantares Savages Stayed with us last night. a nomber of the Mandanes came this morning with corn. the Water has run over the Ice So that it is difficult crossing the river.

Thursday 7th March 1805. clear but Some colder than it has been for Several days past. Some of the perogue men who came to the Fort last night for provisions returned back this morning. two men went up to the villages to day.

Friday 8th March 1805. Some cloudy & cold. a nomber of the Savages continue bringing corn and fat dryed buffaloe meat for to Git Blacksmiths work done.

Saturday 9th March 1805. the wind high from the N. W. cold. Capt. Clark went up to the perogue party for to See the perogues. a nomber of the Savages called the Big Belleys, chiefs came to the Fort to See the Commanding officers[1] Capt. Lewis Shewed them the air Gun quadron[2] & Spy Glass &.C. which they thought was Great Medicines.

1. Among them Le Borgne, or One Eye, principal chief of the Hidatsas.
2. The expedition's quadrant.

Sunday 10th March 1805. a nomber of the Grossvantares called the big-belleys Stayed with us all last night. Capt. Lewis Gave a chief a Meddel, and Some Small Presents. The day clear and cold high winds.—

Monday 11th March 1805. clear Moderate weather. The head chief of the Water Souix[1] Stayed in the Fort last night. one of the perogue party who came in last night returned with provisions this morning. had orders for two more perogues to be made.

1. Another variation of Watersoon, the Hidatsas.

Tuesday 12th March 1805. a little Snow last night. a clear cold morning the River raiseing fast. two men of the party went up to the Grossvantares Village in order to Git Some tobacco from the tradors.

Wednesday 13th March 1805. clear and cold the wind high from the South. Mr Larouck[1] one of the N. W. Compy tradors came to See our officers &.C.

1. Clark has McKenzie rather than Larocque.

Thursday 14th March 1805. clear & warm. Mr. Sharbono a frenchman who we expected would go with us has lately too[k] another notion and has pitched a lodge outside of the Garrison and moved out.[1] Mr Gravelleen has joined in his place.—

1. See Clark's entries for March 11 and 12.

Friday 15th March 1805. clear pleasant and warm. all the Indian Goods put out to air. Some men employed Shelling corn.

Saturday 16th March 1805. Cloudy & warm two men employed halling corn. the wind high from the East. look likely for rain.—

Sunday 17th March 1805. clear and pleasant. all the Indian Goods put out to air also the parched Meal. Mr. Sharbonow began to move his baggage across the river in order to Go up to the Grossvantares to live. had Got the most of his things across the River he concluded and agreed to Go with us. then moved his effects back to the Fort, & pitched a lodge near the Fort. the wind high from the West. Warner[1] has lost his Tommahawk, expect the Indians Stole it.

1. William Werner of the party.

Monday 18th March 1805. Cloudy. 2 men came down from the perogues for provisions. 2 men went up to Grossvantares. Capt. Clark went to packing up the Indian Goods— 2 men with him—

Tuesday 19th March 1805. cloudy a light Squawl of Snow. cold air. about 10 oClock Sergt. Gass came down to the Fort and informed us that the perogues were finished, and more men wanting to draw them to the River which is about one mile & a half.

Wednesday 20th March 1805. a cloudy cool morning. Capt. Clark and Six men went up to help draw the perogues to the River Missouris. the after part of the day pleasant.

Thursday 21st March 1805. Cloudy. the wind from the S. E. about 2 oClock Capt. Clark and 4 men returned from the perogues. had carried them all to the River and left three men with them to cork and take care of them. a little Snow fell the after part of the day.—

Friday 22nd March 1805. a clear pleasant morning. the wind from the S. E. Savages continue to bring us Some corn a nomber of the Grossvantares Savages came to visit our officers with Mr. McKinzey & Mr Larouck. our Captains made a chief & Gave him a meddel and an artillery coat a Shirt knife &.C. Rives took home his perogue.[1]

1. Probably Rivet, but the meaning is unclear.

Saturday 23rd March 1805. clear and pleasant. about 10 OClock the Grossvantares who Stayed in the Fort last night returned home. rained a little the latter part of the day.—

Sunday 24th March 1805. cloudy. 6 men Sent up to take the perogues down to the Fort, but they returned about noon without them as they were not corked nor made ready. [*several words erased, illegible*] two men making cages for the Magpyes and the prarie hens which is to be Sent down the River.[1]

1. Lewis and Clark sent live specimens of four black-billed magpies, a prairie dog (not mentioned here), and a sharp-tailed grouse, *Tympanuchus phasianellus,* to Jefferson in April 1805. The grouse did not survive, but Jefferson did receive a lone magpie and a single prairie dog.

Monday 25th March 1805. clear and pleasant. 2 men Set at making a Stearing oar for the Big Barge &.C. others Shelling corn &.C.—

Tuesday 26th March 1805. clear and pleasant. Several men went for the perogues. about 2 oClock they returned with the perogues, but before they had landed the Ice Started So that we had to draw them out with Speed we halled 4 of them had not got down to the Fort but they took them on Shore So that took no Injury. all hands turned out and took them on the Bank of the River and carried one down to the Fort. the Ice Stoped and jamed up. Started Several times but Stoped entirely before night.

Wednesday 27th March 1805. clear and pleasant. we brought all the perogues down to the Fort and went at prepareing them and Gitting everry thing ready to Set out on our voiage. the Ice kep Breaking and Starting the Most of the day.—

Thursday 28th March 1805. The Ice run in the River all last night. a pleasant morning. The Ice continues to run. the party employed fixing their perogues oars and poles, So that we may be ready to Set out as Soon as the Ice is done running.—

Friday 29th March 1805. clear and pleasant. the River fell 22 inches in 22 hours.— we continue gitting ready to Start up the River.

Saturday 30th *March 1805.* clear and pleasant The [river] raised 10 Inches last night. the Ice runs thick in the R. to day. The Indian Goods all put out to air. The Big Barge corked & Got ready to descend the Missouri.

Sunday 31st March 1805. cloudy. rained Some at three oclock this morning. the Ice does not run So thick in the River as it did yesterday.

Monday April 1st 1805. Cloudy. thunder and large hail, hard rain followed about half an hour then the party turned out and put the Barge and the 8 perogues in to the River commenced raining again at 4 oClock P. M. and continued raining untill 12 oClock at night.

Monday 1st April 1805.[1] Thunder and hail & hard rain about 8 oClock this morning for about an hour. the party then turned out and put the Big Barge and the 8 perogues in to the River. began to rain again about 4 ock. P. M. rained untill 12 o.C. at night & ceased.

1. The second entry for April 1 begins a new section and a new page of Ordway's first journal notebook. He repeats entries for April 1 and 2.

Tuesday April 2nd 1805.[1] the wind blew high from N. W. all the later part of the night. a Cloudy morning. the wind rises from N. W. the River fell 5 Inches Since yesterday morning

Tuesday 2nd April 1805. cloudy. the wind blew high all the later part of last night from the N. W. the later part of the day plsant.

1. Following this first entry for the day, Ordway left a portion of the page blank, then three more blank pages.

Wednesday 3rd April 1805. clear and pleasant. The articles which was to be Sent back to the States in the Big Barge was packed and boxed up ready to go on board.

Thursday 4th April 1805. clear and pleasant. the Indian Goods and bags of corn all put out to air. the articles for St. Louis carred on board the barge ready to Set out but the wind blew high from the N. W. so we did not load the perogues.

Friday 5th April 1805. clear and pleasant. we Sorted all our loading and divided a proportion of each Sort for each perogue, and loaded all the perogues and got ready for a Start, on our Journey. the wind high from the N. W.—

Saturday 6th April 1805. clear and pleasant. we took all our Baggage on board the perogues in order to Set off. Some of the Mandans Indians informed us that the Rick a Ree nation was all comming up to their villages, as they Supposed to Stay and live with them. our officers wished to wait and know their business, as the indians sayed that they were near this on the opposite Side of the River. So our Intrepeter[1] one of the party and two frenchmen was Sent across the River in order to go & See if the report was true. the wind Gentle from the South.

1. Probably Gravelines.

Chapter Forty-Four

Great Falls of the Missouri

April 7–July 14, 1805

Sunday 7th April 1805. clear and pleasant. about 9 oclock our Intrepter and them that went with him returned brought with them 4 of the Rick a Ree Savages. 2 of them Chiefs.[1] they Informed us that only 10 of their nation had come up to the Mandanes villages to treat & Smoak a peace pipe with them &.c. they brought a letter from Mr. Tabbo who lives with R. Ree to our officers with news that 3 of the Souix chiefs was going down on the Big barge to see their Great father and that Some of the Rick a Ree chiefs was going also. one of our hunters went out at 11 oclock and killed a deer. we Set three of Sd. Rick Rees chiefs across the River. the other one being lame Stayed in order to go down to his nation in the Barge.

About 5 oClock we all went on board fired the Swivel and Set off on our journey. at the Same time the barge Set off for St Louis 2 frenchmen in a perogue in company with them.[2] they took down the letters and all the writings which was necessary to go back to the States also Some curious animals such as Goat Skins & horns, a barking Squirrell Some Mountain Rams horns a prarie hen & badgers Some birds cauled magpies & a nomber of other curious things too tedious to mention &.c.[3] we took with us 2 large perogues and 6 small ones which we had loaded with provisions, Indian Goods, ammunition &.c. we went on verry well with a hard head wind about 4 mls. & Camped[4] opposite the 1st village of Mandans on N. S. wind high from N. W. the greater part of the night their is 30 of the party which continues to Go on.[5] their was 10 which went down in the barge, but only two who had engaged for the route.—

1. Clark mentioned only one chief, Kakawita or Raven Man.

2. Information on the members of the return party is found under Lewis's entry for this day.

3. For lists of the materials sent to St. Louis, see Clark's entry for April 3. The animals Ordway mentioned are pronghorn (goat), prairie dog (barking squirrel), bighorn sheep, *Ovis canadensis* (mountain ram), sharp-tailed grouse (prairie hen), badger, and black-billed magpie.

4. Opposite Mitutanka, McLean County, North Dakota, about three miles below Stanton.

5. On this day both Lewis and Clark name the members of the permanent party and others who made the trip to the Pacific and back.

Monday 8th April 1805. clear and cold. we Set off eairly. proceeded on. passed the 2nd took breakfast at 2nd vil. & 3rd villages of Mandans[1] the [wind] high from the W. we Saw Some Snow on the N. S. of the hills, and thick Ice on and under the banks of the River. the current Swift. we passed two villages of the Grossvantares or Bigbelleys[2] at the lowermost one comes in a handsom River called Knife River. these 2 vill. are in a bottom but little timber. back of which is high open plains which is the Same on the N. S. we halted on a Sand beach on N. S. for the crafts to come up which was behind as we was informed that one of the Small perogues was in danger. capt Clark went back to see what was the matter. they Shortly returned the perogues had evidently filled and every thing in the perogue was wet damiged a keg of powder a bag of buiscuit and a nomber of other articles. we dined and proceeded on passed an Isld [(]covered with timber) on the N. S. high bluffs on the S. S. passed a timbered bottom on the N. S. in which is a Village of the Grossvantares[3] in the lower part of the bottom of cottonwood timber. we proceded 14 mls. to day and camped at the bottom N. S. an Indian came from the Mandan nation and joined us to Go and Show us the River as he tells us that he has been near the head.—

1. Somewhat confusing since there were only two Mandan villages, Mitutanka and Ruptáre.

2. The Hidatsa villages Mahawha and Metaharta.

3. The final Hidatsa village, Menetarra, known as the Big Hidatsa site, and the last of the Knife River settlements.

Tuesday 9th April 1805. clear and pleasant. a gentle breese from the South we set off at day light. Sailed on Shortly took in a large Beaver which one of our men had caught in a Trap which he Set last evening. we passed a bottom on the South Side coveered with handsome groves of Sizeable cotton wood timber. came about 5 mls. & halted took breakfast. then proceeded on passed a Small creek[1] on the N. S. & Ruged Bluffs on each Side of the River &.c. proceeded on about 1 oClock we passed a Bottom covered with c. w. timber on the S. S. where we Saw a hunting party of the Grossvauntares they assembled on the bank of the River our officers halted and Smoaked a Short time with them. went a Short distance further and halted for to take dinner at a bottom covered with Small cotton wood on N. S. the wind Shifted in to the West and blew Steady. proceeded on passed handsome bottoms on each Side of the River. Saw Gravelly bars[2] which was the first we Saw on this River. they were round and large. Saw Some on Shore also we Saw a nomber of wild Geese on the River & brants flying over[3] Some ducks. the Musquetoes begin to Suck our blood this afternoon. we camped at the upper end of a bottom on the N. S. after working our crafts 22 miles to day.—

1. Snake Creek, McLean County, North Dakota.

2. It was apparently Nicholas Biddle who wrote "Qu" (for "question" or "query") across the entry at this point when he was working with Ordway's journal in 1810. It is not clear what Biddle meant to query.

3. The geese are probably the Canada goose, *Branta canadensis,* and the brant is probably the familiar brant, *Branta bernicla.*

Wednesday 10th April 1805. we Set off eairly. a clear and pleasant morning. proceeded on passed a handsome high plain on N. S. and a beautiful bottom covered with c. wood the current Swift. we halted for breakfast at 10 oClock above a falling in Sand bank & a Small willow Island, proceeded on a Short distance further. Saw the track of a verry large white bare. Capt. Clark & G. Drewyer went out hunting on S. S. in a bottom of timber. bare hills on N. S. we Saw a nomber of large Eagles which had nested on large cottonwood trees. the wind raised from West. about one oClock we overtook 3 frenchmen who were trapping for beaver on the river. they had Caught 12 beaver in a fiew days they were fat they Gave us the tails and Some of the meat which eat verry Good; at 2 oClock we halted took dinner. one of our men Shot a bald Eagle.[1] I took the quills to write. proceeded on Capt. Clark killed a prarie hen & joined us. Saw two large Elk in a bottom on S. S. passed round a verry crooked bend in the River, and Camped[2] on a Sand beach on N. S. of the River. about 27 mls. to day as.—

1. Bald eagle, *Haliaeetus leucocephalus.*
2. Just above the later site of Fort Berthold, McLean County, North Dakota.

Thursday 11th April 1805. Clear and pleasant. we Set off at light. one of the party caught a beaver in a trap which he Set last night. the frenchmen killed a Goos & caught one beaver. proceeded on. one of the party went on Shore in the bottom. N. S. came to the crafts at breakfast. had killed & brought in a deer we passed bare barron hills on S. S. & a bottom covered with timber on the N. S. one of the party killed 2 Geese. we halted and dined about 2 oClock at a bottom on N. S. we had a Gentle breeze from the South So that the large perogues Sailed verry well. the day verry warm. Some of the men worked naked. only a breech cloth. the River being low we have to waid at Some places. proceeded on verry well about Sunset we Saw a nomber of Indians on S. S. they had Some horses. we Supposed them to be Grossvantares who had been up the River to Some other nation after corn. we camped[1] on handsome bottom covered with Strait tall cottonwood timber N. S. came this day 21 Miles.

1. A few miles below the mouth of the Little Missouri River, McLean County, North Dakota.

Friday 12th April 1805. a clear pleasant and warm morning we Set off eairly. proceeded on passed high range of hills[1] on the South Side of the River. one of our hunters Shot a verry large beaver which was Swimming in the River. proceeded on about 5 miles which took us till abt. 9 oClock we arived at the Mouth of the little River Missourie[2] about 90 mls. from the Mandans. we halted in the mouth of this R. for our officers to take observations. this River is 120 yards wide at the mouth, but rapid and muddy like the big Missourie. Several of the hunters went out hunting. Capt. Clark went out a Short distance and killed a white rabit. found wild Inions &.c. one of the hunters killed a deer. another killed a bald Eagle. the men all returned but had not killed any thing more. The frenchmen came to us had caught 2 beaver last night. about 3 oClock their came up a Squawl of verry high wind and rain. Some thunder. the wind lasted untill afer Sunsed. then clear up pleasant evening. one of the hunters discovered a fine Spring of water which came from under a high hill on S. S. high mountains back from the River on the S. S. the country in general from the Mandans to this place on the river is hilley and broken except in the bottoms in the bends of the River which is low Smoth & Sandy, covered with cottonwood & Small arsh[3] timber which is all the timber in the country is on the Streams & in the bends of this Missourie the Soil back from the River is tollarable Good but barron plains without timber or water &.c.

1. Killdeer Mountains, Dunn County, North Dakota.
2. Little Missouri River, McLean County.
3. Green ash, *Fraxinus pennsylvanica* Marsh.

Saturday 13th April 1805. clear pleasant & warm Som of our men caught 2 beaver and one fish last night at Sun rise we Set off and proceeded on over took the frenchmen who came on yesterday trapping. they had caught Seven beaver last night. a handsom timbred bottom on the South Side passed a creek on the N. S. proceeded on under a fine breeze of wind from the South. in the afternoon we Saw three Goats under a Steep bank on N. S. the attempted to git up the bank Several times &.c. some of the men Shot at them they then took in to the River & Swam across. Some of the men on S. S. Shot 2 of them. proceeded on passed a high Stoney bank on the S. S. Saw a gang of Elk on a plain near a bottom of wood on the N. S.— Camped[1] the N. S. at a handsome plain. came 22½ miles to day.— Saw a Goose nest on a tree one man clumb it found only 1 Egg.—

1. In Mountrail County, in what was once called Fort Maneury Bend, now under Garrison Reservoir.

Sunday 14th April 1805.[1] clear & pleasant. we set off eairly. one of our men Set a trap for a beaver last night, & caught a large otter that broke the trap chain & got a way. we Saw where it had dragged it along the beach, but could not find it.— proceeded on one man Shot a musk rat[2] which was Swimming in the river. passed a bottom on S. S. Saw a buffaloe feeding in a holler, but we did not Stop to kill it. passed bottoms on each Side of the River covered with C. w. timber. halted about 2 oclock to dine at Some barron hills on the S. S. of the river. Some of the men Saw a gang of buffaloe in the vallies back a little from the river ⟨they⟩ Fraser killed one of them by Shooting Sevl. times (musket) & took the best of the meat on board. the wind Gentle from the South. Sailed the most part of the afternoon. passed a creek or Small river[3] on the S S Side about 15 yards wide at the mouth & Several Small runs which run from under verry high rough raged hills which are barron and broken. Some Small ceeder[4] on the sides of Sd hills. A high mountain back of the hills S. S. Camped on the N. S. of the river in a beautiful bottom covered with thin cottonwood timber came 16 miles to day. camped at a point on N. S. N. B. the above mentioned Small River which we passed this afternoon on the S. S. is named after our Intr. *Charbonoe river* as he has been to the head of it which is further up the Missourie Than any white man has been. Capt. Lewis killed an Elk this evening.— an Indian dog came to us this morning & continues along with us.—

1. Preceding this entry Biddle wrote in red ink the words "From this not consulted. mem.," meaning perhaps that he ceased to use Ordway's journal beyond this point for his narrative history of the expedition.

2. Muskrat, *Ondatra zebethicus.*

3. Bear Den Creek, the party's Charbonneau's Creek, enters the Missouri River near the Dunn-McKenzie county line, North Dakota.

4. Ordway could be seeing either Rocky Mountain red cedar, *Juniperus scopulorum* Sarg., an upright tree found on hillsides, or creeping juniper, *J. horizontalis* Moench, a low, dwarf species. Later, in some cases, his description makes it clear which of the species he is seeing.

Monday 15th April 1805. a clear pleasant morning. we Set off eairly. proceeded on. Sailed under a fine breeze from the S. E. passed Several runs on each Side of the river and handsome bottoms plains hills & vallies &.c. we Saw flocks of Goats on S. S. and Gangs of buffaloe on Sand beach

S. S. Saw a large black bair and 2 white ones on the N. S. Capt. Clark was near Shooting one of the white ones. Sailed on one man killed a Goose. came 22 miles this day. the river Shallow only about 8 feet deep in some places. we poled across in one place with a Small canoe. passd. goat pen creek[1] on N. S. & the river is nearly as wide here as it was at St. Charles near its mouth. Camped on a large Sand beach on the South Side of the river.—

1. Little Knife River, Mountrail County, North Dakota. Clark named the creek after the Indian pen, or pound, for catching pronghorns which he found there.

Tuesday 16th April 1805. a clear pleasant morning we Set off eairly as usal. proceeded on the wind gentle from S. E. passed a Sand beach on the N. S. covered with Ice in Some heaps it lay 4 feet thick where the Ice was drove in When the river broke up. Capt. Clark walked on Shore on S. S. came to us at breakfast had killed a antilope or Goat. we Saw a gang of buffaloe on a Side hill on the S. S. also a gang of Elk near them. See one Elk in a bottom near where we breakfasted. one of the party by the name of John Colter caught a verry large fat beaver in a Steel trap last night. proceeded on The trees are puting out Green. the Grass begin to Grow in the bottoms & plains which look beautiful. we Sailed Some with a Southerly flawey wind.[1] the river crooked So that we could not Sail much of the time Saw Some Scatering Sizeable Stone on the Sides of the hills. halted about 7 oClock to dine at a bottom covered with c. w. timber on the N. S. proceeded on passed Several bottoms and plains on each Side of the river. came 17 miles as the courses was taken but by water the way we came it was about 26. Camped[2] at a point called Grand point on the South Side. Saw different gangs of Elk S. S.

1. Flawy or gusty.
2. A little above Beaver Creek, on the opposite side in McKenzie County, North Dakota.

Wednesday 17th April 1805. a clear beautiful morning. we Set off eairly. Some of the men caught 2 beaver and Several Small fish. a fair wind we Sailed on Saw large Gangs of buffaloe on the Side hills S. S. proceeded on passed a beautiful plain on the N. S. passed Several bottoms on each Side of the River. abt. 1 oClock we halted to dine Saw a gang of buffaloe

Swimming the river. one of the hunters killed one Capt. Lewis killed one large one in a fiew minutes they being poor we took only the tongues of them Saw Several gangs of Elk on each Side of the river. late in the afternoon we Saw a gang of buffaloe on S. S. R. Potts[1] killed one of them. passed Several runs in the course of the day & red hills on each Side and high raged hills which are rough barron broken & Steep. Came 26 miles this day *by Sailing &c.* Camped[2] on a large Sand beach S. S. one of the men caught a nomber of Small cat fish in the river.

1. Actually John Potts.
2. In McKenzie County, North Dakota.

Thursday 18th April 1805. a clear pleasant morning. we Set off eairly. Some of the men who Set traps for beaver last night they caught only one beaver & that in 2 traps by one hind foot and one fore foot. they belonged to 2 owners. they had Some difference which had the best rite to it. proceeded on a Short distance one of the men killed a goose in the river. the wind from the West. proceeded on passed high hills on each side of the River. Saw a gang of buffaloe on the hills on S. S. and a gang of Elk in a handsom [bottom] covered with c. w. timber on the N. S. one of the men wounded one of them another man killed another goose. The wind Shifted in to the N. W. and blew hard against us. Saw a nomber of bald Eagles in Sd. bottom one of them had a nest in a low tree one of the men clumb up and got 2 Eggs (all there was.) The wind rose so high that we could not go with the cannoes without filling them with water. detained us about 3 hours. one man killed another goose Seamon b. out we then proceeded on. Capt. Clark who walked on Shore killed one Elk and one deer which we halted & took them on board. came about 15 miles to day and camped[1] at a bottom covered with Cottonwood and arsh Elm timber also on N. S. the river has been verry crooked and bearing towards the South the most of the day. the Game is gitting pleantyier every day.—

1. They remained here until April 20, in Williams County, North Dakota.

Friday 19th April 1805. Cloudy. the wind blew high from the Northward So that we were obledged to lay at our last nights harbour all day. caught one large beaver last night the hunters killed one Elk and three Geese & Robed Several of their nests of their Eggs. Some of the men caught a quantity of Small cat fish in the river the evening clear blustry & cold. Winds.—

Saturday 20th April 1805. cloudy. the wind is not So high as it was yesterday this morning. we Set off about 7 oClock. we found it Cold polling. the air chilley. proceeded on. Some of the men caught two beaver in traps which they Set last night. Saw a buffaloe Swim the river close before us but would not Shoot him for he was not fat. the wind rose & blew Same as yesterday So that we could hardly make any head way. halted took breakfast about 10 O.C. 2 of the hunters Shot four beaver directly in the edge of the river. delayed Som time the [wind?] abated a little. we proceeded on the wind Shortly rose again and blew so hard that the canoes were near filling they took in considerable of water. the Sand blew off the Sand bars & beaches So that we could hardly See, it was like a thick fogg. it took us about two hours to come about 2½ miles. halted at a bottom on the N. S. Capt. Lewis who walked on Shore this morning killed a deer and hung it up on the bank of the river near an old Indian Camp where he made fire & Eat the liver of the deer, and went on. we took it on board and went up the bottom about 3 miles where we found a good harbour for the perogues to lay out of the wind we halted and dryed the things which was Wet & Camped[1] for the night. we found Some little notions which Some Indian had hung up. Viz. a Scraper a paint bag with ½ an ounce in it, kinikaneck[2] bags, flints &.c. the hunters killed 2 Elk Capt. Lewis a white taild. deer. one man killed a Goose. Drewyer Shot a beaver. we Saw gangs of Elk running along near our Camp we did not want any more meat or we might have killed a pleanty. high Squawls of wind & flights of round Snow this day. we took in Some water in the Canoe I was in. the water came up to my Box So that a part of my paper Got wet.

1. In Williams County, North Dakota.

2. Kinnickinnick, a mixture of bark, perhaps with some tobacco, used by many western tribes for smoking.

Sunday 21st April 1805. a hard white frost last night. froze water in the buckets Setting near the fire. a Clear and pleasant morning, but verry chilly & cold. we proceeded on. Saw the hills and vallies on S. S. covered with buffaloe. Some calfs among them. one of the party clumb a Stump of a tree which had a Goose nest in the top of it found four Eggs in it. passed round the bottom covered with timber which we camped on last night. about 10 oC. we halted & took breakfast. proceeded on passed hills and round knobs on S. S. and a large bottom on N. S. Capt. Clark went on the S. S. to hunt. Came to us at dinner. had killed 4 Deer in a bottom covered with Small timber he attempted to kill a buffaloe Calf but could not git near Enofe without being discovered by them, the plain being So open. about 3 oClock clouded up cold the wind began to blow as usal. we dined at a redish bluff on N. S. Saw large gang of buffaloe & calfs Elk also on the opposite Shore. delayed about one hour & proceeded on passed the mouth of a large Creek on the N. S. Called White Earth River.[1] it is about 15 yards wide at the mouth & Clear water & Gentle current. Camped on the South Side at a bottom came 15 miles to day. Some of the men killed 2 buffaloe Calfs, & one Elk. We Saw this day 4 otter on a drift. Potts shot one of them in head but it Sunk. the rest plunged in to the water and swam down the river, and Drewyer killed & Got one of them. a Cool evening.—

1. Not to be confused with the present White Earth River, which the party passed on April 16 without Ordway noting it. This is Little Muddy River, Williams County, North Dakota.

Monday 22 April 1805. clear and cold. we Set off as usal passed a high bluff on S. S. and a handsom bottom and plains on the N. S. which was covered with buffaloe & buffaloe calfs, Elk deer &.c. and large gangs on the opposite Shore I think that we Saw at one view nearly one thousand animels. they are not to day verry wild for we could go within a 100 yards of them in open view of them before they would run off and then they would go but a Short distance before they would Stop and feed again, We delayed about 2 hours & proceeded on. passed bluffs on N. S. where we dined & delayed again on acct. of the high wind, aired Some articles which got wet in a Small canoe proceeded on with the towing lines. Saw a buffaloe Calf which had fell down the bank & could not git up again. we helped it up the bank and it followed us a Short distance (the river raised 4 Inches last & a white frost) we have Seen a great nomber of dead buffaloe lying on each Shore all the way from the little missourie R. we Suppose that they Got drownded attempting to cross on the Ice last fall before it got Strong. we Camped[1] in a bottom covered with c. w. timber & rabbit berry bushes on the S. S. the beaver has cut down large trees along this bottom. Saw a great nomber of their houses. Capt. Clark Shot a large one. G. Drewyer went after dark to set his traps & Shot another. (N. B. Came only 10 miles today) one man found killd a Spoted Snake.

1. In McKenzie County, North Dakota, a few miles above Williston, on the opposite side.

Tuesday 23rd April 1805. a clear and pleasant morning. not quite as cold as it has been for Several morning. we Set off as usal proceeded on. Some of the men caught two beaver last night passed high bluffs on the S. S. and a bottom in a bend on the N. S. the river verry crooked halted and took breakfast on a sand beach S. S. one man Shot a beaver in the willows. another Shot a Goose in the river, proceeded on the wind blew So hard that the large perogues Sailed in a bend where the wind came fair verry high the Small canoes took in Some water. the large perogues Sailed verry fast. a Short distanc we were obledged to halt the first Safe place untill the wind abated which was about 3 hours. dryed the articles which was wet. towards evening the wind abated and we proceeded on round a point and Camped[1] in a bottom covered with c. w. timber on N. S. came 14½ miles to day. Capt. Clark killed to day one buffaloe Calf, and three black taild deer.—

1. The party remained here until April 25, in Williams County, North Dakota.

Wednesday 24th April 1805. Clear and cold. The wind high from the N. W. So that we had to delay here all this day. we dryed and aired Some of the loading which had got wet yesterday. Severall of the party went out a hunting. they killed Several buffaloe Elk deer &.c. one of them found Several young wolf papppies and brought them to camp. the wods got on fire.

Thursday 25th April 1805. a clear cold morning. the river rose 2 Inches last night. we Set off eairly. the wind blew from the N. one of the men caught a beaver last night. we proceeded on passed high land on N. S. and timbred bottom on S. S. Sailed Some in a bend of the river. came about 12 miles by 12 oClock. the perogues could go no further as the wind blew them a head So that they halted for it to abate on the N. S. Capt. Lewis myself and 3 more of the party crossed over to the S. Shore to go up by land to the Mouth of the river *Roshjone* or *yallow rock* river[1] (for observations). we walked along the high bluffs, Saw a large gang of buffaloe in the bottom. we killed one young one and took our dinner of it and proceeded on. Capt. Lewis Shot a goose on hir nest we got 6 eggs out of it, towards evening we killed 2 cow buffaloe and a calf in a handsom Smoth bottom below the mouth of *Yallow Rock River.* we Camped on the bank of the yallow R. River, about 2 miles above its mouth. little above the bottom on the Sand beach large & Small cottonwood & arsh in Sd. bottom

1. The French term is *Roche Jaune,* Yellowstone, for the river of the same name which joins the Missouri near the North Dakota–Montana state line.

Friday 26th April 1805. a Clear pleasant morning. Capt. Lewis Sent one man[1] about 6 miles up the River Roshjone to See what discoveries he could make. one man killed a Goose another killed a buffaloe cow & calf. Saw a flock of Goats Swimming the river this morning near to our Camp. Capt. Lewises dog Seamon took after them caught one in the River. Drowned & killed it and Swam to Shore with it. Capt. Lewis took an observation at 9 oC. and at 12 oClock, also at 4. he caught Several Small fish in the River Roshjone at 4 the man returned who went up the River this morning he Informed us that he went about 8 miles up it to a large creek which came in on the S. S. & that the bottoms was large and covered with timber. &.c. he brought in a live buffaloe calf, which had followed him about 4 miles. we then heard that Capt. Clark & the party had come at the Mouth of the River Roshjone about 12 oClock to day. Capt. Lewis Sent a man[2] down for a perogue to come up for our meat and baggage. Capt. Clark Immediately Sent up a canoe We moved down to their Camp[3] which was about two miles. our officers Gave out one Gill of ardent Spirits per man. So we made merry fidled and danced &.c. Camped for the night on the point between the 2 Rivers. a handsom place thinly covered with timber & a verry large bottom. Capt. Clark Measured these two Rivers to day and found the Missourie to be 337 yards wide only the water but at high water mark 529 yards wide at this place. the River Roshjone is 297 yds. water, high water mark 858 yards wide. the distance from the mouth of the Missourie to the mouth of the River Roshjone is 1888 miles, from Fort Mandane 279 miles from the little Missourie River 186 miles. the River Roshjone is not quite as rapid as the missourie the men killed to day Several buffaloe & buffaloe calfs the Calfs are the best meat we find at this time one man killed a White Swan[4] in a large pond 4 or 5 miles from this, between the two Rivers. this pond the men that Saw it Judged it to be 4 miles long, & 200 yds across, &.C. on the River Roshjone and the Missourie the Game is verry pleanty, viz. buffaloe Elk Deer Goats Some bair. pleanty of bever, fish &C and a beautiful country around in every direction. considerable of timber Such as cottonwood Elm arsh &.c. the Latidude at this place is [*blank*] North.

1. Joseph Field, according to Lewis.
2. Drouillard, according to Clark.
3. In McKenzie County, North Dakota; shifts of the Missouri and the mouth of the Yellowstone make determination of the exact spot difficult.
4. Trumpeter swan, *Cygnus buccinator*.

Saturday 27th April 1805. a clear and pleasant morning. we aranged our loading in the perogues and Set off about 9 oClock, proceeded on passed a beautiful level plain which lay between the River Missourie & River Roshjone, about 12 oC. the wind rose So high from the N. W. and the Sand flew So thick from the Sand bars that we halted about 1 oClock, to wait untill the wind abates, at a bottom of large scatering timber on the N. S. about 4 oClock the wind abated So that we proceeded on till dusk, and Camped[1] at a bottom covered with Small timber on the N. S. came only about 10 miles to day. the current Swift.—

1. The party's first camp in Montana, in Roosevelt County, about a mile below and opposite the village of Nohly, Richland County.

Sunday 28th April 1805. clear and pleasant. one of the Men caught a large beaver last night. we Set off eairly. the wind had Shifted to S. E. and blew gently So that we Sailed Some part of the time. proceeded on passed high bluffs on N. S. of a whiteish coulor rough hills and knobs on each Side. Some Smoth bottoms of cottonwood on each Side of the River. Saw large flocks of Cabberrie or antilope which is a Specie of the Goat kind, on the Sides of the hills on S. S. Saw Some dead on the edge of the river, which I Suppose the wolves had killed. Capt. Clark and our Intrepter walked on Shore on the S. S. we proceeded on untill abt. 3 oClock. came to where Capt. Clark had made a fire. we then halted to dine in a bottom above high bluffs on S. S. Capt Clark had killed one Deer & a goose. he Saw Several bair proceeded on towards evening we Saw a large black bair Swimming the River we went on Shore to head him in hopes to kill him. one man Shot & wounded it but it ran in to thick bushes So that we could not find it. Some of the party Saw Several more bair on the hills, on S. S. the bluffs make neare the river all this day and are verry Steep in some places & other places high & rough Some of which are White Stone and Clay, others are of a redish coulour, nearly like brick. we Camped[1] in a handsom bottom of c. w. timber on N. S. high steep bluffs on S. S. Came 24 miles this day.—

1. Near Otis Creek (not mentioned by Ordway), Richland County, Montana, but on the opposite side in Roosevelt County.

Monday 29th April 1805. a clear pleasant morning. we Set off eairly. proceeded on round a bend Saw a bay horse in a beautiful Smooth plain on the N. S. where we Saw a great quantity of wild Hop[1] Growing we Suppose that this horse had Strayed from Some Savages he appeared to be a tollarable Good horse but wild. proceeded on a Short distance. Saw a Mountain Sheep[2] on a high Steep bluff on N. S. which had a lamb with it one man went up the bluff to Shoot them. they took down the bluffs and ran along whare it was nearly Steep where there was a black Stripe in the bluffs he Shot at them but at too Great a distance. they run untill they got round the bluffs and ran in to the prarie. the coulour of the Sheep was white had large crooked horns, & resembled our tame Sheep only much larger Size & horns. Capt. Lewis and one hunter who walked on Shore this morning. came to us about ½ past 9 oClock had killed a Whiteish bair what is called the white bair, but is not white but light coullour we delayed untill ½ past 10 to git the meat on board. then proceeded on passed high bluffs & bottoms on each Side. Saw large flocks of the Cabberree or antilopes and handsom bottom on S. S. also buffaloe & elk.[3] Saw a nomber of Mountain Sheep & lambs on a verry high bluffs as nearly like rough mountains Some red ceeder in the hollows & gullies in the Mountains. these Sheep are verry wild, and keep mostly in these bare hills or mountains Some of these hills are red Earth resembling Spanish brown, but the most of them are whitish & naked. Some large Stone at the foot of the bluffs, the country back from the river is I belive is barron & no timber & Good for nothing but Game. proceeded on passed a large timber bottom on the S. S. Camped[4] after dark at the Mouth of a Small river which came in on the N. S. at a beautiful Smoth plain. we named it little yallow River.[5] Came 25 *miles* this day.—

1. Probably the "wild hyssop" noticed earlier by Lewis, and if so, it is big sagebrush, *Artemisia tridentata* Nutt.

2. Bighorn sheep; see also Lewis's entry of April 26 for a discussion of a possible subspecies. The party also used the name "ibex" for the animal.

3. Biddle again wrote his "Qu" across several lines near this point but without any indication of the purpose of his query.

4. Camp was just above Big Muddy Creek, Roosevelt County, Montana.

5. In fact, Clark named it "Martheys river in honor to the Selebrated M. F," whose identity remains unknown.

Tuesday 30th April 1805. clear and pleasant. we Set off eairly. proceeded on Saw large gangs of buffaloe Swimming the River just before our cannoes & we would not Shoot them as we had meat enofe on board. passed high rough hills on S. S. the wind blew from the N. proceeded on verry well. towards evening, one of the men Shot a verry large beaver & a Goose in the edge of the River that would have weighed 70 or 80 pounds. it had large young ones in it. Capt. Lewis killed an Elk in a bottom on the N. S. Came 24 miles to day & Camped[1] on a large Sand beach on the N. Side

Some men went for the meat with Capt. Lewis. we Sailed a little in the bends of the River this afternoon.—

1. In the vicinity of Brockton, Roosevelt County, Montana.

Wednesday 1st day of May 1805.[1] a clear pleasant morning, but cold. we Set off at Sun rise. the wind from the East. we Sailed on verry well passed broken bluffs and round knobs on the S. S. and bottoms covrd with cottonwood timber on each Side of the River and the hills in general are not so high as they have been below and the country is more pleasant, and the timber is gitting pleantier. about 12 oClock the wind rose So high that the Small canoes could not go on without filling. we halted at a bottom covd with timber on S. S. one of the canoes lay on the opposite Shore and could not cross the water ran so high. Some men went out in this bottom a hunting & killed one buffaloe one Deer & a Goose & 2 beaver also. the wind continued So high that we delay and Camped[2] for the night. the sd cannoe lay on the opposite Side all night. came only 10 miles to day.

1. This entry, and the next three, are especially faint and difficult to decipher.
2. In the vicinity of later Elkhorn Point, Roosevelt County, Montana.

Thursday 2nd May 1805. at day light it began Snowing & continued Snowing & blowing So that we did not Set off. Some of the party went out a hunting. they killed Some buffaloe & Deer, & found Several pieces of red cloath at one old Indian camp that we expect they left their as a Sacrifice as that is their form of worship, as they have Some knowledge of the Supreme being, and any thing above their comprehention they Call Big Medisine— &.c. about 3 oClock it left off Snowing. the wind Shifted in to the West. we Set off & proceeded on. the Snow lay on the edge of the Sand bars & Sand beaches where the wind had blew it up one foot deep, but on the hills it was not more than half an Inch deep. Capt. Clark & one of the hunters[1] Shot 3 beaver in the edge of the River s. s. the air & wind verry cold. we Camped[2] at a handsom bottom on the N. S. which is a very large bottom part c. w. timber & part prarie high plains back from the River. Came only abt. 5 miles to day.

1. Drouillard, according to Clark.
2. In Richland County, Montana, near the crossing of Montana Highway 251.

Friday 3rd May 1805. clear but verry cold for May. we Set off about 7 oClock, & proceeded on. Saw the Standing water froze Over the Ice froze to ore poles as we poled where the sun Shined on us. a hard white frost last night. the Ground covered with Snow. the wind rose high from the W. about one o.C. Capt. Clark Came to us where we halted to dine had killed an Elk, as he had been by land Since morning. this place where he killed the Elk is in a bottom covered with c. w. timber. we found a goose nest a little below this on some drift wood. we took 3 Eggs out of it. one man went along the bank of the River a fiew minutes and killed a beaver. we have Sawn Great Sign of beaver for several days but more this day than usal. the wind verry high & cold. we proceeded on. Saw a nomber of buffaloe on the ridges and in the plains. passed large bottoms of timber, & plains on each Side but no high hills. passed a creek on the S. S.[1] Came 20 miles and Camped in a bottom on the N. S. after dark. had passed a large creek on the N. S. which is two thousand miles from the mouth of the M. 2000 ml. creek.

1. Ordway has the streams transposed in this entry. The stream on the south side (the actual 2000 Mile Creek) is Redwater River, McCone County, Montana, and the river on the north side, called Porcupine River by Lewis and Clark, is Poplar River, Roosevelt County, above which the party camped for the night.

Saturday 4th May 1805. clear and moderate this morning. the Snow is all melted off the hills. we delayed Some time to mend the rudder of the red perogue which got broke landing last evening. we Set off about 9 oCock and proceeded on passed large bottoms covered with timber on each Side of the River and high Smoth plains back from the River. at 11 oC. we passed the Mouth of a Creek came in on the S. S.[1] proceeded on passed a beautiful large plains on the N. S. Saw buffaloe and Elk passed large bottoms on S. S. Came 22 miles and Camped on a bottom of timber on the N. S. one of the party killed two deer in a fiew minutes. Came 22 miles today.

1. Nickwall Creek, McCone County, Montana.

Sunday 5th May 1805. Clear and pleasant. we Set off eairly proceeded on. one hunter who [s]tay on the S. Shore all night came to us at breakfast time. had killed two buffaloe Calfs which we took on board. we proceeded on. passed bottoms of timber on each Side. passed a large handsom plains on the N. S. where we saw a great nomber of buffaloe and white geese.[1] we halted for to dine about 2 o.C. on the S. S. at a bottom of timber where we Saw buffaloe and Goats our officers gave the party a half a Gill of ardent Spirits. Jo. Fields who was taken Sick yesterday is some worse to day. jest as I went Set off with the canoe the bank fell in & all most filled it. we directly took out the Sand & bailed out the water and proceeded on towards evening Capt. Clark and Several more of the party killed a verry large bair which the natives and the french tradors call white but all of the kind that we have seen is of a light brown only owing to the climate as we suppose. we shot him as he was Swimming the River. the place where he dyed was Shallow or perhaps he would have Sunk to the bottom. with the assistance of Several men was got on board a perogue and took him to the Shore on N. S. and dressed it after taking the measure of him. he was verry old the tushes most wore out as well as his claws. the measure of the brown bair is as follows round the head is 3 feet 5 Inches. do the neck 3 feet 11 Inches do the breast 5 feet 10½ Inches. do the middle of the arm 1 foot 11 Inches. the length from the nose to the extremity of the hind toe is 8 feet 7½ Inches. the length of tallons better than four feet [inches]. we found a Cat fish in him which he had Eat. we Camped[2] and rendered out about 6 gallons of the greese of the brown bair. he was judged to weigh about 4 hundred after dressed. one of the party went out and killed an Elk, and Saw another brown bair. we Came 16 miles to day before we killed the brown bair. we Sailed considerable in the course of the day with an East wind.

1. Probably the snow goose, *Chen caerulescens.*

2. Southeast of Wolf Point, and on the opposite side given the river's present course, in McCone County, Montana.

Monday 6th May 1805. pleasant and warm. we Set off early Sailed on under a gentle breeze from the East. Some of the party caught two beaver last night. we Saw a brown bair Swimming the River before us. Saw beaver looking out of their holes along the bank. we came 16 miles by 2 O.C. then halted to dine Capt. Clark killed an Elk on N. S. in a bottom covred with timber. one man killed a beaver. we proceed on passed a large Creek or Small River which came in on the S. S. about 200 yards wide named [*blank*][1] Some Sprinkling rain, but did not last long. proceeded on passed high land on S. S. Smoth plains on N. S. and timbred bottoms on each side. Came 26½ miles in all this day, and Camped in a bottom of Small timber on the S Side.

1. The party passed three streams on the south side during the day's course, this last and most prominent is Prairie Elk Creek (Lewis and Clark's Little Dry River), McCone County, Montana, above which the party camped.

Tuesday 7th May 1805. clear pleasant and warm. we Set off eairly. the wind rose from the East. we Sailed verry fast untill about 12 o.C. one of the canoes filled with water, but we got it Safe to Shore, and halted for the wind to abate at a bottom on s. s. Some men went out to hunt. two beaver was caught last night by Some of the party, & shot five more at this place. about 4 oClock we proceeded on as the wind had abated Some. Saw large gangs of buffaloe on each side of the River. handsom plains on the N. S. Capt. Clark and one hunter walked on Shore on S. S. towards evening they killed 2 buffaloe in a bottom of timber on S. S. where we Camped[1] for the night and dressed the 2 buffaloe. Came 15½ miles this day,

1. In either McCone or Valley County, Montana, depending on shifts in the river, and a few miles southwest of Frazer.

Wednesday 8th May 1805. we Set off eairly. it clouded up of a Sudden, and rained Some. we Sailed on under a fine breeze from the East. came 20 miles by one oClock, passed the mouth of a large River on N. S. Called Scolding or named milk River.[1] about 200 yards wide and deep, and 2100 miles from the mouth of the Missourie.— we halted in a handsom bottom abo. the Mouth of Sd. River to dine. Sergt. Pryor killed a Deer. about 2 o.C. we proceeded on passed in the course of this day timbred bottoms on each Side of the river. a little back from the River their is no timber but high beautiful plains on the N. S. and river hills on S. S. Came 27 miles today and Camped in a handsom bottom covred with Groves of timber on the S. S. one man Shot a large beaver.

1. Milk River stills bears the name Lewis and Clark gave it; it reaches the Missouri in Valley County, Montana. "Scolding" comes from the name the Knife River Indians had given them for this stream, "River which Scolds at All Others" (see the discussion at Lewis's entry for this day).

Thursday 9th May 1805. Clear and pleasant. we set off about Sun rise and proceeded on passed an Island in the Middle of the River partly covd with Small timber and willows. about 9 oC. we halted to take breakfast in a beautiful Smoth bottom partly covred with timber &c on the S. S. where Capt. Clark who walked on this morning had killed 2 deer. the Game is gitting So pleanty and tame in this country that Some of the party clubbed them out of their way. about one oCock we passed the Mouth of a river on S. S. named [*blank*] [1] it is at high water mark 220 yards wide, but at this time the water is So low that the water all Sinques in the quick Sand we halted to dine above the mouth of this R. Capt. Clark killed 2 buffaloe we proceeded on passed large bottoms covred with timber and Smoth plains on N. S. hilley on S. S. Saw large gangs of buffaloe and elk. Saw great Sign of beaver where they had cut the Small timber on the bank of the River for a large peace of Ground all Smoth and carried the most of it away to their lodges. we Came 25 miles to day and Camp[2] at the mouth of a creek (named Warners R.[)] on the N. Side the country for Several days back is handsom and pleasant the Soil rich the Game pleanty. but the timber back from the river Scarse &.c.

1. Big Dry Creek, the boundary between McCone and Garfield counties, Montana; it is Big Dry River on expedition maps.

2. The party camped a few miles above the town of Fort Peck, Valley County; "Warners R." (for expedition member William Werner) is Duck Creek.

Friday 10th May 1805. a clear cold morning. we Set off about Sun rise, and proceeded on about 4 miles. the wind rose So high from the N. W. that obledged us to halt at a bottom covred with timber on S. S. where the beaver had cut & fell a peace of Small timber on the bank. Several of the party went out to hunt. the wind rose verry high. Some Squawls of rain. one man caught a nomber of fish. the hunters killed a fat buffaloe 4 Beaver & 2 black tailed deer and one white taild deer. they Saw Several moose deer[1] which was much larger than the common deer and the first we have Seen our officers Inspected the partys arms & ammuntion &.c. Camped[2] at this place for the night.

1. Ordway must mean mule deer again, rather than the moose, but it is unclear why he says it was the first they had seen.
2. In either Garfield or Valley County, Montana, on a site inudated by Fort Peck Reservoir.

Saturday 11th May 1805. a clear cool morning & white frost we Set off eairly. Some of the party caught 2 beaver last night we proceeded on passed black bluffs & hills on the S. S. low ceeder on the hills in places & Spots on each Side of the River. Saw verry large gangs of buffaloe in the bottoms on Each Side of the River. one of the party which had a lame hand was walking on Shore. towards evening he came running and hollowing to the perogues chased by a brown bair which he had wounded, bad. Some of the hunters went out with him and killed it. it was nearly of the Same description as the one killed Some days past, but much fatter. we Camped[1] before night to dress the bair, after comming 17 miles today. Capt Clark who walked on Shore killed 2 buffaloe 2 deer and one beaver. he went on some broken hills on the N. S. which was partly covred with pitch pine[2] and another Sort of pine which resembles the pitch pine only the bark & leaf Smaller. these hill bair the first pine we have Seen on this River. the country back from the River is broken, but the Soil verry rich and good. the River bottoms are Smoth and level thinly covred with cotton wood timber, and filled with all most all kinds of Game. Some Smoth plains under the black broken hills which is covered with wild hysop. passed Several Small runs in the course of the day,

1. In Garfield County, on a site inundated by Fort Peck Reservoir.
2. Ponderosa pine, *Pinus ponderosa* Laws. Lewis and Clark do not mention another pine.

Sunday 12th May 1805. a clear pleasant & warm morning. we Set off Soon after Sun rise, and proceeded on passed the pitch pine hills on N. S.

one of the hunters killed a deer on a bottom on s. s. Capt Clark killed a beaver in the River. passed a creek or Small river on the N. S.[1] about one o.C. P. M. we halted to dine at a bottom covred with timber on S. S. opposite the lower point of a willow Island, which is in the middle of the River. the wind rose high from the N. W. the detained us the remainder part of the day. Some men went out hunting. we camped for the night. the hunters killed Some Elk & deer &.c. we had come [*blank*] miles this day. Some Squawls of rain this evening.—

1. Seventh Point Coulee, Valley County, Montana.

Monday 13th May 1805. the wind blew verry hard all last night. Some Sprinkling rain and high wind this morning. Some men out hunting about one oC. P M the wind abated So that we Set off though the hunters had not all returned. the afternoon pleasant. we proceeded on passed the bottoms and bluffs on each Side passed the mouths of three creeks 2 on S. S. and one on the N. S.[1] we came 9 miles and Camped in a large bottom on S. S. the hunters all joined had killed several Elk & deer and wounded a brown bear on the hills. the current Swift (came 9 mls.)

1. The two creeks on the south side are Sheep Creek and Crooked Creek, Garfield County, Montana; neither of the captains mention a creek on the north side, nor is one shown on expedition maps.

Tuesday 14th May 1805.[1] a hard white frost last night. our mocassons froze near the fire. a clear and pleasant morning. we Set off at Sun rise. proceeded on passed the mouth of a creek on N. S.[2] passed black bluffs which make near the River on each Side. high hills back from the river Some pitch pine on them. Saw verry large gangs of buffaloe about 11 oClock we passed the Mouth of a large Creek on the S. S. called [*blank*][3] we proceeded on about 12 oC. it was verry war[m] or much warmer than it has been before this Spring. we Saw Some banks of Snow laying in the vallies at the N. S. of the hills. about one oClock we halted to dine at a bottom on the S. S. Capt. Clark killed a buffaloe. about 3 oC. we proceeded on. Capt. Lewis and Capt. Clark crossed the River where we Saw a large gang of buffaloe & went on Shore abt. 4 oClock the men in the canoes Saw a large brown bear on the hills on S. S. 6 men went out to kill it. they fired at it and wounded it. it chased 2 of them into a canoe, and anoth[er] [into?] the River and they Steady fireing at him. after Shooting eight balls in his body Some of them through the lites,[4] he took the River and was near catching the Man he chased in, but he went up against the Stream and the bear being wounded could not git to him. one of the hunters Shot him in the head which killed him dead. we got him to Shore with a canoe and butchred him. we found him to be nearly the Same discription of the first we killed only much larger. about 5 oClock the white perogue of the Captains was Sailing a long, there came a violent gust of wind from the N. W. which was to the contrary to the course they were Sailing. it took the Sail and before they had time to douse it it turned the perogue down on one Side So that she filled with water, and would have turned over had it not been for the earning [awning] which prevented it. with much a diew they got the Sail in and got the [pirogue] to Shore and unloaded hir at a bottom where we camped on N. S. came 18½ miles this day one man wounded another b. bear.

1. The latter part of this entry and the entries of the next few days are very faint and difficult to read.

2. Probably the party's Gibson's Creek (after expedition member George Gibson), now Sutherland Creek, Valley County, Montana.

3. Either the party's Stick Lodge Creek or Brown Bear Defeated Creek, now Hell Creek and Snow Creek, Garfield County.

4. The lungs.

Wednesday 15th May 1805.[1] cloudy. we delayed to dry the goods. Some men went up the River a hunting the day unfavorable to dry the goods. a Small Shower of rain about 11 oClock. continued cloudy all day towards evening the hunters returned. had killed one buffaloe Seven deer and four beaver. the party dressed Skins.

1. At the top of the page preceding this entry are the words, "Journal continues," apparently in Ordway's hand.

Thursday 16th May 1805. a heavy diew last night. a clear & pleasant morning. we opened the goods &.c. to get them dry before we packed them up. one of the party wounded a large panther[1] he had killed a deer & was covring it up Capt. Clark made Search to find him but in vain about 12 I killed a goat or antilope about one we packed up the goods and loaded the Captains perogues one of the party caught another goat which was mired in the mud. about 3 oClock P M we Set off proceeded on passed high rough broken hills and round knobs on each Side of the River and narrow bottoms. passed a Small willow Island on or near the N. Shore towards night we killed 3 buffaloe 2 Deer and one buffaloe calf we Came [*blank*] miles and Camped[2] on the S. Side at a bottom covered with timber & ran back like the most of the bottoms for a long distance back.

1. Mountain lion, *Felis concolor.*

2. In Garfield County, Montana, now under Fort Peck Reservoir (see a discussion for this day's campsite at Lewis's entry).

Friday 17th May 1805. a clear pleasant morning we [*page faded and worn, perhaps two lines missing*][1] by rains Saw Spots of pitch pine but the knobs are washed so that their is not ever any grass on them the River hills look mountainous and make near the river on each Side we saw large gangs of Elk which are gitting more pleanty than the buffaloe we saw a nomber of geese and goslins in the River about 2 oClock P. m. we halted to dine at a narrow bottom on the S. S. where their was Some old Indians camps. about 3 we proceeded on. towards evening I and Several more of the party killed a femail brown bear, the first female we killed. passed a creek on S. S.[2] verry high hills and white knobs, which are washed by rains. Some Spots of pitch pine on each Side of the River. came [*blank*] miles and Camped on a narrow plain on S. S. where Capt. Clark killed 1 Elk.

1. Whitehouse has, "we Set off eairly and proceeded on. passed high broken whiteish couloured hills, which wash by rain."

2. Ordway probably means the party's Burnt Lodge Creek, now Seven Blackfoot Creek, Garfield County, Montana (see Lewis's entry for this day). The party camped upstream from the mouth of this creek.

Saturday 18th May 1805. a clear warm morning. one of the party caught a beaver last night. another killed a rattle Snake[1] this morning at 7 oClock Set off and proceeded on passed verry high rough hills, which look mountainous and make in to the River on each Side. the bottoms verry narrow, but little timber only Spots of pitch pine on Sd hills. the bottoms are generally covered with rose[2] bushes & Rabbit berry bushes [*two lines illegible*][3] to dine at a large bottom covered with timber on N. S.[4] which was filled with buffaloe Elk deer &.c. Capt. Clark killed a fat deer. one of the party killed 2 Elk. another killed a beaver about one oC. P. M. cleared up pleasant, about 2 we proceeded on passed pitch pine hills on each Side of the River about 3 oC. we passed a large Creek[5] on N. S. & a large timbered bottom on the S. S. the Missourie is gitting clear and gravelly bottom, & Shore we passed no falling in banks as we did below these pitch pine hilly country. a pleasant warm afternoon. Capt Clark killed three Deer. we came 19 miles to day and Camped in a Smooth bottom thinly covered with c. w. timber on the South Side.

1. Prairie rattlesnake, *Crotalus viridus viridus*, described by Lewis on May 17.

2. Unknown rose, *Rosa* sp.

3. Whitehouse has the following for these missing lines, "about 10 oC. clouded up and began to rain. about 12 oC Capt. Clark killed a fat deer. we halted to dine. . . ."

4. Above these letters, in the top right-hand corner of the page, is the word, "May."

5. Wiser's Creek to the captains, after Peter Weiser of the party, now Fourchette Creek, Phillips County, Montana.

Sunday 19th May 1805. a heavy diew fell last night. one of the party caught a beaver. we Set off about 7 oC Clear and pleasant. we proceeded on. about 10 oC. A. M. we killed a young brown bear, on the S. Shore. passed pitch pine hills on each Side of the River and timbred bottoms. Semon Capt Lewiss dog got bit by a beaver. one of the hunters on Shore killed a Deer. about one oC. we halted to dine on N. S. at a bottom of c. wood timber. Capt Clark killed three deer. about 2 we proceeded on passed a willow Island near the N. Shore passed high pitch pine & ceeder hills as usal. passed bottoms on each Side covered with c. w. timber. we Came about 18 miles this day & Camped[1] on a timbred bottom on N. S. [*illegible words*] place Capt Lewis killed an Elk. Some other of the hunters killed 3 deer & 3 beaver to day.

1. In either Phillips or Garfield County, Montana, depending on shifts in the river, and a few miles below the entrance of the Musselshell River. From "18" to "place" the text is partly

missing from the bottom of a worn page. Considering other entries for this day, the missing words might be, "at this."

Monday 20th May 1805. a clear pleasant morning. we Set off as usal. one of the hunters or trapers caught a large beaver last night. about nine oClock A. M. we passed the mouth of a large Creek[1] on the S. Side & a handsom bottom of C. wood timber. proceeded on passed pitch pine & ceeder hills on each Side of the River. the river narrow and crooked[2] at 11 oClock we arived at the mouth of Shell River[3] on the Lard Side and formed a Camp for the present. the large Creek which we passed about 4 miles below on the Lard. Side we Call Blowing fly Creek from the emence quantities of those insect which geather on our meat in Such nombers that we are obledged to brush them off what we eate Mussel *Shell* River falls in on Lard. Side 2270 miles up contains a greater perportion of water than River of its Size below. Capt. Clark measured it and found it to be 110 yards wide. the water of a greenish yallow coulour and appears to be navagable for Small crafts, the natives Inform us that this river heads in the 1st rocky mountains & passes through a broken Country. its head at no great distance from the Yallow Stone river the Country about this river as described yesterday. our Captains took the Meridian altitude and found the Latd. to be 47° 0 24″ the Missourie at the mouth of Shell River is 222 yds wide with a Small current. the Missourie water is not So muddy as below but retains nearly the usal colour. and the Sands principily confined to the points. Capt. Clark killed two Deer and an Elk. the hunters killed Several Elk and Several Deer, mearly for the Skins to make Leagins [and moccasons?] &.c. Some men was Sent out in [every?] Direction the Country generally verry broken Some level plains up the Shell river. the bottoms of the Shell River is well timberd as also a Small river[4] which falls into that river on the upper Side 5 miles abo. its mouth the hills on the Lard. Side contain Scattering Pine and ceeder but of no great value. Small & Scrubby.— (*Came 7 miles* to day)

1. Squaw Creek, Garfield County, Montana.

2. From this sentence to the end of the entry Ordway is largely copying from Clark. He continued to do so for the next two weeks. That Ordway is doing the copying and not Clark seems apparent from his use of such words as "larboard" and "starboard," where the sergeant would normally use "south" and "north."

3. Musselshell River, dividing Garfield and Petroleum counties, still bears the expedition's name.

4. Today's Sacagawea River, Petroleum County, after the party's name and honoring Sacagawea, the Shoshone interpreter.

May 21st Tuesday 1805. a butiful morning. wind from the west. river falling a little. we Set out at an eairly hour and proceeded on in the usal way by the assistance of the chord principally, but little use for the oars & less withe the poles, as the bottom are muddy. we See no great bodies of pure Sand the bars & points are rich mud mixed with fine Sand. Capt Clark walked on Shore Stard. Side the river makes a great bend to the South in a Northerly direction is a rich vallie contain Some Short grass, and prickly pears[1] without timber the Country on the South Side of the Missourie is high Soil and mineral appearence as usal Some Scatering pine &.C. ceeder on the hills. The wind which moderately all the fore part of the day increased and about dusk Shifted to the N. W. and blew high & Stormed all night Several loose articles were blown overboard, our Camp[2] which was on a Sand bar on the Stard. Side at the lower point of an Island we were obledged to move under the hills the dust & Sand blew in clouds. the bends of the river are Short and points covered with cotton wood under grooths wild rose bush. Capt. Clark killed 2 Elk to day. Several deer killed and a buffaloe cow. we Came *20 miles* to day.—

1. Probably plains prickly pear, *Opuntia polyacantha* Haw.

2. In Phillips County, Montana, now inundated by Fort Peck Reservoir.

May 22nd Wednesday 1805. the wind continued to blow So violently hard we did not think it prudent to Set out untill it luled a little about 11 oClock we Set out the [morning] cold. passed a Small Island in the bend of the river to the Lard. Side, and proceeded on at 5 miles higher passed a Isld in a bend to the Stard. Side & a creek[1] a Short distance [above] on the Stard. Side Capt. Lewis walked on Shore and killed a deer in the fore part of the day, after dinner Capt. Clark walked out a fiew miles to view the Country, which he found verry rich Soil produceing but little vigitation of any kind except the prickly pairs but little grass & that verry low. a great deal of Scatering pine on the Lard. Side & Some fiew on the Stard. Side. the mineral production as described yesterday or in the proceeding days. the game not So a bundant as below the river continues about the Same width. a fiew Sand bars, and current more regular. River falls about an Inch a day, we Camped on the Stard Side eairlier than we intended on account of Saveing the oil of a yallow bear which the party killed late this afternoon. Came 16½ miles to day.—

Many of the creeks which appear to have no water near their mouths have Streams of running water high up which rise & waste in the Sand or gravel the water of those creeks are so much impregnated with the Salt Substance that it cannot be drank with pleasantness.—

1. The party's Grouse Creek, now probably Beauchamp Creek, Phillips County, Montana. The party camped below their Teapot Creek, which they passed the next day.

May 23rd Thursday 1805. a Severe frost last night. the Thurmomiter Stood at the freezeing point this morning wind S. W. the water freezes on the ore Ice on the edge of the river. we Set out at an eairly hour and passed the mouth of a Creek[1] at 1 mile on the Stard. Side which heads in a mountain N. W. of its mouth 10 miles the country on each Side is as passed yesterday. passed 2 Small creeks Stard & 2 on the Lard. Side to day.[2] a Mountain[3] which appears to be 60 or 70 miles long bearing E. & W. is about 25 miles distant from this river on the Stard Side. Northerly of us passed an Island. Capt. Clark walked on Shore and killed 4 Deer one Elk & a beaver.— in the evening we killed a large fat brown or yallow bear, which we unfortunately lost in the River after being Shot took the water & was carried under a drift passed in course of this day three Islands two of them covered with tall timber & a 3rd with willows the after part of this day was warm & the Musquetoes troublesome Saw but fiew buffalow a nomber of Elk & Deer & 5 bear & 2 antilopes to day. the river begining to rise, & current more rapid than yesterday in many places we Saw Spruce[4] on the hills Sides Camped on Stard. Side Came 27 miles to day.

1. Teapot Creek of the expedition, now CK, or Kannuck, Creek, Phillips County, Montana.

2. In addition to CK Creek, as indicated by nameless streams on expedition maps. They include Sevenmile Creek, Phillips County, and Carroll Creek, Fergus County, Montana.

3. Little Rocky Mountains.

4. Perhaps Engelmann spruce, *Picea engelmanii* Parry, but apparently not known from this area. See entries of Lewis and Clark for this day.

May 24th Friday 1805. a cold night the water in the Small vessels froze ⅛ of an Inch thick & the Thurmot. Stood this morning at the freezeing point we Set out at an eairly hour and proceeded on at 9 oClock we had a breeze of wind from the S. E. which continued all day this Breeze aforded us good Sailing the River riseing fast current verry rapid passed Several Small Islands two large & 2 Small creeks the 1st of these creeks or small rivers[1] ½ a mile above our Camp is 30 yds. wide and contains water and appears to take its rise in the North Mountain which is Situated in a Northely direction abt. 20 miles distant. 2½ miles higher up a creek[2] falls in on the Lard. Side opposite a large village of Barking Squerrells 3 miles Still higher a Small Creek falls in on the[3] Lard. Side which is 40 yards wide & has running water this Stream appears to take its rise in the South Mountains[4] which is Situated in a Southerly direction 30 or 40 miles distant. Capt. Clark walked on the high Country, on the Stard. Side found it broken & dry Some pine, Spruce & Dwarf ceeder on the hills Sides. one man went 10 miles out he reported a Simelarity of a country back. Capt. Clark killed a fat buffalow a Short distance below the place we dined 2 canoes & 6 men waited & got the best of the meat. did not joine the party this evening. Camped on the Lard. Side on point the cotton wood in this point is begining to put out a Second time the first being killed by the frost. Came 24½ miles to day.—

1. The party's North Mountain Creek, now Rock Creek, Phillips County, Montana.
2. Lewis's Little Dog Creek, now Sand Creek, Fergus County, Montana.
3. At this point Ordway drops a line of Clark's writing. The missed portion from Clark reads: "Stard. 13 miles higher up a Small river falls in on the." The small stream on the north is probably Siparyann Spring Creek, Phillips County, and the small river on the south is the party's South Mountain Creek, now Armalls Creek, Fergus County, Montana.
4. Judith Mountains, possibly including Moccasin Mountains.

May 25th Saturday 1805. the 2 canoes left for meat did not join us untill 8 oClock this morning at which time we Set out. the morning cool & pleasant wind a head all day from the S. W. we passed a creek[1] on the Lard. Side about 20 yards wide, which does not run we also passed 7 Islands. Capt. Clark walked on Shore and killed a female *Ibex* or big hornd animel:

two of the hunters killed 2 others this animel is of a blackish colour or dark duskey colour over the body. they have great resemblance of the deer kind, especally the leggs, but the head & huffs resemble a Sheep. they are verry active & keep freequently on the Sides of Steep bluffs & places where wolves & bears cannot hurt them. the Country on each Side is high broken and rocky the rocks are soft Sand Stone and of a dark brown hard & rough, the hills also contain Coal &.C the bars in the river covered with corse gravel the bottom of the river are Small do. [ditto] we Saw a pole cat[2] to day being the first we have Seen for a long distance. the air of this country is pure & healthy the water of the Missourie fine and cool. Came 18 miles to day.—

1. Two Calf Creek, Fergus County, Montana.
2. A skunk, *Mephitis mephitis.*

May 26th Sunday 1805. Set out eairly. wind from s. w. the river nearly closed by the high hills on boath sides. the Country thro which borders the River is high broken & rockey generally imbeded with a Soft Sand Stone higher up the hills the Stone are of a brownish yallow, hard & gritty those Stone wash in to the River down the brooks and cause the Shore to be rockey for some distance in the water which we find troublesome to assend. their is Scarce any bottom under the hills, & but fiew trees to be Seen, on either Side except a fiew pine on the hills, we passed 2 creeks[1] on the Starbord Side boath of them had running water in one of them saw Soft Shell Turtle.[2] Capt. Lewis in his walk killed a fat Buffalow, which we were in want of the hunters killed 2 Mountain Rams, or big horned animel in the evening late we passed a rapid[3] which extended quite across the river. the waves roled for Some distance below, we ascended it by the assistance of the chord & poles the crafts all crossed on Stard. Side except one which with Some difficulty got up the Lard Side we Saw a dow Elk & faun, which gave rise to the name Elk & faun riffle. bluffs on Labord Side, and jist over the opposite Side is a livel plain. we Camped a little above in a Small grove of Cotton trees on the Lard. Side. we had a fiew drops of rain at dark. the Salts coal & burnt hills Still continue. Game Scarser. this country may with propriety be called the Deserts of North america for I do not conceive any part of it can ever be Setled as it is deficient of or in water except this River, & of timber & too Steep to be tilled. we passed old Indian Camps & lodges in the woody points everry day, & 2 at our Camp &.C. we Came 22¾ miles this day.—

1. The party's Windsor's Creek (after expedition member Richard Windsor), now Cow Creek, Blaine County, Montana, and their Soft Shell Turtle Creek, Bullwhacker Creek, also in Blaine County, Montana.

2. Western spiny softshell turtle, *Trionyx spiniferus hartwegi.*

3. Elk Fawn Rapids is now Bird Rapids, near which the party camped in Fergus County, Montana.

May 27th Monday 1805. the wind blew hard from the S. W. which detained us untill about 10 oClock at which time we Set out & proceeded on. passed a Small necked Island on the Lard. Side immediately above the timber in which we Camped the river is verry Shoaley and the bad places are verry numerous.— at the mouth of every dreen the rocks is thrown Some distance in the river which causes the riffles. this day is verry warm. we Saw only a fiew herds of Big horned animel on the hills, & 2 Elk, one of which we killed. we Camped[1] at 2 dead top trees on the Larboard Side. the river is generally about 200 yards wide & current verry Swift to day, and has a verry prosperous falls in all its course it rises a little. Came 14 miles to day.—

1. In Fergus County, Montana, near later McGarry Bar.

May 28th Tuesday 1805. a cloudy morning. Some fiew drops of rain & Smokey wind from the S. W. we Set out at an eairly hour. the Shoaley places are verry numerous & Some bad to git around. we have to make use of the cords & poles, our cords are all except one made of Elk Skin & Stretch & Some time brake which indanger the Pirogues or canoe, as it immediately turns and if any rock Should chance to be below the rapidity of the water would turn hir over if Should Strike, we observe great caution at these places. Capt. Clark walked on Shore, found the country ruged and as described yesterday. he saw great nombers of the Big hornned animels, one of which he killed their faun are nearly half grown. one of the party saw a verry large bear. we picked up a pole on the Shore which has been made use of by the natives for a lodge pole & halled by dogs & it is new & a certain Sign of the Indians being on the River above a foot ball & Several other articles are also found to Substantiate this oppinion. at 1 oClock we had a fiew drops of rain & Some Thunder which is the first Thunder we have had Since we Set out, from Fort Mandans, at 10 miles the river the hills begin to widen & the river Spreads and is crouded with Islands, the bottoms contain Some Scatering cottonwood the Islands also contain timber. passed a creek[1] of running water on the Stard. Side about 35 yards wide, and Camped imediately opposite to a Small Creek[2] on Lard. Side. Came 21 miles to day.—

1. Thompson's Creek to the party (after expedition member John B. Thompson), now Birch Creek, which meets the Missouri in Chouteau County, Montana.
2. The party's Bull Creek, now Dog Creek, Fergus County, Montana.

May 29th Wednesday 1805. in the course of last night we were alarmed by a Buffalow Swimming across from the opposite Shore & landed opposite the white perogue in which our Captains Stay. he crossed the perogue, & went with great forse up the bank to the fire where the men were Sleeping & was within 18 Inches of their heads when one man Setting up alarmed him and he turned his course along the range of men as they lay, passing between 4 fires & within a fiew Inches of Several mens heads, it was Supposed if he had trod on a man it would have killed him dead. the dog flew at him which turned him from running against the lodge, were the officers lay. he passed without doeing more damage than bend a rifle & breaking hir Stalk & injuring one of the blunder busses in the perogue as he passed through. we Set out this morning at the usaul hour and proceeded on. at 2½ miles passed the mouth of a river[1] [*blank*] yards wide, dischargeing a great quantity of water, and containing more wood in its bottoms than the Missourie. this river Capt. Lewis walked up a Short distance and he Saw an old Indian encampment. we Saw also great encampments on the Stard. Side at the mouth of a Small creek[2] of about 100 lodges, which [a]ppeared to be about 5 or 6 weeks past. our Indian woman examined their moccasons &.C and told us that they were the Indians which resided below the rockey Mountains, and to the North of the river that hir nation made their moccasons differently. at 6½ miles passed a considerable rapid[3] at which place the hills approach near the river on both Sides, leave a narrow bottom on the Starboard Side (ash rapid) and continue close all day but little timber. we Saw the remains of a number of buffalow which had been drove down a Steep clift of rocks, from appearence their was upwards of 100 of these animels all picked off in a drove, great nombers of wolves were about this place & verry gentle Capt. Clark killed one of them with his Sphere.—[4] the hills above ash rapid contain more rocks & coal, and the more rapid points. we come too for dinner at or opposite the entrance of a Small River[5] which falls in on the Lard. Side, & no timber for Some distance. has a bold running Stream. Soon after we came too it began to rain, and blew hard, and as we were in a good harbour a point of wood on the Stard. Side, & no timber for Some distance above, induced the Captains to Stay all night, they gave each man a dram though Small was enofe to efect Several of the men one of the hunters killed an Elk. in the evening Capt. Clark killed 2 beaver on the Side of the bank. Some of the hunters who went out on the high land, Said it Snowed & hailed on the hills. we Came 18 miles this day.—

1. Judith River, Fergus County, Montana; so named by Clark after his future wife, Julia Hancock.

2. Valley Run to the party, now Chip Creek, Chouteau County, Montana.

3. Deadmans Rapids, the party's Ash Rapids.

4. The captain's espontoon.

5. The captains called it Slaughter River because of the number of dead buffalo found nearby; it is today's Arrow Creek, the boundary between Chouteau and Fergus counties.

May 30th Thursday 1805. the rain commenced yesterday evening & continued moderately through the course of the night. more rain has now fallen than we have experenced Since the 15th of September last, the rain continued this morning, and the wind too high for us to proceed, untill abt. 11 oClock at which time we Set out & proceeded on with great labour we were oblidged to make use of the tow rope & the banks were So muddy & Slippery that the men could Scarsely walk notwithstanding we proceeded as well as we Could, wind hard from the N. W. in attempting to assend a rapid our toe cord broke of the white perogue, they turned without injury. those rapids are Shallow points & are numerous & difficult one being at the mouth of every dreen. Some little rain at times all day. one man ascended the high country & it was raining & Snowing on those high hills, the day has proved to be raw and cold back from the river is tollarably level. no timber of any kind on the hills, & only a fiew Scatering trees of cotton willows &.C. we discover in many places old encampments of large bands of Indians, a fiew weeks past & appear to be makeing up the River. those Indians we believe to be the Blackfoot Indians or Manetare who Inhabit the Country on the heads of the Saskashoarr North of this place & trade a litto [little] in the *Fort Deprare* establishments.[1] we Camped[2] in a handsome grove of cotton trees on the Stard. Side. River rise 1½. Came 8 miles to day

1. Ordway, still copying Clark, mentions the Blackfeet and Atsina Indians, the Saskatchewan River, and the North West Company post of Fort des Prairies where the two tribes traded.
2. In Chouteau County, Montana, nearly opposite Sheep Shed Coulee.

May 31st Friday 1805. a Cloudy morning. the canoes all dispached eairly to collect the meat of 2 buffalow killed last night. the perogues proceeded on it continued to rain moderately untill about 12 oClock when it ceased & continued cloudy. the Stones on the edges of the river continue to form very considerable rapids. we find them difficult to pass. the tow rope of the white perogue which we were oblidge to make use of broke & was in Some danger of turning over. we landed at 12 oClock the Capts. gave the or refreshed the party with a dram we are oblidged to undergo great labour and fatigue in ascending this part of the Missourie as they are compelled from the rapidity of the current in many places to walk in the water & on Slippery hill sides on the Sides of rocks &.c. on gravel & thro Stiff mud, bear footed & we cannot keep on moccasons from the Stiffness of the mud & decline of the Steepp hill sides— the hills and river cliffts of this day exhibit a most romantick appearence[1] on each Side of the river is a white Soft Sand Stone bluffs which rises to about half the hight of the hills, on the top of this Clift is a black earth. on points in many places this sand Stone appears like antient ruins Some like elegant buildings at a distance, Some like Towers &.C. &.C. in many places of this days march we observe on either Side of the river extroardanary walls of a black semented stone which appear to be regularly placed one Stone on the other. Some of those walls rise to the hight of 100 feet. they are from about 9 foot to 12 feet deep or thick and are perpinticular. those walls commence at the waters edge & in some places meet at right angles. those walls appear to continue thier course into the Sand clifts. the Stone which for those walls are of different Sizes all Square edged. great nombers has fallen from the walls near the river which causes the wall of unequal hite, in the hollars & gullies I Saw Some Scrubby ceddr. the low walls Strait White & handsom, like ancient elegant buildings. towards evening the country becomes lower and the bottoms wider. no timber on the uplands, except a fiew ceddr & pine on the clifts. a fiew Scatering cottonwood trees on the points in the river bottoms. The appearence of coal continues. Capt. Lewis walked on Shore & observed a Species of pine[2] we had never before Seen, with a Shorter leaf than common & The burr different, he also collected Some of the Stone of one of the walls which appears to be a Siment of Sun glass black earth. we Camped[3] on the Stard. Side in a Small timberd handsom bottom above the mouth of a creek on the Stard. Side. the hunters killed 2 animels with big horns. 2 buffalow an Elk & a black taild or mule deer. we Saw a nomber of those big horned animels on the clifts. but fiew buffalow or Elk, no antilope, a fiew mule Deer. Saw a fox to day. the river rises a little it is from 150 to *250* yards wide. Came 18 miles to day.—

1. Ordway, copying from Clark who copied this passage from Lewis, describes the White Cliffs area of the Missouri River Breaks, Chouteau County, Montana.

2. Limber pine, *Pinus flexilis* James.

3. At the party's Stonewall Creek, present Eagle Creek, Chouteau County.

June 1st Saturday 1805. a Cloudy morning. we Set out at an eairly hour and proceeded on as usal with the toe rope. the Country appears to be lower and the clifts not So high or common. a Mountain or a part of the north Mountain about 8 or 10 miles N. of this place. more cotton trees Scatering along the river & Islands than yesterday. no timber on the high land. The river from 2 to 400 yards wide & current more jentle than yesterday. but fiew bad rapids points to day. the wild animels not So pleanty as below we only killed a ram & mule deer to day. we Saw buffalow at a [d]istance in the plains. perticelarly near a lake on the Lard. [s]ide about 8 eight miles off from the river. we passed Six Islands and Camped[1] on the

7th all night. all those Islands are Small but contain Some timber on them. The river riseing a little. wind to day from S. W. Some fiew drops of rain in the morning and also in the evening. flying clouds all day. Saw Several Indians Camps made of Sticks & Set up on end and do not appear to be long evacuated. The roses are in full bloom we saw yallow berrys, red berry bushes great nombers wild or choke Cherries, prickly prairs are in the blossom we Saw great nombers of them. Came 23 miles to day.

1. In the vicinity of Boggs Island, Chouteau County, Montana.

June 2nd Sunday 1805. we had a hard wind & a little rain last night. this morning fair. we Set out at an eairly hour. wind from S. W. Some little rain to day wind hard a head. the Country much like that of yesterday, as described. Capt. Lewis walked on Shore, himself and the hunters killed 6 Elk a bear and 2 mule Deer, and 2 buffalow, which was all in good order a beaver also killed this evening. passed 9 Islands to day. the current Swift but regular. we Camped[1] on the Larboard Side at the mouth or at the forks of the river. the current & Sizes of them we could not examine this evening. a fair night. the Captains took Some Lunr. observations, of moon & Stars—. Came 18 miles to day.

1. In Chouteau County, Montana, opposite the mouth of the Marias River, named by Lewis in honor of his cousin, Maria Wood.

June 3rd Monday 1805.[1] we formed a Camp[2] on the point in the junction of the two rivers, & two canoes & 3 man were dispached up each river to examine and find if possable which is the most probable branch.[3] the left fork which is the largest we are doubtful of. the Indians do not mention any river falling in on the right in this part of the Missourie. The Scolding river, if their is Such a one Should have fallen in below agreeable to their accts. men were dispached also in different directions by land, to a mountain covred with Snow to the South. & others up each river. the Captains walked out & assended the hill in the point, they observed a level Country to the foot of the mountains which lye South of this, also a River[4] which falls into the Right hand fork about 1½ miles above its mouth on the Larboard

Side. this little river descharges a great deal of water & contains as much cotton timber in its bottoms as either of the others. they Saw buffalow & antilopes wild Cherries red & yallow berrys, Goose berrys &.C. abound in the river bottoms. prickley pairs on the high plains. the Capts. had a meridian altitude and the Latitude produced was *47° 24′ 12″* North. the after part of the day proved Cloudy. Capt. Clark measured each river & found the one to the Right hand 186 yards wide of water, & the left hand fork 372 yards wide and rapid. the right hand fork falling the other at a Stand, and clear. the right fork and the river which fall into it is couloured & a little muddy. Several of the party complain of their feet being Sore by walking in the Sand, & their being cut by the Stones we to be Sure have a hard time of it oblidged to walk on Shore & hawl the rope and 9/10 of their time barefooted— in the evening the parties all returned to Camp had been about 15 miles up each river, but could not determine which would be our most probable branch for our Course &C. our officers are not Satisfied in their minds which River will be best to for us to take. So they determine to leave the crafts & the most of the men here & go one day & a half up each river with a Small party to find out which will be the most probable River for us to take &.C. the hunters killed 4 buffalow 3 Elk 3 beaver & Several Deer our officers Gave Each man a Dram.—

1. From this day Ordway's copying of Clark's journal ceases, although part of this material is from the captain.

2. Below the present mouth of the Marias River, Chouteau County, Montana, where the party would remain until June 12, 1805, while they investigated the two streams to determine which course to take.

3. Pryor and his men went up the Marias while Gass with a party went up the Missouri; Whitehouse says he was with the latter.

4. Teton River, a tributary of the Marias, which the captains called the Tansey River.

June 4th Tuesday 1805. Capt. Lewis and 6 men Set out to go up the right hand fork.[1] Capt Clark & 5 more Set out at the Same time to go up the left hand fork in order to go one day & a halfs march up the River and see if they can find out which will be our best River to proceed on. Some of the men at Camp killed 2 faun Elk near the point for their Skins to dress. the day proved Cloudy. 2 men who had been from Camp a hunting returned towards evening. had killed one Elk & a Deer & Set traps for beaver &C. a fiew drops of rain towards evening & high cold wind from the North.

1. Clark listed the men in each of the detachments in his entry for this day. Ordway remained behind with the main party.

Wednesday 5th June 1805.— the wind blew high from the North all last night a Cloudy Cold windy morning. one beaver caught last night. the men engaged Dressing Skins for to make themselves moccasons leggins &C. one man by the name of Goodrich has caught a considerable quantity of fish. Some of which are Shell fish, but the most part are Small cat fish. we have caught none as large this Season as we did last as yet, as we have a great pleanty of meat we do not trouble ourselves for to catch fish.—

June 6th Thursday 1805. a Cloudy Cold morning. The wind high from the north. Some of the men went a Short distance from Camp and killed 2 buffalow 1 mule deer 1 common deer 2 antilopes & a fat Elk. about 2 oClock P. M. Capt. Clark and his party returned to Camp had been about 40 miles up the South fork & Capt. Clark thinks that it will be the best course for us to go. they Saw a beautiful Spring[1] about eight miles up the South fork from this place where they refreshed themselves with a drink of grog as they had a canteen of old Spirits with them, the middle river[2] is only about 200 yards across from the South fork, at the Spring, they Saw but little game on the South fork but returned back on the middle fork, where they found abundance of Elk Deer buffalow antilopes & wolves. they Saw Several brown or yallow bear also. one of the men by the [name?] of Jos. Fields was attacted by an old hea bear & his gun missed fire and he was in danger of being killed by that venimous animel had the rest of the party not been in hearing, who fired at him and he turned his course and left the man. they killed three bear & eat a part of one of them. they killed on the little R. a nomber of fat Elk Deer &C &.C— the bottoms on the little river is like those below the forks, a considerable of a kind of cotton wood which has a leaf like the leaf of a cherry.[3] we Saw wild tanzey[4] in these bottoms. nothing groes in the high plains but Short grass and prickley pears, they Saw a large Mountain[5] to the South of them covred with Snow, which was but a

Short distance from where they turned back. a light Sprinkling of rain this afternoon. Capt. Lewis and his party has not returned this evening. Capt. Clark revived the party with a Dram.

1. See Clark's entry of July 12.

2. Teton River, with the Missouri being the south fork.

3. Probably narrowleaf cottonwood, *Populus angustifolia* James. Only Ordway and Whitehouse compare its leaf to the leaf of a cherry.

4. Perhaps western yarrow, *Achillea mellefolium* L. See Clark's entry of June 6, 1805, Lewis's of July 31, 1805, but especially Lewis's of June 5, 1806, for a most likely determination of the plant's identity.

5. Probably the Little Belt Mountains with the Big Belt Mountains behind.

June 7th Friday 1805. rained all last night. a rainy cold morning the wind N. W. Some men went out a hunting, & killed two Deer. rained moderately all day. Capt Lewis and his party did not return this evening we expect the reason is owing to the badness of the weather as it is muddy & Slippery walking

Saturday 8th June 1805. Some cloudy. the wind blew cold from the N. W. Several men went out from Camp to hunt— about 9 oClock A. M. cleared off pleasant. the Indian goods &.C. put out to air. we Saw the high Mountains to the West. our Camp covered with Snow the greater part of which has fell within a fiew days. the South fork of the Missourie is high & of a yallow coulour. the N. fork is more white than common owing as we expect to the late rain which has melted the Snow on the mountains. about 3 oClock P. M. Capt. Lewis & his party returned to Camp, & Informed us that they had walked through high plains for about 60 miles up the north fork. they found that it holds its bigness, & depth of water bottoms of timber which is covered with game. they killed a nomber of buffalow, 16 Deer 6 Elk & a brarow. they Saw a range of Mountains[1] to the South of them. Capt. Lewis think that the N. fork bears too far north for our course for if we Should take the wrong fork we Should have much further to go by land & more mountains to cross to git over the Columbia River which descends to the western ocean. So our Captains conclude to assend the South fork and burry Some articles which we can do without & leave the largest perogue. they named the North fork River *Mariah* and the middle or little River named *Tanzey River.* the water & bottoms in everry respect of each resimbles the Missourie below the forks. only Smaller. we put a brand on a tree which Stood on the point. the men generally in camp has been employed dressing Skins &.C—

towards evening the hunters all came in had killed 13 m. mule & common Deer & one beaver. The wind blew from the East a light Shower of rain this evening.

1. Probably the Highwood Mountains.

Sunday 9th June 1805. a clear pleasant morning. we unloaded the red perogue, & put out the Indian Goods &.C. to air. 2 of the hunters went out in the plains and killed the fattest buffalow that we have killed this year. it took Eight men to bring in the meat. 7 men went out to the high land to dig a cash. a hole in the ground for to burry Some of the articles So that we may find them Safe when we return back. the wind rose high from the west all day. in the evening the Capts. revived the party with a dram. they had a frolick fiddled & danced & Sang untill late in the evening. we had a light Shower of rain about 11 oClock at night.

Monday 10th June 1805. a beautiful pleasant morning. Some men employed makeing a towing line for the white perogue. we burryed a canister of powder & Some led &.C. in the point. we halled out our largest perogue in the middle of an Island in the North fork opposite the point, and made hir fast between Some trees, & branded Several trees to prevent the Savages from disturbing hir the blacksmiths[1] fixed up their bellowes & repaired the air gun & Several other fire arms. The Canoe Calked, the Baggage aranged & loaded the Crafts, about 4 oClock P. M. we had a light Shower of rain which lasted about an hour. high wind. the evening pleasant Capt. Lewis concludes to go on with a fiew men to the South Mountain & See the course of the River &.C. *Sah cah gah* our Indian woman verry Sick & was bled.—

1. Shields, according to Lewis.

Tuesday 11th June 1805. a clear pleasant morning. about 8 oClock Capt. Lewis, George Drewyer G. Gibson Jos. Fields & Silas Goodrich Set out for the Snowey Soth Mountains, we burryed on the high land 1 keg of powder 1 bar led, 1 keg flour, 1 keg pork 2 kegs parchd meal the bellowes & tools, augur plains, Saws axes, tin cups dutch ovens, bear Skins packs of beaver Skins buffalow Robes, & a nomber of other articles, all of weight, Such as Rams horns &.C. The blacksmiths compleated repaering the arms &.C. we Compleated burrying the articles &C got in readiness to assend the South fork. the wind from the S. West hard. the evening fair & fine wind from the N. W. after night became cold. high wind we have caught a considerable quantity of Small fish Since we lay at the forks. one kind of flat Scalled fish[1] that we never Saw the kind before.

1. Probably the goldeye, described this day by Lewis.

Wednesday 12th June 1805. a clear pleasant morning. we burryed 3 traps which was forgot when we made the Deposite yesterday, about 7 oClock we Set out from Camp on point Deposite which is 2508¼ miles from the Mouth of the Missourie. we proceeded on the South fork which we continue to call the Missourie. we passed 5 or 6 Islands before we got out of cite of the point. one man caught a large beaver on one of them last night. we passed verry high black & yallow bluffs on each Side of the River. Saw Elk antilopes & Geese & Goslings &.C. found penerial[1] along the Stoney banks. the current verry rapid. 2 Canoes were in some danger to day one came near turning over. Several rattle Snakes has been Seen by the party to day one man took hold of one which was in a bunch of bushes as he was taking along the towing line, but luckley escaped being bit. our Intrepters wife verry Sick. Capt. Clark killed this evening 1 Elk & a deer Some of the men killed 1 Elk & a deer also—. we passed in the course of the day a nomber of Gravelly Islands & bars in the River. the Shore on each Side is covred with Small Stone of different Sizes, we Came 18 miles to day & Camped[2] at a handsom bottom of cotton timber, where the Elk & Deer was killed.— on Stad. Side—

1. The pennyroyal is a European species; it is not clear what plant Ordway notices.
2. About five miles downstream from Fort Benton, Chouteau County, Montana.

Thursday 13th June 1805. a beautiful pleasant morning. we Set out at an eairly hour a heavy diew. proceeded on. passed the mouth of a Small River[1] on the Lard. Side about 50 yds. wide at the mouth of a muddy coulour and verry rapid. bottoms of cotton timber for Some distance up we named it Snowey River as it heads in the mountain covred with Snow to our left. we passed verry high bluffs on each Side of the River. Some Small bottoms of cotton timber. Saw abundance of wild or choke cherrys, the Goose berrys are now ripe & abound in the River bottoms. also a yallow current[2] the kind I never Saw before. they are nearly as large as the goose berrys, but Sower & yallow when ripe we Came 14 miles to day and Camped on the South Side, Some of the hunters killed a buffalow and 2 Deer to day—

1. Clark passed it on his trip on June 4; it is now Shonkin Creek, Chouteau County, Montana.

2. Probably the buffalo currant, *Ribes ordoratum* Wendl. f., but possibly the golden currant, *R. aureum* Pursh. See Clark's entry of April 30, 1805.

Friday 14 June 1805. a fare pleasant morning 3 men lay out last 2 of them had Sore hands the other Sick. proceeded on passed a bottom on N. S. where Capt. Lewis & men had Camped 1 night & killed 2 bears & one Deer & left the Skins & fat for us to take on board. the 2 men who lay out on that Side we found here. at breakfast we came up with the other man who had killed the evening before 2 buffalow & 2 Deer. we proceeded on passed verry high bluffs on each Side of the River and Several Islands covered with cotton timber. the current verry rapid all day. our Intrepters wife verry Sick. one of the men a light feaver. we Came 10 miles to day through a verry rapid current, and Camped[1] on the Lard. Side at a Small bottom of cotton timber.—

1. Near the entrance of Black Coulee, Chouteau County, Montana.

Saturday 15th June 1805. a clear pleasant morning. we Set out at the usal hour & proceeded on passed through the rapidest water I ever Saw any craft taken through. passed high bluffs & clifts on each Side. at noon we halted at the mouth of a Small River on the Lard. Side, which we named

Strawberry River[1] as their is a Great many vines about it. it is a handsom rapid Stream. Small bottoms of cotton timber on it. 2 hunters went a Short distance up the branch & killed 2 Deer. wild or choke cherrys Goose berrys & yallow currents abound in these bottoms. the afternoon verry warm we proceeded on passed redish bluffs on each Side of the River, & clifts of blackish rocks in some places, passed over Some rapids where the waves came over the Canoe which I was in and I expected everry moment to have filled.—. in the evening we came to a bad rapid which we concluded to camp below it all night as we would be too late gitting through— So we Camped on the Stard. Side. one man[2] Sent up to the falls for Capt. Lewis &.C. the wood Scarse. we Came 12 miles to day by exerting ourselves as much as possable with the towing line to the best advantage.—

1. The name given also by Gass and Whitehouse, but Clark called it Shields' River, for John Shields of the party; it is Highwood Creek, Chouteau County, Montana.

2. Joseph Field, according to Clark.

Sunday 16th June 1805. a Small Shower of rain and high wind from the west the fore part of last night. a clear morning. all hands took the canoes up over the rapids. then came back and took over the large perogue about 1 mile then halted to wait the arival of Capt. Lewis their being another rapid near above which was impossable for loaded craft to pass. we caught considerable quantity of Small flat Scale fish while we lay here. about 12 oClock Capt. Lewis and his men joined us. Capt. Lewis had been about 15 miles up the River above the 1st rapid, or Shoot, and that the falls continue all that distance in 5 different Shoots.[1] the highest about 50 feet perpinticular, & Shoots & brakers all the way between each other. Capt. Lewis & men had killed Some fat buffalow and dryed the best of the fat meat for us. they caught a great many fine fish like our Sammon trout.[2] they had dryed a considerable quantity of them for us also. Capt. Lewis concluded that the Lard. Side would be the best for us to carry our baggage through the plains above the falls as that is the Smoothest Side we crossed over to the Lard. Side & unloaded the canoes & crossed them back to the Stard. Side & halled them up the rapid about 1 mile empty. then crossed them back again So that we could take them in the mouth of a Small River[3] which puts in close under the next Shoot or fall, then we could have a more convenient place to take them up the bank, on the Smoth plains. opposite to the mouth of this little River on the N. Side of the Missourie is a beautiful Sulpher or mineral Spring[4] which falls out of the Side hills. it has a Strong taste of Sulpher. we drink of it freely. in the bottoms is a great quantity of flax[5] growing all in blue blossoms &C.

1. Great Falls of the Missouri, a series of five falls in Cascade County, Montana.
2. Probably the cutthroat trout, *Oncorhynchus clarki* (formerly *Salmo clarkii*), named for Clark.
3. Portage or Red Creek to the expedition, where the party established their lower portage camp; it is now Belt Creek, the boundary between Chouteau and Cascade counties, Montana. At least a part of the group would remain here until July 1 as they made their way around the falls.
4. Sulphur, or colloquially, Sacagawea, Springs, where healing waters were found for the Shoshone woman.
5. Perhaps blue flax, *Linum perenne* L., or roundleaf harebell, *Campanula rotundifolia* L., which resembles flax. See Lewis's entry of July 18.

Monday 17th June 1805. a clear morning. Some men employed taking the canoes up the little River.[1] 6 men employed making Small low waggons for the purpose of halling the canoes, Goods & baggage through the plains by the falls. Capt. Clark and five men[2] went to Survey and measure the distance &.C. to the head of the falls to where we could take the water again 2 hunters out in order to git Elk Skins to cover or bottom our Iron boat when we git abo. the falls, as we will Stand in need of it as we leave our largest craft at this place. the timber is verry Scarse about the falls. the buffalow pleanty. in the evening we got the canoes up the Small River about 1¾ miles to the falls of it of about 4 feet prepinticular. we had some difficulty in gitting them up the rapids to this place one canoe turned over. was near hurting the 2 men in hir. Several others filled with water halling them up Such Steep rapids, but we got them all up Safe to this falls of the little River, and carried them out on a level, turned them on one Side to dry &.C.

1. Belt Creek.
2. Including Willard, Colter, and perhaps Joseph Field.

Tuesday 18th June 1805. this morning all hands halled out the long perogue. we leave in a bunch of bushes below the Camp. we covered hir over with bushes & dry wood. Secured hir Safe. 3 men Sent to a knob a short distance out to dig a cash or hole to put a fiew heavey articles in which we can Spare, to deposite at this place. the day pleasant we repacked the Indian goods &.C. moved all the baggage near to camp. about 12 oClock the hunters came in had killed 10 deer but no Elk. in the evening we saw some buffalow on the opposite Shore. Some of the hunters crossed and killed 2 of them the little low waggons Compleated. all made of wood & of a ordinarry quallity though they may answer the purpose. the wind high from the west. our Intrepters wife Some what better than She has been for Some time past. we are now 2580¼ miles from the mouth of the Missourie River.—

Wednesday 19th June 1805. a clear pleasant morning. Several men Sent over the River for the meat which was killed last night. three hunters[1] sent up to the head of the falls to a river called medicine River[2] on the N. Side. we Set them across here in a canoe we kept a canoe to cross the River in. the wind verry high from N. W. we prepare to move the Goods & baggage &.C.

1. Drouillard, Reubin Field, and Shannon, according to Lewis.

2. Sun River, which meets the Missouri at the city of Great Falls, Cascade County, Montana.

Thursday 20th June 1805. Some cloudy & cold for the Season. the wind continues high from the west off the mountains. 4 men Sent across the river to hunt. a light Sprinkling of rain about noon we are now waiting the arival of Capt. Clark. late in the afternoon 2 of the hunters Came in and informed us that they had got 11 buffalow killed & the most of them fat. the other 2 Stayed to butcher. all hands in Camp turned out for the meat, & brought about the half of what was fat 3 men Stayed all night to dress the remainder. verry large gangs all around the place within Shot of the butchers &C. a light Sprinkling of rain. late in the evening Capt. Clark and party returned to Camp they informed us that they traversed & measured the River and falls, as they went up. measured all the Small or little falls which were common & of different hites. the highest catteract or falls is 87 feet perpinticular. the next highest 47 feet 8 Ich the next or 3rd about 30 or upwards. a nomber of Small ones & a continued rapid the whole way for 17 miles to where we can take water again. those large falls all have a mist which rises about 200 yards from the Shoot. about a mile above the falls of 47 feet, 8 Inches, the largest fountan or Spring[1] falls in that we ever Saw before and it is the oppinion of Capt. Clark that it is the largest Spring in america known. this water boils up from under the rocks near the River & falls immediately in to the river 8 feet & keeps its colour for ½ a mile, which is verry clear and of a blueish cast &C— two of Capt. Clarks party was attacted by a large white bear on an Island[2] near where they had camped one night. one of them A. Willard like to have been caught. the other chased in the water after Willard made his ascape towards camp. Capt. Clark and 3 others went to their assistance. the bear ratreated. night came on the bushes thick. So they did not kill him, they Saw but little timber. the country up the medicine River above the falls is level with low banks. they Saw a chain of Mountains[3] to the west Some of which perticular those to the N. W. and S. W. are covered with Snow, and appear to be verry high. they turned back in order to look out the levelest way for the portage. Capt. Clark lost a part of his notes which could not be found. Capt. Clark Saw a rattle Snake out in the plains a long distance from timber or water. they Saw verry large innumerable quantyties of buffalow while they were gone. they killed 7 buffalow & Saved as much of the meat as possable. killed a beaver also,

they Saw buffalow attempt to Swim the River above the falls. Some of which was Sucked over and Seen no more. great numbers of those animels are lost in these falls which is the cause of our Seeing So many below for a long distance washed up on Shore. Some make the Shore above the falls half drowned.—

1. Giant Springs, now located in a park northeast of the city of Great Falls, Cascade County, Montana.

2. The party's White Bear Islands, since nearly disappeared, a short distance north of Sand Coulee Creek, Cascade County. It became the upper portage camp.

3. Probably the Lewis Range and the main Rockies.

June 21st Friday 1805. a fine cool morning. the wind from the S. W. off the mountains and hard. Capt. Lewis with the men except a fiew took a part of the baggage & a canoe up a hill on to the plain above a mile in advance. Several men employed in Shaveing & graneing Elk hides from the Iron boat as it is called, the remainder of the meat which was dressed last night was brought in this morning & the men returned Some of them had killed 2 or 3 deer & a buffalow calf and a Small Elk. we Saw thousands of buffalow on the high lands the calfs verry numerous among them they come in gangs to the river to drink &.C.

June 22nd Saturday 1805. a clear pleasant morning. the wind as usal the party all raised eairly the 2 Captains with all but 3 of the party[1] set out with more baggage to take the canoe and loading we took on the plains yesterday up to the upper end of the portage to where we can take water again with the canoes. Capt. Lewis and 3 more of the party who went took their baggage all in order to Stay at the upper Camp[2] to prepare whatever may be necessary for the Iron boat, &C. large gangs of buffalow all around the lower Camp to day. one gang Swam the river near the camp Capt. Clarks Servant York killed one of them. a light Sprinkling of rain. The Country in general is verry high land, no timber back a little Scatering along the Shore on the points &C. high bluffs & clifts along the Shores. Some pine in the drift wood along the Shores. we are a little South of the Mandans but have had cold weather as yet. it must of course be a healthy country. we all enjoy good health as yet. our Interpreter wounded a cabberee or antelope this evening.

1. Ordway remained with Silas Goodrich, Charbonneau, and Sacagawea, according to Clark. Lewis's list adds York, whose presence Ordway confirms.
2. The upper portage camp, where they remained until July 12.

June 23rd Sunday 1805. a cloudy morning. the wind from East. a light Sprinkling of rain. in the afternoon one of the hunters[1] came to the lower camp from the medicine River. he informed us that George Shannon left them the Same day they Stearted from this, & they could not account where he went. The other 2 hunters[2] had killed 16 buffalow and 5 Deer but no Elk. they had Dryed considerable of the buffalow meat at their Camp. in the evening Capt. Clark & party returned to the lower Camp, they informed us that they had Some difficulty. the truck wheels, or Some part of them broke Several times &.C. the tongue broke near the upper Camp & they were obledged to leave it and formed the Camp about 3 miles above the Medicine River. Capt. Clark Straightned the road considerable from that he went on yesterday. they took 2 canoes up the hill from the creek this evening. the men mended their mockisons with double Soles to Save their feet from the prickley pear (which abound in the plains) and the hard ground in many places is So hard as to hurt our feet verry much. the emence numbers of buffalow after the last rain has trod the flat places in Such a manner as to leave them uneaven, and dryed as hard as frozen Ground. the men all much fatigued this evening &C. the Distance Staked out for the portage is 18¼ miles from the lower Camp or lower rapid.

1. Reubin Field.
2. Field and Drouillard.

June 24th Monday 1805. a cloudy morning. all hands rose eairly. had halled the remaining canoe out of the water to dry. we divided the baggage in to 3 percels, one of which the party took on their backs and one waggon with truck wheels, to the canoes 3 miles in advance loaded and proceeded on with 2 canoes being in 2 parties. put the baggage in to the canoes & went on verry well to the creek called willow creek.[1] one of the waggon tongues broke which detained us a Short time. then proceeded on towards evening when we got within about three miles of the upper Camp, a volent Shower arose from the N. W. hard thunder caught us in a verry hard rain So that in a fiew minutes the ground was covered with water. So that we got a hearty drink of water in the holes & puddles &.C. the rain continued about half an hour, at dusk we arived at the upper Camp all wet and much fatigued. Capt. Lewis revived us with a dram. we found Shamnon their who had been up the medicine River hunting. he had killed 3 buffalow 8 Deer several antelopes but no Elk. the wind was considerable assistance to us in the course of the day, as we were drawing the canoes the wind being Sufficently hard at times to move the canoe on the Trucks. this is Saleing on dry land in everry Since of the word,

1. Or Willow Run, now Box Elder Creek, Cascade County, Montana.

Tuesday 25th June 1805. a cloudy morning. we Set out with the 2 truck waggons and returned back to the lower Camp for another load. took 2 canoes up the hill on the high plains the day proved pleasant and warm the men much fatigued. we Saw large gangs of buffalow and antelopes to day. we got our loads ready for a Start in the morning. below the falls the plains are inferior in point of Soil to those below, more Stones on the Sides of the hills, grass but a fiew Inches long or high and but a fiew flowers in the plains. Great quanties of choke cherryes Goose berrys red & yallow berrys & red purple currents on the Edges of the water. we catch great quantitites of Trout and a kind of muttel [mussel] flat backs and a Soft fish resembling Shad.[1] caught but fiew cat fish this Season. Sergt. Pryor Sick the party amused themselves dancing untill 10 oClock all in cheerfulness and good humour. we tied up all the baggage ready for an eairly Steart in the morning—

1. The mussels could be from either the family Margaritanidae or Unionidae. "Flat backs" are unknown, but perhaps suckers, of the family Catostomidae. Much of this entry is from Clark and many of the sergeant's entries during the portage period are taken from the captains' journals.

June 26th Wednesday 1805. Some rain last night. this morning cloudy. we Set out eairly with our loads to the Canoes consisting of pearched meal pork powder lead axes tools Bisquit and portable Soup.[1] we put it in the canoes and proceeded on verry well to willow creek, where we halted to cook & then proceeded on The day proved fair. we Saw great numbers of buffalow in the plains in every direction considerable of the plains as far as our Eyes could extend appear to be black with buffalow. Some antelopes and Deer also wolves Whitehouse took Sick this evening a little before we got to the upper Camp. we arived at the u. camp a little before night. the men went with Capt. Lewis on a Small Island below the Camp to hunt for a white bear which had been about the Camp the night before and cut Some meat near the tents &C.

1. Lewis purchased this soup in Philadelphia; it may have been kept in the form of dry powder or as a thick liquid. It was a staple army ration of the time.

June 27th 1805, Thursday a fair warm morning. Whitehouse Some better. a heavey dew last night. I and three more of the party Set off eairly to return by the way of the falls. the men Stearted with the truck waggons at the Same time. I passed Some Indian Camps above medicine River on the Shore Lard. Side Saw a large gang of buffalow out of which I killed a cow and calf, and went on passed the upper falls which is a great catteract and look remarkable. I Set and looked at them a few minutes and went on untill I came to the Spring which was the finest tasted water I ever Saw and the largest fountain which up through a ledge of rocks near the River and forces its way up about 10 feet for Some distance around then forms a fall in to the River. it is clear as a cristal I could have Seen to the bottom of the fountain to pick up a pin. the water cold and pure. the Rocks green which the water run over. proceeded on about noon we killed a fat Bull and took out the hump and went down a Steep hill to git to water where we broiled the hump and eat a hearty meal of it. went on passed the lower high falls which is the highest known except the falls of Neagra. all these fall measured and added together is 300 60 [360] odd feet in hight and is a great Site to See them. I proceeded on to the mouth of willow Creek. a hard Shower of rain and hail came on of a Sudden So I got under a Shelving rock on one Side of the creek where a kept dry through the hardest of it. hard thunder. large hail the creek rose So high in a fiew minutes that I had to move from the dry place and proceeded on. the wind blew So high that the hail cut verry hard against me and I could hardly keep my feet. the rain has made it So muddy and Slipperry, but we arived at the lower Camp a little before night the party had arived a little before, with the truck wheels look likely for more rain So I and one man more went and Slept in the carsh or hole which was dug to deposit Some baggage in which we intend to leave. cloudy all night. Some buffalow came down the River dead.

June 28th Friday 1805. a fair morning. wind from the South we Set out with the remaining canoe and baggage took it to the top of the hill three miles. the men who remained at the camp was employed carrying those things we intend to deposite to the whole or *carsh.* Some repairing one of the trucks &C. the water is riseing and of a redish brown cholour. after covering the carshe or whole, and loading the 2 carriages with the remaining part of the Baggage, we all Set out passing red creek[1] which had rose a little and the water nearly red and bad tasteed. we ascended the hill to the place the canoe lay with great labour, at the canoe at which place we left some boxes & kegs of pork & flower for another load, and proceeded on with the canoe and what baggage we could draw on the wheels to willow run 6 miles where we camped. this run nearly dry some water remaining in wholes. Soon after we halted, we had a Shower and at dark we experienced a most dreedful wind from off the Snow Mountains to the S. W.[2] accompanied with rain which lasted nearly all night. Capt. Clark refreshed the men with a dram. killed 2 buffalow great numbrs. about this run

1. An alternate name for the party's Portage Creek, modern Belt Creek, Chouteau and Cascade counties, Montana.
2. Probably the Lewis Range of the Rockies.

June 29th Satturday 1805. a little rain verry eairly this morning after clear & warm we find that the prarie is So wet as to render it impossable to pass on to the end of the portage, So. Capt Clark Sent all back except one man to take care of the baggage after the remainder which was left yesterday on the hill. Capt. Clark Set out to go to the falls at the Same time his Servant Intrepter and Squaw accompanied them. I went with the p[arty] for the remainder of the baggage. we got all and was returning. Saw a black cloud rise in the west which we looked for emediate rain we made all the haste possable but had not got half way before the Shower met us and our hind extletree broke in too we were obledged to leave the load Standing and ran in great confusion to Camp the hail being So large and the wind So high and violent in the plains, and we being naked we were much bruuzed by the large hail. Some nearly killed one knocked down three times, and others without hats or any thing about their heads bleading and complained verry much. Soon after we had got all Safe to the run cleared off. Capt. Clark & them that went with him returned Capt. Clark informed us that when he Saw the Shower comming he looked out for Some Shelter about ¼ of a mile above the falls he observed a deep reveen in which was Shelving rocks under which they took Shelter near the river and placed their and Compass &C &C. under a Shelving rock in a place verry secure from rain the first Shower was moderate to them then a torrent of rain fell and hail violent than they ever Saw before. the rain fell like one voley of water falling from the heavens and gave them time only to git out of the way of a torrent of water, which was poreing down the hill with amence force tareing everry thing before it, takeing with it large rocks and mud. Capt Clark took his gun and Shot pouch in his left hand and with his right he Scrambled up the hill pushing the Intrepters wife who had hir child in hir arms. the intrepter himself makeing attempts to pull up his wife by the hand much Scared and narely without motion, at length reached the top of the hill Safe, where Capt. Clark found his Servant york who was in Search of them greatly agitated, for their well fare Capt. Clark informed me when he went in to the revene it was a flat dry rock, but before he got out of it, it was up to his waist so he wet his watch, lost the large *Compass*, an elegant fusee, tommahawk, an *Humbrello* Shot pouch & horn with powder and ball mockinsons and the woman lost hir childs Cloaths & bear bedding &C. &.C.— The Compass is a Seerious loss, as we have no other large one. the plains are So wet that we could doe nothing this evening. we got revived with a dram of grog and got some warm Soup and took our rest.

June 30th Sunday 1805. a fair morning. we went after the remaining Baggage left in the plains. 2 men went to the falls to look for the Compass &.C. 2 men went out to hunt. about 4 oClock the hunters came in loaded with fat meat the men returned with the baggage ecty [etc.?] 4 men Set at makeing axtletrees and repair the carriages &C. this run has fallen a little. last evening it was up to a mans waist at the crossing place where it was dry before the Showers, and verry riley and bad tasted. Some took the Baggage up the hill the 2 men in Search of the articles lost yesterday returned and brought the Compass which they found in the mud and Stones near the mouth of the revene. no other articles found. one man killed an Elk at 12 oClock we Set out with a load to the 6 mile Stake and return this evening. we intend takeing the remainder through to the upper Camp tomorrow if the prarie will permit. at 3 oClock we had a Storm of wind from S. W. after which a fair evening great numbers of buffalow in everry direction I think 10000 may be Seen at one view

July 1st Monday 1805. we Set out eairly this morning with the remaining loads and proceeded on verry well to Capt. Lewiss Camp where we arived at 3 oClock the day warm and party much fatigued found Capt. Lewis and party all employed in fitting the Iron boat &C the wind hard from the S. W. one man verry unwell. his legs & thighs broke out and Swelled. the hail which fell at Capt. Lewis Camp was 7 Inches in Surcunference and weighed 3 ounces. fortinately for us it was not so large in the plains where we was if it had we Should most certainly fallen victims to its rage as the most of the men were without hats or any thing on their heads and mostly naked. the hunters at the upper Camp killed 3 White bear one large the fore feet of which measured 9 Inches across. the head [hind] feet 11¼ Inches long and 7 Inches wide. a bear nearly catching Joseph Fields chased him in to the water. bear about the Camp everry night, and Seen on the Island in the day.

July 2nd Tuesday 1805. Some rain at day light this morning after which a fair morning we Set out eairly with the truck waggons for the kegs and boxes &C. left at the Six mile Stake. the men at camp Set at gitting timber &C for the Boat Musquetoes verry troublesome to day. we went to the 6 mile Stake and got the remander of our loading &C returned back. Saw buffalow as usal one hunter killed 3 buffalow and one antelope in a fiew min[utes] we arived at Camp about 2 oClock and rejoiced that we have got through Such a laborious & fatiguing portage The day warm the men put their fire arms in good order and towards evening the most of the hunters with the 2 Captains went over on an Island to hunt bear they killed one and Saved the Skin and Greese. the Musquetoes troublesome this evening.—

July 3rd Wednesday 1805. a clear pleasant warm morning. Sergt. Gass and 4 men[1] Set out to go down the River and take a view of the falls and Big Spring &.C. the men at Camp employed Some at makeing tar or pitch for the Boat others puting the leather on it &C. we over halled the Baggage and killed a large curious kind of a rat[2] with hair on his tail. the mice are pleanty also. light Sprinklings of rain in the afternoon. we fixed Scaffels and put our Baggs &C from the ground, & a little more from the rats & mice &C. Some men Sowing the leather on the Iron boat. the men not other ways directed are dressing Skins to make themselves mockinsons as they have wore them all out in the plains one pair of good mockins will not last more than about 2 days. will ware holes in them the first day and patch them for the next.— George Drewyer one of Capt. Lewis hunters at the upper Camp killed 2 large handsom otter and three beaver. 2 men went out a short distance that evening and killed a fat buffalow. Some men out for meat &.C. the 2 men returned from the falls and had killed 6 buffalow, and Saved only the tongues, & brains for to dress Skins. we got the leather on the Iron boat in 8 seperate Sections & put them in the water to Sook. 2 men attempting to burn a Small tar kill.

1. Gass says one man, apparently Hugh McNeal. Whitehouse counts two others. Lewis notes "several others."

2. Probably the pack rat, or bushy-tailed woodrat, *Neotoma cinerea,* noted by Lewis on July 2.

July 4th Thursday 1805. a beautiful clear pleasant warm morning. the most of the men employed putting the sections of the Iron boat together &C. one of the hunters went on bear Island a Short time and killed an Elk and a beaver. we Saved the Skins and Some of the meat. we finished puting the Iron boat together and turned hir on one side to dry. it being the 4th of Independence we drank the last of our ardent Spirits except a little reserved for Sickness. the fiddle put in order and the party amused themselves dancing all the evening untill about 10 oClock in a Sivel & jovil manner. late in the evening we had a light Shower of rain but did not last long.—

July 5th Friday 1805. a clear pleasant morning. 3 men Set out to go down to See the falls &C. a gang of buffalow Seen on the hills Some distance from Camp. Capt Clark and 12 men went out to attempt to kill Some of them but we could not git near them before they Smelled us and ran off Capt. Clark and Some of the men then returned to Camp the rest went after another gangue towards the South Mountain. towards evening they all came in had killed 3 buffalow 4 miles from this. they brought in Some meat and Skins. the 3 men returned fr[om] the falls & had killed Several buffalow might have killed hundreds if they had wished where they were pened under high clifts of rocks at the falls. they went So close among them as to reach them with the muzzle of their guns, &.C. they brought home Several tongues & Some brains, but had not time to take care of their meat & Skins &C—

July 6th Saturday 1805. verry hard Showers of rain and hail through the course of last night, hard Thunder & lightning, at day light this morning a hard Shower came up of a Sudden attended with high wind, & large hail one of the men Saved a Small tin kittle full of the hail which did not all disolve through the day. the morning cloudy. 4 men dispached with 2 canoes to go down to the head of the falls in order to kill buffalow & git Skins to cover our crafts & meat to dry &.C. Some men employed finishing the Iron boat &.C. a part of the day clear. light Showers of rain in the afternoon. Some men dressing Skins to make themselves cloaths &.C. the wind high from the west. this evening the hunters did not return this evening (Caught a fiew Small fish).

July 7th Sunday 1805. a clear pleasant morning. one man caught a beaver last night. two hunters Set out across the river eairly in order to hunt Elk for 1 or 2 Skins &C. we finished off the Iron boat and put hir up in an open place to dry &C. the day warm. in the afternoon Some Thunder the musquetoes troublesome at this Camp a light Shower of rain. about 4 oClock the hunters returned. had killed Several buffalow and buffalow calfs one Elk and Several wolves. they brought in the Skins which will answer to cover our crafts &C. the 2 hunters returned from the other Shore. had killed 4 Deer & one antelope.—

July 8th Monday 1805. a clear pleasant morning one man went across the river a hunting eairly this morning about 9 oClock A. M. Capt. Clark and all the men that could be Spared from Camp Set out to go down the river a hunting down past the falls and big Spring &.C. the men that remained in Camp employed in paying[1] over the outside of the Iron boat with coal Tallow and base wax[2] in Stead of pitch. we went about 6 miles through the plains then went to the big Spring. Capt. Clark measured the width of t[he] River at the Spring and middle falls and found it to be [*blank*] yards wide at the Spring and [*blank*] yards wide at the middle falls. in the afternoon we all returned to Camp had killed Several buffalow one of which was fat. killed 1 or 2 antelopes and a curious yallow fox[3] and Several rattle Snakes. towards evening the hunter returned from across the river had killed one buck Deer and a buck antelope &C. Some Thunder and light Showers this afternoon The River falling. The Musquetoes troublesome.

1. In the nautical sense meaning to coat with tar, pitch, and the like.
2. Beeswax.
3. Apparently the swift fox, *Vulpes velox* (see Lewis's entry for this day).

July 9th Tuesday 1805. a beautiful pleasant morning. the Island near the Camp is covered with black birds.[1] we put the Iron boat which we covered with green hides in to the water. Corked Some of the canoes in order to git in readiness to depart from this place in the afternoon we loaded the 6 canoes but did not load the Iron boat as it leaked considerable Soo[n] after we got the canoes loaded Thunder and high wind came on So that we had to unload again. our officers concludes for to leave & burry the Iron boat, as we cannot git tar or pitch to pay the over the out Side of the Skins. the coal Tallow & bease wax would not stick to the hides as they were Shaved the time is So far expended that they did not think proper to try any more experiments with it. So we Sank hir in the water So that She might be the easier took to peaces tomorrow. our officers conclude to build 2 canoes more So that we can carry all our baggage without the Iron boat. about 10 men got ready to up the river to build 2 canoes.—

1. Perhaps rusty blackbird, *Euphogus carolinus*, or Brewer's blackbird, *E. cyanocephalus*. The party also apparently called the common grackle, *Quisculus quisculus*, a blackbird.

July 10th Wednesday 1805. a clear morning. we took the Iron boat out of the River and loaded 4 canoes one of which was the men baggage & tools who were going to make canoes. we Set out eairly, with the canoes. Capt. Clark and about 10 men Set out to go by land after we Set them over the river. it is only about 5 miles by land to the bottom where they git the timber for the canoes and it is about 20 miles round by water.[1] we proceeded on with the canoes 5 or 6 miles then the wind arose So high that we were obledged to lay by untill towards evening. we passed 2 Islands covered with cotton and box elder[2] also choak cherrys & yallow currents which are now ripe. halted near a village of bearking Squerrells. one of the hunters killed one of them on the N. S. late in the afternoon the wind abated a little So we proceeded on within about 3 miles of the upper Camp and halted for the night in a grove of cottonwood high banks of Sand along this Shore on N. S. we killed a large rattle Snake near our Camp.—

1. Clark and party remained at this camp until July 15 making canoes; it is in Cascade County, Montana, on the north side of the Missouri, a few miles east of Ulm. Ordway led another group to help with the baggage to this point.

2. Boxelder, *Acer negundo* L.

July 11th Thursday 1805. a clear morning. the wind verry high from the N. W. which oblidged us to lay at Camp untill late in the afternoon, except the Canoe which had the baggage and tools. they went on to Camp 2 men went by land to the Camp & got Some meat. towards evening the wind abated So that we went on and arived at Capt. Clarks Camp at a Sunset, and unloaded. the hunters had killed 2 fat buffalow and Several Deer. we took on board Some fat meat and 4 of us Set out with 3 canoes to return back to the other Camp for the remainder of the baggage &.C. we floated about 8 miles and the wind rose So high that drove us to Shore So we landed untill morning. (*Capt.* Clark and party had got 2 fine trees cut for 2 canoes & ready to dig out.[)]

July 12th Friday 1805. a clear morning. the wind as usal. we proceeded on down the wind rose So high that one canoe filled with water the other 2 took in water the waves high but with difficulty we got down to

Camp about noon the men at Camp had killed 2 buffalow and put the Irons of the Iron boat and other articles in the ground. Several men had Set out this morning for to join Capt. Clarks party. we Scaffelled up what meat we had to dry. the wind continues verry high all day.—

July 13th Saturday 1805. clear and calm this morning. we loaded the canoes eairly and Set out with all the remainder of our baggage for the upper Camp.[1] Capt. Lewis a Sick man[2] & our Intrepters wife went across by land which is only about 6 miles distant by land and 20 by water we proceeded on verry well with the canoes about 5 miles. the wind rose so high that 2 of the canoes took water. it oblidged us to halt and dry our baggage. the wind continued untill towards evening. then abated a little and we proceeded on about 7 miles and Camped. the Musquetoes verry troublesome in the evening.

1. Clark's canoe-making camp, not the camp at White Bear Islands, which they are now abandoning.
2. Lepage.

July 14th Sunday 1805. The morning clear and pleasant. we Set out eairly and proceeded on very well. passed 3 Islands covered with timber and arived at the upper Camp about noon. Capt. Clark and party at Camp had got the 2 large canoes nearly done. we unloaded the canoes, and put the large niew one in the River about 4 oClock P. M. we expencerenced a Small Shower of rain. warm the Musquetoes verry troublesome we put the other niew canoe in to the River and make ready to leave this tomorrow. we have considerable of fat buffalow meat dryed, which the hunters killed at or near this Camp. the weeds and Grass in this bottom is as high as a mans knees but the Grass on the high plains & praries is not more than 3 Inches high no time in this Season.

Chapter Forty-Five

Across the Rockies

July 15–October 10, 1805

July 15th Monday 1805. rained the greater part of last night. a clear morning. the wind high from the N. W. we loaded the 8 Canoes and could hardly find room in them for all our baggage about 10 oClock A. M. we Set out with the 8 canoes and all our baggage and proceeded on verry well. passed a large creek or Small River[1] on the S. Side. passed Several Islands covered with cotton timber. fine pleasant bottoms & plains on each Side of the river. the current verry gentle & river Smoth Since we left the falls. our officers and a hunter[2] who walked on Shore killed two Elk and 2 Deer also an otter. we Came about 26 miles by water to day and Camped on the N. S. of the River.—

1. Smith River, named by the party in honor of Robert Smith, Jefferson's secretary of the navy, meets the Missouri River in Cascade County, Montana.
2. The hunter was Drouillard.

July 16th Tuesday 1805. a clear pleasant morning. I went about 4 miles back down the River after an axe forgot last evening. the party proceeded on with the canoes. we passed a round hill on N. S. which at a distance look like a large fort or fortifycation. so we called it fort mountain.[1] passed a large creek on S. S.[2] Saw large Indian Camps on N. S. back of the bottoms in the edge of the Smooth plains. the hunters killed 2 buffalow. I Saw verry large gangs of buffalow on the plains under the rockey mountains, which we are now approaching. in the afternoon I joined the party. Capt. Lewis and 2 men was gone on a head. the current Swift towards evening we Came

20 miles this day and Camped near the entrence of the Rocky Mountain, which appear verry high & rocky. Some pine &C.

1. Mentioned by Lewis the previous day; it is Square Butte, south of the town of Fort Shaw, Cascade County, Montana.

2. Bird Creek, Cascade County; not mentioned by the captains.

July 17th Wednesday 1805. Capt. Lewis and the two men Stayed out all last night. a clear morning we Set out at Sunrise & proceeded on about 4 miles. Came to a verry bad rapid[1] where we found Capt. Lewis & the 2 men. the Mountains make close to the River on each Side. we left Some articles and doubled maned the canoes and them all over Safe which was about half a mile long, & roled white over the rocks, but by the assistance of the towing lines we got up all the canoes without Injury Sent back for the other articles. passed a large Spring jest above the rapids which heads about half a mile above or back under the mountain on Lard. Side. proceeded on. the mountains make close to the River & verry steep high pricipicies about 700 feet from the Surface of the water perpinticular & a Solid rock. Some Spots of pine and balsam fir[2] timbers & narrow bottoms on the points and high grass &C. Some willow & currents[3] of different kinds. the current Swift. the River about 100 yards wide. we Came 11 miles this day and Camped on the Starbord Side in a narrow bottom. a little cotton timber—[4]

1. Probably the later Half-Breed, or Lone Pine, Rapids, Cascade County, Montana.

2. The pine is ponderosa pine, and the balsam fir for this region is Douglas fir, *Pseudotsuga menziesii* (Mirb.) Franco.

3. The willow could be any of a number of species. Lewis discusses the currants and berries of the region in his entry for this day.

4. In this region the cottonwood species begins to shift from the eastern cottonwood, *Populus deltoides,* to the western variety, *P. angustifolia.*

July 18th Thursday 1805. a clear pleasant morning. we Saw Mountain Sheep or Ibex on the top of a high Steep pricipice. they ran along the rocks where it was all most perpentickelier and about 200 feet from the Surface of the water. we set out at sun rise and proceeded on about 3 miles passed the mouth of a river[1] on the N. S. about 100 yards wide at its mouth. one mile further Capt. Clark killed an Elk. Saw Several others. we Saw a flock of mountain Rams on the Side of a hill which had large horns. Capt. Clark his Servant and 2 other men[2] Set out to go 1 or 2 days march a head to make discoverys &.C. we proceeded on verry well with the canoes. towards evening we passed a River[3] which came in on N. S. about 60 yards wide. the mountains continues but not So high as yesterday. we Came 19½ miles and Camped in a narrow bottom on the Larbord Side considerable of fine flax in this bottom now going to Seed. we found a Deer Skin and Some meat which Capt. Clark had killed.

1. Dearborn River, named by Lewis and Clark for Jefferson's secretary of war, Henry Dearborn, forms the boundary between Cascade and Lewis and Clark counties, Montana, for a short distance above its mouth.

2. Clark was joined by York, Joseph Field, and Potts.

3. Named Ordway's Creek by the party, it is Little Prickly Pear Creek, Lewis and Clark County.

July 19th Friday 1805. a clear pleasant morning. we Set out as usal and proceeded on. Capt. Lewis and one hunter walked on Shore & Shortly killed a cabberee or antelope we took on board the Skin and some of the meat. the current Swift. the Mountains high. Some Spots of pine ceeder, and bolsom-fir trees &C. one of the men killed an otter with a Socket pole they are pleanty &C. Some beaver also along these mountains. passed the mouth of a Small River[1] on the South Side. in the afternoon we passed through a verry high part of the Mountain, which is Steep on each Side & about 6 or 700 feet perpinticular up from the Surface of the water & a Solid rock this curious looking place we call the gates of the Rocky Mountains.[2] Several fine Springs Issues from under the clifts or in md. near the edge of the River. about one oClock P. M. we had a Thunder Shower which lasted about one hour a little hail attended it. Saw Some Spots of pine Spruce ceeder and bolsom fer timber on the Sides of the Mon. and in the vallies &C. we Came 19 miles this day through verry rapid water & Camped on a narrow bottom on the Lard. Side.

1. Willow Creek, Lewis and Clark County, Montana.

2. Today's Gates of the Mountains stretches for about six miles between Holter and Hauser dams in Lewis and Clark County, still retaining the name Lewis gave it.

July 20th Saturday 1805. a clear morning we Set out as usal and proceeded on. about 8 oClock A M we Came to a lower part of the Mountain. one of the hunters killed an Elk in a bottom on L. S. we find pleanty of ripe currents of different kinds red yallow and black. the black is the most palatable.[1] Some of the hunters find an excelent berry which is called Servis berrys.[2] we found the Skin of an Elk & a note which Capt. [Clark] had left for us, letting us know that he would wait our arival after he got over the Mountain. passed a Small creek[3] on the L. S. about 2 oC. P. M. we got through this range of Mon. Saw another range Some distance off on our course. Saw a Smoak in the valley between. we cannot determine whether is was made by the natives or Capt. Clark. passed a level Smooth plain in the valley. Some timber Scatering along the River. Came 15 miles this day and Camped at a Spring on the L. S. the prickley pears are So thick we scarsely could find room to camp without being on them.—

1. Ordway's taste is in agreement with Lewis's for the golden currant.
2. Serviceberry, *Amelanchier alnifolia* Nutt.
3. Beaver Creek, Lewis and Clark County, Montana.

July 21st Sunday 1805. a clear morning. we Set out as usal and proceeded on. Saw a nomber of large Swans Some of the men killed two of them. passed a Small creek on the Lard. Side and one on the Starbord Side.[1] the grass in the valley and on the hills look dry and pearched up. passed a hill & clifts of rocks in the afternoon the River divides in many channels and full of Islands and Spreads about a mile wide. the current Swift our hunter on Shore killed a deer. we Came 15½ miles this day and Camped on a Smooth plain on the Larbord Side. the party in general are much fatigued.—

1. Trout Creek (not mentioned by Lewis and Clark) and Spokane Creek, respectively, Lewis and Clark County, Montana. This is a very confused day in the captains' journals and on the maps. See their entries of this day.

July 22nd Monday 1805. a clear morning. we Set out as usal and proceeded on passed large Islands mostly covered with grass Some fiew trees. the currents [currants] Still abound. Some of the canoes I being one went about 5 miles behind an Island through a verry narrow crooked channel. these large Islands are mostly level Smooth plain. one of the hunters killed a deer. about 2 oC. P. m. we halted to dine on the N or Stard. Side then went on Capt. Lewis forgot his Thurmometer where we dined I went back for it. it Stood in the heat of the day at 80 degrees abo. O, which has only been up to that point but once before this Season as yet. we went on took a narrow channel behind Some Islands and at Camping time I came out a head of the party nearly a mile, then went down to Camp.[1] Capt. Clark had joined them, and his men who were with him. they had Seen a great deal of Indian sign the fire we saw was made by the natives. perhaps they were alarmed by our Shooting So at the game and moved off. our Intrepters wife tells us that She knows the country along the River up to hir nation, or the 3 forks.[2] we are now 166 miles from the falls of the M. Came 17 miles of it to day.—

1. A few miles upstream from Beaver Creek, Broadwater County, Montana; the site is now under Canyon Ferry Lake.

2. Meaning the Three Forks of the Missouri River, Gallatin County, Montana.

July 23rd Tuesday 1805. Capt. Clark and 3 men[1] Set out again in order to go on to the 3 forks of the River expecting to find the Snake nation at that place. a little cloudy. the Musquetoes verry troublesome. we proceeded on as usal. passed level Smooth plains on each side. passd. a Small creek[2] on L. Side. passed a nomber of Islands. considerable of good flax now fit to pull in the praries & bottoms. the Thissels pleanty.[3] the pine continues on the Sides of the hills. our hunter who Stayed out last night joined us at noon had killed Several deer. we dryed Some articles which got wet in the canoes. we hoisted up our flags expecting the natives would See them & know the meaning of them. the current verry Swift. we Came 24 miles this day & Camped on the Larbord Side. we find pleanty of wild Inions or what Some calls leeks, or garlick.[4] we gethered a quantity of them to eat—

1. Actually four men: Joseph and Reubin Field, Frazer, and Charbonneau.

2. Whitehouse's Creek, after Joseph Whitehouse of the party, now Duck, or Gurnett, Creek, Broadwater County, Montana.

3. Probably elk thistle, *Cirsium foliosum* (Hook.) DC.
4. Possibly *Allium brevistylum* A. Wats.

July 24th Wednesday 1805. a clear pleasant morning we Set out at Sun rise and proceeded on. the current Swift. we found a goat or antelopes Skin which Capt. Clark killed and left for us— we passed a redish clift of rocks[1] on Stard Side in the aftrernoon we passed a large plain on the Stard Side, the prickley pears abound on it Saw otter and beaver in great abundance &C. the Swift water continues Some bad rapids which it is with difficulty we passed over them. Saw many different kinds of Snakes along the Shores. we Came 19½ miles this day and Camped[2] on the Stard. Side. one deer killed to day. a white bear Seen. considerable of Elk Sign &C.

1. The rocks are shale, formerly a lateritic soil horizon.
2. About seven miles north of Toston, Broadwater County, Montana.

July 25th Thursday 1805. a clear morning. we Set out as usal and proceeded on. Saw a large white bear on an Island. we Saw a flock of goats or antelopes one of the hunters killed one of them. we passed a Camp where Capt. Clark had Stayed all night.[1] we discover Mountains a head which have Spots of Snow on them. passed a large dry plain on S. Side, in the afternoon we passed high rough rocky hills & clifts of rocks. at the entrence we found bad rapids, and Shallow rocks sticking up all the way across. Saw excelent Springs along the Shore on Larbord Side. Saw Some excelent Springs, which ran from under the clifts of rocks. Came 16 miles this day and Camped on the Stard. Side.[2] our hunter killed one goose which was all the game killed to day.—

1. Clark's camp of the July 23, according to Lewis, near Toston, Broadwater County, Montana.
2. Above Toston Dam, Broadwater County. The camp is misdated July 24 on *Atlas* map 64.

July 26th Friday 1805. a clear morning. we Set out as usal and proceeded on. the current verry Swift. Saw Several Springs along the Shore. one of the party killed a large beaver. pleanty of those animels along the

Islands and Shores. Saw Some pine & ceeder timber also Some cotton timber passed clifts of rocks on each Side of the River the hills make off lower. we can discover high mountains a head, with Snow on them. The River wide and full of Islands. passed over Several bad rapids. our hunter on Shore killed 4 deer. we found an Indians bow in a plain on L. S. took on board a deer Skin which Capt. Clark had left on Shore for us. also a note letting us know that he had Seen no Indians, but had Seen fresh Sign of horses &C. we Came 19 miles this day, and Camped on the Lard. Side.[1] the party found Servis berrys to day &C.

1. The camp is misdated July 25 on *Atlas* map 64; it is in Gallatin County, Montana, at the landmark of Eagle Rock, a few miles from the mouth of the Gallatin River.

July 27th Saturday 1805. a clear morning. we Set off as usal and proceeded on. the current Swift as usal. passed clifts of rocks. villages of little birds[1] under the Shelveing rocks. the hills not So high as below. the currents abound along the Shores. about 9 oClock we arived at the three forks of the Missourie,[2] which is in open view of the high Mountains covered in Some places with Snow Saw large flocks of Mountain Sheep or Ibex and antelopes &C. on the plain. we passed the South & west forks, and Camped at an old Indian Camp on the point a Short distance up the North fork. this is a handsom pleasant plain considerable of cotton timber about the points of the forks. we unloaded the canoes. Several men went out in the bottoms to hunt. Capt. Clark joined us and the men who were with him. he informed us that he had been about 40 miles up the west fork and over to the North fork and came down that to the forks. they had killed several deer antelopes and a cub bear. Capt. Clark verry unwell. he had Seen a large elagant horse in the plains which appeared to be verry wild. the hunters killed Several or 6 deer, and 3 otter and a musk rat. we had a Shower of rain this afternoon. came 7 mls. to day, which brought us to this Camp where we intend to rest a day or two. we expected to have found the Snake nation of Indians at this place, but as we expect they are further up the River, or perhaps they are gone over the mountains to the Columbian River[3] on the other Side to fish &C. this is the place where our Intrepters wife was taken prisoner by the Grossvauntaus, about 4 years ago, &C.[4]

1. Bank swallow.

2. The Three Forks of the Missouri, Gallatin County, Montana, where the party remained until July 30. The rivers still bear the names given them by Lewis and Clark. They are the Gallatin (south fork), after Albert Gallatin, Madison (west fork), for James Madison, and Jefferson (north fork), for the president.

3. Ordway means a branch of the Columbia River, in this case the Lemhi River. He uses the term "Columbian River" very broadly in the next few weeks.

4. The best evidence is that Sacagawea was captured by Hidatsa (*Gros Ventres*) raiders in about 1800 in this area.

July 28th Sunday 1805. a foggy morning, but clear after. Several men went out a hunting. we put out the baggage to air. Capt. Clark Sick. we built a bower for his comfort. the party though much fatigued are engaged dressing Skins to make themselves cloaths and mockasons &C. towards evening the hunters all returned had killed 7 or 8 deer and 2 Elk. Some of the buck deer were fat. one of the hunters who had been up the South fork a Short distance, and found it not so large as the West & N. forks. we conclude to proceede up the North fork to the Mountains. towards evening we had a fine Shower of rain Some Thunder attended it which cooled the air verry much. the men at Camp all employed dressing their Skins &C.— rushes[1] along here.

1. Sandrush or scouring rush, *Equisetum hyemale* L.

July 29th Monday 1805. a clear pleasant morning. Several men went out eairly a hunting we conclude to lay at this Camp all day &C. Capt. Clark a little better. the day warm. the wind from the East. The Latitude at this place is 45° 22m 34s 5/10ths North. the width of the three Rivers at the forks we alow the North fork to be about 60 yds. wide the middle fork about the Same the South forks not So wide nor large. all appear rapid but not verry deep. towards evening the hunters returned had killed 2 or 3 fat bucks deer, and caught a curious redish couloured long leged crain[1] which they brought in a live, and it ran about the Camp Some time &C.

1. Sandhill crane, *Grus canadensis.*

July 30th Tuesday 1805. a fine pleasant morning. we loaded all the canoes eairly and Set out about 9 oClock A. M. and proceeded on up the North fork Capt. Lewis and Several Inveleeds walked on Shore. we passed large bottoms covered with cotten timber & thick brush willow &C. the River crooked rapid and full of Islands &C. a bundance of beaver & beaver dams along these bottoms. thee currents of different kinds abound in these bottoms. we dined at a Camp where the snake Indians had been camped 4 years ago, and was actacted by the Gross vauntaus. 2 or three of the Snake nation was killed, and Several Squaws taken prisoners our Intrepters wife was one of them. She tells us that She was taken in the middle of the River as She was crossing at a Shole place to make hir ascape. the rest all mounted their horses and cleared themselves as they do not wish to fite, neither were they Strong enofe for the Grossvauntaus. one of the hunters on Shore killed a Deer. we peroceded on passed a verry large plain or prarie on L. S. considerable of fine good flax on it, also wild onions or garlick. passed high land on S. Side we Came 13½ miles this day and Camped on the Stard. Side[1] Capt. Lewis did not join us this evening. these bottoms along the River are low and many beaver dams which causes ponds in many places &C.—

1. Just below the entrance of Willow Creek, the party's Philosophy River, Jefferson County, Montana.

July 31st Wednesday 1805. Capt. Lewis Stayed out all last night. a fine morning. we Set off at Sunrise and proceeded on as usal. the current Swift. about 8 oClock A. M. we came up with Capt. Lewis where he Camped all last night. proceeded on passed the mouth of a creek[1] on the Lard. Side, the water of which is of a redish coulour, and is damed up in many places by the beaver, and runs through a beautiful prarie and bottom of Small timber. the beaver verry pleanty along these bottoms. the River filled with Islands. passed a large plain or prarie on L. S. covered with fine grass Tanzey flax and thissels, wild onions or garlick &.C. considerable of cotton timber along the River bottoms, but no timber back in the country. the hills begin to make near the River on each Sides. we dined under a handsom Shady grove of cotton timber under the hills of the Mountains[2] to our left which has heaps of Snow on the top & sides of it. Capt. Clark Saw a Mountain Sheep thro. glass on a hill towards the mo. the Game is now gitting Scarse. We are now with out fresh meat which is very uncommon to us, for we have generally had double as much as we could eat. the day very warm we proceeded on passed clifts of rocks and high wales &.C. Some pine[3] and ceeder timber along the hill Sides. Some of the hills nearly a Solid rock. we Came 17¾ miles and Camped on a Small Island on the Lard. Side. our hunter on Shore wounded a White bear, but did not kill it dead.

1. Willow Creek, Jefferson County, Montana.
2. Tobacco Root Mountains.
3. Probably limber pine.

Thursday, August the first 1805. a fine morning we Set out as usal, and proceeded on. Some of the hunters killed a goose and a beaver. about 8 oClock A. m. we halted took breakfast under a handsom ceeder tree on S. Side. Capt. Lewis, Sergt. Gass, G. Drewyer and our Intrepter Sharbonoe Set out to go on by land 4 or 5 days expecting to find Some Indians. we proceeded on the current Swift. we find currents of different kinds as usal, and wild or choak cherries which are now gitting ripe. the hills begin to git higher and more pine timber on them, and ceeder along the River. we passed clifts of rocks about 500 feet from the Surface of the water. considerable of pine timber along the Sides of the hills. Saw Some timber or trees along the Shores, resembling ceeder which Some call juniper wood.[1] about noon Capt. Clark killed a Mountain Sheep out of a flock on the Side of a redish hill or clifts on L. Side he Shot it across the River and the rest of the flock ran up the clifts which was nearly Steep. the one killed roled down Some distance when it fell. we got it and dined hearty on it. we proceeded on. passed over a bad rapid at the upper end of an Island jest above high rough clifts of rocks. the towing line of the Captains canoe broke in the pitch of the rapid and the canoe was near turning over nocking again the rocks. little further up passed a creek or large Spring run,[2] which came in on L. S. and ran rapid. came to a large valley which Capt. Clark had Seen before when he came up a fiew days ago. passed large bottoms covered with timber, on each Side of the River. Saw a white bear. took on board 2 Elk which Capt. Lewis had killed and left for us. the hunters killed in these bottoms 5 deer this evening. passed the mouth of a large creek[3] on the Stard. Side and a Spring. came 13½ miles and Camped on the Lard. Side in a bottom of cotton timber. high hills on each Side, and Saw the mountain a Short distance to the South of us.—[4]

1. The trees are Rocky Mountain red cedar; the juniper is common juniper, *Juniperus communis* L.

2. South Boulder Creek, Madison County, Montana, called "Frasures Creek" by the party after member Robert Frazer.

3. Boulder River, Jefferson County, named "R. Fields Vally Creek" for Reubin Field.

4. Again, the Tobacco Root Mountains.

Friday 2nd August 1805. a fine pleasant morning. we Set out eairly and proceeded on. The River is now Small crooked Shallow and rapid. passed bottoms covered with cotton Timber. Saw abundance of beaver lodges & sign Some trees newly cut down by them. Saw ponds where they damed up the water one dam above another which is curious to behold. passed a high bank in which was villages of bank Swallows passed large beautiful bottom praries on each Side and bottoms of timber &C. Saw Several old Indian Camps on S. Side. Some of the high hills look black with pine timber and Solid rocks &C. the day warm. we proceeded on. passed a nomber of Islands, and bottoms covd. with cotton & birch[1] timber. passed Smooth prarie. Saw Several grey Eagles &C[2] we Came 14¾ miles to day and Camped[3] on the edge of a Smooth plain on L. Side. Saw a gang of Elk back under the hills. the country in general back from the river is broken and mountaineous.—

1. Perhaps scrub birch, *Betula glandulosa* Michx., which Lewis notes the next day as dwarf birch, or perhaps the more common water birch, *B. occidentalis* Hook.

2. Golden eagle, *Aquila chrysaetos*.

3. Below Big Pipestone Creek, the party's Panther Creek, Madison County, Montana.

Saturday 3rd August 1805. a clear morning. we Set out as usal and proceeded on. Capt. Clark walked on Shore a Short time and killed a Deer. the River verry crooked and filled with Islands. we proceeded on. Saw 2 deer on the edge of the River one of the hunters R. Fields went after them and killed a panther on an Island. it was 7½ feet in length. it differs from those in the States. it is of a redish brown, and the first we have killed.

passed verry rapid water we have to double man the canoes and drag them over the Sholes and rapid places. we have to be in the water half of our time. passed level praries on each Side. the bottoms has been burned over about 6 months past by the natives, as appears. passed a large Spring on the Lard. Side at a low bottom of willows and high grass. The beaver has made a dam at the mouth on the bank of the River which causes a pond back Some distance and they have lodges all through the pond. the water falls over the dam in the River abt. 4 feet. I drunk of the water found it verry cold. it appears that there is 3 or 4 Springs running from under the mountains a Short distance to the South of us Some Spots of Snow on it. about one oC. we passed over a bad rapid and halted at a bottom covered with timber, to dine the day pleasant and warm. proceeded on passed a large Spring run which is made by the Snow on the Mountains and runs from the foot of the Mo. through a Smooth plain. the River gitting more rapid the rapids longer passed beaver ponds, bottom prarie & bottoms covred with timber &C. Came 17½ miles this day, and Camped[1] on the Lard. Side at a bottom of cotton timber. the currents verry thick & rabit berrys &C.

1. Near Waterloo, with the camp in either Jefferson or Madison County, Montana.

Sunday 4th August 1805. a clear morning. we Set out at Sunrise one hunter Sent on a head to kill some fresh meat for the party. proceeded on about 8 oC. A M. we found a note which Capt. Lewis had left & his camp yesterday morning, letting us know that if he found no Indians or fresh Sign by this evening he would return a fiew miles back & hunt till we come up. we Saw a flock of goats in the high plain under the Mountains, on the top of which is a little Snow & considerable of pine timber. the Mountains are makeing near the River on each Side only a valley along the River which is pleasant, but the Soil indifferent. we proceeded on came up with our hunter who killed 2 deer the rapids continue. we have hard halling over them with the chord, and where the Shore will not admit we have to waid in the water. Some of the Mountains near the River has been burned by the natives Some time ago. the pine timber killed. the cotten timber in Some of the R. bottoms killd. & dry also. not So much timber along the River as below. we proceeded on killed a goose & a duck they are pleanty on the River. we Came 15 miles this day and Camped[1] on S. Side at a bottom covd. with dry trees red willows[2] & rose bush which are verry thick. beaver ponds & Sign pleanty,—&.C.

1. In the vicinity of Silver Star, Madison County, Montana.
2. Red osier dogwood, *Cornus sericea* L.

Monday 5th August 1805. a clear cool morning we Set out as usal 2 hunters Sent on a head to kill Some meat. passd. rapids as usal. one of the hunters killed a deer before brakfast. the wind cold from the South. the Shores and hills rocky the bottom of the River covred with Slippery Small Stone and gravvel. we proceeded on passed over rapids worse than ever it is with difficulty & hard fatigue we git up them Some of which are allmost perpinticular 3 or 4 feet fall in a Short distance. our other hunter joined us at noon had killed nothing but had Seen where the River forks again. about 7 oC. P. m. clouded up wind high we proceeded on about a mile further up came to a another forks[1] one nearly as the other if any difference the right hand fork the largest. we was not certian whether Capt. Lewis was up the left fork or right So ⟨we⟩ Capt Clark[2] left a note for him on the point which is level prarie, & proceeded on up the right hand fork, which is amazeing rapid Some of which falls nearly 3 feet in the length of a canoe, but with hard labour we draged them over. we passed thro a channel which was filled with willows and young cotton wood & brush, Some of which was fell across by the beaver. the currents So rapid we were oblidged to hall by the bushes, and Some places be out in the water where we could Scarsely kick our feet for the rapidity of the current. Saw Several high beaver dams. passed Several Islands. we could Scarsely croud the canoes through the bushes in Several places, night came on and we Camped on the Stard. Side at a bottom which is level and low, has been over flowed lately. it appears this little Stream is verry high, but has been high by the Snow melting off the Mountains. it is now falling a little. was it low we could not proceeded by water any further. our hunter killed a deer. Came 8 to forks miles this day. the party much fatigued and wish to go by land.

1. The forks of the Jefferson River at this point are the Big Hole (right fork) and Beaverhead (left fork) rivers. The Big Hole was called Wisdom River by the party, while they contin-

ued to use the name Jefferson for the Beaverhead. See Ordway's summation of the names of the rivers through this region in his entry of August 10.

2. The words "Capt Clark" may have been added by someone else.

Tuesday 6th August 1805. a clear morning. we Set out as usal and proceeded on halling the canoes over the rapids. the bottoms low and covred with Small timber. about 8 oClock we halted for breakfast. Several men went out a Short distance to hunt. Some of them Saw a large Indian path, or road along the plain. George Drewyer came to us and Informed us that we were on the wrong fork that we could not go far up this for the Sholes & rapids & that their was 3 forks in this valley and the middle one was the best for us to go up.[1] one of the hunters did not return, So we left George Drewyer expecting the hunter in Soon. we turned about and proceeded on down the rapids to the forks, with the crafts. in passing the bad place of bushes & drift which we went up last evening, one canoe turned over another partly filled and was near turning over also. one knapsack, full of cloaths leather &C. lost, allso a Shot pouch powder horn & some mockisons. the rest all got down Safe to the forks and put out all the goods and articles to dry. Several men out to hunt. one man Jos Whitehouse got his leg lamed when the canoe turned over. Several things damaged by gitting wet. found Some difficulty in gitting the canoes down over the Sholes and rapids. one kig of powder Spoild. we found Capt. Lewis and party at the forks. they informed us that they had been about 30 miles up the middle fork and they allowed that to be much the best for us to go up. we Camped on the L. Side of the forks in the evening all the hunters returned had killed 3 deer & a faun Elk the man who left us this morning has not returned and we expect he is lost again. his name is george Shannon. we blew the horn and fired Several guns in hopes he would hear it. the Indian goods &C did not all git dry this evening.

1. They had missed a note from Lewis to this effect; the note had been carried off by a beaver. The other fork is the Ruby River, some distance ahead of the party. The middle fork is the Beaverhead, above the Ruby.

Wednesday 7th *August 1805.* a clear morning. we unloaded one of the Small canoes and halled it out in the bushes in a grove of cotton timber on

L. Side of the forks and left their. we put the goods &.C. not dry out in the Sun Capt. Lewis took an observation & Shoot the air gun. the man G. Shannon not returned yet. the morning cool, but the day warm. the large flys troublesome &C. about one oClock we packed up all the baggage &c. and Set out and proceeded on up the middle fork we find the current not so rapid nor the rapids So bad as the N. Fork. we had Thunder Showers this afternoon, attended with high winds. passed Smooth prarie on each side the River verry crooked, &C. Came 7 miles and Camped[1] at a bottom on L. S. this bottom is covered with bushes & a little timber bryry &C. our hunter G. Drewyer joined us had killed one deer which we Stood in great need off.

1. Just above Twin Bridges, Madison County, Montana.

Thursday 8th August 1805. a clear cold morning. a heavy diew. 4 hunters Sent out at light. we Set out at Sun rise and proceeded on. passed beautiful praries on each Side, but little timber, only willows currents &C. passed the left hand or South fork.[1] has 2 mouths empties in at 2 places but is not as large as the middle fork which we Still take. Saw a little Snow on the knobs back of this large and extensive valley, which is Smooth level prarie. the 3 forks all comes in at this valley. Saw wild onions & golden rod.[2] the prarie is covred with grass which is high in places. the beaver abounds on these Rivers. they have dams and ponds &C. in different places. the Soil of these praries is much better than it has been below for a long distance. proceeded on passed a fine Spring on L. S. one of the hunters brought us a deer which he had killed. Saw a nomber of geese & ducks on the River. passed beautiful prarie on each Side covred with high grass thissels Sun flowers Some clover and different kinds of herbs &C. &C. at noon R. Fields who had been hunting for Shannon returned to us. had not found him. had killed a deer & a goat also. one other of the hunters came in had killed a deer & a goat or antelope. the day warm. a verry pleasant part of the country in this valley, which appears to be 10 or 12 miles wide all Smooth prarie except a fiew groves of cotton trees willows & bushes beaver dams &C. on the River, which is verry crooked but not So rapid as below, and only about 25 yards wide, and verry crooked the bends Short passed upwards of 60 points this day. Came [*blank*] miles & Camped[3] in a thicket of bushes on the L. S. the hunters came in with another Deer.—

1. Ruby River, called Philanthropy by Lewis and Clark.
2. The goldenrod may be any of several varieties, perhaps Missouri goldenrod, *Solidago missouriensis* Nutt. Lewis's botanical notes for this day are quite different, and Ordway is the only writer to mention goldenrod.
3. A few miles above the mouth of Ruby River, Madison County, Montana.

Friday 9th August 1805. a clear cool morning. Several hunters out eairly. we Set out at Sun rise, and proceeded on. the wind high from S. E. took on board a deer which the hunters killed. about 8 oClock we halted for breakfast. George Shannon who had been 3 days lost joined us with 3 buck Skins which he killed & found fat. he brought in a little of the meat also. Capt. Lewis, Shields, Drewyer & Mcneal Set out to go on a head a long distance to make discoveries in hopes to find Indians &C. we proceeded on took on board another Deer which the hunters had killed. the Game is generally Scarse along here. only a fiew Deer to be Seen. The River & bottoms prarie continues as yesterday ⟨back at the 3 forks our Captains named this fork Jeffersons River the North we call Sensable River because we were Sensable of it. the South fork named⟩ not known for certn. yet So I expect the forks ought to be called the head of the Missourie, although we are yet on a branch which we expect to See the head of it in a fiew days. Some thunder the Musquetoes troublesome. the beaver as pleanty as usal, &C. Saw Snow on the Mountains Some distance a head. proceeded passed the head of the old Channel where the River formerly ran along the high land at the South Side of the prarie. Some timber along the old bed. Some part of the prarie is low and boggy and will Shake for Some distance around a man when he walks on it. we expect it would be good turf to burn. Some Showers passed over. we Came 18 mls. and Camped[1] at a fiew trees on L. Side.

1. Near the Beaverhead-Madison county line, Montana.

Saturday 10th August 1805. a clear pleasant morning. we Set out as usal. Several men out hunting. we have now to live on poor venison & goat or antelopes which goes hard with us as the fatigues is hard. the clifts and high land begin to make near the River. passed a high bank along L. S. took on board a deer which one of the hunters killed 2 days past. passed a high clift of rocks on Stard. Side[1] proceeded on the valley wider & covered with high Grass. the hills make further from the River. the River Small & amazeing crooked, our Commanding officers thought proper that the Missourie Should loose its name at the 2 3 forks we passed Some time ago, where we expected to have found the Snake nation of Indians. So they named the North fork *Jeffersons* River, the west or middle fork *Maddisons* River, the South fork *Gallitine* River, on which is a large Spring 2 miles from its Junction with the Missourie. the Small River which falls in to Jeffersons River above the forks on L. S. they call Phillossofy River. So we Still keep on Jeffersons River the last three forks we passed a fiew days past. they call the North fork Wisdom River the ⟨west or⟩ South fork they call Philandrophy, and the west or middle Still retains the name of Jeffersons River, which we are yet on. it is now gitting a Small Stream verry crooked and Shole in places, So that we have to wade and hall the canoes over. about one oClock we halted to dine. a hard Thunder Show arose of rain and large hail which lasted nearly an hour. we then proceeded on the prarie low & Smooth as usal. the beaver abound in this valley which is large and extensive & pleasant &C our hunters killed only one Deer this day. we Came 13 miles this day and Camped on the Stard. Side.—

1. Beaverhead Rock, near the Beaverhead County line, Montana.

Sunday 11th August 1805. a wet rainy morning. Several men out hunting. we Set out after breakfast and proceeded on about 3 miles come to a large prarie Island which three Thousand miles from wood River or from the Mouth of the Missourie. So we call it 3000 mile Island. we went up the L. Side of it and were oblidged to hall the canoes over Several Shole places. Saw a nomber of geese and ducks in the little pond and on the prarie. one of the hunters joined us at noon had killed three Deer and two other a Short distance a head. the day warm the large flys troublesome. we proceeded on passed Several muddy Sunken ponds, and low marshy bottom prarie which is wet and Soft. the beaver have made many channels to their ponds & lodges from the River &C. they are verry numerous in this valley. more So than ever we Saw them before. towards evening we came to a fiew Scattering trees along the Shores but no other but cotton & willow a fiew Small birch.[1] the valley continues 8 or 10 miles wide & all Smooth low prarie without timber. we Saw high Mountains a head some distance large Spots of Snow on them. we Came 14 miles this day and Camped[2] on a wet bottom on Stard. Side.

1. Probably scrub birch.
2. About halfway between Beaverhead Rock and Dillon, Beaverhead County, Montana.

Monday 12th August, 1805. a clear morning. 3 hunters out hunting. we Set out as usal and proceeded on. the current verry rapid the River verry crooked. Some of these rapids is deep and dangerous to pass up one of the large canoes was near turning over. we passed low Swampy land a little timber along the Shore. about 2 oClock we halted to dine. we had a hard Thunder Shower rained some time. we then proceeded on found pleanty of red and yallow currents along the Shores. took on board a goat or antelope which one of the hunters killed yesterday. in the evening the hunters joined us had killed 3 deer & a faun. we Came [*blank*] miles and Camped[1] at a grove of cotten trees & Smooth prarie on the Lard. Side.—

1. A few miles north of Dillon, Beaverhead County, Montana, but perhaps on the opposite side of the river as Ordway has it.

Tuesday 13th August 1805. Cloudy. we Set out as usal and proceeded on. Several hunters to hunt. passed a handsome Spring run[1] which came in on L. Side the hills make nearer the River. the valley not So wide as below & a little higher. Smooth plains covred with grass & Sun flowers &C. Saw Some pine timber on the high hills back from the River. we halted and took breakfast at a high clift of rocks on L. Side the hills above make near the River on the L. Side. we proceeded on the current rapid. the plains continues on the L. Side and hills along the Stard. Side a fiew Scattering cotton trees along the River. in the afternoon the current more gentle. we had caught a nomber of fine Trout this Several days passed high clifts of rocks and fine Springs on S. Side Saw a nomber of large otter diveing in the River before us. Saw bald eagles ducks &C. we took on board a deer the hunters had killed. Came 15 miles this day and camped on the Smooth prarie on L. Side Capt. Clark Shot a duck. considerable of flax in these praries. Some of the party Saw Some of the Seed. 2 of the hunters have not joined us this evening. the mountains appear near a head of us.—

1. Probably Blacktail Deer Creek at Dillon, Beaverhead County, Montana. Lewis and Clark called it McNeal's Creek after Hugh McNeal of the party.

Wednesday 14th August, 1805. a clear cold morning. the 2 hunters Stayed out all last night. we took an eairly breakfast and Set out. the [water?] is verry cold. We have to waid in it which makes our feet and legs ake with cold. we expect it is made of Springs and near the head of the most of them which causes the River water to be as cold as Spring water. the upper part of this valley is Smooth and pleasant passed a large Spring run or creek[1] on the Stard. Side a handsome valley & Small timber Some distance up it. the hills appear verry high to the West about 10 oClock A. m. we came up to the hunters Camp at a grove of cotton timber on L. Side. they have killed 4 Deer and one antelope. we proceeded on the current more rapid oblidged us to hall the large canoes up the rapid & Shole places. the bottom of the River Shores & bars Stoney. about one oC. P. m. we halted to dine at a dry part of the plain a fiew groves of cotton timber along the River the red & yallow currents common. the black goose berry verry Sower to the taste. The wind high from S W. the current continued rapid all day. Capt. Clark killed a buck. one of the men killed a faun deer. we Came [*blank*] miles and Camped on the upper part of the valley a little timber. the plain high. the foot of the mountains near.—

1. Track Creek to the party, it is apparently Rattlesnake Creek, Beaverhead County, Montana.

Thursday 15th August 1805. clear & cold this morning. we Set out after breakfast and entered the Mountains. high clifts of rocks on each Side near the River. S[t]eep up from the River on L. Side 3 or 400 feet. Saw and took on board 4 deer Skins which Capt. Lewis had left at the entrence of the

Mountains. we passed Several bad rapids. caught a nomber of Trout in the Eddys below the rapids. proceeded on passed Several fine Springs on L. Side. the river more Shallow. passed high clifts of rocks & rough knobs &C. about 2 oClock we passed the mouth of a creek[1] on the Stard. Side 10 yds. wide & 3 feet 3 Inch deep, at the mouth. 2 hunters on a head a hunting. we Saw where Capt. Lewis Camped the 10 ult.[2] Some of the high knobs are covred with grass. a fiew Scattering pine trees on them. the River crooked Shallow and rapid. Some deep holes where we caught a nomber of Trout. Capt. Clark was near being bit by a rattle Snake which was between his legs as he was fishing, on the shore. he Shot and killed 2 or 3 others this day. our Intrepters wife found and gethered a fine persel of Servis berrys we Came [*blank*] miles this day & Camped on L. Side at a narrow plain near a grove of cotton trees. Several old Indian Camps here &C.

1. Willard's Creek to the party, named for member Alexander Willard; it is Grasshopper Creek, Beaverhead County, Montana.

2. Ordway means "10th instant" for August 10, not "10th ultimo," which would be July 10.

Friday 16th August 1805. a clear morning but verry cold. the Thurmometer Stood at 47°. the water So cold that we delayed until after we took breakfast. one hunter out this morning. 2 hunters Stayed out last night. we proceeded on as usal. passed a handsom Spring run[1] on L. Side. Some timber on it. we find the current Swift the river Shallow we are oblidged to hall the large canoes the most of the time. Capt. Clark our Intrepter & wife walked on Shore and found a great quantity of Servis berrys the largest & best I ever Saw. they gethered a pale full &C. Gave them out to the party at noon where we halted to dine at a grove of cotton trees on L. Side. Saw a nomber of bald & grey Eagles &C. our hunter who went out this morning killed a verry large buck. the bottoms on the River narrow we name this place Servis berry valley. the 2 hunters who Stayed out last night joined us here and informed us that the River forks[2] again only about 6 miles by land from this & that each fork was Shallow. 2 hunters sent on to the forks to hunt we proceeded on passed up Sholes & rapids towards evening we passed up a verry bad rockey rapid which was difficult to pass over. we were oblidged to waid and hale the canoes over the large rocks &C. we passed a fine Spring on S. Side and a run[3] on L. Side high clifts of rocks & hills on each Side found pleanty of currents on the banks. the water not So Swift above the bad rapid. we Came [*blank*] miles and Camped on a narrow bottom on L. Side no timber. we gethered Small willow Sticks only to boil our vension. the beaver verry pleanty &C—

1. Perhaps the "bold run" on *Atlas* map 66, which may be Gallagher Creek, Beaverhead County, Montana.

2. Red Rock River, the party's East Fork Jefferson, and Horse Prairie Creek, West Fork Jefferson to the party, in Beaverhead County.

3. Probably Clark Canyon Creek, Beaverhead County.

Saturday 17th August 1805. a clear cold morning. we have been cold this Several nights under 2 blankets or Robes, over us. a little white frost. the air chilley & cold. we took an eairly breakfast and set out proceeded on a Short distance heared Some Indians Singing on Shore on L. Side directly came up Several of the Snake nation a horseback. they told us that Capt. Lewis and party was at the forks waiting our arival. Capt. Clark the Intrepter & wife went with them to Capt. Lewis Camp. the natives rode back & forth the Shore to See us come up with the canoes. we halled the Canoes over a great nomber of Shole places and arived at Capt. Lewis Camp abt. 10 oClock A. m. a little below the forks, their was 20 odd of the Snake nation Indians Camped here which came over the Mountains with Capt. Lewis. they appeared verry friendly. Capt. Lewis informed us that he had been over the dividing ridge or mountain to the head waters of the Columbian River & that it is only about 40 miles from this place. they drank at the head Spring of the Missourie & went only about a mile and drank at the head Spring of the Columbian River which ran west. they Saw one Indian comming towards them on horse back a considerable distance from the band. Capt. Lewis wavered a blanket as a token of friendship. he lay close on his horse & Spyed 2 of the party makeing towards him who had been a hunting a little off the road. the Indian turned his horse and ran him untill he got to his band & told the news. the next they met was 3 Squaws digging roots. 2 of them ran off Some distance the other being old Stood her ground. Capt. Lewis Set down and gave hir Some Small presents. She then called the other 2 which came up and piloted them to their Camp which was on a branch of the columbian River they were on their way over to this Side to hunt &C. they had Some Salmon[1] which they caught in the main River they tell us that their is no timber on the head waters for canoes. they also tell us that their is no game, but we do not believe them. they are poor. Capt. Lewis gave them what little presents he had with him and they came about 20 odd with their horses with him across the Mt. 2 chiefs among them. when Capt. Lewis first came near them they appeared frightened untill he & them with him lay down their arms & made motions of friendship. when they met the natives took them round the neck as a great token of friendship. they were uneasy & afraid that they were taken in when they came to the forks & found that we were not their as they had motioned, but when they Saw us they were glad, and were verry friendly to lend us their horses to pack meat &C. we conclude to leave the canoes at this place, So we unloadd and formed a Camp[2] a little below the forks on a Smooth prarie on L. S. no timber. we have to cook with Small willow &C. high hills on the point between the 2 Rivers, & around this valley. a fiew Scattering pitch pine on them. this valley Smooth & pleasant the natives horses appear good and in tollarable order, but they are verry poor nothing to be Seen amongst them but thier horses & 2 or 3 guns, but no ammunition. they are dressed tollarably well in antelope & Mountain Rams Skins well dressed. a fiew beeds hung in their ears with mussel Shells &C their hair Short the most of them. we expect they git their horses from the Spanis and what other little art articles they have, but they have no knives tommahawks nor no weapons of war except their bow & arrows. it is only by their acct. 8 day travel to the South to the Spanish country. our officers Captains Lewis & Clark told the head chief[3] of them that they wanted to by their horses to take our baggage over the Mountains. the Chief Said they would let us have the use of their horses & promised to assist us over as much as lay in their power. So they gave them out considerable of different kinds of marchandize. gave the chief a meddel made another chief & gave him a meddle also. gave the head chief a uniform coat & Shirt & arm bands &C &C. Capt. Lewis Shot the airgun, which they thought a great meddicine & Shewed them a nomber of Strange things to them. 4 deer & 2 antelopes killed by the hunters this day. Capt. Lewis tells us that the game is verry

Scarse on the mountain he was about 3 days with[out] meat. the natives gave Capt. Lewis ear bobs to put in ears and an ornament to Spread over his Shoulders, which was made of white wezels[4] tails & fastened on an otters Skin. they fixed off all the men in the Same way who were returning with Capt. Lewis. they take us round the neck and Sweze us in token of friendship as they have a practice in Stead of Shakeing hands

1. Salmon, *Oncorhynchus* sp., of an unknown type.

2. Called Camp Fortunate by the party, it was located just below the forks of the Beaverhead River, Beaverhead County, Montana. The site is now under Clark Canyon Reservoir. The group would remain here until August 24.

3. Cameahwait, the brother of Sacagawea.

4. Long-tailed weasel, *Mustela frenata*. Lewis received such a tippet from Cameahwait; it is shown in vol. 5, p. xii, of this edition.

Sunday 18th August 1805. a clear morning. one beaver Caught last night in a trap. Capt. Clark and 11 men got in readiness this morning to go with the natives over the Mountain to See if possable to make canoes for us to descend the Columbian river to the western ocian. Capt. Lewis bought three horses of the natives. gave a uniform coat and a knife for one and red leggins & a hankerchief & knife for an other. a fiew arrow points hove in about the Same given for the other Some of the men bought one to carry their baggage on and gave an ordinary check Shirt a pair of old red leggins and a knife only for a tollarable good pack horse. about 10 oClock A. m Capt. Clark & 11 men Set out with the natives all except 2 men & 2 of the women Stayed at our Camp. we put out our baggage & Indian goods to dry and air. we had Showers of rain this afternoon. one hunter out who killed one deer. we got one of the Indians horses to pack it into Camp.—

Monday 19th August 1805. a clear cold morning. we took up the fish net which we set across the River last night, and the Steel traps which were Set for beaver. no fish caught in the net. one beaver caught in a trap. a white frost & the grass Stiff with frost it being disagreeably cold. the day pleasant & warm. 3 hunters out with a horse a hunting. the men at Camp employed in dressing Skins packing the baggage & makeing pack saddles &C. we caught a nomber of fine Trout covred all over with black spots in Stead of red.[1] in the afternoon the hunters returned to Camp & had killed and brought in 2 Deer. light Showers of rain this even,g. this is the place we call the upper forks of Jeffersons River & the extream navigable point of the Missourie close under the dividing ridge of the Western Country. Capt. Lewis takes observations by the Sun and moon &C.—

1. Cutthroat trout and brook trout, *Salvelinus fontinalis.* See Lewis's entry for this day.

Tuesday 20th August 1805. a clear cold morning. a light frost. two men out a hunting. the men at Camp all employed dressing Skins &C. the 2 Indians at our Camp behave verry well and their Squaws mend our mockisons, and make Some &C. and are as friendly as any Savages we have yet Seen. our hunters returned in the afternooon but had killed nothing. the game Scarse. G. Drewyer caught a beaver in a trap last night. it got away and carried the trap 2 miles down the river he got it in the afternoon it was a verry large beaver. the Indians eat it. a nomber of fine Trout caught this day. Capt. Lewis went a Short distance down the River and looked out a place undiscovered from the natives for a carsh or hole to hide Some of our baggage which we can Spare or do without untill our return

Wednesday 21st August 1805. the ground is covred with a hard white frost. the water which stood in the Small vessells froze ¼ of an Inch thick, a little. Some Deer Skins which was spread out wet last night are froze Stiff this morning. the Ink freezes in my pen now the Sun jist ariseing clear and pleasant this morning one hunter out a hunting. took a horse with them. four men sent to dig a hole or carsh. Capt. Lewis took his observations at the place and the Latidude produced is 44d 35m 28.ls North. this evening after dark we carried the baggage to the carsh or hole which we leave at this place. we took it to hide undiscovred from the natives. all the baggage which we carry with us packed up & pack Saddles made ready to cross the diveding ridge as soon as the horses return from the other Side.—

Thursday 22nd August 1805. a white frost and cold as usal. our hunter[1] returned late last night. had killed only a faun Deer, and brought in a load of Indian plunder which he took from Some Indians he met with about 6 or 8 miles from this place. their was only 3 Indians and 3 Squaws our hunter had turned his horse out to feed. one of the Indians took his gun and Sprang on his horse and rode off he rode after him about 20 miles before he got his gun he then jurked or caught hold of his gun & jurked the pan open lost the primeing the Indian then let go and ran. our hunter then returned by their Camp and took all their plunder consisting of Servis berrys dryed different kinds of berrys & cherrys which were dryed for food also roots and a nomber of other kinds of wild fruit dryed. Several Elk Skins which were grained also a nomber of other articles this morning clear and pleasant. three men sent to cover the hiden baggage. the men at Camp engaged dressing their deer Skins, makeing their mockasons, Shirts & overalls[2] &.C. about 11 oClock A. M. our Intrepter his wife and one tribe of the Snake nation of Indians arived here on horse back about 50 odd in nomber besides women and children. they have come to trade horses with us. Capt. Lewis Counciled with them made two of their principal men chiefs & gave them meddles, and told them in council that the chief of the 17 great nations of America had sent us to open the road and know their wants, &C. and told them that their great father would Send them goods and Such things as they Stood in need of to defend themselves with and told them also that we wanted in return their beaver and other Skins if they would take care to save them &C. Capt. Lewis traded with them and bought three fine horses and 2 half breed mules for a little Marchandize &C. they have upwards of fifty good horses here now. we being out of fresh meat and have but a little pork or flower we joined and made a fish drag of willows and caught 520 fine pan fish. 2 kinds of Trout & a kind resembling Suckers.[3] we divided them with the Indians, gave them a meal of boiled corn & beans which was a great thing among them they appear verry kind and friendly do not offer to steel or pilfer any thing from us. we trade any usless article which we have no need of for dressed mo[untain] Rams Skins, &C. they Camp close by us we lend them any thing they want and they are verry careful to return the Same. they appear to live in peace with all nations, but if they should war with them any more their great father would send them arms and ammunition to defend themselves with, but wished them to live in peace with all nations &C.—

1. Drouillard, according to Lewis.

2. Heavy trousers worn for protection over regular clothes.

3. Cutthroat trout and perhaps steelhead trout, *Oncorhynchus mykiss*. The sucker may be the northern sucker, *Castostomus castostomus*.

Friday 23rd August 1805. a clear pleasant morning. 2 of the hunters out a hunting. the natives do not incline to part with any more of their horses untill they cross the mountains, but will carry our baggage over for us. Several of the natives went out with their horses a hunting we took all the canoes in to a pond on the North Side of the River and Sank them in the water So as they may be Safe at our return. the natives who went a hunting returned. drove a deer with them near the Camp and rode it down So that they killed it with their bow and arrows, in that way they caught & killd. 5 or 6 this day. one of them a verry large black taild Deer. they have no other way to kill their game but to run them down with their horses and tire them So that they can kill them. about 3 oClock P. M. another party of the Snake nation arived here about 40 of them on horse back. we expect to Set out to cross the mountain tomorrow. So we Sent 2 men on a head to kill Some meat if possable. towards evening our hunter returned. had killed 2 large deer and three Small ones[1] and brought them all to Camp on the horse.

1. The large deer are mule deer; the small ones are western white-tailed deer.

Saturday 24th August 1805. a clear cool morning. we find that the band of the Snake nation who came here yesterday are going down on the Missourie after the buffaloe and offers Some of their horses for Sale So we delay this morning in order to purchase Some from them. we got three or 4 more horses & hired two and loaded all our horses 12 in nomber. then the Squaws took on their horses the remainder of our baggage we had abt. 20 horses loaded with baggage and Set out about 12 oClock on our journey to cross the dividing mountains. we went about 3 miles up the valley. one of the men P. Wiser was taken of a Sudden with the collick and ditained us So that we got only about 5 miles this afternoon and Camped at the creek on the edge of a large Smooth plain.[1] we had a Small Shower of rain one of the men caught Several large Trout one of the hunters came to camp had killd. nothing.

1. The party crossed the Beaverhead River and went up Horse Prairie Creek along Shoshone Cove, Beaverhead County, Montana.

Sunday 25th August 1805. a clear morning. Some frost. we loaded our horses and Set out soon after Sunrise and proceeded on through the level Sandy plain or desert covred with nothing but wild hysop & golden rod, and prickley pears.[1] we went about 7[2] miles and halted to dine our hunters killed three Deer which we divided with the natives. Some of the Indian hunters rode and chased Several goats or antelopes but did not kill any. the mountains are high each Side of this valley and are covred in Some places with pitch pine. passed Several fine Spring runs which falls from the mountains. the creek is gitting Small and affords but little water. the hills rockey &.C. we proceeded on passed thro a low part of the plain or prarie, which is covred with high Grass and wild onions passed Several fine Springs and forks of the creek ⟨of⟩ one of which had a rapid where it passed a hill little above high clifts which make near the creek on each Side. the plain gitting narrow the upper part of it has lately been burned over. no timber in this valley except the willow on the little branches Saw a fiew cotton trees towards evening. we Came 15 miles this day and Camped[3] at the branch where the mountains made near on each Side. our hunters joined us one of them had killed another Deer which we were oblidged to give to the natives who were all most Sterved. had sent an express across the Mo. for the remainder of their lodges to meet them that they all might go down the Missourie after the baffalow. that they could not Sterve but Capt. Lewis prevailed on the head chief to Send one of his men to contermand the Orders and git the other lodges on the other Side to wait one day longer, as we wish to purchase Some more of their horses & want them to help us over &C.

1. Hyssop is big sagebrush, and goldenrod may be Missouri goldenrod again. There are several varieties of cacti in the region; see Lewis's entry of August 13.

2. The number "7" is written over "6."

3. On Trail Creek, Beaverhead County, Montana, not far from its entrance into Horse Prairie Creek.

Monday 26th August 1805. a clear cold morning. the water in the Small vessells froze. we Set out at Sunrise and proceeded on with our big coats on and our fingers ackd with the Cold. we passed a nomber of large Springs and I drank at the head Spring of the Missourie run South & walked across a ridge only about one mile and drank at the head Spring of Columbian River running west.[1] then went up and down a nomber of high hills passed a nomber of large Springs all makeing west. Saw pitch pine and balsom fer[2] which grow verry tall on the Spring runs and Sides of the mountains, but they are mostly covred with Short grass. Saw considerable of Snow on the mountain near us which appear but little higher than we are. it lies in heaps and a cold breeze always comes from these mountains we came in Site of the valley where the Small river runs. came about 8 miles & halted to dine one of our Indian women was taken Sick rideing a long and halted a fiew minutes and had hir child with out detaining us. we gave the Savages a little corn and proceeded on passed over Several hills and a large Spring run came in Site of the Indian lodges which were on the little River running west. by the request of the chief which was with us we fired 2 rounds and went to their lodges. they had a large one prepared for us in the center. they have about 30 lodges consisting of men women and children. they have but little to eat they catch a large kind of fish in this little Stream. a large Smooth bottoms on this R. back of the bottoms high hills & mountains. Som pitch pine on them. we Camped near the lodge among the natives. we danced a while this evening. they assembled to see us they all appear verry peaceable and friendly. we came here a little before night. found Colter here who had been with Capt. Clark a long distance down this River. he tells us that it is not navigable. no game and verry mountaineous. Capt. Clark Sent Capt. Lewis a note and Says he will meet us here & determine whether we follow the River or go across by land to the wtn. ocean

1. Ordway drank at the source of Trail Creek from waters that would eventually reach the Missouri, and probably from Horseshoe Bend Creek, whose waters feed the Columbia by way of the Lemhi, Salmon, and Snake rivers.

2. Pitch pine here is probably lodgepole pine, *Pinus contorta* Dougl. ex Loud. Balsam fir in this region is probably grand fir, *Abies grandis* (Dougl.) Lindl.

Tuesday 27th August 1805. a beautiful pleasant morning. 4 men went out a hunting with horses. we hoisted the large flag Capt. Lewis gave one to the head chief and one to the next. the [Indians] hoisted them also. Capt. Lewis Settled & paid off the Indian women who helped us over the divideing mountain, then began to trade with the natives for horses. our Intrepter bought one for a red cloak the Indian women are mostly employed githering and drying Seeds & roots for food. they git large quantites of fine black Seed[1] which they grind in to meal between two Stones. they kill but fiew Deer but catch considerable quantity of fresh water Salmon with poles with a Sharpened bone fixed on a pole for a gig. they Some years go down on the Missourie after buffalow and Elk. the country around this place is mountainious and broken Snow now lying a Short distance to the South of us on the broken mountains. our hunters all returned towards evening had killed 4 deer and giged 8 or 10 fine fish which we call salmon. they would wiegh 7 or 8 pound each. but differ from the Salmon caught in the Salt water, but the reason may be there living So far from the ocean in fresh water Capt. Lewis bought 8 or 9 horses this day. the natives do not wish to part with any more of their horses without gitting a higher price for them. the most of those he has bought as yet was for about 3 or 4 dollars worth of marchandize at the first cost, but we will have to give a little more to git a fiew more horses. in the evening the natives had a war dance and danced with their guns those that had any but they had only three or 4 among them. they were verry merry but did not dance So regular as the Indians on the Missourie. their women Sang with them, but did not dance any they tell us that Some of their horses will dance but they have not brought them out yet. they have different kinds of plays and games they have a game[2] which they play most like playing butten only they kick singing and do all by motions they risk all the property they git for their horses or Some of them but it does not trouble them they appear to be easy & well contented let the world go as it may

1. Probably Nuttall sunflower, *Helianthus nuttallii* T. & G. Lewis notes it the previous day; see also Whitehouse's journal for this day.

2. A variation of the widespread Indian hand game, versions of which Clark notes on December 9, 1805, and April 18, 1806.

Wednesday 28th August 1805. a clear pleasant morning. we hoisted the large flag. the chiefs hoisted theirs also. Several men out a hunting Several a fishing with gigs fixed on poles. ⟨the natives have a bone Sharpened and fixed on poles for that purpose.⟩ about 9 oClock A. M. Capt. Lewis began to trade again for horses and gives considerable more than he gave yesterday. about 2 oClock P. M. Sergt. Gass arived here had left Capt. Clark & party abt. 12 miles down the River. Capt. Lewis Sent him back to inform Capt. Clark that we ware waiting here to purchase horses, and wished him & his party to come up & join us. Capt. Lewis bought 5 or 6 more horses to day. we have now in all 25, but the most of them have Sore backs. three men Set at makeing pack Saddles. our hunters killed nothing this day in the evening two Strangers arived here from an other band belonging to this nation who now reside Some distance to the South of this near the Spanish country. all the chiefs and principal men assembled to hold a council & hear the news &C these Savages are fond of Salt. the first we have Seen that would taste it.—

Thursday 29th August 1805. a clear pleasant morning. about 8 oClock A. M. a nomber of Indians arived here who had been gone along time from the nation one of them got Sculped by some Indians in the prarie or plain he did not know what nation they belonged to. Some of their relations cryed when they came in the village. Capt. Lewis bought two more horses. about 11 oClock A. M. Capt Clark and party arived here except 2 men who Stayed to take care of the baggage which they left. they informed us that the mountains were amazeing high and rough. almost impossable to pass over them. they had a guide with them. they came uppon one or 2 lodges in a valley between the mots. they started to run but the guide Spoke to them and they Stood and gave them Some cherries and Servis berrys which they were gethering. they lived 4 or 5 days on Such berrys. killed but one Deer while they were out. they find that the mountains are So bad that we cannot follow the river by land and the river So rapid and full of rocks that it is impossable for crafts to pass down. neither is their any game they got some Salmon from the natives which they caught in the River with their bone & horn gigs, but had suffered considerable with hunger. the natives tells us that we cannot find the ocean the course we want to go for their old men has been a Season or more on that course to find it but could not. and that their was troublesome tribes of Indians[1] to pass. that they had no horses and if they could git hold of any they would eat them as they lived on roots &C their being no game the country So rough and mountaineous. we are not like to purchase any more horses here as the natives tell us that they must keep Some horses unless they could git arms and ammunition in return So that they may be able to defend themselves. but we told them that we could not Spare any guns if we Should git no more horses. So we put up the goods, as we have now 27 horses and intend to Set out on our journey to-morrow and go around or between the mountains and strike the columbia River below if possable. our hunters returned towards evening had caught & giged 6 fine Sammon and killed one Deer.

1. Perhaps the Tukudikas, called Broken Moccasin Indians by Lewis; see Lewis's entry of August 14, 1805.

Friday 30th August 1805. a fine morning. we got up all our horses. bought 3 more. have now got 30 in all. we got our loads ready. the guide[1] who has engaged with us to go on to the ocean tells us that their is 2 ways to go, but the one bearing South of the Ri: is plains and a desert country without game or water. but the road to the North of the River is rough and mountaineous but Sd. he could take us in 10 days to a large fork of the River[2] which came in on the South Side where the River would be navigable or in about 15 days we could go to where the tide came up and Salt water. So we concluded to go that road. apart of the natives went from this village over to the head of the Missouri after the buffalow. about one oClock P. m. our hunter came in had killed three Deer we loaded all but 2 of our horses and Set out and proceeded on down the River bottom crossed Several this Spring runs and Sever[al] old Camps. went about 10 miles and Camped[3] on a Smooth bottom near the River considerable of cotton and alder[4] wood along the Shores.

1. Toby or Old Toby; see Clark's entry of August 20.
2. The Snake River, which the party called Lewis's River.
3. Near the Lemhi River, some miles below Baker, Lemhi County, Idaho.
4. Perhaps Sitka alder, *Alnus sinuata* (Regel) Rydb.

Saturday 31st August 1805. a fare morning. we Set out eairly and proceeded on 2 miles and passd. Several lodges of the Snake nation of Indians who Stay here to fish. they catch Sammon in their pots and wires [weirs] which they have made of willows across the River and have more or less in them everry morng. we bough a nomber of fine large Sammon of them and proceeded on. one hunter on a head. one strange Indian seen which is Supposed to be one of the flat head nation.[1] he ran off, and the Indians could not find him. we then proceeded on over rough high hills. Some deep Gullies of white earth. Several of the natives followed us. went about eight miles without water and halted at a large Spring branch[2] to let our horses feed and dine ourselves. Some pitch pine on the mountains which make near the River on each Side. the River bottoms narrow and verry much dryed up. the Soil verry indifferent. we proceeded on over a level Smooth plain abt. 7 miles then passed the end of a mountain near the River where the Stone lay one on an other & holes So that the horses could Scarsely git along without breaking their legs. we then proceeded on to a large Creek[3] which falls in on the East Side of the River. we took a path up Sd. Creek and proceeded on found wild or choke cherrys along the branch. also Servis berrys which were ripe. we Came [*blank*] miles this day and Camped at Some Indian lodges near the Creek. one of the hunters killed a deer at dusk and brought it to Camp after dark.—

1. Also called Salish Indians, see September 4.
2. Probably Carmen Creek, Lemhi County, Idaho.
3. Tower Creek, Lemhi County.

Sunday 1st September 1805. Cloudy. we Set out at Sun rise and proceeded on up a high mountain at the first pich one of the horses fell backward and roled over, but did not hurt him much. we proceeded on up and down the high mountains Crossed Several Creeks the water of which was verry cold. considerable of pine and cotton timber along each of those branches, and pleanty of Servis berrys which are verry Sweet and good at this time. in the afternoon we had Several Shower of rain and a little hail. we descended a mountain down in to a valley through which runs a large Creek[1] we went on a Short distance up the valley and Camped at Some old Lodges. we giged Several Sammon in this Creek. three men went down to the mouth of the creek and bought about 25 pounds of dryed Sammon and Sammon rose[2] with a fiew Small articles. our hunters killed a Deer and wounded 2 bear at dusk. we Came 23 miles this day. we find abundance of wild or choke Cherries which are now ripe in this bottom we gethered and boiled Some which eat verry well. Several Small Showers of rain this evening.—

1. North Fork Salmon River, the party's Fish Creek, Lemhi County, Idaho.
2. Perhaps salmon roe.

Monday 2nd Sept. 1805. a cloudy wet morning. we loaded our horses and Set out about 7 oClock, and proceeded on. the way we had to go was verry bad Some places thick bushes and logs to pass over. other places rockey. our course about N. E. crossed Several creeks or large Spring runs the water of which was verry cold. Saw a nomber of large beaver dams and beaver ponds on this creek. the pine and balsom fir timber tall and Strait, and pleanty. Some of the pine is large enofe for canoes or boards &C. considerable of common alder along the creeks and runs. we proceeded on up the creek passed through verry bad thickets where we were oblidged to cut a road for our horses to pass through. handsom tall strait pine and balsom fir and a little cotton intermixed. crossed Several branches. Some places muddy. we call this place dismal Swamp.[1] Several beaver dams in it &C. Some places Steep along the edge of the mountains and verry rough and rockey. the mountains make close on each Side of the creek and high covred with pine. this is a verry lonesome place. Some of our weak horses fell backward climeing the Steep rockey hills, and mountains. we had considerable of trouble this day carring Several of the horses loads up the steep rockey mont. one of the horses gave out So that he could not carry his load. we went 13 miles this day and Camped[2] in a thicket near the creek.

it was about six miles through the thicket which we call the dismal Swamp. nothing killed this day by the hunters only a fiew fessents.[3] no game of any kind to be Seen in these mountains.

1. Whitehouse also uses this term (but not Clark or Gass) for the area around Gibbonsville, Lemhi County, Idaho. Ordway or Whitehouse may have been recalling the Dismal Swamp of southeast Virginia and northeast North Carolina.
2. Above the mouth of Hammerean Creek and northwest of Gibbonsville.
3. A species of grouse; see Lewis's entry of September 20.

Tuesday 3rd Sept. 1805. we Set out as usal, and proceeded on up the branch a Short distance further up the branch then took the mountain and went up and down rough rockey mountains all day. Some places So Steep and rockey that Some of the horses fell backwards and roled to the bottom. [one] horse was near being killed. crossed a nomber of fine Spring branches. Some places oblidged to cut a road for to git along thro thickets &C. Some of the balsom fir trees on the branches are about 100 and fifty feet high, and Strait. ⟨towards⟩ the most of them are covred with warts ⟨of⟩ filled with the balsom &C. we dined at a branch eat the last of our pork &.C. Some of the men threaten to kill a colt to eat they being hungry, but puts if off untill tomorrow noon hopeing the hunters will kill Some game. towards evening we assended a mountain went Some distance on the top of it then went down in to a cave near the head of a branch running nearly an opposite course from the branch we dined on at noon. we Camped[1] in this cove. Several Small Showers of rain. So we lay down wet hungry and cold came with much fatigue 11 miles this day.

1. The route and campsite for this day are very difficult to determine. The party apparently crossed the Continental Divide near Lost Trail Pass and reentered Montana, then camped in Ravalli County. See Clark's entry of this day.

Wednesday 4th Sept. 1805. the morning clear, but very cold. the ground covred with frost. our mockasons froze. the mountains covred with Snow. 2 mountain Sheep Seen by one of the men who was a hunting the horses. we delayed untill about 8 oClock A. M. then thoughed our Sailes by the fire to cover the loads and Set out. ascended the mountain on to the dividing ridge[1] and followed it Some time. the Snow over our mockasons in places.

we had nothing but a little pearched corn to eat the air on the mountains verry chilley and cold. our fingers aked with the cold proceeded on descended the mountain down a rough way passed through a large thicket of pine and balsom fer timber in which we killed a dozen partridges or fessents. went down in to a valley on a branch[2] running on about a north course and halted. our hunter killed a deer on which we dined. our guide and the young Indian who accompanied him eat the verry guts of the deer. Saw fresh Sign of Indians. proceeded on down this valley towards evening we arived at a large encampment of the flat head nation of Indians[3] about 40 lodges and I Suppose about 30 persons, and they have between 4 or 5 hundred horses now feeding in the plains[4] at our view and they look like tollarable good horses the most of them. they received us in a friendly manner. when our officers went to their lodges they gave them each a white robe of dressed skins, and spread them over their Shoulders and put their arms around our necks instead of Shakeing hands as that is their way they appeared glad to See us. they Smoaked with us, then gave us a pleanty Such as they had to eat, which was only Servis berrys and cheeries pounded and dryed in Small cakes. Some roots of different kinds. our officers told them that we would Speak to them tomorrow and tell th[em] who we were and what our business is and where we are going &C. these natives are well dressed, descent looking Indians. light complectioned. they are dressed in mo Sheep leather Deer & buffalow robes &C. they have the most curious language of any we have Seen before. they talk as though they lisped or have a bur on their tongue. we Suppose that they are the welch Indians[5] if their is any Such from the language. they have leather lodges to live in Some other Skins among them. they tell us that they or Some of them have Seen bearded men towards the ocean, but they cannot give us any accurate of the ocean but we have 4 mountains to cross to go where they saw white men which was on a river as we suppose the Columbian River. came [*blank*] miles to day and pitched our Camp[6] near the creek on the right of the Indian Lodges. considerable of large pitch pine timber in this valley our hunter killed another Deer this evening.—

1. Saddle Mountain, Ravalli County, Montana.
2. Probably one of the forks of Camp Creek, Ravalli County.

3. More correctly, Salish Indians. Clark has thirty-three lodges and eight people at this place.

4. In the valley of Ross, or Ross's, Hole, near Sula, Ravalli County.

5. Ordway recalls the myth that some interior Indians may have descended from a legendary Welsh traveler. The notion was also applied to the Mandans.

6. Probably on Camp Creek, at Ross Hole.

Thursday 5th Sept. 1805. a clear cool morning. the Standing water froze a little. the Indian dogs are so ravinous that they eat Several pair of the mens Moccasons. a hard white frost this morning. Several men went out to hunt our officers purchased Several horses of the natives after Counsiling with them. they are a band of the Flat head Nation our officers made four chiefs gave them meddles 2 flags Some other Small presents and told them our business and that we were friends to all the red people &C. which they appeared verry friendly to us. they have a great stock of horses but have no provision only roots and berrys, at this time but are on their way to the Meddison River or Missourie whire they can kill pleanty of buffalow. our officers bought 12 horses from them and gave a Small quantity of Marchandize for each horse. our officers took down Some of their language found it verry troublesome Speaking to them as all they Say to them has to go through Six languages,[1] and hard to make them understand. these natives have the Stranges language of any we have ever yet Seen. they appear to us as though they had an Impedement in their Speech or brogue on their tongue. we think perhaps that they are the welch Indians, &C. they are the likelyest and honestest we have seen and are verry friendly to us. they Swaped to us Some of their good horses and took our worn out horses, and appeared to wish to help us as much as lay in their power. accommodated us with pack Saddles and chords by our giving them any Small article in return [towa]rds evening our hunters came in had kild 1 deer.

1. Communication would pass through Salishan, Shoshone (from a Shoshone boy among the Flatheads and Sacagawea), Hidatsa (Sacagawea and Charbonneau), French (Charbonneau and a French speaker in the party), and English.

Friday 6th Sept. 1805. a clear cold morning. we packed up our baggage the natives got up their horses also and Struck their Lodges in order to Set out for the Missourie. we have now got 40 good pack horses and three Colts. four hunters were furnished horses without loads in order to hunt constant. about 1 oClock we Set out again on our journey. the natives Set out at the Same time for the Missourie we proceeded on soon crossed a large creek[1] in this valley then Soon took the mountains. one of the hunters left us. we went over a Mountain about 7 miles and descended down the Mountain on a creek and Camped.[2] eat a little parched corn. light Sprinkling of rain, through the course of this day—

1. East Fork Bitterroot River, Ravalli County, Montana.
2. Perhaps following Cameron Creek back down to the East Fork Bitterroot River and camping on that stream in Ravalli County above Warm Springs Creek which comes in on the opposite side.

Saturday 7th Sept. 1805. a cloudy cold morning. one of our hunters Stayed out all last night. we set out eairly and proceeded on down the creek. our hunter who Stayed out last night over took us had lost his horse. we passed over narrow plains larg pine and cotton timber along the creeks high mountains a little to the Lard. Side which is covred thick with Snow. one of our hunters killed two Deer. Some of the other hunters killed 1 goose 1 crain Several pheasants and a hawk. we proceeded on crossed Several Small creeks and runs we had Several Showers of rain. this valley gitting wider. the plain Smooth & dry. we came 18 miles this day and Camped[1] on the bank of the Creek.—

1. On the Bitterroot River, southwest of Grantsdale, Ravalli County, Montana.

Sunday 8th Sept 1805. cloudy and cold. we Set out eairly and proceeded on down this creek which is now verry large. passed over Smooth plain no timber except along the bank of the creeks. Saw Snow on the mount to our left. high barron hills to our right.[1] about 11 oClock we halted to dine at a branch our hunters joined us. had killed an Elk, and a Deer which they brought with them. the wind cold from the N. W. & Showers of rain, and a little hail. passed over Smooth plains in this valley. the Mountains are rough on each side and are covred with pine and on the tops of which are covd. with Snow. our hunters found 2 Stray horses and a handsom colt, which they took along with them we marched 20 odd miles this day and Camped[2] on a Smooth bottom near the creek, where we had fine feed for our horses. our hunters joined us had killed one Deer.—

1. On their left were the Bitterroot Mountains and on their right the Sapphire Mountains.
2. Near Stevensville, Ravalli County, Montana.

Monday 9th Sept. 1805. Cloudy. we Set out [and proceeded on down?] [*page worn, some words illegible*] the valley the plains Continue crossed Several creeks a little cotton and pine timber along the banks the Snow continues on the Mont. each Side of this valley. one of the hunters killed a goose and a wood pecker.[1] Capt. Clark killed 4 pheasants or prarie hens. we find wild or choak cherries along these branches &C— we passed through a large bottom of rich land which is covred with handsom pitch pine timber. this creek has got to be a Small handsome River and gentle current we have to wade it often and find it as deep as the horses belleys. our hunters killed three deer and several ducks this day we Camped[2] on the bank of a creek which runs in to the Small River about 2 miles below and bottoms of cotton timber. Smooth handsome plains on each Side of this creek, and pleanty of choke cherries. Mountains of Snow back to our left. our course has been lately abt. N. W.—

1. The woodpecker could be either the red-headed woodpecker, *Melanerpes erythrocephalus,* or the pileated woodpecker, *Dryocopus pileatus.* See Clark's entry for this day.
2. On the explorers' Travelers' Rest Creek, now Lolo Creek, a mile or two upstream from the Bitterroot River, on the south side of the creek, and in the vicinity of modern Lolo, Missoula County, Montana. They would remain here until September 11.

Tuesday 10th Sept. 1805. a fair morning. we make a Short halt here to wrest and hunt. all the best hunters turned out to hunt. the day warm. towards evening the hunters returned had killed 4 Deer a faun and Several ducks and geese. one of the hunters[1] Saw three Indians on horse back they appeared afraid of him Signed to him to lay down his gun he layed it down they then came to him [in] a friendly manner. he Signed to them to come with him and they took him on behind one of them and rode down to Camp. they belong to the flat head nation they Signed to us that they lay all day in hearing of our guns but was afraid to come to us. they Sign to us also that 2 of the Snake Nation had Stole 2 of their horses, and they were in pursuit of them—

1. Colter, according to Clark.

Wednesday 11th Sept. 1805. a clear pleasant morning. we went out to look up our horses. the Latidude at this place is 46° 48° 28s 8/10 North. we did not find all our horses untill afternoon. about 4 oClock P. M. we Set out and proceeded on up this creek[1] course nearly west. the narrow bottoms on this Creek is thinly covred with pitch pine passed a large tree on which the natives had a number of Immages drawn on it with paint. a part of a white bear skin hund on Sd. tree. we came about 7 miles this evening and Camped[2] on a narrow plain near where had been a large Camp of Indians a Short time past. Saw one lodge made of Earth. the pine trees pealed for some distance around. the natives eat the enside bark.

1. The party was starting west along Lolo Creek on the Lolo Trail, a route used by the Nez Perce Indians to cross the Bitterroot Mountains.
2. About one half mile east of Woodman Creek, Missoula County, Montana.

Thursday 12th Sept. 1805. a fair morning. a white frost. the hunters Set out eairly we loaded and Set out Soon after and proceeded on Soon took the Mountains came up and down Several Steep places crossed Several Small creeks and we descended a bad Step part of the Mout. and came down on the creek again and halted to dine our hunters had killed this day 4 Deer and a pheasant we dined and proceeded on crossed 2 more creeks ascended up a mountain on a high ridge a verry bad trail rough and rockey.[1] we found no water nor place to Camp[2] untill 10 oClock at night. then descended a Steep part of the Mountain. came down on the creek which we left this morning or at noon and we had came 17½ miles this day. and near Sd. creek where we could not find a level place to Sleep, and Scarcely any feed for our horses

1. The party passed along the north side of Lolo Creek, crossing Woodman and Grave creeks and a number of smaller streams, all in Missoula County, Montana.
2. About two miles east of Lolo Hot Springs, Missoula County.

Friday 13th Sept. 1805. cloudy. we got all our horses up except one which Capt. Lewis rode we could not find, and a colt also. we then loaded our horses and proceeded on a Short distance and came to a warm Spring[1] which run from a ledge of rocks and nearly boiled and issued out in several places it had been frequented by the Savages. a little dam was fixed and had been used for a bathing place. we drank a little of the water and washed our faces in it. a handsome green on the creek near this Spring. we had Some difficulty here in finding the direct trail. we went round a bad way came on the trail again and halted to dine at or near the head of Sd. Creek at a beaver dam. then proceeded on ascended a high rough mountain over took the hunters who had killed a deer. 2 of them sent back to look for Capt. Lewises horse. we crossed the dividing ridge[2] and a number of Spring runs and found it to be only about half a mile from the head Spring of the waters running East to the head Spring of the waters runing west. each heading in an open marshy Swamp which is level and full of Springs. we came on a creek running west on which we Camped.—[3]

1. Lolo Hot Springs, Missoula County, Montana.
2. The explorers crossed from Montana back into Idaho near Lolo Pass and followed Pack Creek down to Packer Meadows, Idaho County.
3. At the lower end of Packer Meadows.

Saturday 14th Sept. 1805. we Set out as usal, and ascended a mountain about 4 miles, then descended it down to on the forks of the creek[1] where it ran verry rapid and is full of rocks. we then assended a verry high mountain about 4 miles further to the top of it and verry step. Came Some distance on the top then descended down about 6 miles Some places verry Steep. came down on another fork where the creek[2] is got to be verry large. the Savages had a place fixed across the River and worked in with willows where they catch a great quantity of Sammon in the Spring, as our guide tells us. we Crossed the right hand fork where it was very rapid. we proceed on passed several old camps. we followed down the main creek about 4 miles had nothing to eat but Some portable Soup we being hungry for meat as the Soup did not Satisfy we killed a fat colt which eat verry well at this time a little Thunder hail and rain. Saw high Mountains covred with Snow and timber.—

1. Brushy Creek and Crooked Fork, Idaho County, Idaho.

2. Crooked Fork and Colt Killed Creek (formerly White Sand Creek but now restored to Lewis and Clark's name) merge to form the Lochsa River, Idaho County. The night's camp was on the north bank of the Lochsa, about two miles from where the streams merge and in the area of Powell Ranger Station.

Sunday 15th Sept 1805. cloudy. we Set out as usal and proceeded on a Short distance down the creek. crossed Several Small creeks and Swampy places covred with tall handsome white ceeder and Spruce pine &.C—[1] we crossed a creek a pond[2] a little below then assended a high Mountain[3] Some places So Steep and rockey that Some of our horses fell backwards and roled 20 or 30 feet among the rocks, but did not kill them. we got on the ridge of the mountain and followed it. came over several verry high knobs where the timber had been mostly blown down. we found a small spring before we came to the highest part of the mountain where we halted and drank a little portable Soup and proceeded on to the top of the mount found it to be abot. 10 miles from the foot to the top of sd. mount and most of the way very Steep. we travvelled untill after dark in hopes to find water. but could not find any. we found Some Spots of Snow so we Camped[4] on the top of the Mountain and melted Some Snow. this Snow appears to lay all the year on this Mount we drank a little portable Soup and lay down without any thing else to Satisfy our hunger. cloudy and cold this mountain and all these Mountains are covred thick with different kinds of pine timber. Some high rocks appear abo. the timber

1. White cedar is western redcedar, *Thuja plicata* Donn., the spruce is Engelmann spruce, and the pine is probably lodgepole pine. It may be that Ordway is using the term "spruce pine" for a single species, as Clark did on September 12. The next day's entry seems to indicate such a usage. Spruce pine is Engelmann spruce.

2. Now known locally as Whitehouse Pond, it is on U.S. Highway 12, a short distance west of Powell Ranger Station, Idaho County, Idaho.

3. The explorers ascended Wendover Ridge in order to get back to Lolo Trail which they had left on this misguided loop to the south.

4. About where they rejoined the Lolo Trail, near Forest Road 500, Idaho County.

Monday 16th Sept 1805. when we a woke this morning to our great Surprize we were covred with Snow, which had fell about 2 Inches deep the later part of last night, & continues a cold Snowey morning. Capt. Clark Shot at a deer but did not kill it. we mended up our mockasons and Set out without any thing to eat, and proceeded on could Scarsely keep the old trail for the Snow. kept on the Mountn. rather descending more than ascending. about one oClock finding no water we halted[1] and melted Some snow and eat or drank a little more Soup, and let our horses graze about one hour and a half then proceeded on. Saw considerable of old snow passed several bald knobs and high points of rocks &C. towards evening we descended a Mountain down in to a deep cove where we Camped[2] on a small creek in a thicket of Spruce pine and balsom fer timber. the Snow is now about 4 Inches deep on a levl. we came about 15 miles this day. the clouds So low on the Mount that we could not See any distance no way. it appeared as if we have been in the clouds all this day. we all being hungry and nothing to eat except a little portable soup which kept us verry weak, we killed another colt & eat half of it.

1. Perhaps on Spring Hill, Idaho County, Idaho.

2. Near some rock mounds, later called Indian Post Office (which none of the journalists mention), perhaps on Moon Creek, Idaho County.

Tuesday 17th Sept. 1805. Cloudy and cold we went out to look for our horses found Some of them much Scattered. we did not find them all untill about 12 oClock at which time we Set out and proceeded on. the Snow melted of the timber. the trail verry rough we came up and down bad Steep places of the Mountain, the afternoon clear and pleasant & warm. the Snow melted fast. the water Stood in the trail over our mockns Some places Slippery. we assended a steep high rockey part of the Mountain high rocks and high pricipicies. we Camped[1] on this Mountain at a small creek and dry pine timber. we being verry hungry oblidged us to kill another colt the last we had. one of the hunters chased a bear up the Mountain but could not kill it. we hear wolves howl Some distance a head.

1. A short distance from Indian Grave Peak, Idaho County, Idaho.

Wednesday 18th Sept. 1805. a clear pleasant morning. Capt. Clark and Six hunters[1] Set out at Sunrise to go on a head expecting to kill Some game.

one of our horses lost. we Set out and proceeded on the Mountains rough and rockey up and Steep places Some logs and bushes &C. about 3 oClock P. M. we halted on a ridge[2] to let our horses graze a little and melt a little Snow and made a little portable Soup. the Mountains continue as fer as our eyes could extend. they extend much further than we expeted. we proceeded on untill dark before we found any water then Camped[3] on the Side of a Mountain. had come 14 miles this day. took our horses down a Steep gulley to a run to water them. we Supped on a little portable Soup and Slept on this Sidling Mountain.—

1. Including Reubin Field and Shields.
2. Probably Bald Mountain, Idaho County, Idaho.
3. About three miles west of Bald Mountain.

Thursday 19th Sept 1805. a clear norning. we eat the verry last morcil of our provision except a little portable Soup, and proceeded on to the top of Sd. mountain[1] and as we were descending the Same we discovred a very large plain[2] a long distance a head, which we expect is on the Columbia River, which puts us in good Spirits again. the Mount. bad this day. we descended a Mount. about 4 miles down where it was verry Steep came down on a creek[3] running abt. East. we followed up the creek Some distance the way very rockey and bad, then went along the side of a Mountain a little to the write of the creek. high steep timbred mounts. on each side of Sd. creek. one of our horses[4] fell backwards out of the trail and rolled down over the Steep rocks abt. 200 feet with 2 boxes of Ammunition and plunged in to the creek with Some difficulty we got the horse up again and load it hurt the horse but did not kill him. we Came 17 miles this day and Camped[5] at a Small run in a thicket of pine and balsom timber &C—

1. Probably Sherman Peak, Idaho County, Idaho.
2. Open prairies in Lewis and Idaho counties, northwest of Grangeville, including Camas and Nez Perce prairies. See Clark's entry of September 18.
3. This is probably Hungrey Creek, Idaho County.
4. Frazer's horse, fortunately without Frazer.
5. On Hungrey Creek, near the mouth of a small, nameless stream.

Friday 20th Sept. 1805. a cold frosty morning we found a handful or 2 of Indian peas[1] and a little bears oil which we brought with us we finished the last morcil of it and proceeded on half Starved and very weak. our horses feet gitting Sore. came a Short distance and found a line which Capt Clark had left with the meat of a horse which they found in the woods and killed for our use as they had killed nothing but 1 or 2 phasants after they left us. we took the meat and proceeded on a Short distance further one horse Strayed from us yesterday with a pair of port Mantaus with Some Marchandize and Capt. Lewises winter cloths &C— 2 men went back to hunt for him. we proceeded on along a ridge where we had a bad road which was filled with logs. our horses got Stung by the wasps.[2] we came on untill after dark before we found any water. came 14 miles this day.—[3]

1. The peas may be the hog peanut, *Amphicarpa bracteata* (L.) Fern., which the party would have gathered on the Missouri River in North Dakota and carried with them, perhaps forgotten, to this place.

2. Whitehouse identified them as "yallow wasps," perhaps the western yellow jacket, *Vespula pensylvanica.*

3. The main party camped between Dollar and Sixbit creeks, Idaho County, Idaho.

Saturday 21st Sept. 1805. a clear pleasant morning. we could not find all our horses untill about 10 oClock at which time we Set out, and proceed. on Soon crossed a creek[1] and proceed. on nearly a west course, over a rough trail. Some of the ridges the timber has been killed Some time past by fires, and is fell across the trail So that we have Some difficulty to pass. towards evening we descended down a Mount. and came on a large creek[2] running S. W. we came down it a Short distance and Camped[3] had come 11 miles this day. Capt. Lewis killed a wolf Some of the party killed three pheasants and a duck. we eat them and caught a fiw craw fish[4] in the creek and eat them.—

1. Either Eldorado Creek or Dollar Creek, Idaho County, Idaho.

2. Lolo Creek, Idaho County.

3. On Lolo Creek, Clearwater County, Idaho; the creek at this point forms the boundary between Idaho and Clearwater counties.

4. Some variety of crayfish, *Astacus* sp.

Sunday 22nd Sept. 1805. a clear pleasant morning. and white frost. we were detained Some time a hunting our horses. about nine oClock at which time we Set out assended a Mountain and proceeded on came on a Small Smooth prarie or plain,[1] and run came through it. we met Reuben fields who Capt. Clark Sent back to meet us, with a bag of Sammon and excelent root bread[2] which they purchased from a nation of Indians who are Camped on a plain at the foot of the Mount. about 8 or 10 miles distance from this place— we halted about one hour and a half eat hearty of the Sammon and bread, and let our horses feed. then we proceeded on the two men who had been back to look for the lost horse overtook us they had found the horse and portmantaus, but had lost the horse they took with them. we proceeded on over a mountain and descended it down in to a valley[3] which is Smooth and mostly handsome plains. Some groves of handsome tall large pitch pine timber about 3 miles further we came to a large Indian village of the flat head nation[4] they appeared very glad to see us ran meetting us with Some root bread which they gave us to eat. we Camped[5] by a branch near the village. the natives gave us dryed Sammon and different kinds of their food. Capt Clark joined us this evening and informed us that the[y] had been on a branch of the Columbia River where he expected it is navagable for canoes and only 15 or 20 miles from this place &C— these natives have a large quantity of this root bread which they call Commass. the roots grow in these plains. they have kills [kilns] engeaniously made where they Sweet these roots and make them Sweet and good to the taste—

1. Crane Meadows, Clearwater County, Idaho.
2. Camas, *Camassia quamash* (Pursh) Greene.
3. Weippe Prairie, Clearwater County.
4. Actually, Nez Perce Indians.
5. On a branch of Jim Ford Creek, Clearwater County.

Monday 23rd Sept. 1805. a fair morning. we purchased considerable of Sammon and commass roots from the natives. these Savages are now laying up food for the winter and in the Spring they are going over on the medicine River and Missourie River to hunt the buffalow. Some of them have fine copper kittles and different kinds of trinkets hanging about them. also they are fond of any kind of marchandize, but the blue beeds they want mostly. our officers gave the chiefs of this nation a flag a meddle and Some other Small articles their is another village about 2 miles further down the plain they gave the chief of that village a flag and meddle also. these natives have a great many horses and live well. are well dressed in Elk deer and Mountain Sheep Skins. well dressed they have but a fiew buffalow Robes. the most of them have leather lodges and are now makeing flag[1] lodges &C. we got up our horses towards evening all except one which we could not find. we loaded up left one man to look for his horse and proceed. on down to the other village and Camped. had a Thunder Shower this evening. we bought Some more Sammon and Commass, Some dressed Elk Skins &C. from these villages who live like other.

1. Probably common cat-tail, *Typha latifolia* L.

Tuesday 24th Sept. 1805. a clear morning. we went to look for our horses but found them much Scatered and mixed among the Indian horses which were numerous. Saw a number of Squaws digging commass roots in the plain the Soil verry rich and lays delightful for cultivation about 8 oClock A M. we loaded our horses Several men Sick. one man[1] Sent back to look for 2 horses which was lost on the road. we Set out and proceeded on the day warm we had a good road mostly plain but no water. Some Scattering pine timber. towards evening we came down on a fork[2] of Columbia River and followed it down Some distance then went on a small prarie Island and Camped.[3] our hunters joined us had got 4 deer and two Sammon which they killed. Several of the natives followed us and Camped near us &C—

1. Colter, according to Clark.
2. Clearwater River.
3. Later China Island, on the Clearwater River about a mile above Orofino, Clearwater County, Idaho.

Wednesday 25th Sept. 1805. a fair morning. three men went out a hunting. Capt. Clark went with an old chief down the River to look for timber which would answer for canoes. the Natives have Several Small canoes at this place. this River is about 60 yards wide Some clifts of rocks along its Shores. the natives have a fishery little above our Camp. they caught Several fine Sammon this day. towards evening Capt. Clark returned and informed us that he had been 4 or 5 miles down to a fork[1] of the River which came in on the east Side he Saw Some pitch pine timber which he thought would answer for canoes near this forks on the opposite shore in the evening the man who Stayed at the village joined us had got his horse by hireing Indians to git him

1. North Fork Clearwater River.

Thursday 26th Sept. 1805. a clear pleasant morning. about 8 oClock we Set out and proceeded on down the River crossed a creek,[1] then crossed the River at a shole place the water to the horses belleys. we proceeded on down the South Side and formed an Encampment[2] opposite the little River which came in on the N. E. Side on a narrow plain thinly covd. with pitch pine timber. made a pen round the officers lodge to put the baggage in. a number of the natives come down with us with droves of horses. Some came down the N. E. fork with a Small raft, who had been Some distance a fishing and bring down wood &C. Several of the party Sick with a relax by a Sudden change of diet and water as well as the change of climate also. Several Indians came down in a Small canoe & Camped near us.—

1. Orofino Creek, Clearwater County, Idaho.
2. The party's "Canoe Camp," where they remained until October 7, 1805. It is about five miles west of Orofino, Clearwater County, on the south bank of the Clearwater River and opposite the mouth of the North Fork Clearwater.

Friday 27th Sept. 1805. a fair morning the party divided into five differeent parties and went at falling five pitch pine trees for 5 canoes, all near our Encampment. in the afternoon the man who went back to the Mountain for the 2 horses returned. had found one of the horses, and had killed a large deer and brought a part of it with him.—

Saturday 28th Sept. 1805. a clear morning. two men went out a hunting. all the party that were able to work went at makeing the canoes and oars. the natives visit us and catch Some fresh Sammon which we purchase from them we fixed Some gig poles &C.—

Sunday 29th Sept. 1805. a fair morning. 2 men[1] went out a hunting. all hands employed at the canoes as usal. the Indians caught and Sold us Several Sammon, &C—

1. Drouillard and either Collins or Colter, according to Clark.

Monday 30th Sept. 1805.[1] 2 hunters Stayed out last night. a fair morning. we continued on with the work. the party So weak that we git along Slow with the canoes. towards evening our hunters returned one of them had killed a deer and a pheasant.—

1. This is the last daily entry in Ordway's first notebook journal (see Ordway's entry for May 14, 1804). Then follows a table of "Computed distance" (next) from the party's Camp Fortunate, below the forks of the Beaverhead River, to the Pacific Coast.

[*undated*][1]

The Computed distance in miles from Jeffersons River at the head of the Missourie The place the canoes of the party of N. W. discovery was lift in 1805.—

	miles
From the mouth of the Missouri canoe deposit—	3096
To the dividing Mountain head Spring—	24
To the first fork of the Columbia River	14
To the first large fork down the River	18
To the forks on the raod at mouth of Tower Creek	14
To fishing Creek (after leaving the River)	23
[To] flat head River at first Camp—	41
To the mouth of travvellers wrest ⟨creek⟩—	76
To the foot of the mountain East side	12
To the Flat head village in a plain—	3
To the first of koskoskia River Canoe Camp	21

	miles
To the Ki moo e nem down the kos kos kia	60
To Columbia River down ki mo e nem R.	140
To Snake Indian River on South Side—	162
To the great falls of Columbia River—	6
To the Short Narrows—	3
To the long narrowns on Timn—	3
[To] the mouth of Catterack River N. Side—	[2?]
To the grand Shoote or rapids—	4
To the east rapids at Strabury Island—	6
To the Mouth of quick Sand River South Side—	26
To Shallow bay on N. Side at Salt water	
To blustery point on N. Side—	13
To point open Slope below perminent Encampment of the party of N. W. Discoveries in 1805—	3
To Chim nook River in the bottom of Haileys bay	12
To Cape disappointment on the western ocean—	13
Capt. Clark & party proceeded on 10 miles on the Coast North west.—	
Total	4120

1. This table postdates the entries in this notebook. Ordway could have entered the material any time after the party arrived at the Pacific Coast. The notes may have been added to blank pages in the notebook during the extended stay at Fort Clatsop. The table is placed here to indicate its placement in the original.

Tuesday 1st October 1805.[1] a clear pleasant morning. we Continued on makeing our canoes as usal. built fires on Some of them to burn them out. found them to burn verry well our hunters killed nothing this day.—

1. This begins Ordway's entries in his second notebook journal, covering the period October 1, 1805, to May 15, 1806. It is one of the marble-covered books of 184 pages measuring approximately 6½ by 3¾ inches (see Appendix C, vol. 2). Preceding the initial daily entry is the following on the first two pages of the journal.

"Sergt. Ordays Journal Commencing the first Oct. 1805— it being a minute relation of the various transactions and occurrences which took place during a voiage of two years 4 months ⟨Years⟩ and 9 days from the United States to the Pacific Ocean through the interior of the Continent of North America.—

"A Scatch of the beginning of Sergt John Ordways journal which commenced at River Duboise in Year 1804, 14th of May under the directions of Capt. Meriwether Lewis and Capt. William Clark, and patronised by the Government of the U. States. The individuals who composed the party engaged to essay the difficulties dangers & fatigues of this enterprise with the said officers; consists of the persons whose Names are in the later part of this book as well as the begining as above, not bein room here. So all that is on each Side of this leaf is coppied in the later end of this book and this is no account."

The material at the end of the notebook to which Ordway refers is found in this volume at his entry of March 22, 1806.

Wednesday 2nd Oct. 1805. a fair morning two men[1] Sent with Six horses up to the villages in order to purchase a quantity of Sammon and root bread which the Natives call Commass. one hunter out in the hills we continued on with the work. towards evening the hunter came to Camp had killed nothing but one prarie wolf which we eat. the party are so weak and unwell living without meat that our officers thought proper with the oppinion of the party to kill a good horse which was done and we eat the meat as earnest as though it had been the best meat in the world. in the evening we bought a fiew fresh Sammon and a little Commass from the Savages who are Camped near us.

1. Frazer and Goodrich, according to Clark.

Thursday 3rd Oct. 1805. a clear morning. we Continue on with the canoes as usal. Some of them forward.—

Friday 4th Oct. 1805. a fair morning. two men out to hunt Some of the canoes ready to dress out. Some of the party bought a fat dog. the hunters killed nothing this day.—

Saturday 5th Oct. 1805. a clear cool morning a little white frost. the two men returnd from the villages late last evening with their horses loaded with commass roots and Some more in loaves and a considerable quantity of dryed Sammon &C. Several dressed Elk Skins and otter &C we continued dressing off the canoes. got up all our horses 38 in number. we branded[1] them on the near fore Shoulder with a Stirrup Iron, and cropped their fore mane So as we may know them at our return. the old chief[2] who we leave the care of our horses with has engaged to go on with us past his nation and leave the horses in the care of his two sons our officers gave them Some Small presents &C. another Chief[3] engaged to go with us also. towards evening we put two of the canoes which was finished in to the water.—

1. Now in the possession of the Oregon Historical Society, Lewis's branding iron bore the inscription "U.S. Capt. M. Lewis."

2. Twisted Hair of the Nez Perce. See Clark's entry of September 21, 1805.

3. Tetoharsky, also a Nez Perce. See Clark's entry of October 7, 1805, and Lewis's and Clark's entries of May 4, 1806.

Sunday 6th Oct 1805. a pleasant morning. a hole or carsh dug hide our pack Saddles in. we got oars and poles ready. towards evening we got the other canoes ready to put in the river. Some gig poles got ready. an Indian raft seen floating down the koskoskia River.[1] one of the men killed two ducks. after night burryed the pack Saddles &C.—

1. The Clearwater River. "Kooskooskee" is probably a Nez Perce term, but opinions differ about its meaning; see Clark's entry of this day.

Monday 7th Oct. 1805. a clear morning. we put the other three canoes in to the River. got them in readiness and loaded them about 3 oClock P. m. we Set out on our journay to descend the River. proceeded on over Several Sholes and rapids where we halled the canoes over Sholes. Some part of the River is deep and current gentle &c. the hills and clifts make near the River on each side. Saw old Indian Camps on Lard. Side Came 21 miles and Camped[1] on the Stard. Side.—

1. Near Lenore, Nez Perce County, Idaho.

Tuesday 8th Oct. 1805. a fair morning. we delayed here Sometime changing the officers canoes &C. hid a canister of Powder by a broken top tree. about 9 oClock we Set out and proceeded on Saw Some Indians horses on the Side of the hills on Stard. Side. passed over Several bad rapids took in Some water by the waves. passed Some clifts of rocks and barron hills on each Side. about 12 OClock we halted at Some Indian Camps about 6 lodges of well looking Savages who had Several Small canoes and catch considerable of Sammon. we bought some from them. 2 dogs also. we proceeded on a Short distance and halted at Some more Camps at the foot of an Isld. and rapids where we bought Some more Sammon and Some white roots &C. then proceed on descended a rockey rapid at the foot of an Island where was Several Indian Camps. one of the canoes Struck a rock in the middle of the rapid and Swang round and Struck another rock and cracked hir So that it filled with water. the waves roared over the rocks and Some of the men could not Swim. their they Stayed in this doleful Situation untill we unloaded one of the other canoes and went and released them. 2 Indians went in a canoe to their assistance also. we got the men and the most of the baggage Safe to Shore. a fiew articles lost one tommahawk and a fiew light things. we put the baggage out and Camped[1] on the Stard. Side at high plains. a number of Savages visited us this evening— had Come about 18 miles to day

1. Below the confluence of the Potlatch and Clearwater rivers, Nez Perce County, a few miles from Spalding. The party remained here until October 10.

Wednesday 9th Oct. 1805. a fair morning, and warm. we delayed to Repair the canoe and dry the baggage &C. the natives brought fresh Sammon and trade with us. the River hills Still continue high and broken on each Side. Some Scatering pine timber &C. the natives are very troublesome to us two Sentinels placed to keep them from Stealing from us. as the baggage was exposed. we got the canoe repaired in the evening we bought a considerable quantity of Sammon, a little commass roots. in the evening Some of our party fiddled and danced, which pleased the natives verry much. one of their women was taken with fit by one of our fires. She began Singing Indian and to giving all around hir Some commass roots, and brasslets which hung about hir one of our party refused to take them from hir. She then appeared angry threw them in the fire. took a Sharp flint from hir husband and cut both of hir arms in Sundry places So that the blood gushed out. She Scraped the blood in hir hand and Eat it, and So continued ⟨for⟩ in this way about half an hour then fainted or went in to a fit Some time then came too by their puting water on hir and Seemed to take great care of hir &C—

Thursday 10th Oct. 1805. a clear morning. the two guides[1] who came with us from the Snake nation left us yesterday, and we expect they have returned back again. we Set out eairly and proceed on down passed over a number of bad rapids took water in the canoes by the waves. passd Several Camps of Indians where they had large fisherys we bought Some from them. they have pleanty of Small canoes for the purpose of fishing. about 11 oClock we came to a verry bad rapid which was full of rocks, we halted and took one canoe down at a time one of them Struck a rock in the rapid and broke a hole in hir Side but with Some difficulty we got hir Safe to Shore unloaded & repaired hur. the Indians caught some of the oars &c for us. we bought a little more Sammon and one or two dogs, and about 2 oC. we Set out again and proceeded on as usal. passed Several Sholes where we had to wade and hale the canoes over passd several more fishing camps. about 5 oClock P. M. we came to the Columbia River[2] which is wide and deep. we went on down it a short distance and the wind blew so high from N W that we had come 20 miles to day and nearly a west course. this great columbia River is about 400 yards wide and afords a large body of water and of a greenish coulour. the country on each Side is high barron and mostly broken Some high plains which look pleasant, but no wood only a fiew willows in Some places along the Shores.—

1. Toby and his son.
2. Actually, the group had reached the Snake River, on the Idaho-Washington border.

Chapter Forty-Six

Winter on the Coast

October 11, 1805–May 1, 1806

Friday 11th Oct. 1805. a clear morning. we Set out eairly. two Indians accompy. us in a Small canoe. we proceeded on. at 8 oClock we halted at a large fishing Camp of Indians[1] where we bought Some Sammon and 8 or 10 fat dogs &C. these Savages have among them pleanty of beeds and copper trinkets, copper kittles &C which must have come from white people we proceeded on passed Several more fishing camps, where they have the Stone piled up in roes, So as to gig the Sammon at the Sides of the rocks &C. the country is barron and broken Some high plains. no timber. we can Scarsely git wood enofe to cook a little victules a fiew willows in places along the Shores. passed over Some rapids where the waves roled high. we roed 30 miles this day and Camped[2] at a fishing party of Indians, where we bought 3 or 4 more dogs and a little Sammon &C—

1. Probably a band of Nez Perces, but perhaps including Palouse Indians, as well.
2. In the vicinity of Almota, Whitman County, Washington, where a band of Nez Perces resided near Palouse Indians.

Saturday 12th Oct. 1805. a fair morning. we Set out eairly, and proceeded on as usal. passed a number of old fishing camps along the Shores. high plains no timber. we came 35 miles this day and Camped[1] on the Stard Side little above a bad rockey rapid. our Small pilot canoe and the Indian canoe went over [the rapids?] this evening

1. In the area of Riparia, Whitman County, Washington.

Sunday 13th Oct. 1805. a rainy morning. wind high. delayed untill about 10 oClock then took down one canoe at a time below the rapids. all the men who could not Swim Carried each a load of baggage by land. about 12 we got Safe below the rapids at 2 oClock cleared off. Saw a great number of fishing camps where the natives fish everry Spring. they raft all their wood down the River a long distance and they put it up on Scaffels and take great care of it. towards evening we passed through a place in the River where it was all confined in a narrow channel of about 15 yards wide for about 2 miles and ran like a mill race large fisherys below in the Spring. Saw 2 Indians Swim their horses across the river to the N. Side and went on down the River. passed a creek[1] which came in on the Lard. Side this afternoon the current Swift. the barrons and plains continue as usal.

1. Tucannon River, Columbia County, Washington.

Monday 14th Oct. 1805. a clear cold morning. the wind high N W. we Set out as usal and proceeded on the current rapid. about noon we came to a bad rockey rapid where 2 canoes ran fast on a rock but we got off without Injury. a Small Island on the Lard. Side of the rapids we halted jist below to dine. then proceeded on about 8 miles then came to another bad rapid at the head of an Island. the canoe I had charge of ran fast on a rock in the middle of the river and turned across the rock. we attempeted to git hir off but the waves dashed over hir So that She filled with water. we held hir untill one of the other canoes was unloaded and came to our assistance considerable of the baggage washed overboard, but the most of it was taken up below when the canoe got lightned She went of[f] of a sudden & left myself and three more Standing on the rock half leg deep in the rapid water untill a canoe came to our assistance. we got the most of the baggage to Shore two mens bedding lost one tommahawk, and some other Small articles a Small copper kittle &C. we Camped[1] on an Island Stard. Side at an old fishery where the natives had dryed Sammon burryed their wood covred over it. we took Some for our use &C. one of the men killed 8 ducks the country continues barron and broken in places &C—

1. On an island now inundated by Lake Sacajawea. The area is downstream from Burr Canyon, Franklin County, Washington.

Tuesday 15th Oct. 1805. a clear cool morning. we delayed to dry the baggage which was wet. Some of the men went out and killed three geese and Several ducks. about 3 oClock P. M. we loaded the canoes and Set out again and proceeded on the current very rapid. the country continues barron as usal. Came 27 miles this day and Camped[1] little above a bad rapid—

1. Above Fishhook Rapids, Franklin County, Washington.

Wednesday 16th Oct. 1805. we Set out as usal and proceedd on over the rockey rapids one of the canoes run fast on a rock in a bad rapid and Stayed untill we went with a canoe to their assistance. got all Safe to land loaded and Set out again and proceeded on. in the afternoon we Came to the last bad rapid as the Indians Sign to us. we halted little above and carried Some of the baggage past by land abt. one mile then took the canoes Safe down and loaded them again and procd. on passed over Several rapid places in the River. towards evening we arived at the big forks.[1] the large River which is wider than the Columbia River comes in from a northerly direction. the Country around these forks is level Smooth plain. no timber. not a tree to be Seen as far as our Eyes could extend. a fiew willows Scattering along the Shores. about 200 Savages[2] are Camped on the point between the 2 rivers. we Camped near them. they Sold us eight fat dogs and Some fresh sammon. in the evening the whole band came Singing in their way to our Camp around our fires and Smoaked with us, and appeared verry friendly. they have pleanty of beeds Copper & brass trinkets, about them which they Sign to us that they got them from Some tradors on a River to the North of this place—

1. The juncture of the Columbia and Snake rivers. Ordway continues to consider the river on which he has been traveling the Columbia; it is actually the Snake. The party camped this day and the next at the point where the rivers join, in Franklin County, Washington.
2. Yakima and Wanapam Indians.

Thursday 17th Oct. 1805. a clear pleasant morning. we delay here this day for our officers to take observations &C. the natives Stole a large ax from us last night. we bought Several more dogs from them as we can git no other meat to eat, &C. a number of the Savages have red and blew cloth, but no buffalow Robes among them. the River which we came down looses its name and is now Called Kimo e num[1] the North fork which is the largest is Called the Calumbia River. Capt. Clark and 2 men went up it abt. three miles to the Indian lodges. they Saw a great quantity of Sammon in the R. they giged a verry large Sammon. they Saw a great number lay dead on the Shores which the Indians had giged. a great number of large fowls in the praries a Size larger than haith [heath] hens.[2] Some of the men killed Several of them. our officers took down Some of the language found these to be of the flat head nation but another tribe.[3] our officers gave Some of the principal men meddles & flags and Some other Small articles these Savages are verry poor but peacable. Some of them naked and Some have dressed Elk and Deer Skins with the hair on. Some fiew rabit Skins also. they have a numbr of horses among them. their grave yards are picketed in. and the place about these forks is verry pleasant— and Smooth &C—

1. This is the name the captains gave to the Tucannon River, but which they seem to have attached to the Snake in error for a time. See Clark's entries of October 10, 13, and 16, 1805. The river they came down was the Snake which the leaders named the Lewis in honor of the captain.

2. The party's first specimen of the sage grouse, *Centrocercus urophasianus*.

3. The Flatheads are Salish speakers, whereas the Yakimas and Wanapams are of the Shahaptian-language family and totally unrelated. Perhaps the word "not" was left out of the sentence or Ordway may have been using the term "flat head" for all the Indians they had met since descending from the Rocky Mountains.

Friday 18th Oct. 1805. a clear pleasant morning. we delayed here untill after 12 oClock to day Capt. Clark measured Columbian River and the Ki mo e nem Rivers and found the Columbia River to be *860* yards wide, and the ki moo e nem R. to be *475* yards wide at the forks.[1] Capt. Lewis Compleated his observations and found the Latitude to produce [*blank*] North our officers compared several of the natives languages and found these to be of the flat head nation but another tribe. about 2 oClock P. M. we Set out. two chiefs continued on with us. we proceeded on down the great Calumbia River which is now verry wide about ¾ of a mile in General the country in general Smooth plains for about 10 miles down then the barron hills make close to the River on each Side passed Several Smooth Islands on which was large fishing Camps. large quantity of Sammon on their Scaffels. we Saw a great many dead Sammon floating in the River, and Saw the living jumping verry thick. we Saw a great nomber of horses near Some Indian villages the lodges of which was made of flags and large grass verry neatly worked.[2] we passed over Several rapids. no timber along the Shores. we Camped[3] on the Lard Side at a fiew willows which we got to burn. a nomber of the Savages came to our Camp in Small canoes.—

1. Clark has the distances as 960¾ yards and 575 yards.

2. Flag is common cat-tail, while the grass is probably beargrass, *Xerophyllum tenax* (Pursh) Nutt.

3. Beyond the mouth of the Walla Walla River, Walla Walla County, Washington, and near the Washington-Oregon border.

Saturday 19th Oct. 1805. a clear cold morning. the natives brought us Some pounded Sammon. about 7 oC A M we Set out proceeded on passd high clifts of rocks on each Side of the River. the natives are verry numrous. our officers gave one[1] a meddle and Some other small articles. this morning passd. Several Small villages the Savages all hid themselves in their flag loges untill we passed them. the Indians are numerous along the River. the villages near each other and great quantitys of Sammon drying. we passed over Several rapids which are common in this River. we discovred a verry high round mountain[2] a long distance down the River which appears to have Snow on the top of it. we came 36 miles this day and Camped[3] on the South Side an Indian village on the opposite Shore a nomber of the natives came over the River in their Small canoes to see us. when any of these Savages dye they bury them and all their property with them and picket in their grave yard. even their canoes are put around them.—

1. Yelleppit, chief of the Walula, or Walla Walla, Indians.

2. Probably seeing Mt. Adams, east of the main Cascade Range in Yakima County, Washington.

3. Apparently between Irrigon and Boardman, Morrow County, Oregon.

Sunday 20th Oct. 1805. a clear frosty morning. we Set out eairly. proceeded on passed a pleasant part of the County level Smooth plains but no timber. the River Smooth. we Saw Some pilicans and abundance of ravens and crows,[1] as the Shores are lined with dead Sammon. about 12 oClock we halted at a village to dine where we bought a fiew roots &C. and Saw among them a number of articles which came from white people. Such as copper kittles Scarlet &C. passed many rapid places of water. the country continues as yesterday our hunters who went in the small canoe killed nine ducks and a goose to day. we came 46 miles this day. and Camped[2] on the Starbord Side no wood except a fiew Small willows.—

1. The common raven, *Corvus corax,* and the western variety of the common crow, *C. brachyrhynchos hesperis.*

2. In the vicinity of Roosevelt, Klickitat County, Washington.

Monday 21st Oct. 1805. a clear cold morning. we Set out eairly and proceeded on as usal we then halted at an Indian village where we bought a little wood and cooked breakfast. bought Some pounded Sammon from the natives, and Some white root cakes which is verry good. we Saw among them a number of fisher and rackoon Skins.[1] Some otter Skins[2] also. these Savages gave us any thing we asked them for, by our giving them any Small article as we pleased, as if they were in fear of us. we proceeded on passed River hills and cliffs of rocks on each side. passed over a number of bad rockey rapids where the River is nearly filled with high dark coul-oured rocks the water divided in narrow deep channels, bad whorl pools. passed several Islands and fishing camps. Saw a great quantity of pounded Sammon Stacked up on the Shores. we Saw a fiew Scattering pine on the hills. we came about 32 miles this day and Camped[3] at some Indian lodges close under high clifts of rocks on the Stard Side a handsome Spring flowed out of the clifts. these Savages have a fiew Elk and Deer Skins dressed with the hair on which they wear for covering. they have also a fiew blue cloth blankets &C—

1. Fisher, *Martes pennanti,* and raccoon, *Procyon lotor.*

2. Perhaps the river otter, but notice confusion about the sea otter and harbor seal in the next entry.

3. In the vicinity of John Day Dam, Klickitat County, Washington.

Tuesday 22nd Oct. 1805. a fair morning. we Set out at Sunrise and proceeded on. passed a number of fisheries and a high Island which had towers of Solid rocks and verry high and rough. a roaring rapid at the Stard Side we went down a narrow channel on the Lard. Side a large river[1] puts in verry rapidly of the Island about 40 yards wide Several perpinticular falls near its mouth. large fishing Camps at the lower end of the Island. this Isd. is about 4 miles in length and high rough & rockey. a Short distance below we came to the first falls of the Columbia River.[2] we halted about noon a Short distance above at a large Indian villages. the huts of which is covred with white ceeder bark these Savages have an abundance of dry and pounded Sammon we bought Some from them and Some flag & grass mats &C. they have a number of small canoes and a fiew horses our officers viewed the falls and found that we had a portage of about ¾ of a mile, on the Stard. Side. So we went at carrying the baggage past the portage. hired Some horses from the natives to take the heavey baggage past, &C. [*illegible letters*] we got all except the canoes below the falls and camped[3] close under a high range of clifts of rocks, where the body of the River beat against it and formed a verry large eddy. we Saw a number of large Sea otter[4] below the falls in the whorl pools and eddys the natives are verry troublesome about our Camp—

1. The Deschutes River, forming the line between Wasco and Sherman counties, Oregon. The island is later Miller Island.

2. The Celilo, Great Falls, of the Columbia River, near Wishram, Klickitat County, Washington, and Celilo, Wasco County, Oregon.

3. Beyond the falls near Wishram where the group remained until October 24.

4. Not a sea otter, *Enhydra lutris,* which never leaves salt water, but evidently the harbor seal, *Phoca vitulina richardii.*

Wednesday 23rd Oct. 1805. a clear pleasant morning. about 8 oClock Capt. Clark went with the most of the party and took all the canoes across the River and halled them about a quarter of a mile over the rocks past a perpinticular fall of 22 feet and put them in a verry rapid channel below. this portage has been used by the natives takeing their Small canoes round and close below the great falls is a large fishery in the Spring of the year and the flies at this time are verry numerous and trouble us verry much as the ground is covred with them we got the canoes all in the channel below the big fall then the best Swimmers went on board and took them through the whorl pools a little more than half a mile then came to two more pitches of abt. three feet each we let the canoes down by ropes. one of them broke loose from us and went over Safe and was taken up by the natives below. towards evening we got the canoes all Safe down to camp without dammage—

The Latitude at this place which is called the grand falls of the Columbia River as taken by Capt. Lewis is 45° 42′ 57.3′ North. the hight of the particular falls in all is 37 feet eight Inches, and has a large rock Island in the midst of them and look Shocking the water divided in several channels by the rocks. Some of the cooks at camp bought several fat dogs this day. in the evening one of our chiefs Signed to us that the natives had a disign to kill us in the night, So we prepared for them &C—

Thursday 24th Oct. 1805. the natives did not attempt to trouble us last night. a clear pleasant morning. we loaded the canoes and Set out about 9 oClock and proceeded on the current rapid we went through a narrows[1] where the river is all confined in a narrow channel of about 20 yds and verry rapid and bad whorl pools, and went on verry well towards evening we came to another narrows[2] we camped[3] little above at an Indian village which was made half under the surface of the ground and the upper part well formed and covred with white ceeder bark. they are verry comfortable houses. we bought a number of fat dogs, crambries and white cakes of root bread. high prarie and barron hills near the River but appears to be Some timber back from the River.

1. The Short, or Little, Narrows, and the Long Narrows, which the party would pass the next day, together constitute The Dalles of the Columbia River above the town of The Dalles, Wasco County, Oregon. The narrows have disappeared under the waters of The Dalles Dam.

2. Long Narrows.

3. In the vicinity of Horsethief Lake State Park, Klickitat County, Washington, among Wishram-Wasco Indians.

Friday 25th Oct. 1805. a fair morning. we carried some of our baggage by land about one mile past the worst of the narrows. then took one canoe at a time down the narrows and whorl pools. one of the canoes filled with water running through the narrows we got all below and loaded the canoes we have now 16 bags of Sammon on board about 3 oClock P. M. we Set out and proceeded on the narrows continued about 2 miles and verry rapid. 2 Small Islands of Sollid rock Stood in these narrows one of the canoes was near dashing in peaces by Strikeing hir bow against the upper point of one of them. the River between these narrows and the great falls rises at high water 48 feet perpenticular by its being confined by the different narrows. near the lower end of the narrows we Saw a war party of Indians which had jest Swam the River to the Stard Side with their horses. they had some vension &C with them. we halted a fiew minutes and our officers Smoaked with them they gave us some bears oil and a little vension and Some fresh fish. we went on 2 chiefs told us that their was a nation below which they were at war with and they did not wish to go any further with us so our officers Settled with them and they returned back to their nation. we then went on Saw Some drumm fish[1] jumping in the River the River gitting Smoth. Saw pine and oak timber near the Shores we can Still See the round high mountain Some distance a head yet. we Camped[2] below the mouth of a creek on a point of rocks on the Lard. Side. the country timbred back a little from the River.—

1. The fish is not identifiable; see Clark's entry for this day.
2. At the mouth of Mill Creek at the town of The Dalles, Wasco County, Oregon, the party's "Fort Camp" or "Fort Rock Camp," where they remained until October 28.

Saturday 26th Oct. 1805. a clear pleasant morning. our officers delay here for observations &c. and to repair the canoes also. Several men went out in the timbred land to hunt. we unloaded the canoes and halled them out of the water to Smooth their bottoms and repair them. one of the men giged a Sammon Trout[1] in the River. towards evening the hunters returned to Camp had killed 5 Deer a goose and a gray Squerrell.[2] a number of Savages came in canoes made in form of Sciffs to our Camp. our officers took down Some of the language from these Savages and Compared with all other we have passd. and find them to be all of a flat head nation but different tribes. we think the flat head nation to be more than ten thousand Strong. the River raised considerable this afternoon

1. Apparently the steelhead trout.

2. Probably the western gray squirrel, *Sciurus griseus*.

Sunday 27th Oct. 1805. a fair morning. the wind high from the west. Six men went out to hunt. Some of the Indians Stayed with us our officers gave one of the principal men a meddle and Some other Small articles. towards evening the hunters returned to camp had killed four Deer. we Set the Indians across the River. the waves roled verry high.—

Monday 28th Oct. 1805. rained hard the later part of last night. cleared up this morning we then loaded the canoes and Set out proceeded on down a fiew miles and halted at a Small village[1] on the Stard side where we bought several dogs Some berrys &C. Saw a british musket copper tea kittles &C. among them. we then went on a Short distance further the wind rose So high N W that obledged us to halt on the Lard. Side under Some clifts of rocks.[2] the Indians came in their canoes to our camps. one of the party killed a Deer and wounded another this evening a Short distance back near a pond. a little rain this evening.

1. The party's Chiluckittequaws (variously spelled), probably Wishram-Wascos.

2. A few miles below The Dalles, Wasco County, Oregon, in the vicinity of Crates Point, and above Rowena.

Tuesday 29th Oct. 1805. a cloudy morning. we Set out eairly, and proceeded on about 6 miles and halted at Some Indian lodges where we bought a number more dogs and proceeded on the current gentle passed a great number of Indian villages[1] on the Stard Side. passed a creek on the Stard. Side and one on the Lard. Side.[2] Saw 2 or 3 cabbens on the Lard. side which is the first we Seen on that Side on this River. Saw a beautiful Spring on the Lard. Side, which run off a high clift of rocks, and fell of the clift upwards of a hundred feet perpinticular. the country Mountaineous. high clifts on the River. mostly covred with pine timber. Some cotten wood[3] on the narrow bottoms. Some willow also we bought several more dogs at one of the villages. we Came 26 miles this day and Camped[4] at a village on the Stard. Side Saw Snow on a mountain on the Lard. Side.—

1. More Chiluckittequaws, living in Klickitat County, Washington.

2. The party's Cataract River, now Klickitat River, Klickitat County, on their right, and their Labiche River for François Labiche, now Hood River, Hood River County, Oregon, on the left.

3. Probably black cottonwood, *Populus trichocarpa* T. & G.

4. A little above the mouth of Little White Salmon Creek (Little Lake Creek to the Corps), Skamania County, Washington.

Wednesday 30th Oct. 1805. a cloudy morning. we bought 3 dogs of the Indians and Set out and proceeded on the River wide and Strait the current gentle. the timber thick on each Side. Saw a number of beautiful Springs which came in on each Side. the narrow bottoms along the Shores are covred with cotten timber and under brush. the after part of the day rainy and foggy. one of the hunters killed a Deer we Saw a great number of Swan[1] and geese along the Shores. Some turkey bazzards[2] which had white under their wings. Capt. Clark killed a black loon.[3] towards evening we heared a great roaring a Short distance a head which we expect is another falls. we passed the mouth of a River[4] which came in on the Stard. Side about 40 yards wide we passed a large Indian village on the Stard. Side a Short distance above the big Shoote. we Camped[5] close above the Shoote. a number of the Savages came to our Camp and Signed to us that they were Surprized to See us they thought we had rained down out of the clouds. Several of the party went to the village and was treated verry friendly. we had come about 15 miles this day.—

1. Probably Lewis and Clark's whistling swan, now the tundra swan, *Cygnus columbianus.*

2. California condor, *Gymnogyps califorianus.*

3. Not mentioned by Clark, it may be either the red-throated loon, *Gavia stellata,* or the Pacific loon, *G. arctica pacifica,* of the coastal area. It might also have been the widely dispersed common loon, *G. immer.*

4. "Crusat River" to the party, named for member Pierre Cruzatte, now Wind River, Skamania County, Washington.

5. Until November 1 they camped here, just above the Cascades of the Columbia (Ordway's "Shoote"), on an island in Skamania County, nearly opposite Cascade Locks, Hood River County, Oregon. The Indians are Yehuhs.

Thursday 31st Oct. 1805. Cloudy. we unloaded the canoes and went at halling them past the Shoote took one down at a time over verry high rocks. this Shoote is full of rocks and roles verry high waves &C. the after part of the day pleasant.

Friday 1st November 1805.— a fair morning. the wind high from the N. E. and cold. we carried all our baggage past the portage a number of Indians with canoe loads of pounded Sammon are going down the River tradeing. they are carrying their loads past the portage with us & their canoes also. we then took down the rest of the canoes. got them all Safe below the big Shoote and Camped[1] their on the Stard. Side.

1. In Skamania County, Washington, above Bonneville Dam and near the communities of Fort Rains and North Bonneville.

Saturday 2nd Nov. 1805. a fair morning. we carried Some of our baggage past the last rapid about one mile further and took one canoe down at a time partly loaded. about 10 oClock A. M. we got all Safe below the last bad rapid we can git any account of from the natives. then loaded up the canoes. 2 Indians came to us from a village below who had red and blue cloath blankets which appeared new one had a brass musket and powder flask a little powder &C. about 12 we Set out passed a large Island mostly prarie which our officers name Strabery Island.[1] we halted a fiew minutes and killed Several geese. passd. Several old villages about or a little below the big Shoote on the Stard. Side. at the foot of Said Island we passd. over a rapid which high waves in it the hills high on each Side but mostly covred with pine timber. proceeded on about 4 miles further the River got more Smooth the current gentle wide and Strait. passed the mo. of a creek[2] on the Lard. side Saw a number of Spring runs flowing from the high clifts and Mountains. Some of which falls off about 100 feet perpinticular[3] we came 21 miles this day & Camped[4] under a verry Shelving clift on the Lard. Side—

1. Hamilton Island, Skamania County, Washington.
2. Perhaps Tanner Creek, Multnomah County, Oregon.
3. Perhaps scenic Multnomah and other falls in Multnomah County.
4. In the vicinity of Latourell, within Rooster Rock State Park, Multnomah County.

Sunday 3rd Nov. 1805. a foggy morning. the geese verry pleanty on a marshey green below the Camp one of our hunters Shot Several flying. Several Savages Stayed with us last night they have 2 canoes with them. we perceive the tide rise and fall a little at this place. one of the hunters[1] went out a Short distance to hunt and killed a large Deer. about 9 oClock we set out and proceeded on the fog So thick that we could not See across the River. passd. Several Sand Islands about noon we halted to dine at the mouth of a River which is filled with quick Sand and is wide and Shallow our officers name this River Quick Sand River[2] on the Lard. Side. here we perceive the tide water. we Saw the round mountain some distance a head which we expect is the Same which was discovred by Lieut. Hood and is called Hoods Mountain.[3] the after part of the day pleasant the River is better than a mile wide in general. towards evening we met several Indians in canoes they Signed to us that their was Some white people and vessells &C. passed Several bottoms covred with cotten and oak pine &C. the Country not so Mountaineous as above. we came 13 miles this day and Camped[4] on a verry large Island which is mostly prarie and large ponds, which is full of Swan Geese brants and ducks &C. Several Indians Camped with us. at Sunset we got a small canoe and carried in the pond Several Swan geese and brants killed by the party to day and this evening.—

1. Collins, according to Clark.
2. Sandy River, Multnomah County, Oregon.
3. Mt. Hood, Hood River County, Oregon, was named in 1792 for British Admiral Sir Samuel Hood by Lieutenant William Robert Broughton of George Vancouver's expedition.
4. On either Government or McGuire islands, opposite and upstream from Portland, Multnomah County.

Monday 4th Nov. 1805. cloudy. the tide Ebbs and flowes abt. 3 feet at this place one of the hunters killed a Deer on Said Island. about 7 oClock we set out and proceeded on passed Several large Islands partly covred with cotten timber & partly prarie. proceeded on about 8 miles came to a large new village[1] on the Lard. Side consisting of about 35 Cabbens and have 50 fine canoes they have considerable of cloaths of different kinds among them, wool hats &C. we bought Several dogs, and Some excelent roots nearly like potatoes[2] these Savages killed and brought in Several

Deer to day. we then went on a Short distance farther & halted to dine on the Stard. Side two canoe loads of Savages followed us and Stole Capt. Clarks pipe tommahawk which he had been Smoaking with them. we could not find it with them. they had Several muskets on board of their canoes. we then proceeded on passed Islands the most of the way on the Lard. Side and timbred bottoms on each Side Some oak mostly cotton timber the pine continues back from the River. we passed Several large villages on each Side the natives verry numerous the country appears good the Soil rich. towards evening we met several Indians in a handsom canoe which had an Immage on the bow. one of the Indians could talk & Speak Some words English Such as curseing and blackguard they had a Sturgeon on board and have five muskets on board. we discovred a high round mountain Some distance back from the River on the Stard Side which is called mount rainy—[3] Saw a number of sea otter in the River. we Came 28 miles this day and Camped[4] after dark on the Stard Side the geese and brants verry thick

1. Called Shahala Village by Clark, it was home to the Watlala Indians, an Upper Chinookan-language people. The village, long since destroyed, was within the limits of modern Portland, Multnomah County, Oregon.

2. Wapato, *Sagittaria latifolia* Willd.

3. Not Mt. Rainier, but the closer Mt. St. Helens in Skamania County, Washington.

4. Probably near Salmon Creek, Clark County, Washington.

Tuesday 5th Nov. 1805. hard rain the later part of last night. we proceeded on about 10 miles and passed a verry large village at the foot of an Island[1] on the Stard. Side they have a number of canoes Some of the Savages came out in the River in their canoes to See us they wanted to trade with us for muskets offered us dressed Elk Skins. passed Several Islands Some of the hunters killed one Swan and Several brants. we had Several Small Showers of rain we Came 31 miles to day and Camped[2] on the Lard. Shore— the pine hills make close to River

1. The party's Green Bryor Island, now Bachelor Island, near the mouth of Lewis River, the boundary between Clark and Cowlitz counties, Washington.

2. Southeast of Rainier, perhaps near Prescott, Columbia County, Oregon.

Wednesday 6th Nov. 1805. Several Showers of rain in the course of last night. we set out as usal and proceeded on Shortly passed a Small village on the Lard. Side Several Indians came out in a canoe to trade with us we bought Some fresh fish and some roots. we passed large bottoms covred with cotton timber passd. 2 old villages which was Evacuated. the wind rose from the west towards evening So that the waves run high. we Came 29 miles this day and Camped[1] on the Stard. Side close under a clift of rocks—

1. In southwestern Wahkiakum County, Washington (see Clark's entry of this day).

Thursday 7th Nov. 1805. a foggy cool morning. we Set out eairly and proceeded on about 10 oClock we halted at an Indian Village[1] where we bought Some fresh fish and Some roots. we proceeded on passed a number of Islands which are low and marshy. partly covred with willows &C— the hunters killed a Swan and Several geese to day and Camped[2] on the Stard. Side at a Spring run—

1. A Wahkiakum Indian village in Wahkiakum County, Washington
2. Opposite Pillar Rock, between Brookfield and Dahlia, Wahkiakum County.

Friday 8th Nov. 1805. a Cloudy morning. we Set out as usal. the waves high tossed us abt. passed round a point in to a bay which we Call Shallow bay[1] where the River is 5 or 6 miles wide we can See along distance a head we expect we can See the mo. of the Columbian River. we but it appears a long distance off. we halted in the Shallow bay at some old Indian Camps to dine. the Swan and geese are verry pleanty in this bay. Some of the party killed Several ducks &C. we then proceeded on an Indian Canoe and Several Indians in met us we bought Several fresh fish from them. the waves roled So high that we were obledged to land on the Same Shore Stard. Side and took great pains to keep the canoes from filling with water. the River water is gitting so brackish that we cannot drink of it at full tide. the evening rainy.—

1. Grays Bay, in Pacific and Wahkiakum counties, Washington.

Saturday 9th Nov. 1805. rained hard the greater part of last night, and the wind rose so high N. W that we had to unload the canoes in the night. this morning wet rained the most of the day and the wind So high up the River that Caused the tide to raise much higher than common So we had to moove our loads and Some of the Camps further from Shore. Some of the party killed Several ducks in the course of the day.—

Sunday 10th Nov. 1805. considerable of rain fell last night. a rainy morning. the waves not So high as yesterdy we loaded the canoes and Set out and went on passed high clifts of rocks, and fine Springs. we Saw porpises[1] in the River. Saw a number of Sea otter, Sea gulls,[2] ducks &C. continued raining hard abt. noon the wind rose So high that obledged us to turn back from a point of rocks and roe about 2 miles back into a cove before we could git a place to unload the canoes. we got in to the harbour and unloaded the canoes and Stayed untill towards evening. then loaded again thinking to find a Safer harbour. we went on a Short distance to a Spring run where we Camped.[3] the wind contind. So high that we could not proceed. the hills and pine timber make close to the River on each Side. we had Scarsely room for to camp.—

1. The harbor, or common, porpoise, *Phocoena phocoena*.

2. The gulls could be any of a number of species of *Larus*.

3. On the eastern side of Point Ellice, Pacific County, Washington, near the town of Meglar, where they stayed until November 15 except for a short move on November 12.

Monday 11th Nov. 1805. rained hard the greater part of last night. a rainy wet morning. our Robes all wet as we have no Shelter that will keep the rain from us. the wind continued So high that we did not attempt to move this day abt. 10 oClock four Indians came in a canoe to our Camp we bought a number of Sammon Trout from them. they tell us that they have Seen vessels in the mouth of this River and one man by the name of Mr. Haily[1] who tradeed among them, but they are all gone. these Savages went in their canoe across the River in the high waves. Some of our party giged and Shot 16 Sammon Trout

1. Perhaps Samuel Hill of Boston, skipper of the brig *Lydia,* who traded with the Indians of the lower Columbia (see Clark's entry for November 6, 1805).

Tuesday 12th Nov. 1805. a hard Storm continued all last night, and hard Thunder lightning and hail this morning we Saw a mountain[1] on the opposite Shore covred with Snow. the rain continued hard all day. we moved our Camp a Short distance further up the River to the mouth of a creek and got a more comfortable Camp. we giged Several more Trout in this creek.

1. Perhaps Mt. Hood, some distance to the southeast in Hood River County, Oregon.

Wednesday 13th Nov. 1805. hard rain continued all last night a rainy morning. in the afternoon three men[1] Set out in the Small canoe in order to go down towards the mouth of the River and See what discovrees they could make. as the wind continues So high that obledges us to stay—

1. Colter, Willard, and Shannon, according to Clark.

Thursday 14th Nov. 1805. the Storm continues, and obledges us to Stay in this disagreeable harbour with nothing but pounded Sammon to Eat. one of the men[1] returned who had been down the River and informed us that they went down to an Indian Village in the bay about 10 miles down but Saw no white people. Capt. Lewis and four men[2] Set out by land to go down the River to the mouth.

1. Colter, according to Clark.
2. Drouillard, Joseph and Reubin Field, and Frazer, says Clark.

Friday 15th Nov. 1805. a wet morning. about 10 oClock A. M cleared off the after part of the day calm and pleasant we loaded up the canoes and at low tide we Set out and went down about 5 miles passed an old Indian village a little below the clifts passd. Several Small creeks. the country below the clifts is lower and covred with Small timber. we Camped[1] in a verry large bay on a Sand beach on L. Side. one of the men[2] who went down the River first joined us. Several Indians with him. he informed us that the Savages at the village Stole two of their guns when they were asleep last night, but when Capt. Lewis went to the village they Scared them So that they gave them up again. we took plank from the old village to make us Camps &C.

1. Southeast of Chinook Point, on the east side of Baker Bay, Pacific County, Washington, and west of McGowan. Here the main party remained until November 25, with perhaps a short move on November 16 (see Clark's entry, November 16, 1805).

2. Shannon, according to Clark.

Saturday 16th Nov. 1805. a clear cool morning. Several men went out a hunting. we put our baggage out to dry. towards evening the hunters all except one returned to Camp had killd. four Deer and a number of geese brants and ducks. a number of Savages Stayed with us all day.—

Sunday 17th Nov. 1805. a clear morning Several of the party went out a hunting, and Several more for meat. in the after part of the day the hunters returned to Camp had killed two Deer and Several geese and brants &C. Capt. Lewis and party returned to Camp also, and informed us that they had been about 30 miles down which took them on the Sea Shore and a verry bad road the most of the way.[1] they Saw the harbour where the vessells had lain but they were all gone.—

1. Lewis's party reached the Pacific Coast near Cape Disappointment and went up the coast some miles in Pacific County, Washington. There is no known account of this reconnaissance.

Monday 18th Nov. 1805. Cloudy. Capt. Clark myself and 10 more of the party[1] Set out in order to go down and see the passiffic ocean. we proceeded on round Hailys bay[2] crossed two Rivers[3] in Sd. bay. one of the party[4] killed a verry large turkey buzzard which had white under its wings, and was nine feet from the points of the wings, and 3 feet 10 Inches in length, and everey way proportined. we proceeded on round high clifts of rocks where we had much trouble to pass.— towards evening we arived at the Cape disapointment on the Sea Shore. went over a bald hill[5] where we had a handsom view of the ocean. we went on a Short distance on the coast and Camped[6] for the night.

1. Clark gave the other men's names in two inconsistent lists, those named included Clark, Ordway, Charbonneau, Pryor, the Field brothers, Shannon, Colter, Weiser, Labiche, Bratton, and York.
2. Baker Bay, Pacific County, Washington.
3. Chinook and Wallacut rivers, Pacific County.
4. Reubin Field killed the expedition's first specimen of the California condor.
5. Probably McKenzie Head in Fort Canby State Park, Pacific County.
6. Near McKenzie Head.

Tuesday 19th Nov. 1805. cloudy a light Sprinkling of rain the later part of last night we proceeded on the coast over high rough hills Some places prarie and bald hills. one of the hunters killed a Deer. we halted and eat a part of the Deer and went on over a verry bad rough way along the coast. high towers of rocks Standing out in the edge of the ocean. we got over these rough hills the country appears low further on the coast. So we went on the Sand beach about 10 miles distant from Cape dissipointment, then turned back,[1] cut across the woods a new way, and Camped[2] at Chi neck River in Hailys bay.

1. The party went as far as the area about Long Beach, Pacific County, Washington.
2. On the east side of Wallacut River, a mile or more northeast of Ilwaco, Pacific County.

Wednesday 20th Nov. 1805. a fair morning. one of our hunters[1] went out a Short distance to Some ponds & killed several brants & ducks. we eat them and went on up the other River and village the Indians had all left the village, So we made a raft and one man went across and got a canoe. we then returned to Camp.[2] a great number of Indians at Camp. our men at Camp had killed Several Deer, geese and brants &C.—

1. Labiche, reports Clark.
2. The men returned to the camp of the main party at Chinook Point; see November 15.

Thursday 21st Nov. 1805. a cloudy and a little rain The Latitude of Hailys bay or at our Incampment at the point above is 46° 19′ 11 7/10″ Min North. the Natives value their Sea otter Skins verry high. our officers being anxious to purchase a robe made of two of those animels, they offered great prices in cloaths trinkets &C. but they would not take any thing except blue beeds. at length they purchasd the Robe for a beeded belt which our Intrepters Squaw had these animels are Scarse & hard to kill.

Friday 22nd Nov. 1805. a hard Storm arose the later part of last night and continues raining and the wind high from the S. W. the waves rolled So high and the tide raised much higher than common dashed one of our canoes against the logs and was near Splitting it before we got it out. dammaged it and obledged us to move Some of our Camps.—

Saturday 23rd Nov. 1805. Still continues rainy and high wind Several men went out a Short time a hunting and killed 3 Deer and 21 fowls. a number of Savages visited us &C—

Sunday 24th Nov. 1805. a clear pleasant morning. a white frost Several men went out a hunting we put out our baggage to air. The Calumbian River at this place is three miles 660 yards wide. Some of two nations of Indians came to our Encampment the Clatsop and Chinuck nations[1] they behave very well as yet. our officers conclude with the oppinion of the party to cross the River and look out a place for winters quarter[2] Some where as near the ocean as possable on the account of makeing Salt.

1. The Clatsop Indians are discussed under Clark's entry of November 21, while the Chinook Indians are considered at November 15.

2. See notes on the discussion and the record of the vote at Clark's entry of November 24.

Monday 25th Nov. 1805. a clear pleasant morning. we put the canoes in the River loaded up. our officers bought two more Sea otter Skins of the natives. we then Set out and Came about 9 miles up the River and attempted to cross over to the opposite Shore but the waves So high that the canoes were near filling. So we turned back to Shore again and kept along the Shore about 4 miles above Shallow bay and Camped.—[1]

1. Near the party's camp of November 7, opposite Pillar Rock, Wahkiakum County, Washington.

Tuesday 26th Nov. 1805. a Cloudy wet morning. we Set out eairly went about one mile then crossed the River and went down along the South Shore passed Several Islands, halted at a village of the Clotsop nation.[1] they gave us pleanty to eat and appeared verry friendly. we bought a fiew wapatoes roots, &C the day rainy and cold. we went on passd. Several low marshey Islands which was covred with course grass, and willows the Shore is high land covred thick with pine timber and under brush. we Campd[2] in a thick part of wood

1. The Indians were Cathlamets, living along the south shore of the Columbia River; see Clark's entry for November 11.

2. In Clatsop County, Oregon, near Svenson.

Wednesday 27th Nov. 1805. rained all last night. Several Indians came from the village to trade their wapetoes roots with us. we went on across a bay then turned a cape & where we could perceive a considerable of current in the River we went on about one mile further the waves ran So high that obledged us to halt at an old fishery.[1] hard rain.

1. The party moved along the shore and crossed the neck of Tongue Point, the group's Point William, to its west side and camped there, east of Astoria, Clatsop County, Oregon. Most of the party, including Ordway, would remain here until December 7, while Lewis and several men sought a winter camp.

Thursday 28th Nov. 1805. a hard Storm. the wind high from the N. West. Several men went out to hunt the but killed nothing hard rain all day—

Friday 29th Nov. 1805. Capt. Lewis and five men[1] Set out with the Small canoe in order to go down the River to look out a place for winters quarters. Showery and Some hail in the course of the day.

1. Drouillard, Reubin Field, Shannon, Colter, and Labiche, according to Lewis.

Saturday 30th Nov. 1805. Some of the party killed three ducks. the after part of the day clear.

Sunday 1st December 1805. a cloudy morning. Several of our men are unwell living on pounded Sammon only.

Monday 2nd Decr. 1805. a Cloudy wet morning. Several men went out a hunting. one of them returned towards evening.[1] had killed an Elk Six men went with a canoe after the meat—

1. Joseph Field, Pryor, and Gibson went hunting; Field returned that evening.

Tuesday 3rd Decr. 1805. Cloudy about 10 oClock A. M. the men returned with the meat. 2 hunters[1] Stayed out a hunting a number of Indians came in a Canoe to our Camp. in the evening the two hunters returned had killed Six Elk about 5 miles distance from this place.—

1. Pryor and Gibson.

Wednesday 4th Decr 1805. a rainy wet morning. Sergt. Pryor & Six men Set out to go and dress and take care of the Elk meat. continued Storming & high wind all day.—

Thursday 5th Decr. 1805. rainy dissagreeable weather. about noon Capt. Lewis and three men returned and informed us that they had found a tollarable good place for our winters quarters about 15 miles down the South Shore, a Short distance up a Small River.[1] they had killed 7 Elk and five Deer. 2 men stayed to take care of the meat—

1. The site of Fort Clatsop on Lewis and Clark River, Clatsop County, Oregon, called Netul River by the party.

Friday 6th Decr. 1805. about noon the Storm arose and the tide raised about 2 feet higher than common So that the water came in to our Camp So that we moved our Camps to higher ground. the Storm cont. all day.

Saturday 7th Decr. 1805. the morning clear we put our canoes in the water loaded up and set out and proceeded on down the River. the Shore is covred thick with pine and under brush. passd. Several Spring runs.

the waves ran verry high. we could not land untill we turned a point in a bay[1] where we halted and cooked a young Deer which the hunters had killed the other day. the men who had been out to take care of the meat joined us with 4 Elk hides but no meat the distance so great and the weather so bad that they brought no meat. Capt. Clarks servant did not come up with the rest. Capt. Clark Stayed with one canoe and waited for him a Short time we proceeded on the waves roled verry high. the canoe I was in ran on a Sand barr and was near filling. but the waves took hir off without injury. we proceed. on round a bay then went up a River abt. 3 miles and landed at the place appointed for winters quarters.[2] this River is about 100 yds wide at this place but the tide water extends further up. we unloaded the canoes and carried all our baggage about 2 hundred yards on a rise of ground and thicket of handsom tall Strait pine and balsom fir[3] timber and Camped here we intend to build a fort and Stay if game is to be found thro. this winter Season.—

1. Youngs Bay, Clatsop County, Oregon, called Meriwether's Bay by the party, in honor of Lewis.

2. Fort Clatsop on Lewis and Clark River, near Astoria, Clatsop County, the party's camp until March 23, 1806.

3. The pine may be Sitka spruce, *Picea sitchensis* (Bong.) Carr.; the "balsom fir" is probably grand fir.

Sunday 8th Decr. 1805. one canoe taken away from the landing by the tide last night. a hard white frost this morning, and cold. 12 men was dispached with two canoes after Elk meat. Capt. Clark and 5 men[1] went across by land to the Ocean in order to blaze a road and look out a place to make Salt &C. in the evening the men returned with a fine chance of Elk meat. we formed an Encampment &C.

1. Including Drouillard and Shannon, according to Clark's entry of December 9.

Monday 9th Decr. 1805. rained the greater part of last night I went with Eight men after the remainder of the meat. rained hard all day. we returned towards evening with the meat and found the canoe which the tide took off the other night. 4 Indians came in a canoe to See us &C—

Tuesday 10th Decr. 1805. the Indians left us this morning. all hands wen[t] at clearing away the ground for the huts. rained hard the most of the day, towards evening Capt. Clark and 3 of his party returned from the ocean and informed us that it was about 7 miles to the ocean the way they blazed a road. they was at a Small village[1] of the Clatsop nation of Indians on the Coast. they treated them in a friendly manner. considerable of prarie land on the Coast &C. Some low marshes also.—

1. At Seaside, Clatsop County, Oregon; see Clark's entry for December 9.

Wednesday 11th Decr. 1805. we began raiseing one line of our huts. rained the greater part of the day. George Gibson Sick.

Thersday 12th Decr. 1805. a number of the Clatsop Indians visited us.[1] we finished raiseing one line of our huts.

1. Including Coboway, a Clatsop leader, according to Clark.

Friday 13th Decr. 1805. cloudy & rain we raised another line of our huts and began the last line of our huts forming three [sides of a] Square and 7 rooms 16 by 18 feet large. the other Square we intend to picket and have gates at the 2 corners, So as to have it a defensive fort. Capt. Lewis bought Several kinds of curious Skins from the natives as a curiousity Such as wild cat[1] and Some other Small Skins which the Indians Call Shugolell[2] which they make Robes of. in the evening our 2 hunters returned had killed 17 Elk.

1. Probably the Oregon bobcat, *Lynx rufus fasciatus*.
2. Ordway attempts the Chinookan term now Anglicized as "sewelel," for the mountain beaver, *Aplodontia rufa*. It is Lower Chinookan *swalál;* see Lewis's entry of February 26, 1806.

Saturday 14th Decr 1805. continues wet and rainy. we continued on with the huts. 2 men employed Splitting out plank to cover our huts with. we finished raiseing the other line of huts & began covring one room for a meat house.—

Sunday 15th Decr. 1805. Capt. Clark and the most of the party set out with three canoes to go after the 17 Elk. went up as far as possable with the canoes then packed each man 2 loads each, and went after the third and got Scattered night over took Some of us and I Whitehouse Collins and Hugh Mcneal got lost and Stayed out all night with out fire.[1]

1. Clark also counted Colter in this group.

Monday 16th Decr. 1805. rained hard all last night and cold we Suffered with wet & cold all last night, and could not make fire for everry thing we had was wet. we Soon found ourselves this morning and went to Camp put the meat on board the Canoes and the loads the men brought in this morning, and all except 5 or 6 went down to Camp or fort hard rain and high wind. those men who Stayed in the woods went after the rest of the meat. we put the meat in house—

Tuesday 17th Decr. 1805. a little Snow and hail fell last night and continues this morning. we went at chinking up our huts and Splitting plank &C. cut our meat & hung it in the meat house &C

Wednesday 18th Decr. 1805. cloudy and rain. Several men Sent with 2 canoes across the bay after Some plank. they returned towards evening with the canoes loaded with plank which they took from Some old fishing Camps. a little hail and frozen rain & cold—

Thursday 19th Decr. 1805. rained all last night, and continues hard this morng. I was taken verry unwell last night. the men in general are in good health. Several of the Clatsop Savages came to visit us &C.

Friday 20th Decr. 1805. cloudy and rain. about 10 oClock cleared off, but rained again before evening.—

Saturday 21st Decr. 1805. Still continues raining but we Still kept at work finishing our huts to make ourselves comfortable &C.—

Sunday 22nd Decr. 1805. high wind all last night. the weather rainy warm & wet.

Monday 23rd Decr. 1805. nothing extraordinary hapened more than common this day.—

Tuesday 24th Decr. 1805. hard rain as usal. we finished covering our huts and made fires in them. Some of the men moved in them this evening—

Wednesday 25th Decr. 1805. rainy & wet. disagreeable weather. we all moved in to our new Fort, which our officers name Fort Clotsop after the name of the Clotsop nation of Indians who live nearest to us. the party Saluted our officers by each man firing a gun at their quarters at day break this morning. they divided out the last of their tobacco among the men that used and the rest they gave each a Silk hankerchief, as a Christmast gift, to keep us in remembrence of it as we have no ardent Spirits, but are all in good health which we esteem more than all the ardent Spirits in the world. we have nothing to eat but poore Elk meat and no Salt to Season that with but Still keep in good Spirits as we expect this to be the last winter that we will have to pass in this way.—

Thursday 26th Decr. 1805. we found that our huts Smoaked by the high winds and hard Storms hard rain continues as usal.—

Friday 27th Decr. 1805. we built backs and enside chimneys in our huts which made them much more comfortable than before. in the evening Several Savages came to the fort.[1] hard rain all day.—

1. The group included Coboway again, according to Clark.

Saturday 28th Decr. 1805.— the Savages Stayed at the fort all last night and informed us that a verry large fish was drove to Shore on the coast and that their women wer packing the oil and meat. our offi Capt. Lewis and three men got ready to go with a canoe to See the whail as we expect it is, but the wind and Storm arose So high that they could not go five men Set out by land with kittles to go over to the Sea coast to form a Camp and make Some Salt.[1] three men[2] went across the River a hunting in the evening 2 hunters returned had killd. one Deer.—

1. Joseph Field, Bratton, and Gibson were accompanied by temporary hands Willard and Weiser to set up a saltmaking camp at Seaside, Clatsop County, Oregon. It operated until February 21, 1806, under varying personnel.
2. Clark names five men hunting this day: Drouillard, Shannon, Labiche, Reubin Field, and Collins.

Sunday 29th Decr. 1805. a fair day. the men at the fort are employed gitting pickets &C. Several of the Chin ock nation[1] came to the fort with wapatoe roots and dry Sammon to trade we bought Some from them &C.—

1. Clark says they were Wahkiakum Indians.

Monday 30th Decr. 1805. a fair morning and a little Sun shine which is verry uncommon at this place. we finished puting up our pickets and gates of the fort. about 2 oClock P. M. three hunters[1] came to the fort had killed 4 Elk. Seven men Set out immediately and brought in the meat. a centinel placed in the fort to look out for the Savages for our Safety, &C.—

1. Including Drouillard, according to Clark.

Tuesday 31st Decr. 1805. a cloudy morning Several more of the natives[1] came to the fort with wa pa toe roots we bought Several bags from them. we built a box for the centinel to Stand in out of the rain dug 2 Sinques[2] &C—

1. They were Wahkiacums and Watlalas ("Skillutes"), reports Clark.
2. Latrines.

Wednesday 1st Jany. 1806— The party Saluted our officers at day break this morning by firing at their quarters as a remembrence of the new year a pleasant morning. 2 men went out a hunting. Several of the natives[1] visited us. they go bare leged all winter and bare footed Some kind of a little Robe over their Shoulders &C. the women have Short peticoats made of Some kind of grass Some of which are twisted like twine, and are nearly naked otherways the general part of them are verry poor and ask a large price for any thing they have to part with. in the evening the two hunters returned & had killed two large buck Elk.—

1. Clatsop Indians, according to Lewis and Clark.

Thursday 2nd Jany. 1806. rained the greater part of last night and continues this morning 14 men went out and brought in the meat our officers issued an order[1] for the regulation of the Garrison at this place, charging the party to treat the natives will &C.—

1. The order was issued January 1; see the Orderly Book entry at that date with Lewis's and Clark's materials.

Friday 3rd Jany. 1806. hard Thunder hail and rain the greater part of last night one of the hunters caught a large otter. Sergt. Gass went over to the Salt Camps, about 10 oClock a number of the natives[1] came to the fort. in the evening three of our hunters[2] came to the Fort had killed nothing but one Deer one Swan and 4 ducks, also a raven which they eat on new years day to Satisfy their hunger.—

1. Including Coboway and six other Clatsops, according to Lewis and Clark.
2. Reubin Field, Collins, and Potts, according to Lewis and Clark, but Potts was not included in Clark's enumeration of December 28.

Saturday 4th Jany. 1806. Small Showers of rain and hail as usal. the Clatsop Indians trade to us Some excelent Sweet roots. one of the party bought a dog also.—

Sunday 5th Jany. 1806. a wet rainy morning. in the afternoon one of the hunters[1] returned to the Fort had killed nothing except one brant and 2 ducks Shortly after 2 men[2] came from the Salt Camp with about 2 gallons of Salt. they had killed three Elk and one Deer. they informed us that the Savages brought loads of the whail that they had informed us of. Our men bought Som of the meat from them which was good.

1. Colter, according to Lewis and Clark.

2. Willard and Weiser, who had caused some concern to the captains due to their long absence since accompanying the saltmakers on December 28.

Monday 6th Jany. 1806. Capt. Clark and 12 men[1] Set out with one large canoe and the Small one in order to go after Some of the whail on the coast. about 9 oClock A M. cleared off pleasant and warm.

1. Including Charbonneau, Sacagawea, Pryor, Frazer, McNeal, and Werner. Others who may have been in the party were Jean Baptiste Charbonneau, Colter, Lepage, Reubin Field, Potts, Labiche, Windsor, Shields, and either Cruzatte or Weiser. See Clark's entry of this day.

Tuesday 7th Jany. 1806. clear and pleasant. George Drewyer went out to his traps abt. 3 mls. and found in them one large beautiful black otter and a beaver. he brought the beaver in to Eat. contn. clear all day which is a very uncommon thing at this place.

Wednesday 8th Jany. 1806. a clear warm morning— two men[1] went out from the fort a hunting.

1. Drouillard and Collins, according to Lewis.

Thursday 9th Jany. 1806. rained the greater part of last night but cleared off pleasant this morning, and continues warm

Friday 10th Jany. 1806. a clear pleasant day about noon the 2 hunters returned had killed one Elk. towards evening 12 Savages[1] came to the fort with wap a toes roots to trade. we bought Some from them and 2 dogs also. in the evening Capt. Clark and the most of his party returnd. to the fort and informed us that they had been abt. 25 miles along the Sea coast about a South course. they passed over verry Steep high rough rockey mountains to git to the whail. the natives Shewed them the fraim of a verry [large?] whail which had been some time dead it was 100.5 feet in length,[2] and proportined accordingly. they brought some of the jaw bones and some other black bones which are handsome. their was Several villages along the coast of different tribes which lived mostly on whail meat, and fish, Some Seals &C. they had a large quantity by them. they Saw a great many bones of whails along the Shore. one night our men were Camped near a Small village on a Small River, one of our men Hugh Mcneal went to the village by himself withot any arms. an Indian which belonged to Some other nation came to Mcneal and took him out with a design to kill him for his blanket. Some of the other Indians who wishd us well called across the creek to our men. Several went with arms to his assistance the indian hearing the alarm ran from him with his long knife without injury.[3] this Creek was named by Capt. Clark Mcneals folley[4] and the Mountain which they crossed made out in the ocean he called Capt. Clarks view.[5] they bought and brought in considerable of whail meat, and the oil Several of the men Stayed at the Salt Camps.

1. Including Shar-har-war-cap, a chief, and eleven others of the Cathlamet tribe.

2. Clark on January 8 says the whale was 105 feet long; it may have been a blue whale, *Balaenoptera musculus.*

3. Clark reports this incident in his entries of January 8 and 9.

4. Clark does not mention this name for the river he called Ecola Creek after the Chinookan word for whale, but Whitehouse uses it. The creek's name, formerly Elk, has been restored to Clark's designation; it is in Clatsop County, Oregon.

5. Tillamook Head, Clatsop County.

Saturday 11th Jany. 1806. our Small canoe got loose from the landing last night, & went away. Some time last night 7 men went with a canoe after the Elk meat. Several more went to look for the Small canoe. towards evening we returned with the meat &C.

Sunday 12th Jany. 1806. a fair morning. 2 men[1] went out a hunting. 3 men went again to look for a canoe but did not find it. Several men[2] returned from the Salt Camp. towards evening the 2 hunters who went out this morning came in had killed 7 Elk within about 2 miles of the ft.

1. Including Drouillard, according to Lewis and Clark.

2. Including Gass, Shannon, Frazer, and Gibson.

Monday 13th Jany. 1806. rained hard all last night and continues this morning. Capt. Lewis and all the party except the guard went after the Elk meat. Six men Set jurking the meat to keep it from Spoiling.

Tuesday 14th the tide water took away one of our canoes but we Soon found it again.

Wednesday 15th rained hard the greater part of the day.

Thursday 16th the rain & Storm high winds continues as usal.

Friday 17th Jany. 1806. three men went out a hunting a number of the natives[1] came to the fort. about noon one of the hunters[2] came in with a Deer which he had killed.—

1. Coboway again.
2. Colter.

Saturday 18th hard rain all last night, and continues as usal. 2 Indians came to the fort and Stayed a Short time.

Sunday 19th 4 men[1] went out a hunting. moderate Showers of rain. the men in the fort are employed dressing Elk Skins for Mockasons, &C. Several of the natives visited us, and Sold us Several handsome Hats[2] made of Some kind of Splits curiously worked &C.—

1. Including Willard, Labiche, Shannon, and probably Colter. See Lewis's entry for this day.
2. Besides the entry for this day, see Lewis's and Clark's entries for December 29, 1805, and January 29, 1806, for descriptions of and notes on the native hats.

Monday 20th Jany. 1806. rainy and wet. the Crows and ravens verry pleanty about the fort.

Tuesday 21st Cloudy and rain. in the afternoon 2 of our hunters Shannon & Labuche came to the fort had killed three Elk.—

Wednesday 22nd I and 14 more of the party went with one canoe after the Elk meat. a hard Storm of rain and verry high wind. we had a disagreeable time of it. three of the hunters[1] Stayed out to hunt.

1. Reubin Field, Shannon, and Labiche.

Thursday 23rd a little Thunder and hail in the course of last night 2 men[1] Set out to go over to the Salt Camps after Some Salt. high wind &C—

1. Howard and Werner, according to Lewis and Clark.

Friday 24th Jany. 1806. a light Snow fell the later part of last night. Several Showers of rain and hail this day. in the afternoon G. Drewyer & Batteast Lapage came to the fort. 3 Indians came with them in a canoe. Drewyer had killed 4 Elk 2 of the other hunters killed 2 deer. they brought the meat in the indians canoe except what they gave them for packing &C.

Saturday 25th Jany. 1806. froze a little last night, and a little more Snow fell intermixet with hail. continues Squawlly this morning. 2 men[1] came from the Salt Camps. had been a hunting but killed nothing except the deer which was brought in yesterday.

1. Collins was one of the two, according to Lewis and Clark.

Sunday 26th Jany. 1806. considerable of Snow fell in the course of last night and continues this morning, and cold freezing weather the Snow is this evening about 5 Inches deep on a level.—

Monday 27th Jany. 1806.[1] froze hard last night a clear cold morning. one man[2] Set out to hunt for the Salt makers about noon George Shannon came to the Fort and informed us that he had killed five Elk and informed us that R. Feilds had killed three Elk and Labuche 2 Elk.— but Some of them too far to pack in.

1. Ordway left a portion of the page blank after this entry and began his next entry at the top of a new page.
2. Collins again, say Lewis and Clark.

Tuesday 28th Jany. 1806. a clear cold morning, and freezeing hard. 14 of the party[1] Set out eairly to go after the meat. the hunters could not find but 3 Elk in the thickets So we took them and returnd to the fort. 2 men[2] came from the Salt Camps had killed a large otter—

1. Including Whitehouse, according to his own journal.
2. Howard and Werner, report Lewis and Clark.

Wednesday 29th Jany. 1806. froze hard last night a clear cold morning. we do nothing except git wood for our fires &C.

Thursday 30th Jany. 1806. Cloudy and cold. Some fine Snow fell this morning. the evening clear and cold.—

Friday 31st Jany. 1806. a clear cold freezeing morning. Sergt. Gass and Six men set out a hunting took a canoe found Ice in the River So that they turned back. in the evening one[1] of the hunters returned from the Salt Camps he had killed two Elk which is the 1st that has been killed by the Salt makers a long time.—

1. Joseph Field, write Lewis and Clark.

Saturday 1st February 1806. a clear cold morning. Sergt. Gass and five more of the party Set out a hunting, and 4 men Set out with a hunter[1] to help with the meat to the Salt works.

1. Joseph Field again, record the captains.

Sunday 2nd Feby. 1806. the weather moderate. in the afternoon cloudy & a little Snow—but not any worth menting.

Monday 3rd Feby. 1806. a little frozen rain. about noon George Drewyer & Batteast[1] came in from hunting had killed Seven Elk & caught one large beaver. Six men[2] Set out with a canoe after the meat, but the wind So high that obledged them to return five men came in from the Salt works with about 2 bushels of good Salt, and Some whail meat which the natives call Ecoley.[3] we mix it with our poor Elk meat & find it eats verry well.—

1. Lepage.
2. Directed by Pryor, according to the captains.
3. The Lower Chinookan term for "whale," *íkuli*.

Tuesday 4th Feby. 1806. a clear pleasant morning. about noon the Six men Set out again with the canoe after the Elk meat tide high.—

Wednesday 5th Feby. 1806. a beautifl. pleasant morning. about noon one[1] of our hunters came in. had killed Six Elk. a party[2] who went across the river found our Sciff or Small canoe which was drove up on a marsh up a creek &C

1. Reubin Field, say Lewis and Clark.
2. Led by Gass, write the captains.

Thursday 6th Feby. 1806. I went with nine more of the party[1] after the Elk meat. we went out to the Elk and butchred them this evening & packed Some together & Camped. found 2 of the Elk in good order.—

1. Including Gass, Reubin Field, and Weiser, according to the captains.

Friday 7th Feby. 1806. we packed the meat to the River or marsh. I and one man[1] went to the Fort with the canoe and some meat hard rain &C.—

1. Weiser, say the captains.

Saturday 8th Feby. 1806. rained verry hard all last night we went with a canoe over and got the men & meat. the party[1] returned from down the River & went up this little River[2] for meat. we had several showers of hail this evening.

1. Pryor, Shannon, Labiche, and others, report the captains.
2. Lewis and Clark River.

Sunday 9th Feby. 1806. 2 men[1] went out to hunt. Six men went at jurking the meat. Several Showers of hail in course of the day.

1. Collins and Weiser, report Lewis and Clark.

Monday 10th Feby. 1806. a fair morning. a little Snow fell last night. in the afternoon two men[1] came in from the Salt works and informed us that Gibson is verry Sick at the Salt works and Bretn[2] verry unwell. the 2 men who came had killed 5 Elk but got only a little of it at the Salt works.—

1. Willard and Colter are named by the captains.
2. Bratton.

Tuesday 11th Feby. 1806. Sergt. Pryor and five men[1] Set out with a canoe to go round to the Salt works after the Sick men. 2 more men[2] were to Stay in their places three men[3] went out to hunt. the after part of the day rainy.

1. Only four, according to Lewis and Clark.
2. Colter and Weiser, report the captains.
3. Gass, Reubin Field, and Thompson, say the captains.

Wednesday 12th Feby. 1806. continues raining. one of the Clotsop Indians came to the Fort and Stayed all night.—

Thursday 13th Feby. 1806. cloudy and rain. one of the men bought a Sea otter Skin from the Indian for a peace of Tobacco not the half of a carrit.[1]

1. That is, a carrot of tobacco.

Friday 14th Feby. 1806. the morning warm and Showers of rain through the course of this day.—

Saturday 15th Feby. 1806. a fair day. in the evening the party returned Bratton came by land Sick they brought Gibson in a blankt up from the canoe. he is very Sick, and low.

Sunday 16th Feby. 1806. hard rain in the course of last night. three men[1] went out to hunt.

1. Shannon, Labiche, and Frazer, relate the captains.

Monday 17th Feby. 1806. a little Snow fell this fournoon. three hunters[1] came in with the meat of an Elk which they took out of a creek where some of the hunters had killed in the after part of the day Sgt. Gass and 2 men[2] returned to the Fort. they had killed Eight Elk, and jurked 2 of them. Some of the men killed a gray Eagle and a new kind of a Turkey buzzad.[3] one man[4] came from the Salt works for help to move in the Salt & kittles. Drewyer & Whitehouse came in had killed one Elk.—

1. The three from yesterday.
2. Reubin Field and Thompson; see the entry of February 11.
3. The California condor noted on October 30 and November 18, 1805.
4. Joseph Field, report the captains.

Tuesday 18th Feby. 1806. I and five more of the party Set out with a canoe for the Salt works. 10 more set out for the Elk meat.[1] we found the wind so high at the bay that we had to return to the Fort. had Several Squawls of wind & rain.

1. Led by Gass, as he reports.

Wednesday 19th Feby. 1806. a hard Storm of wind and rain myself and Six[1] more of the party Set out eairly to go by land to the Salt works to bring in the Salt & baggage we proced. on to the praries crossed the prarie where the land is in ridges like the waves the frozen rain beat in our faces verry hard. we got on the coast crossd. a river where we waided to our middles and was glad to git in an old Indian house where we made a fire and Stayed all night. Sand flew & waves rold.

1. Including Whitehouse, as mentioned in his own journal.

Thursday 20th Feby. 1806. the wind continued verry high from the S. W. we Set out eairly and proced. on along the coast faceing the wind the Sand cut our faces waided a creek rapid curret about noon we arived to the Salt works and bought a little Ecoley[1] and oil &C from the natives. the waves roles verry high and white froth flying &C.

1. That is, some whale meat.

Friday 21st Feby. 1806. we Set out eairly with all the Salt and baggage.[1] took an Indian canoe and crossed the River and travelled verry hard. when we got half way Set in to Storming & rained verry hard & the wind blew So high that we could not cross the creek in a canoe and waided across and got to the Fort about half past 12 oClock. much fatigued and I am at this time verry Sick, and wet to my Skins waiding the Slashes and marshes. the day verry disagreeable and Stormey &C. the party who went after Elk meat brought it in on evening of 19th inst.

1. Abandoning the saltmaking camp at Seaside, Clatsop County, Oregon.

Saturday 22nd Feby. 1806. a fair morning. George Gibson Some better. I am full of pains but not verry Sick. the rest of the Sick are mending a little. Several of the natives came to the Fort with some of their Split a[nd] chip hats which are Engeaneously made. Drewyer went to the village &C.

Sunday 23rd Feby. 1806. a fair morning. Six of the party are now Sick[1] I think that I and three others have the Enfluenzey.—

1. Ordway may have been the most ill, according to Lewis.

Monday 24th Feby. 1806. Cloudy. in the afternoon George Drewyer retorned and a number of Indians[1] with him they brought some hats and fresh fish. our officers bought a Sea otter Skin and Several hats for the party. the two hunters[2] came to the Fort had killed only one Elk.—

1. Coboway with a retinue of either twelve or fourteen as noted by Lewis and Clark.
2. Shannon and Labiche had been unsuccessful in the hunt, according to the captains.

Tuesday 25th Feby. 1806. a hard Storm of wind and rain. I feel a little better. the Storm contnd. thro the course of the day.—

Wednesday 26th Feby. 1806. the morning fair 4 men went out a hunting and 3 went with a canoe to the Clotsop and cathle mahs villages to purchase fresh fish and wa pa-toes &C.—[1]

1. The composition of the parties is somewhat different in Lewis's and Clark's entries for this day.

Thursday 27th Feby. 1806. a rainy wet morning. one man went out a hunting. in the afternoon one of our hunters[1] returned had killed one Elk. willard verry Sick the rest of us are Some better.

1. Collins, say the captains.

Friday 28th Feby. 1806. rained very hard the greater part of last night. Seven men[1] Set out eairly with a canoe after the Elk meat, and brought it to the Fort. two men Stayed[2] out to hunt. in the evening the other three hunters[3] returned had killed five Elk near a Small River 7 or 8 miles from this place—

1. Apparently led by Pryor.

2. The phrase "and brought . . . men Stayed" is written over some erased words that are illegible. The captains indicate that Reubin Field and Collins stayed out.

3. Shields, Joseph Field, and Shannon, report the captains.

Saturday the 1st March 1806. a fair morning. twelve men[1] Set out after the Elk meat. the day Showery and wet. in the evening the party returned except four[2] who Stayed out to hunt & brought in the meat. the Indian Name of the River they went up is Kil how-a-nàk-kle[3] and this River which we are on Ne-tul.[4]

1. Led by Gass, as he himself relates.

2. Thompson joined the three from the previous day.

3. Youngs River, Clatsop County, Oregon; see notes at Clark's entry of November 30, 1805. The term is Chinookan, *giławanaẋł*.

4. The Chinookan *nít̓ul;* it is Lewis and Clark River.

Sunday 2nd March 1806. a rainy morning. in the evening the three men returned from the village with a considerable quantity of the little fish[1] resembling herren only a Size Smaller—and some Sturgeon[2] and a fiew wapa-toes, which they purchased from them. the natives catch a vast quantity of fish &C—

1. The eulachon, or candle fish, *Thaleichthys pacificus*. Lewis and Clark called them anchovies and drew sketches of the fish in their journals; see vol. 6, figs. 41 and 42.
2. Either the white sturgeon, *Acipenser transmontanus*, or green sturgeon, *A. medirostris*. See Clark for November 19, 1805, and Lewis for February 25, 1806.

Monday 3rd March 1806. hard rain all last night. a rainy wet day. the most of the men are dressing Skins &C—

Tuesday 4th March 1806. rained hard all last night and continues all this day.

Wednesday 5th March 1806. a fair morning a number of the natives[1] came to the fort and brought us Some little fish and Sturgeon &C.

1. Clatsops, say the captains.

Thursday 6th March 1806. a fair morning Six men[1] Set out a hunting in different directions. Sergt. Pryor and 2 more men Set out with the Small canoe to go up the Columbia River to the Cath le mahs village after fish and wa-pa-toes, our old Clotsop Chief[2] visited us. we halled out our canoes to repair them &C.—

1. Including Drouillard, Labiche, and Collins, write Lewis and Clark the next day.
2. Coboway.

Friday 7th March 1806. a little hail last night and Showers of hail and rain this morning. Sergt. Gass and one man went at repairing the canoes. towards evening 2 hunters[1] returned had killed one Elk and Seen a number more.—

1. Drouillard and Labiche, say the captains.

Saturday 8th March 1806. we had Showers of hail and rain last night and continues this morning four others of the hunters[1] Came in. one of them had killed 2 Elk the others killed nothing but 1 deer and had lost the canoe which they took with them. Six men[2] Set out by water after the meat of one Elk. Drewyer & Jo Fields went out a hunting. the day cold and Showery. in the evening the men returned to the fort with the meat of the Elk.—

1. Collins, Shields, Reubin Field, and Frazer.
2. Including Labiche, say Lewis and Clark.

Sunday 9th March 1806. a little [snow?] & hail this morning and cold. I and 10 more of the party went and brought in the meat of the 2 Elk. Shortly after we returnd Several of the Clatsop Indians came to the Fort with Some Small fish and a little bears wax to trade to us. we bought a fiew &C.

Monday 10th March 1806. Showers of hail and a little Snow intermixed. Several men[1] went out a hunting. high winds &C.

1. According to the captains (this day and the next) two parties went on the Lewis and Clark River and another, consisting of Drouillard, Reubin Field, and Frazer, was to go beyond Youngs River.

Tuesday 11th March 1806. a little Snow fell last night. the morning three hunters[1] went out a hunting. Sergt. Pryor returned with a considerable quantity of Small fish and Sturgeon and a fiew wa-pa-toes &C— 4 men[2] went to look for the lost canoe but could not find it.

1. Drouillard, Joseph Field, and Frazer, note Lewis and Clark.
2. Led by Gass, say the captains.

Wednesday 12th March 1806. a white frost. clear and cold. one man went out a hunting. I went and made Search for the lost canoe but could not find it. the other canoes corked & pitched.

Thursday 13th March 1806. a fair cold morning. high winds. our three hunters returned to the fort. had killed two Elk and two deer.

Drewyer Sent to the Clatsop village in order to purchase a canoe. I went with Six more of the party after the meat of an Elk. Sergt. Pryor and 2 men went to look again for the lost canoe. in the evening all returned to the fort. Collins who went with Sergt. Pryor had killed two doe Elk and wounded 1 or 2 more

Friday 14th March 1806. Cloudy. four men went out a hunting and 7 of the party went for the Elk meat. they soon returned with the meat of 2 doe Elk. in the afternoon Drewyer returnd. and a number of the Clotsop Indians came with him brought a canoe to trade to us & some Hats &C.—

Saturday 15th March 1806. a fair morning. the Savages Stayed in the fort last night, but do not incline to Sell us their canoe. Drewyer and five men Sent up to the Cathlemahs village to purchase a canoe if possable our hunters returned had killd. four Elk.[1] all hands turned out and brought in the meat. a number of the Chin-nock nation[2] of Savages came to the fort. Some of the Clotsops[3] also

1. Collins, Joseph Field, Shannon, and Labiche, the last having killed the elk, according to the captains.
2. Including Delashelwilt, his wife, and six women, write Lewis and Clark.
3. A Clatsop man, Catel, and his family, say the captains.

Sunday 16th March 1806.— a rainy wet morning. the Savages Stayed in the fort. rained the greater part of the day. nothing else Extraordinary. our officers Sealed up some papers and letters for Mr Haily[1] and gave them to the Savages

1. Perhaps the ship captain Samuel Hill; see November 11, 1805.

Monday 17th March 1806. Showers of rain intermixed with Snow. we fixed our canoes and git in readiness for a Start expecting G. Drewyer to return from the Cath le-mahs. Showery all day. in the evening Drewyer returnd with a canoe which he had bought for Capt. Lewises Uniform coat and a small peace of Tobacco. we Should have Started this day had we been ready. &C—

Tuesday 18th March 1806.— a Showery morning of rain and hail. Some Thunder. we repair the Small canoes. 4 men went over to the prarie near the coast to take a canoe which belongd to the Clotsop Indians, as we are in want of it.[1] in the evening they returned 2 of them by land and killd. an Elk.[2] the others took the canoe near the fort and concealed it, as the chief of the Clotsops is now here.

1. The captains gave little notice to the incident; see their entries for March 17 and accompanying notes.

2. Joseph Field killed the elk.

Wednesday[1] 19th March 1806.— we went out and packed in the Elk meat. hard Showers of rain intermixed with Snow and hail.

1. Beginning with this day and for the next four entries Ordway apparently got the day of the week wrong, erased his mistakes, and then corrected his errors over the erasures.

Thursday 20th March 1806. rained hard the grater part of last night and continues this morning. So we are only waiting for good weather to Start. their has been 150 odd Elk killed by this party in the course of the last winter and 20 deer. the party has now got in all 338 pair of good Mockasons the most of them good Elk Skins Mockasons.

Friday 21st March 1806. rained hard all last night, and continues this morning. a number of natives visited us with Some dryed Small fish to trade which they call in their language oll-can.[1] we bought a fiew from them.

1. The captains wrote it "ol-then," a Chinookan term, *ú-ɬxan,* for dried eulachon; see Lewis's entry of March 25.

Saturday 22nd 1806. continues rainy. three hunters[1] Set out with a Small canoe to go on a head to hunt untill we come up. carried their baggage with them. 6 men Sent out a hunting. a number of the Clatsop Indians[2] visited us Sold us a dog & Some Small dry fish and Some fancy Hats &C. in the evening the hunters returned except one.[3] had killed nothing.

Fort Clatsop 22nd March 1806[4]

A Scetch of the beginning of Sergt. John Ordway's journal which he commenced at River Dubois (14 May) in the Year 1804.— Under the directions of Captains Meriwether Lewis and Capt. William Clark, and patronised by the Government of the U. States.— The individuals who composed the party engaged to essay the difficulties, dangers, and fatigues, of this enterprize with the Said officers; consists of the persons whose Names are here unto anexed. Viz: George Drewyer to act as interpreter and Hunter John Ordway Nathl Pryor, Charles Floyd & Patrick Gass Sergts John Shields William Bratten John Colter Hugh Hall John Collins Joseph Fields Reuben Fields Silas Goodrich Alexander Willard William Werner John Potts Thomas Proctor Howard Peter Wiser George Gibson George Shannon John B. Thompson Richard Windsor Robert Frazer Hugh McNeal, Peter Cruzatte Francois Labeech and Joseph Whitehouse—also Capt. Clarks Black man York.— At the Mandans Toussaint Sharbono and his Indian woman & child joined as Interpreters and Interpretess to the Snake Indians. also it being a Minute relation of the various transactions and occurences which took place during a voiage of two Years four months & 9 days from the U. States to the Pacific Ocean through the interior of the continent of North Amnerica.—

1. Drouillard and the Field brothers, according to the captains.
2. Including Coboway.
3. Colter stayed out.
4. This entry appears near the end of Ordway's second book of his three-volume journal. At least part of it must have been written after the return to St. Louis, since he counts the passage of time for the entire trip. It is placed here by date.

Sunday 23rd March 1806.[1] the one hunter stayed out last night rained hard the greater part of last night.[2] this morning proved so rainy and uncertain that our officers were undetermined for Some time whether they had best Set out & risque the [wind?] which appeared to be riseing or not. John Colter returned having killed an Elk about 3 miles towards point adams.[3] the rain Seased and it became fair about meridian at which time we loaded our canoes & at 1 P. M. left Fort Clatsop on our homeward bound journey. at this place we had wintered and remained from the 7th of Decr. 1805 to this day, and have lived as well as we had any right to expect, and we can Say that we were never one day without 3 meals of Some kind a day, either poor Elk meat or roots, notwithstanding the reputed fall of rain which has fallen almost continualy Since we passed the long narrows on the [*blank*] of Novr last, indeed we have had only [*blank*] days fair weather Since that time. Soon after we had set out from fort Clatsop we were met by a party of the Chinooks,[4] the old baud and hir Six Girls, they had a canoe, a Sea otter Skin dryed fish & hats for Sale. we purchased a Sea otter and proceeded on thro Meriwethers Bay. their was a stiff breeze from the S. W. which raised considerable Swells around Merewethers Point,[5] which was as much as our canoes could ride above point william[6] we came too at the Camp of G. Drewyer & the 2 Fields they had killed 2 Elk which was about 1½ mile distant. here we Encamped[7] for the night, having made 16 miles.—

1. From this point to the end of this notebook Ordway's writing gets smaller and he adds more lines to each page.
2. From this point to the end of the entry Ordway copies Clark nearly word for word.
3. Point Adams at the mouth of the Columbia River, Clatsop County, Oregon.
4. Delashelwilt, his wife, and her train.
5. Astoria, Clatsop County.
6. Tongue Point, Clatsop County.
7. At the mouth of John Day River, Clatsop County.

Monday 24th March 1806. I and 14 men went out eairly this morning and brought in the flesh of the 2 Elk killed by the hunters yesterday.[1] at half past 9 we Set out and proceed on to the Cath lah-mah village[2] at 12 m. and remained till ¼ after 3 p. m. at this village, this is the dirtiest & Stinkenest place I ever Saw. we proceeded on thro Some narrow channels between the Seal Islands[3] and the South Shore to an old village on South Side opposite to the lower war kia come village and Encamped[4] to the old village a verry considerable deposit of the dead at a Short distance below, in the usual customary way of the natives of this coast in canoes raised from the Ground. Soon after we landed and made fires 2 Indians came from the opposite Side which could Speak Some words of English and repeated the names of the tradors and a number of the Sailors &C.—

1. From this point Ordway largely copies Clark's entry of this day.
2. See Ordway's entry of November 26, 1805.
3. Karlson and Marsh islands in the Columbia River.
4. Northeast of Brownsmead, Clatsop County, Oregon. The village is discussed at Clark's entry of November 11, 1805.

Tuesday 25th of March 1806. we met a canoe of the Clatsops going down with their canoe loaded with fish and wa pa toes. the winds hard a head and tide against us So we delayd untill 1 oClock P. M. at which time we set out met 2 canoes of the Clotsops loaded with dried fish and wa pa toes &C & Sturgeon which they had purchased above. we crossed over to an Island[1] on which was a fishing Camp of the Cath le mahs. they had a vast Site of Sturgeon one of the men purchased a Sea otter Skin, the price of which was a dressed Elk Skin and a Silk hankerchief. we proceeded on from thence the after part of the day the wind rose high after dark we arived at another fishing Camp of the Cath le mahs where we Camped[2] for the night.

1. Puget Island, Wahkiakum County, Washington.
2. Below the mouth of the Clatskanie River, Columbia County, Oregon; see the captains' entries for this day.

Wednesday 26th March 1806. the wind ran high last night and the tide rose higher than common and came in under my blankets before I awoke and obledged me to move twise Several more of the party camps were routed also.— our officers gave one of the Cath lih mahs a meddel. he gave them in return a large Sturgeon. we proceeded on our way and halted on fanneys Island[1] to dine then proceed. on as usal Camped[2] on an Island in thick brush &C.—

1. Supposedly named for Clark's sister, Frances; later Crims Island, Columbia County, Oregon.
2. Below Longview, Cowlitz County, Washington, perhaps nearer the opposite side in Columbia County. The island may be Walker or Dibblee or some other small island in the area.

Thursday 27th March 1806. rain commenced this morning and continued thro the day. we halted at a village of the Chilutes nation[1] they treated us in a friendly manner Gave us Some wapa toes & anchoves to eat. Several Indians followed after us with Small canoes. our officers purchased a large Sturgeon from them we proceed on to the mo of a River named Calams River and Camped[2] on the South Side little above Said River— Six of our hunters Sent on this afternoon to deer Island[3] with the Small canoes in order to hunt.

1. The name is given as Skillute or a variant in Lewis and Clark. See Lewis's and Clark's entries for November 4, 1805, March 25 and 27, and April 16, 1806.

2. In the vicinity of Goble, Columbia County, Oregon, with the Kalama River on the opposite side in Cowlitz County, Washington.

3. Still Deer Island, Columbia County.

Friday 28th March 1806. rained the greater part of last night. we Set out eairly and proceeded on to deer Island at the Camp of our hunters. about 11 oClock the hunters joined us had killed 7 deer. we drew out the Small canoes and repaired them. the day proved Squawlley high winds &C. packed in the venison. the Snakes[1] are as thick as the Spears of Grass on this Island, of different kinds &C Several of the hunters being out our officers concluded to Stay and we Camped[2] for the night one of the hunters killed a Small wild cat.[3] the grey Eagles are pleanty on this Island they eat up three deer in a short time which our hunters had killed some of the hunters killed Several of them. The game is pleanty about this place & the Soil rich &C

1. The Pacific red-sided garter snake, *Thamnophis sirtalis concinnus,* for the most part, according to the captains.

2. On Deer Island, Columbia County, Oregon.

3. Oregon bobcat.

Saturday 29th March 1806. we Set out early and proceed. on. Saw blossom and wild onions[1] along the South Side in the afternoon we passd the mo. of [*blank*] River[2] which came in on N. Side which is high and puts in with a Swift current. little above we arived at the village of the [*blank*] nation[3] which is a large village and the most of their huts join. this village is more decent than any I have Seen below. we delayed at this village about 3 hours. Capt Clark bought a Robe which was made of 2 Sea otter Skins from the princepal man who he made a chief Gave him a meddle. he put it on his wife. Capt. Clark Gave the chief a blue blanket edged with red & Small also an old flag, which he was Satisfied with. we bought Several fat dogs and some wa pa toes from the natives. towards evening we proceed. on a Short distance further and Camped[4] on a handsom Green where had once been a village. Some of the natives visited us. thier women instead of wearing the Straw & bark Short peticoats wear a Soft leather breach cloth all above this Side of the Mountains are dressed in this way & nothing more to cover the most part of them, but those below on the coast wear the Short pticoats. Some among them all have a kind of a fur garment beaver &C. dressed and cut in narrow stripes & sewed together &C—

1. Wild chive, *Allium schoenoprasum* L. var. *laurentianum* Fern.
2. Lewis River, Cowlitz and Clark counties, Washington.
3. The Cathlapotle village Nahpooitle is discussed at Clark's entry of November 5, 1805.
4. Behind Bachelor Island, Clark County.

Sunday 30th March 1806. we Set out eairly and proceed on the River Still riseing & is now So high that the tide has no effect to be perceived at this time considerable of drift wood floating down the River. Saw 2 large villages on a large long Island which is named wa pa-toe Isld.[1] & is about 25 miles long, partly timbered & partly prarie & soil rich. a number of the Savages followed us Some distance with their canoes I must give these Savages as well as those on the coast the praise of makeing the neatest and handsomest lightest best formed canoes I ever Saw & are the best hands to work them. Saw mount rainey and Mount Hood which is verry white with Snow &C about Sunset we Camped[2] at a handsom prarie & Groves of oak timber &C— the country is lower & more Smooth than below.—

1. A number of tribes lived on Sauvie Island, Multnomah County, Oregon. See Lewis's entry of March 29.
2. Within Vancouver, Clark County, Washington.

Monday 31st March 1806. a clear pleasant morning. we Set out eairly and proceed. on passd. a village[1] which was a large one when we went down last fall but the Savages are more Scattered along the River in fishing parties &C. only 2 cabbins left at this village on the South Shore in a large bottom. the wind rose from the Southward. a number of the Savages followed us with their canoes. one of our hunters[2] killed a deer & Saw a great number more Deer & Elk in these bottoms &c. this morning. in the evening we passed the mo of Seal River[3] on N. Side the waves high. we Encamped[4] a Short distance above Sd. River on a handsom high plain of rich land & timber near this is opposite the mouth of Quick Sand River[5] which puts in on South Side & is high at this time.

1. A village of the Watlala Indians, Portland, Multnomah County, Oregon. See Clark's entries of November 2 and 4, 1806.
2. Perhaps Drouillard; see Lewis's entry of this day.
3. Washougal River, Clark County, Washington.
4. The party would remain here in Clark County until April 6.
5. Sandy River, Multnomah County, Oregon.

Tuesday 1st of April 1806. Sergt. Pryor & three men was Sent 5 or 6 miles up Quick Sand River to make discovries & Several hunters went up the—Seal[1]—River a hunting & others went out in different directions a hunting. a number of the natives visited us as they were passing down the River late in the afternoon Sergt. Pryor returned had been about 4 miles up quick Sand River found the current rapid & only about 4 feet deep. he killed one deer. the other hunter returned had killed 4 Elk and 2 deer and an otter the hunters tells us that the country back from the River is rich land Some praries and rich plains &C. a number of Savages passing down the River in their canoes. we discovred yesterday the top of a high white Mountain Some distance to the Southward our officers name it Mount Jefferson.[2] 2 canoe loads of Savages Camped near us.

1. "Seal" may have been added later to a blank space.
2. The captains named Mt. Jefferson, Linn County, Oregon, on March 30.

Wednesday 2nd April 1806. 9 of our men who went out last evening for meat of the 4 Elk Stayed out all night. our officers determined to delay at this place untill the hunters kill 9 or 10 Elk and jurk the meat to take along with us. So all the best of our hunters[1] turned out the most of them went over to the South Shore & in different directions a hunting. the natives informed our officers that their is a large River[2] comes in on the South Side Some distance below quick Sand River which we had not Seen So Capt. Clark & 6 men[3] Set out with a canoe to go and examine the Sd. River. took an Indian along for a guide. the after part of the [day?] clear & pleasant in the evening 3 of the hunters came in had killed two Deer. 30 odd Savages Camped with us men women & children.

1. Including Gass, Windsor, Collins, Drouillard, and the Field brothers, according to Lewis's entries for the next few days.

2. The Willamette River enters the Columbia at Portland, Multnomah County, Oregon.

3. Actually seven—neither Clark nor Ordway seems to have counted York, but Lewis had the number right. They were Thompson, Potts, Cruzatte, Weiser, Howard, Whitehouse, and York.

Thursday 3rd of April 1806. a foggey morning. one hunter[1] came across the River & informed us that the hunters had killed 4 Elk 2 of which is about 3 miles from the River so Sergt. pryor and 3 more men were Sent over to help jourk the meat Slight Showers of rain in the course of the day. the Savages who Stayed with us last night were of five different nations and had Several prisoners among them these Savages tells us that they are going down the River after wapatoes &C &C. in the evening Capt. Clark & party returnd. to Camp and informed us that they had been and took a view of the River which the Indians informed us of, and that it is a verry large River & is 500 yd. wide and is Supposed to head with the waters of the California. they went 7 miles up Sd. River. their guide informed them that a large nation lived up the fork of this River by the name of Clack-a-mus Nation[2] of 30 Towns, and that another Nation lives along distance up this River where it gits Small by the name of Callah-no-wah Nation[3] who are verry numerous. on their return they halted at a new discovred village behind Swan Island[4] where they bought 5 dogs, a fiew Commass roots and some wa-patoes &C

1. Drouillard, says Lewis.

2. The Clackamas were a Chinookan-language people living on the Clackamas River in Clackamas County, Oregon.

3. Ordway may mean the Indians Clark gave as "Cal-lar-po-e-wah." They are the Kala-

puyas, or Calapooyas, of the Kalapuyan-language family living in the vicinity of the Willamette Falls at Oregon City, Clackamas County, and beyond.

4. Apparently "Nech-e-co kee" village behind Government and McGuire islands, east of Portland, Multnomah County, Oregon. Lewis and Clark called the islands Diamond Island, but neither used the term "Swan Island." Whitehouse, who was with Clark, used that designation in his journal, so it may have been from him that Ordway obtained his information.

Friday 4th of April 1806. I and 2 men went over the River to see what success the hunters had met the hunters & returned with 5 of them they had killd. one Elk Six Deer and a handsome black bear & 2 Geese the hunters Soon went out again 4[1] was Sent on with a Small Canoe a head 5 or 6 miles to a bottom on S. Side to hunt untill we come up. the after part of the day pleasant. one of the men killd. 2 deer. in the evening 2 of our hunters[2] came in had killd. 2 deer and caught a beaver

1. Gibson, Shannon, Howard, and Weiser, according to Lewis and Clark.
2. Joseph Field and Drouillard, say the captains.

Saturday 5th of April 1806. Sergt. Gass & 2 other of the hunters returnd. with 3 Small black cubs which was sold to the Savages I and 5 more men went over to the S. Side and climbed a high River hill on which is excelent rich land. went to the Camp of our hunters and brought in the jurked meat. three more hunters Sent on a head with their Small canoe a hunting great numbers of Savages visited the Camp continually Since we have lay [in?] at this Camp, who were passing down with their famillys from the country above into the vally of Columbia in Search of food. they inform us that the natives above the great falls have no provisions and many are dieing with hunger. this information has been so repeatedly given by different parties of Indians that it does not admit of any doubt and is the cause of our delay in this neighbourhood for the purpose of procureing as much dryed Elk meat as will last us through the Columbia plains in which we do not expect to find any thing to kill &C. the River hills are high above Quick Sand River Some of the clifts is 200 feet high. on the tops of those hills the land is excessively rich and thickly timbred with different Species of Fir intermixed with white cedder. I Saw one of the Fir trees which is 100 and 4 feet in length. Some dog wood[1] and Small Shrubs, in the River bottoms of the fertile valley of Columbia which we are now leaveing, and which extends for about 70 miles on the River below, the growth is ash cottonwood, large leaffed ash & Sweet willow[2] principally with sundry other Shrubs and bushes many of which bear a fruit which the natives make use of for food. those bottoms also produce various Species of plants. the roots of many of which the natives make use of prepared in different ways for food. Such as the root of the anual rush pasnaque wa pa toe which is the common arrow head & a Species of Fern[3] the wapatoes they geather in the ponds but all other grow spontaineously in every part of the Columbian valley—

1. Nuttall's dogwood, *Cornus nuttallii* Aud. ex T. & G.; see Lewis's entry of this day.

2. The ash is Oregon ash, *Fraxinus latifolia* Benth.; cottonwood is black cottonwood; large leafed ash is bigleaf maple, *Acer macrophyllum* Pursh; and sweet willow is probably the Pacific willow, *Salix lasiandra* Benth. See Lewis's entries of March 25 and 27.

3. The rush is probably giant horsetail, *Equisetum telmateia* Ehrh.; "pasnaque" may be Ordway's rendering of the Shoshone term *pasigoo,* designating camas (see Clark's entry of September 20, 1805); arrowhead is another name for wapato; and the fern is western bracken fern, *Pteridium aquilinium* L. This material largely follows Clark's entry of this day.

Sunday 6th of April 1806. a clear pleasant morning. we loaded up and Set out proceeded on verry well about 8 miles and halted at the Camp of our hunters they having killed 3 Elk in a bottom S Side 8 men went out for the meat Ruben Fields killed a curious handsom bird[1] which made a curious noise it had blue feathers on its breast and under its throat and 2 long feathers on the top of its head the longest 3 Inches long & a handsome Small bird. he Skined it and it is taken care of to carry home with us. in the evening the men returned with the meat of 5 Elk having found 2 more than they expected which the hunters had killed. So we Camped[2] here for the night in a Small willow bottom near high river hills on South Side eat & fleased the greater part of of the Elk meat to dry &C.

1. Mountain quail, *Oreortyx pictus,* an expedition discovery.

2. The camp of this day is somewhat difficult to locate. It is most likely above Latourell Falls and Rooster Rock State Park, Multnomah County, Oregon. See the note discussing this difficulty at Lewis's entry of this day. The party remained here until the morning of April 9.

Monday 7th of April 1806. a fair morning Drewyer & the 2 Fields were sent on a head to ascend the River & hunt untill our arival all hands set at jurking & drying the Elk meat. a number of Savages came down the River in their canoes brought a fiew dogs a little Chapellel[1] & roots for trade, but asked a large price for them So we purchased only one dog. we got the meat all dry towards evening and packed it up &C the Musquetoes trouble us a little &c— Drewyer returned with the Savages and killed 2 ducks this evening &c—

1. Usually spelled by the captains with "s" instead of "c" at the beginning; it is cous, *Lomatium cous* (Wats.) Coult. & Rose. The Chinookan word is *a-sáblal,* "bread."

Tuesday 8th of April 1806. a fair morning. the wind raised So high a head that in Stead of our Setting out as we intended had to unload our canoes. the waves ran high and filled them with water &C Several men Sent out a hunting put our dry meat on a Scaffel & dry it a little more &C. the wind still raiseing. the River Rises a little the wind continued high all day &C

Wednesday 9th of April 1806. a fair morning and calm we bailed our canoes found Some of them to leak loaded up & about 9 oClock we departed and proceed on along the South Shore overtook the 2 Fields who had killed nothing about noon Some of the men killed an eagle. we crossed over to the North Side & halted at a village of the wa-cla-lah nation[1] where we bought 5 or 6 fat dogs. found Capt. Clarks pipe tommahawk which was Stole from him last fall, below Quick Sand River. we took it from them. they Signd. that they bought it below and appeared to be highly afronted at our taking it but were afraid to Show it a number of these natives are moveing up to the big Shoote[2] to fish &C a number of an other nation overtook us who belong up near the big falls[3] &C a large creek[4] puts in close above the village which we did not discover last fall. when we passd. down we dined and proceed. on passd Strabury Island[5] where the Swift water begins. we halted at a village at the foot of the 1st rapid, on N. Side which was lately erected. we purchased 2 fat dogs and crossed over to the South Shore and Camped[6] behind [*blank*] Island commenced raining hard & high winds from N. W. the River much higher at this time than it was last fall when we passd. down. Some Spots of Snow is now on the tops of these Mountains Near the River.

1. Watlala Chinookans, whose village was in the vicinity of Skamania, Skamania County, Washington, which the group visited on November 2, 1805.

2. Cascades of the Columbia River.

3. Celilo Falls.

4. Perhaps Woodward Creek, Skamania County.

5. Hamilton Island, Skamania County.

6. The party camped on shore behind Bradford Island, site of Bonneville Dam, Multnomah County, Oregon.

Thursday 10th of April 1806. rained hard the grater part of last night. a cloudy & Showery morning. 2 men[1] Sent out to hunt pitch who belonged to a Small canoe. we took up the large canoes one at a time up the rapids with the towing line. the Small one also who was left to help up with the other small one. we then crossed over the River to the N. Side and halted at a village where we took breakfast. the men who were hunting pitch came up with their canoe one of them by the name of Collins had killed three Deer and brought them to us. Capt. Lewis purchased a white mountain Sheep[2] Skin for which he gave 2 Elk hides we bought a fiew Salmon trout[3] then we proceed. on Soon came to bad rapids where we had to tow one canoe up at a time. Drewyer & the 2 Fields went on a head with their Smal canoe. their chord broke & their canoe went back down the rapids and taken up by the Indians below, who returnd. it to us. our officers gave them two knives for the kindness. one of the men lamed one of his feet towing over the Stons with Some fatigue we got all the canoes to the lower end of the portage of the big Shoote and unloaded in the large eddy below on N. Side and carried all the baggage on the top of the hill, and Camped[4] a number of the natives visited us Some distance below this place I Saw a large grave yard little below an ancient village.[5] this is a different manner from any I have Seen of burrying the dead in tombs about 8 feet Square made of wood plank and tite flowers [floors?] made of plank layn in them and the corps are layn out on the flower Roped up in Some kind of a Robe, and all thier property is deposited with them Such as copper tea kittles baskets cockle Shells canoes are layn by the Side of Sd. tombs also. Several

Images cut in wood one put up at the ends of Said tombs &C one of the Indians Stole an axe from us another told one of our men and he followed him and took it from him and told him that he was bad and he replied that he was &C—

1. Apparently Collins and Gibson, according to Lewis and Clark and to Ordway in this entry.

2. The mountain goat, *Oreamnos americanus*.

3. Salmon trout was the party's name for the steelhead trout.

4. In the area east of North Bonneville, Skamania County, Washington; see the captains' entries for this day.

5. Lewis places this description under his entry of April 11.

Friday 11th of April 1806. rained the greater part of last night and continues this morning. all of the party except a fiew to guard the baggage turned out with Capt. Clark to takeing up our canoes with the tow Rope up the big Shoote took one large one and one Small one at once the large one filled at the highest pitch where it is allmost perpinticular but with Some difficulty we got the 2 to the head of the portage about noon. then went back took dinner and took another large canoe and a Small one the other Smallest one was taken & carried by land. this large canoe filled twice with water at the worst pitch but with some difficulty & hard fatigue got them Safe up towards evening by the assistance of a number of Indians at the worst pitch &C. and halled the large canoe up by force allthough She was full of water. the most of the mens feet sore towing over the Sharp rocks. our officers made a chief of the [*blank*] nation gave meddle &C.[1] Drewyer and the 2 Fields Sent on a head with their little canoe to a creek on the N. Side to hunt untill our arival.

1. The Clahclellah Indians, as Lewis and Clark called them, were a branch of the Watlala Chinookans. See the captains' entries for this day and for April 9.

Saturday 12th of April 1806. a rainy wet morning. all the party except a guard went with Capt. Lewis to take up the other large canoe. we got it under way verry well but She took a Swing on us and broke away and rid the high waves down the rapids. then all hands went at packing the baggage past the portage which is 1½ miles. carried it all up at 4 loads a peace towards evening to everry thing to the head of the portage and Campd.[1] for the night. our officers finding that the natives do not incline to Sell their canoes So they divided the baggage & men among the 4 canoes. a number of the natives visited us. one of the Squaws told us in the Clatsop tongue that She had Slept with the white tradors &c.

1. Evidently at the camp of October 30–31, 1805, in Skamania County, Washington.

Sunday 13th of April 1806. we loaded up our canoes took a light breakfast of a little dog meat and departed Soon passed the village only one house remaining covred in it which lives a number of the natives. Capt. Lewis and the Small canoes crossed over to the South Side to 2 villages[1] little above the Shoote in order to purchace a canoe from the natives if possable. the current Swift. we proceeded on little above cruzattes River[2] the wind rose So high that obledged us to halt at this bottom where we expected to find our Hunters 2 men[3] went out a hunting the day proved fair the wind cold and Snow laying low on the Mountains near the River. the hunters soon came in had killd. nothing but a bald Eagle we then proceed. on about 5 miles and halted again at a bottom on the N. Side[4] 3 men went out a hunting. Sergt. Pryor & 2 men Sent back to cruzattes River to look again for the hunters one of the hunters killed two Deer. Capt. Lewis & party overtook us had purchased two Small canoes the price of which was 2 Small peaces of blue cloath and two Elk hides, & bought three dogs also. we dryed the 2 Small canoes by fire and pitched them &c.

1. Lewis calls it the "Y-eh-huh village," but it is not shown on expedition maps in Hood River County, Oregon.
2. Wind River, Skamania County, Washington.
3. Shields and Colter, reports Clark.
4. Where they camped in Skamania County, apparently between Collins and Dog creeks.

Monday 14th of April 1806. Sergt. Pryor & men returned with Drewyer & the two Fields they had killed 4 deer. we then departed and proceed on verry well passed Labuche River[1] on N. Side about noon the wind rose so high from the N. W. that we came too at a village[2] on the N. Side where we Saw 25 or 30 horses which are in tollarable good order. we bought a number of dogs from the natives. they gave us Such as they had to eat which was pounded Salmon thistle[3] roots & wild onions & other kinds of roots all of which they had Sweeted & are Sweet. they are makeing Shappalell &C but they had but little to eat at this time but are Scattered along the River expecting the Salmon Soon &C. Mount Hood appears near the River on the South Side which is covd. thick with Snow & very white the wind high we delayed about 2 hours and proceed. on passed Several Small villages on the N. Side Scatered along the narrow bottoms near the River. Saw a number of horses at each village the wind continued aft and high So we run fast. Camped[4] at dark at a village on the N. S.

1. Hood River, Hood River County, Oregon.

2. A village of the Chinookan-language White Salmon people above the White Salmon River, Kliciktat County, Washington.

3. Edible thistle, *Cirsium edule* Nutt.

4. Near Major Creek, Klickitat County.

Tuesday 15th of April 1806. a clear pleasant morning. we delayed untill after breakfast for to See if the natives would Sell us any horses but they did not incline to Sell any without beeds which we have not got So we departed. Capt. Lewis & Clark went on a small high Island[1] to see a large burying ground they Saw Seven large Sepulchers made of wood in a Square form and by appearence is nearly a hundred persons piled in one on another with their robes Sowed round them, and all their heads down the River. we proceed. from thence to a village at the mouth of the [*blank*] River[2] on the N. Side where we halted expecting to purchase Some horses as the natives have a number at this place, but they wanted beeds also and Sign to us that they hunt and go to wa[r] with their horses &C. we purchased only one dog, and proceed. on passed several more Small villages along the North Side. about 3 P. M. we crossed over to the South Side and arived at rock Camp where we Camped on the 25th & 26th of Oct. last. we went up the creek little above and Camped[3] under high clift of rocks in order to lay here tomorrow & See if any horses can be purchased about the narrows or falls the plains are green & pleasant Saw a number of horses feeding in it which are in good order as they have been wintered below in the narrow bottoms where the rushes abound &C. we are Camped where has been an ancient large village[4] only the cellers now to be Seen. George Drewyer killed a deer this evening. a number of the natives visited us &C—

1. The party's Sepulcher Island, now Lower Memaloose Island, Wasco County, Oregon.
2. Klickitat River, Klickitat County, Washington.
3. The "Fort Rock" camp of October 25–28, 1805, at Mill Creek, Wasco County. This time the group would remain here until April 18.
4. No Indian site is shown on expedition maps, nor is such a village discussed by Lewis or Clark.

Wednesday 16th of April 1806. a clear pleasant morning. Several Indians Stayed at our Camp last night. 6 of the party went out eairly a hunting. Capt. Clark and 8 more of the party[1] went across the River and took Some marchandize & other articles in order to purchase horses &C. Capt. Clark intends going up to the falls & See if any is to be had their. a number of Indians Came to our Camp Some of them on horse back. Sergt. Gass and 2 men Set at makeing pack Saddles. Capt Clark Sent back a part of the articles as the Indians asked more for their horses than our goods would admit of, but he was going up to the falls in hopes to git Some their by giving a little more than has been offered as yet. our hunters killed this day only two Deer 2 Squerrells[2] of a new kind of any we ever Saw before. Capt. Lewis had the Skins Stuffed & taken care of. one large new kind of a grey Squerrell[3] also. 1 or 2 ducks the game is verry Scarce about this place.

1. Lewis counts twelve persons with Clark, among whom were Drouillard, Charbonneau, Sacagawea, Cruzatte, Goodrich, Frazer, Willard, McNeal, Weiser, and perhaps Werner. They went across the Columbia to Klickitat County, Washington, and camped in the vicinity of Dallesport.
2. Perhaps the California ground squirrel, *Spermophilus beecheyi.*
3. Western gray squirrel.

Thursday 17th of April 1806. a beautiful warm morning. Several of our hunters went out a hunting. the Small birds of different kinds are Singing around us. Capt. Clark not returned but wrote a line to Capt. Lewis that he had not purchased any horses yet but was going up to another village above the falls where he expected to purchase Some this day. Capt. Lewis wrote back that we Should move tomorrow up to the bason as far as we can go with the canoes. our hunters killed only one Deer this day. towards evening a number of Indians visited our Camp one of them informed us that he had killed 2 Indians on this ground in a battle some years ago as they were at war with Some nations to the Southward.—

Friday 18th of April 1806. a clear cool morning we took breakfast and Set out crossed the Columbia River to the N. Side proceeded on Soon came to a rapid[1] where we made a Short portage and towed up the canoes & proceeded on up a rapid current to the bason & landed[2] on the N. Side about 3 P. M. unloaded the canoes cut the large ones for firewood Capt. Clark had purchased 4 horses. we packed several articles to the village to purchase horses. bought 2 dogs Several cakes of chappalell &C.

1. Perhaps Threemile Rapids below The Dalles Dam, Wasco County, Oregon.
2. Perhaps at Spearfish Lake, Klickitat County, Washington.

Saturday 19th April 1806. a clear cold morning a little Snow fell on the hills last night. all hands went at packing the baggage past the portage which is about 2 miles towards evening we got all the baggag and canoes carried to the head of the narrows above the village & Camped[1] carried our firewood past the portage also as it is so hard about the village that the Savages value it high. Capt. Clark bought 3 or 4 more horses this day. Capt. Clark and 3 men[2] Set out this evening to go up to the Short narrows at a village in order to purchase horses untill our arival.

1. Above the Long Narrows of The Dalles, Klickitat County, Washington, near the camp of October 24, 1805. The party remained here until April 21, 1806.
2. Four men, according to Lewis and Clark: Pryor, Shannon, Cruzatte, and Labiche.

Sunday 20th of April 1806. a clear cold morning. Capt. Lewis went to tradeing for horses &C. Several of our men went out to hunt their horses but could not find all of them we expect the Indians loosed their Spanil[1] and took them away expecting a reward to git them again. So we hired the Indians to hunt them. found all except one who the man we bought him of Gambled him away with Some of an other nation & they had taken him away. all the Indians we have Seen play a game & risque all the property they have at different games. the game[2] that these Savages play is by setting in a circle & have a Small Smooth bone in their hands & Sing crossing their hands to fix it in a hidden manner from the other Side who gass the hand that has it in then counts one a Stick Stuck in the ground for tallies & So on untill one Side or the other wins the propertey Stacked up. this game is played with activity, and they appear merry & peaceable. Capt. Lewis took the property from the man that gambled away our horse. we Sold old Robes Elk Skins &C. &C. for white beeds. these Savages have but little pounded Salmon in their village as they trade it to Several other nations &C. the Indians would not give us any thing worth mentioning for our canoes So we Split & burnt one of them this evening. we tyed up our horses &C. we bought 2 more dogs & Some chappalell &c

1. Ordway must mean spancel, that is, to hobble with rope.
2. Clark discusses the game on April 18; it is another version of the Indian hand game.

Monday 21st of April 1806. a clear cold morning. one of our horses broke away last night we found him after hunting a while this morning we make ready to depart from this place as the Indians are verry troublesome to us have stole 5 or 6 tommahawks Iron Spoons &C &C. we loaded our horses 9 in number. 4 men took 2 small canoes by water. we Set out about 8 oClock and proceed on about noon arived at the village below the big falls. joined Capt. Clark who had not purchased any horses. we bought 2 dogs. the Indians returned us a horses in liew of one of those we lost &C. we carryed the canoes past the portage and mooved all above the portage and dined and proced. on the N. Side to a village opposite the mouth of Clarks River where we Camped[1] as the road leaves the river at this place we bought 3 dogs and a little wood to cook with one of the canoes Stayed on the opposite Side

1. The captains eventually came to call "Clark's River" by another name, "Towanahiooks." It is today's Deschutes River, forming a line between Wasco and Sherman counties, Oregon, on its lower course. The party camped on the opposite side in Klickitat County, Washington.

Tuesday 22nd of April 1806. a clear pleasant cold morning. we loaded up our horses & Set out. assended a high hill one of the horses threw his load & Scattered it one of the Indians Stole a robe & hid it in one of their lodges. we found it & proced on the high Smooth plain which is extensive & Smooth back from the river about noon we halted at a village[1] of the Wal-a-wal tribe where we bought a dog and a little firewood. the wind So high from the N. W. that the canoes being on the opposite Side of the river could not cross we purchased a horse. took a light dinner and proceed. on about 6 miles and Camped[2] at a village where we purchased a horse 5 dogs and a little wood and considerable of new chappalell &c. in the evening Sergt. Gass & R. Fields came across the river & joined us with one of the Small canoes

1. In Klickitat County, Washington, in the vicinity of Maryhill Museum. It was at a village of Tenino Indians (called "Eneshur" by the captains) and not Walula Indians as Ordway seems to indicate.
2. In the vicinity of John Day Dam, Klickitat County.

Wednesday 23rd of April 1806. one of our horses broke loose and Strayed away last night we delayed to hunt for him & made two pack Saddles. we could not find our lost horse. about 10 A. M. Set out proced on through high plains and banks of Sand along the river. the day warm. towards evening we arived at a large village at the mouth of a creek where we Camped[1] our canoes came up. we purchased 4 dogs and a considerable quantity of Chappalell &C. the day warm. these Savages have lately mooved here & have a great number of horses. our horses are troublesome as the most of them are Studs. but the feed is good the prarie covred with flowrs the natives are numerous at this place. they had a dance[2] at our fire this evening. nearly the Same manner & way as those on the Missourie. we played the fiddle and danced &C. Several of the flat heads continue on with us & assist us as much as lyes in their power.—

1. At Rock Creek, Klickitat County, Washington, at a village of Tenino Indians.
2. Lewis and Clark describe the dance more fully in their entries for this day.

Thursday 24th of April 1806. a clear cool morning. we delay to purchase horses so as to leave the canoes. one of our horses Strayed away last night. we hired Indians to hunt him. these Savages are numerous & tribe of wa-hopan,[1] who come from a river to the North of this. a number of them went at playing a game for beeds and other property in the Same manner as those below. we purchased 3 horses & exchanged old axes &C. for beeds. these Savages are tollerable well cloathed in dressed Deer and mountain Sheep Skins & buffaloe robes, but live poor at this time, as they expect the Salmon to run Soon. we git pleanty of new Shappalell for Small articles. they have a great number of horses. the most of them are good to ride or pack. the Indians found our lost horse. we hired 2 more of Some of the flat heads who are going with us. the Indians would not purchace our canoes, as they find we are going to leave them, but when we went to Split them they gave us 6 fathem of white beeds for them. about 11 A. M. we loaded up our horses and Set out proceed on the Sandy road about 12 miles and Camped[2] at a village where we bought a fiew dogs & gathered a fiew willows to Cook with &C.—

1. Lewis and Clark have it as "Wah-how-pum" or some variation; they are the Teninos.

2. In Klickitat County, Washington, opposite the town of Blalock, Gilliam County, Oregon, in the territory of Umatilla Indians.

Friday 25th of April 1806. a clear cool morning. we got up our horses. Set out proceeded on verry well over a pleasant plain, about 10 miles and halted at a large village of the pas-qute-pu tribe[1] who are verry numerous and have a great number of good horses. we bought 5 dogs. our officers gave 2 meddles to 2 of their princepal men. Stayed to purchase horses but they do not incline to Sell any. one Indian brought back broken glasses which he purchased from us last fall & as they broke he wanted other glass in place &C. we dined and proced on a number of Indians followed us. in the evening we Camped[2] at the Commencement of a low Country on this Side. our officers purchased two horses from the Indians who followed us, as they wished to hear the fiddle we played & danced a little to please them. one of the party killed Several ducks to day.

1. "Pish-quit-pahs" to Lewis and Clark, perhaps a Shahaptian-speaking division of Umatilla Indians. See the discussion of these people at Lewis's and Clark's entries for this day.

2. The location of the day's camp is difficult to determine. It may have been near Alderdale, Klickitat County, Washington, or perhaps farther upstream at Glade Creek, Benton County, Washington. See Lewis's and Clark's entries for this day.

Saturday 26th of April 1806. we got up our horses. took a light breakfast of a little dry Elk meat and Set out proced on over a low level Smooth Sandy plain about 12 miles & halted & dined on a little dry Elk meat as we have nothing else. the day warm. we delayed about 1 hour and proceed. on a number of the natives followed us who are mooveing up the river & Some of them are going over the rockey mountn. to kill buffaloe. Saw considerable of Snow on the mountains to the South & S East. came 20 odd miles this day & Camped[1] on the bank of the river. only small willows to burn &C—

1. In the vicinity of Plymouth, Benton County, Washington.

Sunday 27th of April 1806. a little rain fell the latter part of last night. we Set out as usal and proceed. on Soon passd. a Small village of 3 lodges then assended a high plain where we Saw an extensive country around us & not a tree to be Seen came about 20 miles before we halted & delayed a Short time eat a little dry meat & let our horses feed a Short time and proceed on about 5 miles further and arived at a large village of the wal-a-wal tribe, at the commencement of a low barron Smooth country where we Camped[1] bought a fat dog to each mess. these natives are numerous their is another village on the opposite Side of the river & a great number of horses. we get different kinds of roots and fresh Salmon trout & Suckers[2] &C. all these Savages are glad to See us and appear verry friendly.—

1. In Benton County, Washington, opposite and below the mouth of the Walla Walla River, at a village of Walula Indians, where the party would remain until April 29.
2. The suckers are *Catostomus* sp.

Monday 28th of April 1806. a clear pleasant morning. our Indian guides who are going over the mountains with us inform us that their is a nearer way across the plains to the forks of Lewises river at the entrence of Kooskooske[1] which is a Smooth way and only 3 days march to that place which is allmost as near again as to follow the river round.[2] So our officers conclude to cross the river at this place & take the near way. So we purchased

6 dogs from the natives to take with us. our Intrepters wife[3] found a woman of hir own nation who was a prisoner among these Indians, and as they could Speak together our officers Spoke to the head chief[4] & told him our business and that the white people would Supply them with marchandize at the head of the Missourie &C. asked for canoes to cross the river they Said they wished us to Stay with them to day as we lived a great way off, and they wished to See us dance this evening & begged on us to Stay this day. So our officers concluded to Stay this day. the head chief brought up a good horse & Said he wished to give it to us but as he was poor he wished us to give him Some kind of a kittle, but as we could not Spare a kittle Capt. Clark gave his Sword a flag and half pound of powder & ball for the horse. we took our horses across the river. our officers made another chief gave him a meddle &C. in the afternoon an number of Indians came to our officers who were diseased the lame and many with Sore eyes and lame legs & arms &C. our officers dressd. their wounds, washed their eyes & gave them meddicine and told them how to apply it &C. the chief called all his people and told them of the meddicine &C. which was a great wonder among them & they were much pleased &C. the Indians Sent their women to gether wood or Sticks to See us dance this evening. about 300 of the natives assembled to our Camp we played the fiddle and danced a while the head chief told our officers that they Should be lonesome when we left them and they wished to hear once of our meddicine Songs and try to learn it and wished us to learn one of theirs and it would make them glad. So our men Sang 2 Songs which appeared to take great affect on them. they tryed to learn Singing with us with a low voice. the head chief then made a Speech & it was repeated by a warrier that all might hear. then all the Savages men women and children of any Size danced forming a circle round a fire & jumping up nearly as other Indians, & keep time verry well they wished our men to dance with them So we danced among them and they were much pleased, and Said that they would dance day and night untill we return. everry fiew minutes one of their warries made a Speech pointing towards the enimy and towards the moon &C. &C which was all repeated by another meddison man with a louder voice as all might hear. the dance continued untill about midnight then the most of them went away peaceable & have behaved verry clever and

honest with us as yet, and appear to have a Sincere wish to be at peace and to git acquaintance with us &C &C—

1. Where the Clearwater River empties into the Snake.

2. The route they would follow in a few days across Walla Walla, Columbia, Garfield, and Asotin counties, Washington, to the mouth of the Clearwater River at Lewiston, Nez Perce County, Idaho.

3. Sacagawea.

4. Yelleppit, chief of the Walulas, is discussed at Clark's entry of October 19, 1805.

Tuesday 29th of April 1806. we bought 2 more dogs to take us across the plains and a little Shappalell & other roots &C. we borrowed a canoe from the Indians and crossed over the Columbia to the South Side above the mouth of the river which we took to a byo where we passd. down last fall, and got all our baggage across the river and got up our horses. our guide telling us that it was a long distance to water, & further than we could go this day. So we mooved over 1 mile on the bank of the river which is named the wal-a-wal-a River near a large village of the wal-a-wal-a nation where we Camped again.[1] these Savages have wers made of willows across this little river where they catch large quantityes of Salmon trout, Suckers, &C. we bought a little Commass roots, Shappalell and a fiew more dogs &C. the most of the Savages moved across the river also, & they have a vast Site of horses. Capt. Lewis made a chief gave him a meddle. he gave a fine horse in return as a present. another chief who Capt. Clark made yesterday brought up another fine horse and made him a present of. we purchased another by giving a Small quantity of powder and ball. these natives are the kindest and the most friendly to us than any we have yet Seen.— they have lately been at war with the Snake nation and many of them were kild. one of our men lift a Steel trap on the other Side—

1. On the north bank of the Walla Walla River, Walla Walla County, Washington.

Wednesday 30th of April 1806. chilley and cold. the men went out for their horses an Indian brought a women to Capt. Clark which diseased. had not the use of hir limbs. he brought a fine horse and gave Capt. Clark for doctering hir he gave meddicine and told them how to apply it &C.

Capt. Clark gave the Indian a white Shirt which pleased him verry much. about 11 A. M we got our horses up by the assistance of the Indians and Set out. proceeded on over Smooth barron Sandy plains not a tree nor Shrub to be seen except a weed or Shrub like wild hysop[1] which is common. the natives use it when dry for fires to cook with &C. the Indian name of it is cum-cum.[2] we came about 16 miles and Camped[3] on the wala-wal river, which has narrow bottoms partly covred with Small timber 2 or 3 men went out hunting, one of them killed a large beaver and an otter. Several of the horses chokd. by eating Some kind of a weed in this bottom, but they got over it after a while.—

1. Big sagebrush.
2. A term not used by Lewis or Clark. It is Nez Perce *qémqem,* "sagebrush." Haruo Aoki, *Nez Perce Dictionary* (University of California Publications in Linguistics No. 122. Berkeley, 1994), 1276.
3. The party actually camped on an affluent of the Walla Walla River, the Touchet River, in Walla Walla County, some ten miles south of Eureka.

Thursday 1st day of *May 1806.* four hunters Set out eairly to go on a hunting. we Set out as usal & proceeded on up this river over high plains and river bottom which is partly covred with cotton & other timber. the beaver are pleanty. one of the hunters[1] killd. one. no other game to be Seen about noon we halted to dine. Several of the Savages who accompy. us leave us here and take a cross road to the Columbia river. we proceed. on up the branch[2] over Smooth handsom plains and bottoms. Saw a timbred country a long distance to the S. E. & Mount of Snow. Saw Several deer run out of the groves of timber along the branch. about Sunset one of the hunters[3] killed a deer. So we Camped[4] by the branch having made 26 miles this day Soon after we Camped two young men of the wal-awal tribe came up to our Camp & brought us our Steel trap which was forgot at their village. this is an Instance which we had not any right to expect from Savages. we gave them one a knife the other a Sun glass, &.C. and a little vension the wal-a-wal tribe of Flat heads have proved themselves the honnestest Savages we have met with for they had great chance to Steel had they been disposed, but instead of that they helped us as much as lay in their power and believe that we will return and trade with them, as we have told them they disired us to bring them guns and ammunition, copper kittles. knives beeds Scarlet buttens, and allmost any kind of marchandize as other Savages, &C.—

1. Drouillard, reports Lewis.
2. Up the Touchet River, in Walla Walla County, Washington.
3. Labiche, says Lewis.
4. In the vicinity of Waitsburg, Walla Walla County.

Chapter Forty-Seven

Homeward Bound

May 2–September 23, 1806

Friday 2nd May 1806. a clear cold morning. the men got up all but one of our best horses which they could not find. Several hunters went on up the branch a hunting. Several of the men went out in different directions to look for the lost horse. one of them went back to where we took dinner yesterday and turned back. was Soon overtaken by an Indian who had caught our horse & was takeing him to us. as soon as the Indians returned him to us our officers gave a tommahawk knife and a pr. overalls for the kindness. about noon we proceeded on up the branch[1] over high plains & Smooth bottoms. the branch forked in Several places. high hills to our right covred with timber and partly covred with Snow. we crossed the branch in several places, where it was 3 feet deep. our hunters joined us in the evening. had killed only one beaver and one otter.— Camped[2] on a fork of the branch came [*blank*] mls.[3]

1. Touchet River, Walla Walla County, Washington.

2. On Patit Creek, a branch of Touchet River, Columbia County, and several miles south of Marengo.

3. Nineteen miles, according to Lewis.

Saturday 3rd May 1806. a little rain the later part of last night, and continues Showery and cold a little hail & Snow intermixed. one of the hunters horses broke his hobbles and got away. about 7 we Set out proceeded on over high plains and hills. road bearing to the left from the branch. the wind blew verry high and cold Showers of hail & rain about noon we descended a hill. came on an other large creek[1] where we halted to dine on the last of our meat. our hunters Came up had found the lost horse a long distance back the road. our Indians went on this morning intending to git to the forks to day considerable of Snow fell on the high hills Since yesterday. we delayed about 1 hour & left the creek named ke-moo-e-nim Creek ascended a high hill and procd. on over high plains. crossed 2 creeks, and followed up the third creek[2] the big horn chief[3] who we Saw at the big forks last fall met us Several other Indians with him he appeared verry glad to See us and turned back with us we had considerable of hail & verry high winds. in the evening we Camped[4] having made 28 miles this day, having nothing to eat bought the only dog the Indians had with them. the air is very cold.—

1. Tucannon River, reached near the Columbia-Garfield county line, Washington. It is the party's Kimooenem, variously spelled.

2. The last is Pataha Creek, in Garfield County.

3. Lewis and Clark called him We-ark-koomt; his real name was Apash Wyakaikt, *'apáswahayqt,* "flint necklace."

4. On Pataha Creek, east of Pataha City, Garfield County.

Sunday 4th of May 1806. a hard frost & verry cold this morning. we Set out as usal and proced on left the creek and assended high plains came on a Small branch[1] in a deep revean. followed down it. about noon we arived at a small village[2] on the bank of Lewises river where we halted about 10 miles below the forks of koos kooskee & Lewises rivers. we bought a little dark couloured root bread[3] which is not good but will Support nature. bought 2 dogs & a fiew Small fresh fish &C. we dined and proceed. on Soon met one of the chiefs[4] of the flat head or Chopennish tribe who we left our horses with & who went down to the narrows with us last fall. he tells us that tobe our Snake Indn. guide took 2 of our best horses away with him when he left us.[5] we crossed Lewises river to the N. Side to a Small village where we bought only one dog and Camped[6] the head chief of the Chopennish tribe Camped with us and a number more of his tribe who came down to meet us, &C—

1. Alpowa Creek, Garfield County, Washington.

2. In the vicinity of former Silcott, Asotin County, Washington, on the Snake ("Lewises") River and some miles below the entrance of the Clearwater ("Kooskooskee") River, as Ordway mentions. This is the same Nez Perce village that was visited on October 11, 1805.

3. Probably the unidentified species that Lewis discusses on January 20, 1806, and this day, as resembling the sweet potato.

4. Tetoharsky, a chief of the Nez Perces, whom the party met in October 1805. The etymology of the term "Chopunnish" is discussed at Clark's entry of September 17, 1805.

5. Toby left the party on October 9, 1805.

6. In Whitman County, on the Snake River about three miles below Clarkston.

Monday 5th of May 1806. a white frost and verry cold this morning. we Set out having nothing to eat and proced. on up the river about 3 miles came to the forks at the mouth of the kooskooskee river.[1] followed up Sd. river Saw a great number of horses on the high plains passed 2 small villages where we tryed to purchase Some dogs. they did not incline to Sell any as they have but fiew. an Indian gave Capt. Clark a good horse we then proceeded on about noon we came to another Small village opposite the mouth of cottonwood creek[2] where we bought 2 dogs and dined & proceed on to Colters Creek & pah-map village where we Camped.[3] at this village the dogs are verry poor, and these natives have but little to eat except roots which the women are engaged pounding and make it in cakes and put it up over the fire to dry to take with them for provision across the rockey mountains. this villages is all in one joining for about 100 yards long and have different fires & dores but live much compackd. and agreeable together. we could not purchase any thing to eat except a few of those roots or bread which they vallue high in the evening several of the natives which was diseased & Sick came to our officers to be healed who gave & applyed meddicine. the natives promised to reward us by giving us a good horse tommorrow for us to eat as they wished us to Stay two or 3 days with them. finding a man of the Snake nation a prisoner here our officers told the chiefs by intreptation of thro 6 tongues[4] what our business was and that our tradors would come about the head of the missourie and trade with them for furs &C.—

1. The confluence of the Clearwater and Snake rivers at Lewiston, Nez Perce County, Idaho.

2. Lapwai Creek, Nez Perce County.

3. The camp was in the vicinity of Arrow, Nez Perce County, just below the confluence of Potlatch River ("Colters Creek"). The Indian village had been visited on October 8, 1805.

4. Actually five languages (Nez Perce, Shoshone, Hidatsa, French, and English) through six persons (the Nez Perce chief, the Shoshone prisoner, Sacagawea, Charbonneau, one of the French speakers in the party, and Lewis or Clark).

Tuesday 6th of *May 1806.* a rainy wet morning the natives brought us the young horse they promised to give us last night which we excepted and Shot him to eat, as some of the men are gitting Sick eating roots. Several of the natives gambled in the same way as those below had buffaloe robes war axes &C. Staked up the war axes these Indians have they got from the Grousevauntares on the Missourie & they got them from us at the Mandans.[1] about noon we Set out proceeded on up the river passd. a large lodge. Some part of the road is rockey & rough in the evening we Camped[2] near a Small village. the big horn chief and a number other Indians Camped with us.—

1. These *Gros Ventres* are again the Hidatsas; see Ordway's entry of October 29, 1804, and Lewis's entry of May 11, 1806.

2. On the Clearwater River, in Nez Perce County, Idaho, perhaps at the mouth of Pine Creek. See Lewis's and Clark's entries for this day for a more detailed discussion of the day's campsite.

Wednesday 7th of May 1806. a fair morning. we Set out Soon after Sunrise and proceeded on to a creek[1] and lodge where we got our two canisters of powder which we hid about 7 miles above this as we passd. down. they told us that the dogs Scratched open the hole and they finding the powder took care of it for us. we gave them Small articles for being so honest we crossed the river to the South Side. dined and proceed on up the river ascended a high hill. Saw the rockey mountains covred with Snow. the country on these hills is verry rich, thinly covred with pitch pine, thick grass plants wild onions, &C. descended a hill down on a creek. followed up the creek a short distance and Camped[2] at an old In[dian] Camp fishery or were [weir] has lately been made in this Creek. considerable of Cotton wood & pine on this creek. Some of the men killed a duck & a pheasant[3] only.

1. Perhaps Bedrock Creek, Nez Perce County, Idaho.

2. The camp was probably located south of Peck on the east side of Big Canyon Creek, in Nez Perce County.

3. Some species of grouse, most likely the blue grouse, *Dendragapus obscurus*.

Thursday 8th of May 1806. a fair morning. we delay a while to hunt. Several of the hunters went out and killed 4 Deer one of the hunters[1] wounded a deer only broke its leg Capt. Lewises dog Seamon chased it caught it killed it. we finding a Indian here belonging to the Snake nation our officers got some information of the country rivers &C. about 2 P. M. we Set out ascended a high hill. came on a high pleasant plain Scatering pine timber & Soil rich & filled with pine roots and plants &C. we met the twisted hair the chief of the Chopen-nish tribe who we left our horses with. he did not appear Sociable as when we left him our officers asked the Snake Indn. to ask him where our horses were but he did not incline to Speak, So we proced on to a small run where we Camped.[2] the chiefs kept themselves at a distance for a while then by an invitation came and Smoaked and the intreptrs Spoke & we got information concerng our horses and found that the twisted hair & the head chief cut nose[3] as we call him is not at a good understanding with each other respecting our horses, caused by jealousy but informd. us that the most of our horses and pack Saddles were Safe, but Some of boath had been use of by the admittance of the head chief.[4] Several of fowls such as pheasants &C killd this day. N. B. the wolves killd. one of our colts last night.

1. Collins, according to both Lewis and Clark.

2. In Clearwater County, Idaho, on one of several small creeks flowing into Little Canyon Creek, and a few miles from Orofino.

3. Also known as Neeshneparkkeook, spelled variously.

4. Broken Arm, also known as Tunnachemootoolt, variously written.

Friday 9th of May 1806. we Set out & proced. on about 6 miles to the twisted hairs village where we Camped.[1] the chief Sent for our horses & pack Saddles one of our men went for the ammunition we left at canoe Camp[2] a band of Indians came from another village to See us. towards evening Willard returnd. with the ammunition and the pack Saddles the

Indians brought up the most of our horses. Some of them in good order. we caught & hobbled them. Some of them had been rode after Deer &C. these plains are Smooth Soil rich & filled with commass wild onions and white roots calld. halse[3] & other roots good for food which the natives live on at this Season of the year. the evening cold rainy & windy.—

1. In Clearwater County, Idaho, southwest of Orofino, but the exact location is disputed. See the captains' entries for this day.

2. The camp of September–October 1805, where the party built canoes for the downriver trip.

3. A word not used by Lewis or Clark; it is probably the plant cous and perhaps a Nez Perce term. See also the term "uppah" at May 29.

Saturday 10th of May 1806. the wind fell and the rain turned to Snow Some time last night and the Snow fell 6 Inches deep & continues chilly & cold this morning, & we had not any thing to eat. got up our horses & Set out & proced. on over a high Smooth plain no timber. The Snow melts a little but the air cold. wrode about 20 miles descended a Steep hill down in a valley and bottom in which a creek runs through, and Camped[1] near a village of the head chiefs of abt. 15 lodges. they had their flag hoisted and appeared glad to See us. gave us Some commass roots which had been Swetted last fall. Some Shapealell and a little dry fish, but have but little the natives have great numbers of horses gave us two to kill. we killed one to eat. Some of the women pitched a leather lodge[2] and brought wood & made a fire in it and chiefs invited our officers to Stay in it, and talked together our officers told them our business &C. in the evening we played the fiddle and danced a while a number of Indians came from other villages to See us the Snow is gone in this bottom but lyes on the high plains & hills considerable of cottonwood and wild or choke cherry along this creek & Scattering pine on the edges of the hills, &C. we are now as near the Mountains as we can git untill Such times as the Snow is nearly gone of[f] the mountains as we are too eairly to cross. one of the party purchased a dog this eveng. but the most of their dogs are too poor to eat

1. On Lawyer Creek, Lewis County, Idaho, southwest of Kamiah and near Broken Arm's village; the party remained here until May 13.

2. A tipi, showing the influence of Plains Indian culture.

Sunday 11th of May 1806. a fair morning. a number of the natives who were diseased came to our officers to be healed Capt. Clark applyed meddison and done all possable for them. one of the Indians gave Capt. Clark a fine horse. George Drewyer Came in from hunting. had killed two Deer. the Indians brought us Several more of our horses &C. in the evening we fiddled and danced a while. the natives assembled to See us.

Monday 12th of May 1806. a clear pleasant morning. Capt. Clark attended on the Sick natives. three brave men of this tribe painted up three of their horses the best they had & were excelent horses they made a present of them to our officers. our officers then gave them Some ammunition and they locked hands with our officers as a Sincere token of friendship &C. we killed another horse they gave us to eat. our officers gave the chief a musket towards takeing care of our horses. Swapped Several of our horses for better ones &C.

Tuesday 13th of May 1806. a clear frosty morning. we collected all our horses 60 in number now together and all good except 4 which has Sore backs, &C. a number of the natives went at playing the game[1] as those below had considerable property up on each Side Such as beed Strips of otter Skins which was filled with rich Shells, trinkets & Spanish bridles &C &C. about 12 oClock we set out and proced on down the creek.[2] a bold runing Stream about 15 yds wide. considerable of cotton & cherry servis berry also in the bottoms. about 4 miles we came to its mouth a handsom low plain rich Soil & timber around went a short distance down the kooskooskee river[3] and halted to wait for a canoe which we expect the natives to bring us from above this place. we intend crossing the river here and Camp on the other Side untill Such times as the Snow will admit of our crossing the mountains. a number of the natives followed us we Swapped Several horses with them.

1. The Indian hand game again.

2. Down the north bank of Lawyer Creek, Lewis County, Idaho.

3. Actually they went up the Clearwater River about 1½ miles and camped at Kamiah, Lewis County.

Wednesday 14th of May 1806. a clear frosty morning. three men[1] went across the river a hunting. we took our baggage and Swam our horses across the river to the N. Side and mooved a Short distance down the river and Encamped[2] in a Smooth bottom partly covred with young pitch pine in order to stay untill we can cross the mountains. a number of the natives came across the river to our Camp. Some of the principal men gave our officers two fine horses. our hunters returned had killed Collins two bear of the white kind, Labuche three white bear, and Several prarie hens Shannon Several prarie hens and Squerrells. we gave the natives Some of our bear meat as they gave us So much & are So kind to us. they cooked it in the Same manner as they Swet their commass roots. we eat Several of our Stud horses as they have been troublesome to us.—

1. Collins, Labiche, and Shannon, according to the captains, and as Ordway notes later in this entry.

2. Here the party remained until June 10, longer than at any one place on the route except for Fort Mandan and Fort Clatsop. The site is in Idaho County, Idaho, about two miles below the mouth of Lawyer Creek, and near the town of Kamiah. Although Lewis and Clark never used the name, the camp has come to be called Camp Chopunnish.

Thursday 15th of May 1806.[1] a fair morning. one of our hunters[2] Saw a white bear followed it with horses but did not kill it. a number of the party went out to make a camp hunt. we made a Shelter to put our baggage in down in a large celler where had formerly been a wintering house & has been a large village at this place. we formed our Camp around this celler So as in case of an alarm we can jump in the celler and defend our Selves. built a bowery for our officers to write in. we tryed out 5 gallons of bears oil and put it in a keg for the mountains &C.

1. This is the last daily entry in the second book of Ordway's three-volume journal. Then follows, reading from the back of the book to the front, a summary entry listing the names of party members dated "Fort Clatsop 22nd March 1806," which is placed at that date. Finally comes a ten-page table of "Estimated Distances" from Fort Mandan to the Pacific Coast. Ordway's table is similar to ones developed by Clark at Fort Clatsop (see Chapter 30, vol. 6). Minor differences are apparent with Clark's final table in Codex I, so it may be that Ordway took his material from one of Clark's other two versions. One significant difference is that in the final

column for the table Ordway gives only latitudes, leaving out the "remarks" provided by Clark.

2. Reubin Field, say the captains.

Friday 16th of May 1806.[1] Sergt. Pryor and two other men went out a hunting. we eat two more of our unruly Stud horses. a light rain in the fore part of the day. the after part pleasant. in the evening our hunters except two[2] returned had wounded three white bear and killed two Deer, which they brought in the meat

1. Here begins the first entry in Ordway's third and final notebook of his journal. This book is missing its original covers, is about 7½ by 4⅛ inches in size, with 120 unnumbered pages covering the period May 16 to September 23, 1806. The outer, first page of the notebook is quite faded and some words are illegible. This page and the following one appear to be a listing of the animals that the party took for food from March to August 1806. More particularly it may be a listing of the wildlife obtained by Collins. A note to the side on the second page reads, "John Collins game," but not all of the quarry on the list can be accounted for in entries for corresponding days nor can they always be attributed specifically to Collins's hunting. There is also the name "Richardson" at the end of the list, but its relation to the list is unknown and the person's identity cannot be determined. Some of the animals listed are crossed out and there is a large "X" across each page. Apparently there was a heading at the top of the first page, but only the last part is legible; it reads, "[Fort?] Clatsop 23rd March 1806.—" Then follows this list:

in the month of March [two?] Deer—
in the month of April one black bear at Sandy river & 2 Deer & one Elk
on May 14th at kooskooskee river Camp two white bear 16th one white bear [17th?] May [three?] Deer.—
month of June [4th?] two deer 10th one deer
Commas flat
22nd do one Deer
[23rd?] do one black bear and one deer
July 1st two large bucks & [9?] does
2nd three Deer—
4th two Deer—
9th one Deer—
11th two deer—
12th three 3 beaver
13th two deer
14th three deer
15th one fat buck
[16th?] faun Elk

July 16th one faun Elk two Mountn. Sheep [*word illegible*] one beaver—
18th three deer—
23rd three buffaloe
26th one buffaloe & one brarow
27th one deer
28 two buffalo & one beaver [1?] Elk
29th one big horn animal
30th one big horn & one beaver
31st one beaver—
1st August one beaver

At the top of the third page immediately above the first daily entry in this notebook is the heading, "Encampment at kooskooskee river *Sergt. Ordways* journal continued from Small Book."

2. Pryor and Collins, write Lewis and Clark, and confirmed by Ordway in the next entry.

Saturday 17th of May 1806. rained the greater part of last night and continues this morning. about 10 oClock A. M. Sergt. pryor and Collins returned had killed one black bear and one white bear, and brought in one of them. in the evening our officers directed that 10 or 12 hunters turn out a hunting tommorrow. asigned them horses Some three & others 4 to hunt on in turn.

Sunday 18th of May 1806. cloudy. eleven of our hunters[1] Set out on horseback in order to go out Some distance back in the high country to make a Camp hunt. and two men went out for the meat of the bear killed on 16th Inst in the evening 4 of our hunters returnd. had killd. nothing but one hawk & a pheasant.—

1. Including Joseph and Reubin Field, Drouillard, Lepage, Shannon, Collins, Labiche, Cruzatte, Shields, and Gibson.

Monday 19th of May 1806. a light rain. four of the party[1] went up to a village about 4 miles up the river on S. Side to purchase Some roots & Shappalell &C. about noon cleared off pleasant & warm in the evening Several of the hunters returnd had killd nothing. the men returnd from the village with a considerable quantity of white roots &C. which the natives call couse and a little Shappalell &C.—

1. Perhaps Ordway did not include Charbonneau, who the captains listed in addition to Thompson, Potts, Hall, and Weiser.

Tuesday 20th of May 1806. rained all last night and continues this morning, but Snows on the hills. Colter and Shannon returnd. had killd. nothing but had wounded a white bear. Soon after Labuche returnd. with the flesh of a large black taild. Deer which he had killd. but the Deer are Scarse & verry wild. rained the greater part of the day.—

Wednesday 21st May 1806. continues rainy & wet. I and one[1] more of the party went up to a village about 5 miles on South Side on the Side of a hill & Spring run we purchased some white roots Shappalell &C. Some of the women in the village were crying aloud at different times in the course of the day. I Signed the reason of their lamenting & they gave me to understand that they had lost Some of their Sons in battle and that was the custom among them when their relation died they mourn and lement a long time after the aged women only make a loud noise. we Stayed in the village all night.

1. Goodrich joined the sergeant, according to Lewis and Clark.

Thursday 22nd of May 1806. a clear cold frosty morning. the most of the women went out eairly with their horses to dig roots. the women do the most of the Slavery as those on the Missourie the men went eairly to a Swet house built a large fire and put in a large quantity of Small Stone and het them red hot then put them in some water in the swet hole which was prepared for that purpose & only a hole big enofe to git in one at a time. about 12 at on once got in to the hole untill they Sweet then went in the water and bathed themselves. then in the hole again and bathed themselves in that way for about 2 hours. they Signed to me that it was to help them of Some disease & Sore eyes, &C. &C. I then returned with a back load of white roots to the Encampment. Several of the party were employed makeing a canoe for convenience of the fishing &C and 4 men were gone a hunting. Sergt Pryor was Sent down to the mouth of Collins creek[1] to See if their is any good place to encamp as all may moove down in our canoe for a better place to fish and hunt if the place will admit &C. we haveing had no meat of any account for several days we killed a fine colt. Sergt. Pryor returnd without finding the mouth of Collins creek as the clifts were so high he got only 8 miles five of our hunters returnd had killed five deer and brought in the meat. a number of Indians chased a deer down the hills with their horses on South Side of the river it took the river tho the Inds had wounded it with their arrows. Some of the party Shot in [it?] in the river and the Indians got it. in the evening we made a fire on the canoe to burn it out.

1. Lolo Creek runs into the Clearwater River below Camp Chopunnish and forms the boundary between Clearwater and Idaho counties, Idaho.

Friday 23rd May 1806. clear & pleasant. Sergt Pryor wounded a deer at a lick near our Camp it Swam the river to the S. Side two Indians who Stayd with us last night Swam the river with their horses and ran the deer it took the river and Swam back again. Sergt. pryor then killed it and gave the Indians one half of it who Swam their horses back after it. Wm bratton having been so long better than 3 months nearly helpless with a Severe pain in his back we now undertake Sweeting him nearly in the manner as the Indians do only cover the hole with blankits having bows bent over above the hole. we expect this opperation will help him. we continue burning out the canoe &C. about noon our hunters all came in empty had killed nothing except a fiew fowls most of our men went to the village we were camped at Some time past and bought considerable of couse & Shappalell &C. Some of the natives caught 3 Salmon to day.

Saturday 24th of May 1806. a clear pleasant warm day. Several of the natives cam down the river in a canoe. Several of the party went across the river to the village and Several Indians came across to our Camp. Several hunters went out to day a hunting.[1]

1. Including Drouillard, Labiche, and Cruzatte.

Sunday 25th of May 1806. a Thunder Shower eairly this evening. we undertook to Sweet the Sick Indian but he being quite helpless did not carry it into effect. four of our hunters went out a hunting 2 of which went across the river to the South Side[1] the canoe being burnt enofe we went at finishing it &C. two hunters[2] came in this evening had killd. nothing.

1. Five according to Lewis and Clark, with Drouillard, Labiche, and Cruzatte going in one direction, while the Field brothers crossed the river.

2. Gibson and Shields, say the captains. Gass agrees that they had killed nothing, but the captains report that they had killed a sandhill crane.

Monday 26th of May 1806. clear & pleasant. two men[1] went out a hunting. we finished the canoe and put it in the river. a number of the natives visited us. the river riseing. our two hunters[2] returnd from the South Side of the river. the creek being so high they did not go to where was any hunting but purchased considerable of Shappalell and couse roots &C—

1. The captains count three men: Collins, Shannon, and Colter.

2. The Field brothers.

Tuesday 27th of May 1806. J. Frazer and wiser Set out to go over to the kimooenim river[1] for fish & [*page torn, word missing*] Swam our horses and waidd on to [the?] village on commeap cre[ek][2] three young men went on with [us] up Sd. creek about 5 miles left this creek ascended a high hill on a plain and proced. on passd. a lodge where we Struck the creek again followed up Said creek about 8 miles farther and came to the chiefs village[3] which took care of our horses. the [*word illegible*] chief, and as the old man said he was a going on with us in the morning the young men returned and we camped here, and had a hard Thunder Shower. the Indians grass houses leak.

1. Here meaning the Snake River, Lewis's River to the party, while the term "Kimooenem" (variously spelled) was applied to the Tucannon River.

2. Lawyer Creek, Idaho County, Idaho.

3. A Nez Perce village on Lawyer Creek but not necessarily the home village of Twisted Hair, who had cared for the horses and who lived to the north near Orofino, Idaho. Here the men camped for the night.

Wednesday 28th May 1806. we Set out eairly the old chief and an other Indn went with us. we rode on a plain about 2 hours then left the road and bore South thro an unlevel timbred country untill towards evening. Saw Several big horn animel or mountain Sheep and Saw 14 deer in this timbred country Some Spots of Snow & falling timber. had a hard Thunder Shower. towards evening we descended a bad hill down on a creek[1] followed it down Some distance and arived at a village where we Camped.

1. According to John J. Peebles, "The Return of Lewis and Clark," *Idaho Yesterdays* 10 (Summer 1966): 21, the party continued west on Lawyer Creek, then overland southwesterly to Deer Creek, descended it a ways, and camped for the night. The camp would have been near the Lewis–Nez Perce county line, Idaho, above Deer Creek's entrance into the Salmon River. More recently, Merle Wells of the Idaho Historical Society has been at work tracing Ordway's route. Personal communication, September 14, 1990. Wells has the party follow Lawyer Creek west to Mitchell Creek, move northwesterly up it a distance, then go overland to return to Lawyer Creek, follow it a short distance before breaking off overland again, and finally descend to the Salmon along a route paralleling Deer Creek but to the west of that stream. Both accounts have to rely on what seems the most plausible route since Ordway's description is not detailed enough to allow a precise tracing. Lewis summarizes Ordway's journey in his entry for June 2, 1806.

Thursday 29th May 1806. rained the greater part of last night. a rainy morning. we took a light breakfast Frazer got 2 Spanish mill dollars from a squaw for an old razer[1] we expect they got them from the Snake Indians who live near the Spanish country to the South.[2] we proceed. on Shortly arived at a fork of the kimoo-enim or Lewises river[3] followed down it Some distance then left it and bore to the right up a creek.[4] passd one lodge crossed a steep bad hill and descended down a long hill an a run pass a large lodge and descended the worst hills we ever saw a road made down. towards evening we arived at the kimooenim or Lewises river at a fishery at a bad rapid.[5] our chief told us to set down and not go in the lodge untill we were invited so we did at length they invited us in. spread robes for us to sit on and Set a roasted Salmon before us and Some of their white bread which they call uppah.[6] we eat hearty of this fat fish but did not eat ¼ of it. It was Set up for us. this lodge is about 100 feet long and 20 wide and all in one but they have but fiew Salmon.

1. The story and wider implications of this transaction is told in James P. Ronda, "Frazer's Razor: The Ethnohistory of a Common Object," *We Proceeded On* 7 (August 1981): 12–13. Gass elaborates on this incident in his entry of June 2, 1806, saying that the coins came from the neck of a dead Shoshone Indian whom the Nez Perces had killed some time before.

2. Probably modern New Mexico.

3. The fork of Lewis's (Snake) River is the Salmon River; again Ordway uses "Kimooenem" inappropriately.

4. China Creek, Nez Perce County, according to Peebles and Wells.

5. The men followed China Creek in a northwesterly direction for a distance, then went over Wapshilla Ridge to the Snake River. From the ridge Peebles has them come down Corral Creek to the fishery at Wild Goose Rapids, Nez Perce County, on the Snake River. Wells puts the route on a parallel course but more to the south after they cross Wapshilla Ridge. He would have them descend in an area between China Garden Creek and Cave Gulch, reach the Snake River and follow it to McDuff Rapids near the Asotin-Wallowa county line, Washington, some distance to the south of Wild Goose Rapids.

6. A word not used by Lewis or Clark. It may represent the Nez Perce term *'ápa,* "cous cake." Aoki, *Nez Perce Dictionary,* 973. On June 1 Ordway mentions a "large cake of uppah."

Friday 30th May 1806. a number of [Indians?] left this eairly with nearly all the Salmon which was caught so we had to wait here to day expecting to git some Salmon the natives roasted an other Salmon & Set before us to eat. in the afternoon we purchased as many Salmon as we thought was necessary to take home and hung them up the most they catch is on the opposite shore along the rocks in the whorls & eddys. we Saw only three dip nets at 3 places a fishing.

Saturday 31st May 1806. Some of the young Indians Stole Some of our fish and went away in the night. we got up our horses eairly and Set out on our return our old chief and his man stayed as they had got no fish yet, so we followed back the same road we went on to the fork of the kimooenim which the Indian name of it is Toomonamah river[1] which is about 150 yards wide. we followed up to the village we left the day before yesterday. their the chief directed us another way whi[ch] he said was nearer & a better road and Sent 2 boys to show us the way to a village on the road. they took us over a verry bad hill down on to the Thommonama river again then left the river ascended a high long hill near the top of which is a large village we Camped[2] near Sd. village as night came on.

1. Toomonamah (variously spelled) is Nez Perce *tamá·nma,* for the Salmon River.

2. The detachment retraced their steps to Deer Creek. Wells then has the men go east to touch the Salmon River near the mouth of Maloney Creek. From there they must have ascended a hill to the northeast and camped for the night at a spot a short distance northeast of where Maloney Creek empties into a prominent oxbow of the Snake River, in Lewis County, Idaho.

Sunday 1st day of June 1806. we Set out eairly a young man went and put us on the road which he said was a near way & a good road we wrode thro the timbred country struck the head of a creek[1] in the plain followed down Said creek passd. one lodge about noon the road left the creek and kept thro the high plain a good road. towards evening we came down the river hills to a large village above the forks on kooskooskee river.[2] we halted a Short time to let our horses feed a little and git something to eat ourselves. bought considerable uppah and couse from the natives and proceeded on to another village down the river near the forks. night came on and we Camped[3] here at the chiefs lodge that gave us so many horses they appeared verry friendly to us and gave us a large cake of uppah their is a vast site of excellent horses Scattered along this river which they offer to Sell for a Squaw axe pr peace & 2 or 3 for a gun & a little ammunt

1. This could be any of a number of creeks in the area, perhaps Deep Creek, the dividing line between Lewis and Idaho counties, Idaho.

2. To reach the Clearwater (Kooskooske) River Peebles has the men go nearly directly east to the Clearwater River, reaching it near Kooskia, Idaho County, Idaho. Wells has them proceed eastward, passing near Keuterville and Cottonwood in Idaho County, then reach the Clearwater near Stites, Idaho County, south of Kooskia.

3. Apparently the village of Hohots Ilppilp, which Lewis estimated to be six miles below Camp Chopunnish on the Clearwater River. See Lewis's entry of May 10, 1806.

Monday 2nd June 1806. a fair morning. we Set out eairly and turned down the river passd 2 more villages about 12 oClock we arived at our Camp.[1] found the river verry high indeed. Swam the horses across and got across in an Indian canoe as our men informed us that as Some of our men were crossing several days past our large canoe ran against Some trees as they were going to Shore and the canoe upset and Sank emediately. the men got Safe to Shore but lost three blankets one blanket cappo and Several articles, they had for trade &C. they had killed a horse soon after we went away to eat which the natives gave us for that purpose Soon after our hunters killed and brought to Camp 12 Deer. Some of our castrated horses are nearly well and one is Sick and like to dye. So Some of our men went and Shot him &C. towards evening the head chief[2] of the cho-pennish nation came to our Camp with George Drewyer and brought and gave up a tommahawk[3] which Capt Clark lost last fall which the chief kept for us.

1. Camp Chopunnish.
2. Actually two chiefs, Cut Nose and Hohots Ilppilp.
3. Actually two, report Lewis and Clark, one of which had been stolen and was Sergeant Floyd's, which Clark hoped to return to the dead soldier's friends.

Tuesday 3rd June 1806.[1] clouded up and Sprinkled a little rain. a number of the natives visited us. three of our hunters[2] came in had killed five deer and one black bear. my horse that I wrode over to the kimooenim river nearly failed and his back verry sore and poor & in low Spirits and as luck would have it an Indian brought me a large good strong horse and Swaped with me as he knew my horse to be good when in order to run the buffaloe which is their main object to git horses that will run and Swap their best horses for Servis, for them that will run if they are not half as good as otherways.

1. The stubs of several pages of the notebook are apparent between this entry and the previous one.
2. Colter, Joseph Field, and Willard, write the captains.

Wednesday 4th June 1806. rained the greater part of last night a wet morning one of our hunters John Shields came in had killed 2 Deer and brought in the meat. the after part of the day fair.

Thursday 5th June 1806. a fair morning. Several of the party went across the river to Some villages and purchased Some uppah & couse.— towards evening our hunters[1] all came in had killed one black bear and five deer and informed us that an Indian had Set out Some days past to cross the mountains if possable but Soon after dark he returned to our Camp and informed us that he went over one mountain and in attempting to cross a creek which was high and rapid his horse fell and hurt him So he turned back to wait untill the water falls. the river kooskee is falling fast.

1. Reubin Field, Shannon, Labiche, and Collins, say Lewis and Clark.

Friday 6th June 1806. a fair morning. Capt Clark and five men[1] went across the river to Some villages. one of the party[2] who Stayed at the commeap village last night riturnd informed us that 5 of the Sho-Sho-nee of Snake nation had come to make peace or treaty with this nation[3] towards evening Capt Clark & party returned the young chief[4] who gave us Several horses and Several more of the natives of his village accompanyd them &C.

1. Drouillard and three others went to the village of Broken Arm, according to Clark.
2. Frazer, report the captains.
3. This was actually news from Clark about the Cayuse Indians.
4. Again, Hohots Ilppilp.

Saturday 7th June 1806. cloudy & light Showers of rain intermixed with hail & Snow. the air cold. Several of the party[1] went over the river to Some villages all except 2[2] returnd with Some uppah and couse &C.

1. Charbonneau, Gass, McNeal, Whitehouse, and Goodrich, write the captains.
2. Whitehouse and Goodrich stayed, according to Lewis and Clark.

Sunday 8th June 1806. the 2 men returnd from the villages. a number of the natives visited us and gave Frazer a fine young horse a number of the natives joined and got out our canoe which was Sank. our party exercised themselves running and playing games called base[1] in the evening danced after the fiddle as the Indians were anxious to See them.

1. Or prisoner's base, a child's game in which each side tries to make prisoner the members of the opposing side who run out their base area.

Monday 9th June 1806. a number of the natives Stayed with us last night. a chief we call cut nose went Some distance after young Eagles. got

Several by climbing a tree by a rope. the feathers of these eagles the Indians make head dresses war like & paint them & is a great thing among them. we got up our horses and hobbled them as we intend to moove to morrow.

Tuesday 10th June 1806. clear & pleasant. we went eairly for our horses found all except 2. about 10 A. M. we Set out and proced. on ascended a high hill then decended it down on Collins Creek forded it and ascended a high hill on to a livel timbred country 2 or 3 men was left to look for the lost horses. proced. thro. thickets of young slim pines & balsom fer timber about 4 P M. we arived at the Commass ground[1] where we Camped 22 Sept last but no villages here now. we Camped here for a fiew days to kill some deer to take Some meat for the mountains. this level consists of about 2000 ackers of level Smooth prarie on which is not a tree or Shreub, but the lowest parts is covred with commass which is now all in blossom, but is not good untill the Stalk is dead, then the natives assemble and collect their winters food in a short time as it is verry convenient for their villages as points of timber runs out in the praries of higher ground & covred with pitch pine. a fine timbred country all around this rich land the Soil is deep black & verry rich & easy for cultervation our men all came up had found only one of the 2 lost horses. Several of the natives accompanied us. Several of our hunters went out this evening a hunting. they all returned at dark Collins had killed one deer. Some of the rest wounded Several others &C.

1. Weippe Prairie, Clearwater County, Idaho. The party now camped near the location where they had met the Nez Perces on September 20, 1805.

Wednesday 11th June 1806. clear and pleasant all the party that could hunt turned out at day light a hunting. about noon all returned to Camp. Gibson had killed one fine large buck & Labuche killed a black bear and a large buck & a crain. Some of the other hunters wounded Several deer & killed Several pheasants &C. a number Indians went across this commass flat on horse back to another prarie or flat to the North of this a hunting but killed nothing. Several of our hunters went out again this afternoon our horses have excelent feed in this pleasant commass flat. Some of the hunters came in this evening and Several Stayed out in the woods for an eairly hunt in the morning.— the Indians all went away from our Camp &C.—

Thursday 12th June 1806. a clear pleasant morning. a number more hunters went out eairly to hunt. about 10 oClock Some of them came in Shields had killed two fine bucks and brought in the meat. the rest of the hunters that came in killd. nothing. we fleased what meat we have to dry it for the Mountains. towards evening Several of our hunters went out Some distance to Stay all night and take an eairly hunt in the morning.

Friday 13th June 1806. a fair morning. Several men went out eairly from Camp a hunting about noon R. Fields and willard Set out to go on about 10 miles a head and hunt at a small prarie[1] untill we come up. our hunters all came in this afternoon and eight of them had killed each a deer Gibson Shields Shannon Collins Jo. Fields Drewyer Labuche and [*blank*] all the meat except Labuches was brought in & that the ravens & buzzards[2] eat while he was hunting a little more after killing it. one of the other hunters Colter killed a large crain

1. Perhaps Crane Meadows, north of Lolo Creek in Clearwater County, Idaho.
2. Perhaps the turkey vulture, *Cathartes aura*.

Saturday 14th June 1806. Some cloudy Several hunters went out eairly about 10 oClock Colter came in had killed a deer and found eight ducks eggs. the day verry warm

Sunday 15th June 1806. we arose at day light and went out in this flat for our horses. Soon Set in to raining hard. we got up all our horses took breakfast & packed up and Set out about 8 oClock and proceeded on. found the road verry Slipperry & bad took the mountains and the road So bad Several of our horses fell about noon we had Thunder and hard Showers of rain. we crossed Several runs on which is considerable of white ceedder timber balsom fer & diffrent kinds of pine. we have now 66 good horses to take us and our baggage across the mountains. came to the Small prarie where R. Fields and willard had been hunting found 2 deer hanging up which they had killd. we took the meat and proceed. on down the bad hill on Collinses Creek where we found R. Fields and willard they had killed another Deer and were Camped on the bank of the Creek where we dined and proceeded on. found the road very bad falling timber &C. at dark we Camped[1] at a Small glade where was pleanty of feed for our horses

1. On Eldorado Creek, near the mouth of Lunch Creek, Idaho County, Idaho.

Monday 16th June 1806. two of our hunters went on to a glade a Short distance to hunt we took an eairly breakfast the morning fair. we Set out proced on overtook the hunters who had killed nothing. folled up the glade and mountains Some distance then took the hills on to a ridge of falling timber towards noon we passed over high banks of Snow which bore up our horses. Some places 5 or 6 feet deep about noon we halted at a Small branch[1] & green to dine the grass is verry Short and in the woods jest Starting up. delayed about 2 hours and Set forward again. light Showers of rain this afternoon the Snow is more Common and much deeper. towards evening we came on hungry creek[2] followed down it to a green where Capt. Clark killed a horse last fall for the party to eat. here we Camped.[3] the young grass verry Short. the bushes are all bent flat down by the deep Snow lying on them. the Snow must fall in these hollars in the winter 15 or 20 feet deep and perhaps the Snow drifts in and fills the hollars full.

1. On a branch of Fish Creek, Idaho County, Idaho.
2. Hungery Creek, Idaho County.
3. At Horsesteak Meadow on Hungery Creek just below Windy Saddle, Idaho County. Clark's party killed the horse on September 19, 1805, and Lewis's group found it the next day.

Tuesday 17th June 1806. we Set out as usal the morning chilley and cloudy. we proceeded on down Sd Creek about 6 miles then took up a high mountain. when we got about half way up it the ground was covred with Snow 3 or 4 feet deep as we ascended higher it got deeper untill we got to the top of the mountain where it was 12 or 15 feet in general even on the South Side where the Sun has open view but is So Settled So that it bears up our horses.— here is not a sign of any green Shrub or any thing for our horses to eat, and of course no better for 4 days march a head. if we could even find the road which is impossable without a guide as their is no Sign of a road or trail here So we halted on the top of this mountain and our officers consulted on what was best to do. at length determined to our Sorrow to return to where we might git feed for our horses. So we Scaffelled up all our baggage[1] we could do a Short time with out. Set in to hailling & raining at this time verry cold and disagreeable. So we turned back much against our expectations when we Started went back on hungry creek & followed up it about 2 miles & Camped[2] for the night.—

1. The baggage was left at Willow Ridge, just west of Sherman Saddle, Idaho County, Idaho.

2. On the south side of Hungery Creek, Idaho County.

Wednesday 18th June 1806. cloudy Drewyer and Shannon Sent on a head to go to the villages of the pel-oll-pellow[1] nation they took one of the Short rifles[2] in order to git a pilot if possable to go over the mountn. with us. 2 of our horses could not be found this morning, So 2 men was left to hunt them. we Set out about 8 oClock proced. on with 4 men in front to clear the limbs and bushes out of the path. we got but a short distance before one of the men Potts who was of the front cut his leg verry bad with a big knife we halted a fiew minutes Capt. Lewis Sowed up the wound and bound it up we then proceeded on a Short distance further in crossing the creek Colters horse threw him in the creek lost his blanket and hirt him a little. about noon we halted to dine at the Same place we dined on the 16th Inst. at which time came up a hard Shower of hail and rain and hard Thunder, which lasted about an hour and cleared off. the 2 Fields Stayed here to hunt we proceeded on towards evening we arived at the long glades on a branch of Collinses Creek where is fine feed for our horses. so we Camped[3] in order to Stay if the hunters kill game untill a guide comes or untill the road is So that we can go but it depends on the hunters and game in a great measure. the musquetoes verry troublesome at this place. Several Salmon[4] Seen in this branch &C—

1. The term may apply to either the Palouse or Nez Perce Indians. Lewis used his term for the Nez Perces on this occasion, which is probably the case in this context. The expression could also refer to names of villages. See Lewis's entry of June 8, 1806, for a discussion of the term.

2. Meaning the Model 1803 rifle. See Clark's entry of May 10, 1804.

3. On Eldorado Creek, at the mouth of Dollar Creek, Idaho County, Idaho.

4. From Lewis and Clark it is apparent that the fish are steelhead trout. The next day Ordway calls them salmon trout.

Thursday 19th June 1806. a fair morning. Several men went out a hunting & 2 went at fishing with Indin gigs which Some of the party had with them but could See only now and then a Scattering one, and could not kill any. about noon Labuche came in with a deer which he had killed. Shortly after all our men who Stayed back came up R. Fields had killed two deer, but Shields had not found the 2 lost horses. towards evening Gibson giged & killd. one of the fish we took to be Salmon and we found it to be Salmon trout, and poor. we expect they all are that is in this creek. the Musquetoes are verry troublesome

Friday 20th June 1806. a fair morning. Several hunters went out eairly a hunting. about 11 A. M. R. Fields came in had killed a Brown bear about a mile down this glade. Several men went at fishing fixed gigs of Bayonets & Indn. gigs and fixed a dip net &C. and killd and caught 7 Salmon trout towards evening Labuche and Cruzatte came in had killed one deer & caught one Salmon trout.—

Saturday 21st June 1806. a fair morning. we got up our horses all except 4 which we expect has gone back to the Commass ground. we Set out on our return to the Commass flat where we expect we can kill Some more meat to Start again with & to take us back in mount. when we got down on Collinses Creek we met 2 Indians who were on their way to cross the mountn. they had our 4 horses takeing them back to us had 5 horses of their own and provision to last them across the mountains. we halted and dined below the forks of Collinses Creek.[1] these 2 Indians told us that we could have went on if in case we could have found the road, for as the Snow bears up the horses all can cross the high parts which is covred So thick with Snow in about 3 days and our horses cannot git any thing to eat dureing that time. we ascended the hill to the Samll prarie[2] the 2 Indians halted here to stay 2 or 3 days & wait for us to kill some meat & then pilot us across the Snow mountains. Sergt. Gass & the 2 Fields Stayed here to hunt. we descended the mountain down to the Commass flat towards evening and Camped[3] at the old Camping ground. Several went out a Short distance to hunt & came in at dark. Shields had killed & brought in one deer—

1. On Lolo Creek, Clearwater County, Idaho, where Lewis's party had camped on September 21, 1805.

2. Crane Meadows, Clearwater County; see June 13, 1806.

3. The camp of June 10–15, 1806, on Weippe Prairie.

Sunday 22nd June 1806. clear and pleasant. all the hunters turned out eairly this morning a hunting around this Commass flat. one man Set out to go over to the kooskooskee river for Salmon as the 2 Indians told us they catch pleanty at this time. about noon all the hunters came in had killed in all eight deer and two brown bear. towards evening the hunters turned out again and Collins killed a black bear.

Monday 23rd June 1806. a clear pleasant morning. The most of the hunters turned out again a hunting and killed two deer in the afternoon Drewyer Shannon & Whitehouse returned with the young chief[1] and 2 other Indians who has engaged to go over the mountains as guides for us &C. in the afternoon two of the hunters came in had killed 2 two deer. the Strawburys are pleanty about this place.—

1. He may not have been a chief, but was the brother of Cut Nose, a chief, according to Lewis and Clark.

Tuesday 24th June 1806. we got up all our horses and Set out on our homeward bound journey again proceed. on to Collinses Creek the three guides with us. the other 2 Indians who we lift here is gone on and 4 of our men went on after them. we dined and proceeded towards evening we arived at a Small prarie[1] on a branch of Collinses Creek where the 2 Indn.

and our men except 2 were waiting for us. the other 2 had gone on to hunt. the men who Stayed with the Indians had killed one deer.—

1. The camp of June 18–21, 1806, on Eldorado Creek, Idaho County, Idaho.

Wednesday 25th June 1806. a little rain last night. we took an eairly breakfast and Set out proceeded on about noon we came to an open place or Small prarie joined the 2 Fields we find the Snow has melted considerable Since we passd we dined and proceed. on to hungry Creek & found the 2 horses we lost here a fiew days past. the after part of the day Showery and wet we Camped[1] eairly as their is no grass near a head.

1. Probably at or near the main party's camp of September 19, 1805, on an unnamed creek emptying into Hungery Creek, Idaho County, Idaho.

Thursday 26th June 1806. we Set out as usal and proceed. on to the top of mountains covred with Snow where we had left our baggage,[1] and packed up and proceed. on we find the Snow has Settled a little more than 2 feet Since we left this the other day. proceeded on thro. Snow deep. in the evening we Came to the Side of a mountain where the Snow is melted away and a little young grass &C. So we Camped.[2] Soon after we Camped another Indn. Came up who is going over the mountn. with us.

1. The cache on Willow Ridge, Idaho County, Idaho.
2. On Bald Mountain, Idaho County.

Friday 27th June 1806. a fair morning. we took an eairly breakfast and proceeded on verry fast over the high banks of Snow the most part of the day and bad mountains. we came further to day than we went in 2 when we came over. and Camped[1] on the South Side of a mountain where our horses find a little grass. the day warm and Snow melts fast.—

1. On Spring Hill, or Spring Mountain, a little south of the Clearwater-Idaho county line, Idaho.

⟨Saturday 28th June 1806. a fair cool morning. we Set out as usal and proceeded on [*four words illegible*] the vallies on to the ridge [thick?] 2

hunters went on a head to hunt. we descended a mountn. down on a fork of Collinses Creek, found the meat of a deer which one of the hunters had killed. we crossed the creek and ascended a high Steep mountn. came in [our old] road had a bad Shower of hail and [Some?] Thunder⟩

Saturday 28th June 1806. a clear cool morning we Set out as usal and proceeded on verry well the Snow continues as yesterday. our guides took us on a ridge different from that we went last fall, but a better way.[1] about one oClock we halted on the top of a bald mountain[2] on the South Side of which our horses git tollarable feed. So we delay this afternoon to let our horses refresh themselves &C in the evening we had Thunder & hail.

1. Instead of going down to the valley of the Lochsa River as on the westbound route, the party continued eastward on the Lolo Trail along the ridge.

2. The camp was near Powell Junction on Forest Road 500, Idaho County, Idaho, also near Papoose Saddle and a few miles north of Powell Ranger Station.

Sunday 29th June 1806. a fair morning. we got up our horses eairly two hunters went on a head. the fog rose up thick from the hollars we proceeded on a ridge desended down on a fork of Collinses Creek took the meat of a deer the hunters had killed crossed the creek above the forks Some distance ascended a high mountn. came in the old road we went in last year & proceed. on[1] had a Shower of hail and Thunder. about 1 oClock P. M. we arived at the glades of the rockey mountn.[2] Crossed glade Creek Several times and halted at a handsom flat of grass and Commass. found that 2 of our horses got left back on the road 2 men[3] went back for them Shields killed 2 crains we dined and proceed. on Soon came on the head waters of travvellers rest Creek.[4] towards evening we arived at the hot Stream where we Camped.[5] the 2 men came up with the 2 horses. had killed one deer. a number of the party as well as myself bathed in these hot Springs, but the water so hot[6] that it makes the Skin Smart when I first entered it. I drank Some of the water also.—

1. The party moved eastward along the ridge to Rocky Point, then descended to Crooked Fork Creek and crossed it a mile or so above the entrance of Brushy Creek. Then they turned

to the northeast and climbed a ridge to pick up their trail of the previous year, all in Idaho County, Idaho.

2. Packer Meadows on Pack (Glade) Creek, Idaho County.

3. Joseph Field and Colter, say the captains.

4. Lolo Creek, Missoula County, Montana.

5. Lolo Hot Springs, Missoula County.

6. The temperature of the water has been measured at 111° F.

Monday 30th June 1806. a clear morning. we got up our horses as usal R. Fields killed a deer near the hot Springs in Scite of the Camp. two hunters went on a head. we Set out proceed. on a muddy bad road down the creek & over bad hills &C about noon we halted to dine 12th Sept last[1] Shields killed a deer. we dined and proceed. on took the meat of a deer which the hunters had killed. Shields killed another deer. proceed. on to the bottoms or plains of travvellers rest creek Drewyer had killed three deer, we wrode fast untill about Sunset at which time we arived at travvellers rest where we Camped the 9th & 10th of Sept. last. we Camped[2] here in order to Stay 2 or 3 days to refresh our horses and kill Some meat &C. the Musquetoes verry troublesome here.—

1. The party dined at the same spot as the previous year, on September 12, 1805, on Grave Creek, Missoula County, Montana.

2. They would remain here at Travelers' Rest Camp until July 3. The spot is on the south side of Lolo Creek, about two miles up the creek from the Bitterroot River, in Missoula County.

Tuesday 1st July 1806. cloudy. all the hunters turned out eairly a hunting they all returned by noon had killed in all twelve deer & Some of them large fat bucks. in the afternoon our officers had a talk with the guides that came over the mountains with us. they told our officers that they wished to live in peace and bury their war Stripes[1] in the ground. one of them gave Capt. Lewis a good horse.

1. Perhaps the men spoke figuratively of cleaning the war paint off their faces.

Wednesday 2nd July 1806. a clear pleasant morning. Several men went out a hunting. about 10 A. M. Collins Came in had killed one deer. Capt.

Lewis Called for 6 vollunteers[1] to go with him on a route up the River Marriah as he intends going that way they immediately tourned out our guides wished to leave us here but Capt. Lewis prievailed with them to go 2 days march with him and put him on the road to the falls of the Missouri then they intend to return to their nation. 2 Invalleeds[2] is going to the falls to Stay their untill the party comes down with the canoes, and one man to make geers for the 4 horses which is to be left their to draw the canoes past the portage.—

1. Lewis selected Drouillard, the Field brothers, Werner, Frazer, and Gass to explore the Marias River with him. The destinations and divisions of the rest of the party are discussed in the entries of Lewis and Clark.

2. Clark names three men (Thompson, Goodrich, and McNeal) who would accompany Lewis as far as the Great Falls of the Missouri River.

Thursday 3rd 1806 July. we got up our horses and boath parties Set out about one time. Capts. Lewis & Clark parted here with their parties & proceed. on I with Capt. Clark up the flat head River.[1] we kept up the west Side as it is too high at this time to cross. we are now on our way to the head of the Missourie. we wrode fast & Crossed a number of large creeks in which is beaver dams &C. about noon we halted to dine at a branch[2] and bottom of fine feed white clover[3] &C. proceeded on the plains partly covd. with pitch pine timber. Saw a number of deer. in the evening we Camped[4] at a bottom having made 35 miles in 10 hours this day. one of the hunters killed a deer this evening.

1. Clark's party headed south up the Bitterroot River, going from Missoula County to Ravalli County, Montana.

2. Perhaps Kootenai Creek, Ravalli County.

3. Probably longstalk clover, *Trifolium longipes* Nutt., which Lewis noticed on July 2, 1806.

4. On Blodgett Creek, Ravalli County, near U.S. Highway 93 and about three miles north of Hamilton.

Friday 4th July 1806. a fair morning. 2 of our hunters went on eairly a head. we took an eairly breakfast, and proceed. on through a large plain & groves of pitch pine where the hunters had killed 2 deer we took the meat and proceed on crossed Several creeks one so large it Swam Some of our horses.[1] about 12 we Saw a large flock of Mountn. Sheep or big horn animels. they run so near us that Some of the men fired at them. Shortly after we halted at a branch to dine. dined and proceeded on without finding the road. as we cannot ford the river yet. towards evening one of the hunters killed a deer. Soon after we Camped[2] near the forks of the creek. one of the hunters killed a fat buck this evening.

1. The party continued south on the west side of the Bitterroot River in Ravalli County, Montana.

2. On the north side of West Fork Bitterroot River, near its junction with the Bitterroot in Ravalli County.

Saturday 5th July 1806. a fair M. we took breakfast as usal and Set out to cross the right fork of the river which we found nearly Swimming. proceed. on up the river Some distance crossd. the other fork. the hunters killed a deer and a Mountain Sheep or big horn animel. about noon we halted in a bottom to dine. Shannon left his tommahawk back where he killed the deer & went back for it. we delayed about 3 hours and proceed on over the hills towards evening we came to the Smooth plains where we Saw the 1st flat heads or Tus e paw last year as we passd down. we Camped[1] on the branch & plain the hunters killed two deer. Shannon joined us with his tommahawk &C.—

1. The party crossed from the north to the south side of the West Fork Bitterroot River, Ravalli County, Montana, then crossed the East Fork to its east side and continued southeasterly along that stream. From there they reached Ross, or Ross's, Hole, near Sula, where they had met the Flatheads, or Salish, on September 4, 1805. They camped on Camp Creek near Camp Creek Ranger Station and U.S. Highway 93, Ravalli County.

Sunday 6th July 1806. a fair morning. we were detained a while hunting up our horses. then proceed. on as usal up the branch to the mount. and crossed over to the left in an Indian trail. at about 5 or 6 miles we got over on a branch running South[1] Shields killed a hair[2] of a different discription of any we have seen before. our Intrepters wife tells us that we She knows the country & that this branch is the head waters of jeffersons river &C. we proceeded on down the branch. large glades covred with Commass & fine grass about noon we halted at one of the glades to dine and proceeded on down the creek late in the afternooon we came to a large extensive plain contined our course about South in this plain got 5 or 6 miles out in the open plain came up a hard Thunder Shower of hail rain and hard wind. we halted a Short time in the midst of it then proceed. on at dark we Campd.[3] at a branch Saw Indn. signs abundance of Commass on this branch—

1. The group followed Camp Creek, roughly paralleling U.S. Highway 93, and crossed the Continental Divide from Ravalli County to Beaverhead County, Montana, by way of Gibbons Pass. Here they picked up Trail Creek and began their descent to the Big Hole Valley.

2. Perhaps Nuttall's cottontail, *Sylvilagus nuttallii.*

3. The party followed Trail Creek to near its junction with North Fork Big Hole River then moved southeasterly and apparently camped on Moose Creek, in the western part of the Big Hole Valley, Beaverhead County, some seven miles southwest of Wisdom.

Monday 7th July 1806. we went out in the plain eairly to look up our horses. found all except nine hunted in all directions for them could not find them. So Capt. Clark directed me to Stay with 4 men to hunt this day for them. about 9 A m Capt. Clark and the rest of the party set out to go to canoe deposite.[1] I and the 4 men[2] went out in different directions to look for the 9 horses I and Labuiche went up a valley which led in the mountn. towards the ShoShones nation. got on the track of the horses and followed it on untill towards evening and found them still going on an Indn. road. we turned them back to the last nights Camp. the other 3 men had got back their also. we hobled the horses and Camped here.[3] had several Showers of rain & Thunder in the course of this afternoon—

1. Clark's group continued their southeasterly route to Jackson, Beaverhead County, Montana, then turned more easterly and passed through the Big Hole Pass and camped near there.

2. Shannon, Gibson, Collins, and Labiche, according to Clark.

3. Back at the camp on Moose Creek, apparently.

Tuesday 8th July 1806. a clear cold morning & hard frost. we Set out eairly with our horses and proceed. on over this large extensive plains. crossed Several large creeks Saw elk & deers and goats or antelopes. our course abt. South   Struck the trail of the party   at about 12 miles we come to a boiling hot Spring[1] at the edge of this plains which is large and handsom   we halted a fiew minutes at this Spring   found a peace of vinison in it well boiled which we expect the party left for us.   we eat it. I drank Some of the water found it well tasted but So hot[2] that I cannot hold my hand in a Second of time.   it fairly boils out of the ground in Sundry places &C.   we proceeded on   crossd a creek[3] near Sd. Springs and kept our course abt. South up a creek on which Saw many beaver dams &C.   about noon we dined at the head of the creek near the dividing ridge.[4]   then crossd the ridge about one mile and came on a creek running South, which we expect is a branch of jeffersons river   followed down it 10 or 12 mls. and crossed an other ridge and came in the valley & on the east fork of jeffersons river.   followed down on the trail of the party a Short distance and Camped[5] at dark on the branch of the creek.   hobbled the unruley horses and lay down to Sleep fatigued rideing upwards of 40 miles this day.   and nothing to eat this evening but the head of a goat or antelope which the party had droped on the road.—

1. Jackson Hot Spring, Beaverhead County, Montana.

2. The temperature of the water has been measured at 136°F.

3. Probably Warm Spring Creek, Beaverhead County.

4. They are following Clark's route up Governor Creek and Bull Creek, roughly parallel to Montana Highway 278 in Beaverhead County, then crossed through Big Hole Pass.

5. After leaving Big Hole Pass, the men reached Divide Creek and followed it a distance before getting on Grasshopper Creek, a branch of the Beaverhead (Jefferson) River, as Ordway surmised. They camped on an affluent of Grasshopper Creek, to the west and maybe south of Bannack, Beaverhead County.

Wednesday 9th July 1806.   a fair morning.   three of the men went on at light a head to hunt   I and the other man took on the horses.   about 4 miles overtook the hunters who had killd. a deer.   we halted and roasted a quarter of it and the Intrals which we eat and proceeded on down the river   about noon we arived at the canoe deposite[1]   joined the party who arived here last evening and opened our carsh   found everry thing in it Safe. they had killed a deer and one antelope.   they raised the canoes to day   found some tin and nails had been taken of them by the Savages   we halled them out to Sun them we repaired our canoes &C. the party aranged to go with Capt. Clark to the River Roshjone and also to go down with the canoes. I go down with 9 more to take the canoes to the falls of the Missourie than to the forks of Marriah where I expect to join Capt. Lewis & his party.—[2]

1. Ordway apparently followed Clark's route to Horse Prairie and Horse Prairie Creek and then proceeded to the forks of the Beaverhead River and the site of Camp Fortunate, where the party had first stopped on August 17, 1805, and where Clark's group was now encamped.

2. The entire party would travel north to the Three Forks area, then Clark would lead a group across land to the Yellowstone (Roshjone) River and descend it to the Missouri River to link up with Lewis's party after they had been joined by Ordway and his men at the Marias River. See July 13, 1806, for the division of the company.

Thursday 10th July 1806. a Severe hard frost & Ice. chilley and cold this morning. one canoe which we thot of no account cut up for paddles and fire wood. then put the 6 canoes in the water, and put our baggage in them. at the same time Capt. Clarks party got up their horses and packed up took breakfast and all Set out by land & water about one time. I proceeded on by water. the party by land holds way with us. we came fast with the canoes too. Collins killed a goose about noon we halted to dine Capt. Clark & party halted to dine at the Same place as they hold way with us. Capt. Clark and Several of his party came in the canoes as it would be easier for the horses untill we git to the 3 forks of the Missourie where they are to part from us. the rest of Capt. Clarks party took on the horses &C we proceeded on verry well & fast. in the evening we Camped[1] near the 3000 mile Island, having made 97 miles this day by water. Saw considerable of Small game and a great pleanty of beaver Sign.—

1. On the east bank of the Jefferson River, Beaverhead County, Montana; the island is about ten miles northeast of Dillon, Beaverhead County.

Friday 11th July 1806. a fair morning. we took breakfast eairly and Set off proceeded on the wind hard a head which is unfavourable to us. in the evening we arived at the mouth of Wisdom River. Camped[1] where we left the Small canoe last year. wisdom river is verry high at this time

2 hunters went out. Collins killed 2 deer and Gibson killed a fat buck this evening the beaver Sign and lodges without number all this day. they are pleantier in this valley than I have Seen on the route &C

1. On the east side of Jefferson River, opposite the mouth of the Big Hole (Wisdom) River, Beaverhead County, Montana, some two miles northeast of Twin Bridges.

Saturday 12th July 1806. a clear morning. the canoe we left here last year we Split up this morning for paddles &C. Set out as usal and proceed. on down the river fast the canoe Capt. Clark was in got drove to Shore by the wind under Some tops of trees and was near being filled with water. Capt. Clark fired 2 guns as a Signal for help I and the other canoes which was a head halted and went to their assistance. they Soon got him Safe off. about 2 P. M. we halted to dine at the mouth of R. Fields Creek[1] the hunters killed one deer and one beaver. we dined and proceeded on down the little gape of the mount. and Camped[2] about Sunset Collins killed two beaver this evening.—

1. Boulder River meets the Jefferson River in Jefferson County, Montana.
2. About two miles below the mouth of Antelope Creek in either Jefferson or Madison County, Montana, near where U.S. Highway 287 crosses the Jefferson. Ordway's "little gape of the mount." is the area the captains called the third gap in the mountains on the outbound journey, near their encampment of July 31, 1805, and near where they now camp.

Sunday 13th July 1806. a clear morning. the canoe & 2 men went on a head. we Set out as usal and proceeded on down passd. large timbred bottoms about 12 oClock we arived at our last years Camp on 27 & 28 July little above the 3 forks[1] Joined the rest of the party with the horses and had got here only one hour before us. they had killed a deer and one antelope and had wounded a white bear. we all proceeded to the 3 forks of Missouri crossed the men & baggage and Swam the horses to all to the South Side of gallintines River where we dined below the forks the canoe that was a hunting came up they had killed two deer. we delayed about 2 hours Capt. Clark & party leaves us hear to cross over to the River Roshjone. So we parted I and 9[2] more proceeded on down the river with the canoes verry well. the wind a head So we halted[3] little before night. Collins killed 2 large fat bucks and P. Cruzatte killed a deer & Colter killed a large beaver & good fur though the Season is over for them to have good fur in the Southern parts. the Musquetoes more troublesome than ever we have seen them before. the hunters Saw large gangs of Elk in this valley.—

1. That is, south of the Three Forks of the Missouri River, Broadwater and Gallatin counties, Montana.

2. With Ordway were Collins, Colter, Cruzatte, Howard, Lepage, Potts, Weiser, Whitehouse, and Willard.

3. Ordway does not provide enough information to locate his encampment for the night. The men are on the Missouri River, probably in Broadwater County, Montana. Ordway is the only source for the events of this detachment; Whitehouse's journal for this period is lost.

Monday 14th July 1806. a fair morning. we took an eairly breakfast and proceeded on down the river. the wind rose hard a head Colter killed 2 young beaver about noon we halted the wind rose So high that we were unable to proceed. So two hunters went out a hunting. in the evening as the wind fell we mooved down the R. to a bottom and Camped. willard killed one deer. Saw Indn. Sign Collins did not join us this evening. Saw buffaloe Sign &C.

Tuesday 15th July 1806. a fair morning. we Set out at light and proceed on verry well overtook Collins who had killed three deer about 9 A. M. we halted for breakfast & Collins killed a fat buck & P. Cruzatte killed a goat or antelope. we proced. on verry well the currents are common & ripe. Colter killed a panther a deer and a rattle Snake. in the evening we Camped in the mountains. Collins killed 4 Elk. the Musquetoes verry troublesom in deed.—

Wednesday 16th July 1806. a fair morning. we took an eairly breakfast and proceeded on verry well. the wind rose a head and blew so high about noon that obledged us to lay too near the gates of the rockey Mountains[1] Collins killed a large beaver we gathered a little pitch for our canoes &C about 3 P. M. the wind abated a little and we proced. on thro the gates of the mn Saw large gangs of Mountain Sheep and Elk Collins killed a faun Elk and two Mountain Sheep. we proceeded on below ordways river[2] and Camped on a Sand beach. Same Side.—

1. The Gates of the Mountains is a stretch of about five and three-quarter miles, roughly midway between Holter and Hauser dams in Lewis and Clark County, Montana. The party passed here on the outbound journey on July 19, 1805.

2. Little Prickly Pear Creek, Lewis and Clark County; it is one of the few physical features Ordway mentions on his detached trip.

Thursday 17th July 1806. a clear morning. we took an eairly breakfast and proceeded on Collins and Colter Skinned the 2 mountn. Sheep Saved the Skin and bones for our officers to take to the States. the wind rose So high that Some of the canoes were near being filled. about noon we arived at the head of the pine Islands & rapids & halted at the Creek[1] above as the wind too high to pass these rapids with Safety. Cruzatte killed 2 [3?] big horn animels and Colter killed a deer. towards evening the wind abated a little So we passed down the rapids with Safety. at the foot of the rockey mountains large gangs of the Ibex or big horn anim. Seen along the edges of Sd. Mountns. Camped about 5 miles below Sd. rapids at a bottom in groves of cotten timber.—

1. The rapids are Half-breed Rapids, where the party delayed in the vicinity of Hardy Creek, but probably not the creek mentioned here, in Cascade County, Montana.

Friday 18th July 1806. a clear cool windy morning. we set off as usal and proceeded on down the gentle current Saw large gangues of buffaloe out in the plains about noon Collins killed three deer. Saw great numbers of beaver and otter &C. towards evening we passed the mouth of Smiths River[1] a Short distance below Some of the hunters went out after some gangues of buffaloe and we Camped it being late the hunters did not kill any this evening but Saw great numbers in the plains. the Musquetoes and Small flyes are verry troublesome. my face and eyes are Swelled by the poison of those insects which bite verry Severe indeed.

1. Still carrying the expedition name, it meets the Missouri in Cascade County, Montana.

Saturday 19th July 1806. a clear & pleasant morning. two hunters went on Shore to go across a bend after the buffaloe & we proceeded on with the canoes round sd bend. about 11 A. M. the hunters killed 4 buffaloe and a buck deer. we halted and took the best of the meat or fat and proced. on about 3 P. M. we arived at the white bear Camp at the head of the portage.[1] Sergt. Gass and five more of the party were Camped here.[2] they informed us that they had a fine road over. they followed up the Tus-e-paw or buffaloe river[3] a Smooth road, then crossed a low dividing ridge[4] came on Smooth plains. the blanket mountains[5] to the left. they had a large road. a band of Indians had went before them. Saw one of their Sculp poles &C. they Struck the Meddison river[6] above its forks and followed on down it about 3 days travel to this place. considerable of cotten timber on its bottoms. the plain Smooth Soil indifferent except Some of the river bottoms are rich & good land. they arived here on the 11th Inst. they had killed a number of fat buffaloe and fat buck deers. Capt. Lewis and party lost 7 fine horses at this place. they expect they were Stole by the war parties they hunted for them untill the 16th Inst. then gave them out for lost, and then he Set out for to go up morriahs river Drewyer Jo. & R. Fields only with him as he left 4 horses to hall the canoes past the portage. he had not horses enofe to take any more men with him. they had opened the cash or hole at this place & found Several Small articles Spoiled and opened the one below the portage and found everry thing Safe except Some of the mens robes. they have geers fixed for the horses. Mcneal was attacked by a white bear. his horse threw him So near the bear that he had not time to Shoote but drew his gun and Struck the bear across the head and broke off the brich of his gun and Stonded the bear So that he had time to climb a Sapling. the bear kept him on the tree about 3 hours. then the bear left him he caught his horse and returnd. to Camp. we took our baggage out of the canoes and halled them out to dry &C. the Musquetoes verry troublesome indeed much worse than they were last year.—

1. The White Bear Islands, or upper portage camp, was occupied by the outbound party from June 19 to July 12, 1805. The islands have virtually disappeared today. The area is about three-quarters of a mile north of Sand Coulee Creek, Cascade County, Montana.

2. Gass had Frazer, Goodrich, McNeal, Thompson, and Werner with him. Lewis took Drouillard and the Field brothers to explore the Marias River.

3. By "buffaloe river" Ordway probably means a combination of the Clark Fork and Blackfoot rivers that Lewis's party followed out of Travelers' Rest Camp, near Missoula, Montana. The name "Tus-e-paw" was applied to the Flathead, or Salish, Indians who lived in the vicinity of Travelers' Rest.

4. Lewis and Clark Pass, Lewis and Clark County, Montana.

5. Probably the Lewis Range of the Rocky Mountains. Ordway may mean blanketed with snow; Lewis and Clark called them the "Snowy Mountains."

6. Sun River, Lewis and Clark County.

Sunday 20th July 1806. a clear warm morning. we conclude to lay here to day as the truck waggons are not fixed. Sergt. Gass went at putting in the tongues to the waggons. Some of the men are engaged dressing Skins, but we are tormented by the Musquetoes and Small flys. the men engaged dressing deer Skins &c. towards evening we got up our 4 horses tackled them in the truck waggons found they would draw but were covred thick with Musquetoes and Small flyes &C.

Monday 21st July 1806. a fair warm morning. the Musquetoes troubled us all last night. one man went out at day light for the horses, but could not find them. then Several more men went out and hunted for them all day & could not find any of them we got two canoes Started & considerable baggage ourselves & Camped concluded to delay tomorrow for our horses before we give them out. the Musquetoes and Small flyes verry troublesome we made fires of buffaloe dry dung to make Smoaks &c.

Tuesday 22nd July 1806. a fair morning we rose eairly and turned out in different directions in Search of our 4 horses about noon they were found at the grand falls of Missourie[1] and we tackled up the horses and set out with 2 canoes part of the men not returnd from hunting the horses. we proced. about 5 miles then our extletree broke down and we had to turn back with our truck wheels leaving a man to take care of the baggage &C. we made another extletree and Started with 2 more canoes & Camped Some of the men came in from hunting the horses had killed three buffaloe and one goat or antelope.

1. Great Falls of the Missouri River, Cascade County, Montana.

Wednesday 23rd July 1806. a hard Shower of rain hail and wind last evening. we geered up the 4 horses and Set out with 2 Canoes one large &

one Small one   the truck wheels which bore the large canoe broke down often and troubled us much. Wiser cut his leg with a knife So that he is unable to walk & is a bad wound   Collins went on to willow Creek[1] to kill Some fresh meat for us.   with much difficulty we got the 2 canoes & considerable of baggage to willow Creek about Sunset and Camped. Collins had killed three buffaloe. Some of the other hunters killed another fat one this evening.

1. Box Elder Creek, Cascade County, Montana.

Thursday 24th July 1806.   a clear morng.   we returnd. with the waggons to the head of the portage and took on the other Small canoes   we load the other large canoe as our wheels not bear it.   took in the Small one the baggage and proceeded on 8 miles   halted to baite our horses.   had a hard Shower of rain which rendred the plains verry muddy.   we procd. to willow Creek & Campd.   one waggon went with one canoe to the foot of the portage &c.—

Friday 25th July 1806.   we procd. on to portage Creek.[1]   met the other men returning.   we formed a Camp at portage Creek   left 2 men one to Cook & one to hunt and returnd. to willow Creek   hard rain comd. about noon and continued the remainder part of the day, but did not Stop us from our urgent labours.   halted as much as we were able to help the horses as the place So amazeing muddy & bad.   in the evening we got to portage Creek and Camped.   rained verry hard and we having no Shelter Some of the men and myself turned over a canoe & lay under it   others Set up by the fires.   the water run under us and the ground was covred with water. the portage River raises fast   Collins killed a buffaloe and a brarow.—

1. Belt Creek, the boundary between Cascade and Chouteau counties, Montana.

Saturday 26th July 1806.   a wet disagreeable morning.   an Indn. dog came about our Camp   we gave him Some meat.   the portage River too high to waid but is falling fast. Colter & Potts went at running the canoes down the rapids to the white perogue near the carsh.[1]   the rest of us returned to willow Creek took on the other large canoe and halted to asist the horses as the truck wheels Sank in the mud nearly to the hub. Cruzatte killed a buffaloe we took the best of the meat and returned with much hard fatigue to portage River and got the canoes and all the baggage down to the white perogue and Camped having got the carsh opened and all brought to the White perogue & all Safe &C.

1. The white pirogue was hidden in the area of the lower portage camp below Belt Creek on June 18, 1805.

Sunday 27th July 1806. a clear morning. Sergt. Gass and Willard Set out with the 4 horses crossed the river to the N. Side to take them down to the Mouth of Morriah to back [pack] the meat while we lay their, as we expect to arive their before Capt. Lewis & party. we halled out the white perogue out of the bushes and repaired hir. about 12 we loaded and Set out with the white perogue and the 5 canoes. procd. on down the rapid water fast. Camped on S. Side at large gange of Buffaloe the hunters killed in a fiew minutes 5 buffaloe Some of which was fat, and one deer. And R. Frazer killed one buffaloe with his Musquet &C.

Monday 28th July 1806. two hunters went on eairly a head. Howard killed two deer. we proceeded on as usal about 9 A. M. we discovred on a high bank a head Capt. Lewis & the three men who went with him on horse back comming towards us on N. Side we came too Shore and fired the Swivell to Salute him & party we Saluted them also with Small arms and were rejoiced to See them &c. Capt. Lewis took us all by the hand, and informed us that they had good Sucksess in going to their journeys end and Crossd. a number of branches & forks of Marriahs River and followd. up a North fork[1] to Latidude [*blank*] got his observations for the Lat. but the cloudy weather prevented him from gitting the Longitude &c. but found it was not much difference from the Mouth of Morriah they then Set off on their return the day before yesterday and met with eight of the Grousevauntaus[2] Indians with bows & arrows and 2 guns. they at first appeared afraid but after a little wrode up and Shook hands with Capt. Lewis & party and appeared friendly they desired Capt. Lewis to go with them to their Nation which they said was under the blanket mountn. Some distance about 2 days march. but Capt. Lewis told them that he Could not wait but desired them to come down to the Mouth of Morriah promiseing them the horse if they would comply but they were afraid of being killed by us. they had upwards of 20 horses but they were ordinary ones or the most of them. they Camped with Capt. Lewis & men as they expected they were friends, though Capt. Lewis had a watch up all night, and at day break yesterday morning the eight Savages Seased all our mens guns and Capt. Lewises also. they Instantly Sprung up out of their Sleep and Ruben Fields chased an Indian who Capt. Lewis had made a chief gave him a meddle last evening & he was running of with R. Fields and his brothers Jo Fields guns. Reuben overhalled him caught hold of the 2 guns had his knife drawn & as he Snatched away the guns perced his knife in to the Indians heart he drew but one breath the wind of his breath followed the knife & he fell dead they all Seased their arms from the Indians and took one of the Indn. guns and all their bows and arrows and their Shields which they were on their backs at war. they then went at running after our horses Capt. Lewis wounded one more badly but the Indn. partly raised and fired back at him but missed him. they cleared out with Some of our horses and Some of theirs, though Capt. Lewis took as many as he wanted of theirs and left the rest & made all haste towards us and had wrode 100 and 20 miles Since yesterday morning, and much fatigued and turned out the horses in the plain & threw the Saddles in the River & came on board the canoes.[3] then we proced. on with as much Speed as possable. Soon overtook the 2 hunters who had killed Several Elk a buffaloe & one beaver. we now keep to gether and are concerned about Sergt Gass & willard who went down by land. about 1 P. M. we arived at the forks of Marriah opened the carshes[4] found all except 4 Steel traps which were put in a carsh by themselves & we could not find the place. Some beaver skin and Robes &c. Spoiled. the other articles all Safe and dry &C. Sergt. Gass and willard joined us with the horses. we left the horses here crossed to the N. Side found the red perogue Safe but too Rotten to take down. So we took Some of the nailes out of hir and Set out. Sergt Gass & willard had killed Several buffaloe and 7 antelopes as they came down from the falls by land. we Soon had a hard Shower of rain & large hail. Some larger than a musket Ball Thunder and high winds a head but we procd. on untill evening and Camped[5] on South Side and kept a Strict guard. Collins killed a buffaloe. we got the best of the meat of it. late in the evening we had a Shower of rain which lasted about a hour.—

1. Cut Bank Creek on the Pondera-Glacier county line, Montana. Lewis's account of these days is found at his entries from July 17 to this day.

2. Ordway uses the term *Gros Ventres* loosely here. The term was usually applied to the Hidatsa or Atsina Indians but in this case represents Piegan Blackfeet.

3. Lewis recounts the incident in his entry of July 27.

4. One cache was between the Marias and Missouri rivers in Chouteau County, about a mile upriver from the camp of June 3–12, 1805. See Clark's entry of June 10, 1805. Another was at the camp of June 3–12, 1805, at the mouth of the Marias River.

5. On the south bank of the Missouri in Chouteau County, a little below the mouth of Crow Coulee.

Tuesday 29th July 1806. cloudy and rain we Set out as usal and proceeded on fast Saw large gangs of buffals. and Elk. R. Frazer killed an Elk. we took the hide and Some of the meat about 11 A. M. we entered the high clay broken country white clay hills and the white walls resembling ancient towns & buildings &C.[1] Saw a flock of big horn or Ibex on the top of those walls. we halted and the 2 Fields killed two large Rams which had large horns. Capt. Lewis had them Scallintinized [skeletonized] and all the bones & horns as well as the Skin to take to the Seat of government. we dined and procd. on passing the white pleasant walls and Stone wall Creek[2] and on our way this after noon we killed Seven more Ibex along these clay & Stone hills and knobs, where these animels live generally. Capt. Lewis had two of the femail Scallintineized also. we had a Shower of rain. Saw buffaloe &c &c.

1. The Stone Walls and White Cliffs of the Missouri River, Chouteau County, Montana.

2. Eagle Creek, Chouteau County. The party camped for the night some miles below this stream, about a mile above the mouth of Arrow Creek on the north side of the Missouri.

Wednesday 30th July 1806. cloudy and wet. we Set out eairly and proceeded on verry well our hunters killed 2 buffaloe I and willard killed a white bear. Some of the hunters killed 4 Ibex and 2 beavers. rained all day. Camped on an Island.—[1]

1. Lewis, contrary to Ordway and Gass, apparently places the camp above a nameless island in Blaine County, Montana, a few miles below Cow Creek.

Thursday 31st July 1806. cloudy and rain. we Set out as usal and procd. on verry well at 9 Saw large gangs of Elk Swimming the River we killed 15 of them mearly for the hides to cover our Canoes. Jo. Fields killed one Ibex the hunters killed 14 deer and one beaver this day. had Several Showers of rain. the River verry muddy owing to the heavy rains washing those Clayey hills came a long days roeing and Camped[1] at some old Indn. lodges on N. Side.—

1. Eight miles below the mouth of Rock Creek, Phillips County, Montana, according to Lewis.

Friday August 1st 1806. hard rain we Set out early and procd. on about 9 A M a Brown bear and Drewyer and Capt. Lewis killed it we took it on board and procd. on Colter killed a beaver Shortly after about noon we killed a buck Elk Saved the hide and the best of the meat. about 2 P. M. we halted at Some old Indn. Lodges on S. Side. here we delayd.[1] this afternoon to dry our deer Skins Mountn. Sheep Skins &. C. which were near Spoiling as the weather has been Some time wet. about 3 P. M. a large white bear approached our Camp as Soon as he discovred us Stood up on his hind feed and looked at us. Some of the hunters Shot him down, for the Skin & oil. the other hunters killd. four deer and a beaver, this afternoon.—

1. The party's camp was in Petroleum or Phillips County, some two or three miles below the camp of May 19, 1805, just above what was later called Horseshoe Point. The area is now inundated by Fort Peck Reservoir. Lewis says they were about fifteen miles below the mouth of the Musselshell River. They remained here until August 3.

Saturday 2nd August 1806. a fair morning. the two Fields Sent on a head to hunt. we delayed to dry our baggage. the day warm. Some of the men dressed deer Skins, &C.

Sunday 3rd August 1806. a fair morning. we loaded the canoes and procd. on Soon came to the Camp of the two Fields they had killed 24 deer. we procd. on verry well Saw buffaloe in a bundance[1] and Some white bear. we Camped[2] on N. S. having made 73 miles this day.

1. Contrary to Lewis and Gass, who report seeing few buffalo this day.

2. In Valley County, Montana, below the mouth of Cattle Creek and, as Lewis notes, about two miles above the camp of May 12, 1805. Again, the site is inundated by Fort Peck Reservoir.

Monday 4th August 1806. two of the hunters Colter and Collins did not join us last night. I and willard went on eairly with a Small canoe to hunt we procd. on Some distance and hunted in Some of the bottoms and killed a deer and procd. on towards evening we killed a large white or grizzly bear nearly of a Silver Grey. we then procd. on in the evening by moon light as the party was a head about 11 oClock at night we found ourselves in a thick place of Sawyers[1] as the corrent drawed us in and we had no chance to git out of them So we run about half way through and the Stern run under a limb of a tree and caught willard who was in the Stern and drew him out as the current was verry rapid. he held by the limb I being in the bow of the canoe took my oar and halled the bow first one way and the other So as to clear the Sawyers and run through Safe and paddled the canoe to Shore and ran up the Shore opposite willard & he called to me if everry thing was Safe I told him yes but he could not hear me as the water roared past the Sawyers. he told me he had made a little raft of 2 Small Sticks he caught floating and tyed them together, and tyed his cloathes on them and would Swim down through this difficult place and I run down and took out the canoe and took him in as he Swam through Safe we procd. a Short distance farther and came to the Camp[2] of the party. they had killed a rattle Snake[3] and an Elk to day but the two hunters Colter & Colling has not joined us yet.—

1. A submerged tree with one end stuck in the mud, the other bobbing up and down in the current with a sawing motion, a great menace to boats.

2. In Valley or McCone County, Montana, about two miles above the camp of May 7, 1805.

3. Perhaps the prairie rattlesnake.

Tuesday 5th August 1806. a fair morning. we delayed here for Colter and Collins the 2 Fields Sent on a head to hunt. we waited untill

12 oClock and as we are not certain but what Colter and Collins is a head So we Set out and procd. on Saw large gangs of buffaloe we killed a fat cow and took the best of the meat and procd. on untill evening and Camped[1] on a high Sand beach a little after dark came up a hard Thunder Shower of wind and rain and nearly filled our canoes, So that we had to unload them. the Sand flew So that we could Scarsely See & cut our faces by the force of the wind.—

1. In McCone County, Montana, about four miles southwest of the town of Wolf Point. Lewis says they were ten miles below Prairie Elk Creek.

Wednesday 6th August 1806. a fair morning. we loaded up our canoes and Set out as usal and procd. on about 10 A. M. passd. the mo. of 2000 mile Creek.[1] the wind rose high So halted. the hunters went out and killed Several deer. we delayed about 3 hours then proceeded on in the evening we Camped[2] at a large bottom S. Side a fat Elk killd. and 2 fat buffaloe we took Some of the fattest of the meat. the buffaloe Elk and all kinds of game are pleanty and verry tame &C &C.—

1. Redwater River, McCone County, Montana.
2. In Richland County, about ten miles east of the town of Poplar.

Thursday 7th August 1806. a Showery wet morning. we Set out as usal and procd. on verry well. overtook the 2 Fieldses who had killed two large Silver grey bears. we roed on fast about 4 P. M. we arived at the mouth of the River Roshjone where we expected to have found Capt. Clark and party but found they had been here Some time and left a line that we would find them lower down[1] Capt. Lewis wrote a line and left for Colter and Collins who we have reason to think is behind, directing them to follow on after us, and we procd. on Saw Some Camps which appeared fresh 1 of which had fire at it and dry meat hanging up. we procd. on untill dark and as we were Camping[2] killed a buffaloe out of a gang on the bank. the wind high this evening.

1. Clark left his note at the mouth of the Yellowstone (Roshjone) on August 4, 1806.
2. In Williams County, North Dakota, a few miles south of Trenton.

Friday 8th August 1806. a fair morng. we Set out as usal and procd. on verry well untill 10 A. M. then not overtaking Capt. Clark & party Capt. Lewis concluded to halt and dry our baggage dress Some Skins as the party is nearly naked and repair the canoes. So we Camped[1] at a bottom on N. Side drew out the white perogue after unloading and my canoe as they leaked the musquetoes troublesome at this Camp. Drewyer killed two deer.—

1. In Williams County, North Dakota, several miles southwest of Williston.

Saturday 9th August 1806. a cool windy morning we continued on dressing our deer Skins the 2 fieldses went across the river a hunting returnd. towards evening had killed 1 Elk and one deer. all hands employed makeing themselves comfortable.

Sunday 10th August, 1806. a cool windy morning we went at reppairing the white perogue and continued dressing our deer Skins and Smoaking them. about three P. M. we put the canoes in the river, and loaded up and about 4 we Set out and procd. on down untill dark and Camped[1] on St. Side and the musquetoes verry troublesome indeed. we could not all this night git a moment quiet rest for them.—

1. In McKenzie County, North Dakota, nearly opposite Williston.

Monday 11th August 1806. a fair morning we Set out as usal and procd. on verry well we killed a buffaloe in the river. about 12 oClock Capt. Lewis halted at a bottom on S. Side to kill Some Elk Peter Cruzatte a frenchman went out with Capt. Lewis they Soon found a gangue of Elk in a thicket. Capt. Lewis killed one and cruzatte killed two, and as he Still kept firing one of his balls hit Capt. Lewis in his back side and the ball passed through one Side of his buttock and the ball went out of the other Side of the other buttock and lodged at his overalls which wounded him bad.[1] he instantly called to peter but Peter not answering he Supposd. it to be Indians and run to the canoes and ordered the men to their armes. they were in readiness in a moment and Capt. Lewis attempd. to go back for battle but being faint the men purswaded him not to go himself but the party run out found Cruzatte and he had Seen no Indians then peter knew that it must have been him tho an exidant. we dressed the wound prepared a place for him to lay in the white perogue Jo. Fields killed one Elk. we then took the best of the meat on board and proced. on about 4 P. M. we passd. a Camp of Capt. Clark[2] where we found a note or line informing us that Sergt. pryor & party had joined them here as the Indians had Stole all the horses & they came down in leather canoes. they had left here to day. we procd. on untill about Sunset and Camped[3] on a Sand beach on Ld Side high winds.—

1. Lewis recounts the incident in more detail in his entry for this day.

2. Clark had been at this camp since August 9 and had left it just this morning. It was approximately ten miles above Tobacco Creek, Williams County, North Dakota, putting the camp in McKenzie County; see Clark's entry for August 9.

3. Southwestern Mountrail County, North Dakota, a little above the mouth of White Earth River; the site is now inundated by Garrison Reservoir.

Tuesday 12th August 1806. a fair morning. we Set out eairly and procd. on about 8 A. M. we met two trappers Americans by the names of Jos Dixon & forrest Handcock[1] they were from the Ellynoise country, and have gathered a great deal of peltry Since they have been out about 2 years and have carshed the most of it in the ground they tells us that they are determined to Stay up this river and go to the head where the beaver is pleanty and trap and hunt untill they make a fortune before they return. they had 20 odd good traps and tools for building canoes &C. they informed us that Capt. Clark passed here about 12 oClock yesterday and Said that they would go on Slowly untill we come up. Capt. Lewis gave them Some powder and Several articles while we were here Colter and Collins Come up and joined us. they informed us that they had waited expected we were behind they had killed 6 buffaloe 13 deer 5 Elk & 31 beaver. Mr. Dixon concludes to go back to the Mandans in hopes to git a frenchman or Some body to go with him to the head of the river. So we procd. on about 10 A. M. we overtook[2] Capt. Clark and party all alive and well they informed us that they after they left us at the three forks followed on up the South fork or Gallentines River nearly to its head which was about 30 miles, and that the beavers abound on that river that their dams overflowed the bottoms So that they had difficulty to cross the river they then Struck for the River Roshjone leaving the Mountn. a Short distance to the right crossd over a low ridge 10 miles then come on the head waters of the roshjone followed down Some distance before they found any timber that they could make canoes of. they Saw no Indians but Saw Indn. tracks and the Indn. Stole 25 of the horses they having the two Small canoes done lashed them and Sergt. pryor Set out with 3 men and the rest of the horses by land in order to take them to the Mandans 25 in number which now remained, but the 2nd night the Indn. Stole all the horses and they had to return to the Roshjone and killd. buffaloe and made leather canoes of them and followed on down they informed us that the distance from where they Struck the River Roshjone to its mouth is 836 miles and a pleasant river bottoms and timber on this river the buffaloe So pleanty and Swimming the river So that they could Scarsely pass down this river mountn. Sheep also in many places. we fired the blunderbusses and Small arms being rejoiced to meet all together again. 2 of Capt. Clarks party were a hunting and killed a Spotted Elk had white spots about it and different from any we have ever Seen before. we left their buffaloe canoes and after a delay of three hours we procd. on. Mr. Dixon and Handcock accompy. us to the Mandans. we Camped[3] on a Sand beach on acct. of the Musquetoes a little rain this evening &C—

1. Joseph Dickson, or Dixon, and Forrest Hancock; see Lewis's entry for this day.

2. The two parties reunited at the place Clark had stopped for lunch, in Mountrail County, North Dakota, some six miles south of Sanish and a little below Little Knife River.

3. Near the McKenzie-Mountrail county line, North Dakota.

Wednesday 13th August 1806. a fair morning. we Set out eairly and procd. on ⟨about 9 A. M. we arived at our old neighbours the Grousevauntaus and Mandans we Saluted them by fireing our Swivvel our blunderbuss Several times.—⟩[1] verry well a fair breeze from the N. W. came a long distance this day and Camped[2] on the N. Side.—

1. This crossed-out material was rewritten into the next day's entry.

2. Northeast of Riverdale, McLean County, North Dakota, near the mouth of Snake Creek.

Thursday 14th August 1806. a fair morning we Set out eairly and procd. on about 9 A. M. we arived at our old neighbours the Grousevauntaus[1] and Mandans. we Saluted them by firing our Swivvel and blunderbusses a number of times they answered us with a blunderbuss and Small arms and were verry glad to See us we halted a Short time at the Grousevauntaus village then mooved down convenient to boath the Grousevauntaus and Mandans and Campd.[2] in order to Stay 2 or 3 days to try to git Some of these chiefs to do down with us to Show them the power of the united States &C. they gave us corn & beans &C. &C. Capt. Lewis fainted as Capt. Clark was dressing his wound, but Soon came too again.—[3]

1. Here meaning the Hidatsa Indians.

2. Apparently on the west side of the Missouri River in Mercer County, North Dakota, and considerably below the first (or lower) Mandan village, Matootonha, or Mitutanka.

3. Only Ordway records Lewis fainting.

Friday 15th August 1806. a clear pleasant morning. Some of the party went at dressing themselves deer Skins &C. the natives brought us corn and beans &C. they brought us a breakfast of boild siniblins[1] & beans &C. the 2 village of Mandans[2] gave us Considerable of corn and more than we would take away. Capt. Clark went over and tryed to perswade Some of the chief of that village to go down with us but they could not find any one willing to go with us. the chiefs of the 1st village[3] wished us to Stay 1 or 2 days longer with them we gave the Swivvel to the Big Belleys or Grousevauntaus.—

1. Simlins, which are summer squashes.

2. This would be Rooptahee, or Ruptáre, village; see Clark's entry of October 27, 1804.

3. Big White, or Sheheke, and Little Crow were the principal chiefs of Mitutanka, but Clark seems to have visited only with Little Crow on this day.

Saturday 16th August 1806. a clear cool morning. great numbers of the natives visited us and traded us good robes and mockasons. towards evening the Big White a head chief of the 1st village of Mandans concluded to go down with us and Mr. Jessom[1] and their wives and three children Mr.

Jessom two and the Big White one and verry handsome children one of Mr. jessoms has had a little Scooling at the N. W. Company.—

1. René Jusseaume; see Clark's entry of October 27, 1804.

Sunday 17th August 1806. John Colter one of the party asks leave of our officers to go back with Mr. Dixon a trapping, which permission was granted him So our officers Settled with him and fitted him out with Powder lead and a great number of articles which compleated him for a trapping voiage of two years which they are determined to Stay untill they make a fortune, &C. &C. we lashed together Some of our canoes and Colter Mr. Dixon & Handcock parted with us in their Small canoe the natives visits us in great numbers. about 4 oC. P. M. dropped down to the 1st village of Mandans where we took on board Mr. Jessom his wife and two children the big white the head chief of Sd. village his wife or one of his wives. I understand he has two wives. he has only one child and takes that with him took their baggage on board and the chief putting his arm round all the head mens necks of his nation who Set on Shore and a number crying and appeared Sorry to part with him he took his leave of them however and we Set out and procd. on the wind a head Campd.[1] on S. S.

1. Near Hensler, Oliver County, North Dakota.

Monday 18th August 1806. the wind high and a little rain. about 8 A. M. we Set out and procd. on about 1 P. M. our hunters killed two deer. the wind continued high towards evening Saw Some buffaloe we Camped[1] below otter Creek N. S. the hunters killed 5 deer.

1. South of Bismarck, Burleigh County, North Dakota. Ordway is mistaken in using the term Otter Creek for this stream, it is Heart River.

Tuesday 19th August 1806. a Showery morning. Thunder and high wind So it detained us. the hunters went out & killed 5 Elk 10 deer. about 4 P. M. the wind fell a little and we procd. on took on board the best of the meat which was below and Campd.[1] at dark. windy & cold.—

1. In Burleigh County, North Dakota, about ten miles below the previous night's camp and near the party's camp of October 19, 1804.

Wednesday 20th August 1806. we Set out eairly and proceeded on verry well the after part of the day pleasant. in the evening we Camped[1] on a Sand beach the Musquetoes verry troublesome.

1. In Campbell County, South Dakota, probably below the mouth of Spring Creek.

Thursday 21st August 1806. a fair morning. we Set out eairly and proceed. on Soon met three frenchmen[1] one by the name of Revey they have been trapping as high as the river Roshjone but have made out but poorly and have been living at the Rickarees and are now going to the Mandans for their traps and then they Say they will return to St. Louis. So we proced. on about 11 A. M. we arived at the upper village of Rickarees[2] where we halted after fireing our blunderbusses. they gathered on the bank verry numerous a party of the Chiens[3] are here trading with these natives for corn give buffaloe meat dryed meat in return three frenchman are living here & one Spanyard.[4] they informed us that 15 hundred of the Souix nation had gone up to war with the Mandans. our officers gave a principal man of the chien nation a meddle. he gave in return Some fat dryed buffaloe meat. our officers tryed to git Some of these natives to go down with us but they did not incline to go as they Said they had Sent one with Mr. Gravveleen[5] and he had not returnd. this nation of chien or dog Indians live at the heads of chien river towards the black hills. they Say they are afraid of the white people and of any thing they have for they think it to be great medicin. Still Say that they have a great deal of fur in their country and have no trade for it &C. in the evening we mooved down to the lower village of Rickarees and Camped[6] Ross [Roii?] joined us in order to go down with us. we traded for Robes & Mockasons Some of which was handsome &C.

1. Probably Rivet, Grenier, and some unknown person. Rivet had been a member of the party in 1804, and Grenier had probably first encountered the party on October 18, 1804.

2. The Arikara villages were in Corson and Campbell counties, South Dakota, above the mouth of Grand River, now inundated by Oahe Reservoir.

3. Meaning Cheyennes, but the term does not derive from the French *chien,* "dog."

4. One of them may have been the "Ross" (or "Roii?") mentioned later in this entry. He may be an expedition member of 1804, Peter (or Pierre) Roi. See Clark's entry of August 22, 1806.

5. Gravelines. For a discussion of the death of the Arikara chief see Clark's entries of October 8 and 9, 1804, and for this day.

6. At Ashley Island, above the mouth of Grand River, Campbell and Corson counties.

Friday 22nd August 1806. hard Thunder Showers all last night. I Slept in the village. the Chiefs Say that they are all afraid to go down with us. About 10 A. M. cleared off fair and we Set out and procd. on a fiew miles and halted to dry our baggage and bedding &C. we delayed about 3 hours and procd. on to the foot of prarie Islands and Camped[1] on N. Side.

1. In Walworth County, South Dakota, some six miles southeast of Mobridge. They had passed Grand River, in Corson County, during the day. Clark calls the island Grouse Island; it is later Blue Blanket Island, which the party passed on October 7, 1804.

Saturday 23rd August 1806. we Set out eairly a little rain & Thunder. Saw a large gang of Elk on S. Side. about 11 A. M. the wind rose So high that it detained us about 3 hours our hunters killed three Elk and a deer took the best of the meat and procd. on had light Showers of rain all day and Campd.[1] on S. Side.

1. In Potter County, South Dakota, probably below the crossing of U.S. Highway 212. They had passed Moreau River, in Dewey County, during the day.

Sunday 24th August 1806. a clear pleasant morning. we Set out eairly and procd. on verry well about noon the wind rose high from S. W. which detained us about three hours then procd. on though the work against us. Camped[1] on N. Side.

1. Near the upper end of Lookout Bend, Dewey County, South Dakota, on a site now inundated by Oahe Reservoir.

Monday 25th August 1806. a clear pleasant morning. 5 of our hunters Sent on a head to hunt to an Isld. we procd. on about 9 A. M. we halted at the Mouth of Chyenne river[1] N. Side and our officers conclude to delay untill 12 and take an observation the hunters went out and killed two deer. Set off again at 12 and procd on Soon overtook the other hunters who had killed a fat buck & 2 does. we procd on untill evening and Camped[2] on N. S.

1. The party first passed the mouth of the Cheyenne River on October 1, 1804; it reaches the Missouri on the boundary between Dewey and Stanley counties, South Dakota.

2. In Hughes County, South Dakota, below the entrance of Chantier Creek, in Stanley County.

Tuesday 26th August 1806. a fair morning. we set out as usal and procd on verry well passd the Mouth of Teton River[1] about 9 A. M. procd on verry well without halting to cook this day and Camped[2] at a bluff Some distance below Louisells fort and cedders Island which we passd. little before night.

1. They had reached the Bad River on the outbound journey on September 24, 1804.

2. In Lyman County, South Dakota, some four miles above the mouth of Medicine River. Régis Loisel's Fort aux Cedres was on later Dorion Island No. 2, now submerged by Big Bend Reservoir; see Clark's entry of September 22, 1804.

Wednesday 27th August 1806. a fair morning. we Set out eairly and procd. on a Short distance Saw a number of buffaloe halted about one hour to hunt but killed nothing then procd. on passed the mouth of Teton river[1] and passing round the grand turn or grand bend[2] we killed an Elk and took on board all the meat in the evening we Camped[3] on a large Island which was covd with thin timber and tall grass where we killed 4 out of a large gang [of buffalo] and Saved the best of the meat. the Musqutoes verry troublesome indeed

1. Ordway probably means "Tylor's" River, modern Medicine River, in Lyman County, South Dakota.

2. The Big Bend, or Grand Detour, of the Missouri River, in Hughes, Buffalo, and Lyman counties, which the party first passed on September 20 and 21, 1804.

3. On a nameless island at the lower end of the Big Bend; see Clark's entry for this day for a discussion of the possible identification of this island.

Thursday 28th August 1806. a fair morning. we Set out as usal and procd. on about 11 oClock A. M. we arived at pleasant Camp where we Camped about 20 of Sept 1804. we Camped[1] here to hunt. Several hunters went out.[2] we gathered an emence Site of plumbs which are now ripe and good. Several of the men went at dressing deer and goat skins to make themselves cloaths &C. &C. in the evening our hunters returnd had killed 2 buffaloe three deer one porcupine and Several bearking Squerrells the Musquetoes troublesome &C.

1. The party had camped here September 16–18, 1804, near Oacoma, Lyman County, South Dakota.

2. Clark names the various personnel sent hunting.

Friday 29th August 1806. a little rain. Several hunters went on with Small canoes to hunt. about 10 A. M. we Set out and procd. on passed the hunters. one of them had killed a deer. we Still procd. on about 3 P. M. we halted and killed Several buffaloe and deer, and procd. on untill evening and Camped[1] on S. Side our hunters came up had killed Several more buffaloe & deer. we Save all the buffaloe horns we can find to take to the States as they would make excelent kife and fork handles &C &C.—

1. In Lyman County, South Dakota, a little below Round Island and the camp of September 13, 1804. The party passed the White River, in Lyman County, this day.

Saturday 30th August 1806. we set out eairly and procd on as usal abt. 9 A. M. we halted and killed one buffaloe and 2 deer. the buffaloe verry pleanty. procd. on Some distance further halted and killed two Elk and gathered a quantity of fine plumbs. then procd. on. three of our hunters[1] Stayed back with a Small canoe to try and kill Some black taild deer. about [*blank*] oClock P. M. we discovred a number of Indians on the hills on the North Side, and Soon gathered about two hundred on the Shore besides Some boys and young men they were in a body and had a great number of horses we landed on the opposite side of the river. the Savages hooping and fired & we answered them by fireing our blunderbusses and Small arms

2 rounds. we concluded to wait here for the hunters to come up. a number of Indians Set to Swiming the river to us but Capt. Clark took three men[2] in a Small canoe met them on a Sand bar which happened to be near our Side one of our men Spoke to them in pania tongue and told them that we could not Speak their Language but Soon found that they were the Same band of Tetons[3] that held our boat as we passed up the river Capt. Clark told them and Signed to them that they were bad Indians and treated the white people bad and they might keep from us for we would have nothing to Say to them nor Suffer them to come to our Canoes. they then Signed to the rest of the nation to keep back and Capt. Clark returnd. the most of the Indians returned to the nation 2 or three Stayed on the bar a while and Signed that they were friends to us and wished to have us come over to their Side but we Signed to them to keep off and to go back that we would not hear them &C. they then all returned to the band and called over to us. Mrs. Jessom[4] could understand Some words they said and he heared them Say that if we came on their Side of the river they would kill us & that we were good for to kill &C. at length the Savages or the main body of them went their way our hunters came up had killed three black taild deer. we then set out and procd. on several Indians remaining on Shore called to us and Signed and beckned to us to come to Shore but we passed them Safe and procd on untill dark and Camped[5] on a large Sand bar two Sentinels placed to guard the Camp.—

1. The Field brothers and Shannon, according to Clark.
2. Probably Cruzatte and Labiche, and possibly either Jusseaume or Lepage.
3. The incident with the Teton Sioux occurred on September 25, 1804.
4. Ordway may mean "Mr." here or he may have been using a form of "Messrs." incorrectly. Another possibility is that Jusseaume's wife was aiding in the communication.
5. Between Gregory and Charles Mix counties, South Dakota, in the vicinity of later Hot Springs Island, now inundated by Fort Randall Reservoir.

Sunday 31st August 1806. we had hard Showers of rain all last night and verry high winds caused one of our canoes broke loose and I took another canoe and to take it back and with Some difficulty goot it back to Camp[1] a verry disagreeable night. we Set out this morning as usal and roed on hard all this day without makeing any halt to cook. Musquetoes where we Camped[2] on N. Side—

1. Clark adds some detail to this event.

2. In Charles Mix County, South Dakota, near the mouth of Chouteau Creek, which marks the county line.

Monday the 1st day of September 1806. a fair morning. we Set out eairly and procd. on two hunters[1] went on with a Small canoe to hunt about 9 A. M. we passd. the mo. of rapid water river[2] a Short distance below we Saw nine Indians on the N. Shore which run out of a thicket five of them had guns the others bows & arrows. they Signd. to us to put to shore but we floated a short distance below a point at an open place as we expected they were the Tetons as Soon as we halted we heard Several guns fire we expecting that the Indians were fireing at our hunters who were behind Capt. Clark Instantly run up with 10 men but soon returned with the Indians and found that they had been fireing at a kegg we had thrown out above and our hunters came up Safe. we found these to be Yanktons[3] Nation & good Indians and friends to us our officers Smoaked with them and gave them a bushel of corn & Some ribben and then we procd. on towards evening we killed a fat Elk on an Island. in the evening we Camped[4] on a Sand beach N. Side opposite to this Camp we Counceled with the yanktons or babruleys[5] on the last of August 1804. Some Musquetoes this evening.

1. Perhaps three men, the Field brothers and Shannon, according to Clark.

2. The Niobrara River joins the Missouri in Knox County, Nebraska; the party first passed it on September 4, 1804.

3. The Yankton Sioux are discussed at Clark's entries of August 28–31, 1804.

4. The party had camped at the Calumet Bluff in Cedar County, Nebraska, from August 28 to September 1, 1804, and counciled with the Yanktons. Now they camped opposite in Yankton County, South Dakota.

5. Ordway means Bois Brulé Sioux; see Clark's entry of August 28 and September 24, 1804.

Tuesday 2nd Sept 1806. a fair morning. we Set out eairly and procd. on passed the mouth of River Jaque.[1] Saw gangs of Elk got Some good pipe clay about 11 A. M. the wind rose So high a head that it detained us untill towards evening. the hunters killed two buffaloe and 2 Turkeys The Musquetoes So troublesome that we mooved down a Short distance and Camped[2] on a Sand beach for the night.—

1. The James River, first passed on August 27, 1804, meets the Missouri in Yankton County, South Dakota.

2. A few miles below James River. It is unclear whether they are on the Nebraska side in Cedar County or the South Dakota side in Yankton County.

Wednesday 3rd Sept. 1806. we Set out and procd. on as usal. the day warm & Sultry. towards evening we passd. the Calimet bluffs a Short distance below we met an American trador by the name of Herd.[1] he had two Batteaux and 18 hands and are on their way to the babruleys and yanktons near white Stone River[2] in order to trade with those nations and the Mahars also— Mr. Herd informed us of the news of the States &C a verry hard Storm of wind and hard rain this evening.[3]

1. James Aird, a Scotsman, who was now considering himself an American citizen for trading purposes; see Clark's entry for this day.

2. The Vermillion River reaches the Missouri in Clay County, South Dakota, southeast of the town of Vermillion.

3. The site of the party's camp for the night is unclear. It would have been some miles upriver from Sioux City, Iowa, on either the Nebraska or South Dakota side.

Thursday 4th Sept. 1806. a fair morning, but the hard rain and Thunder continued the greater part of last night. the Musquetoes troublesome. Mr. Herd Gave us a berril of flour although he had a boat Sunk and nearly all his provisions lost but they have a good hunter hired for that purpose a malattoe &C. we gave them a quantity of corn which the Mandans gave us. Mr. Heard gave us Some tobacco &C &C we Set out Soon after Sunrise and procd. on verry well towards evening we arived at the Mahars village[1] found that this nation were out a hunting but had fields of corn growing at the back part of the bottom where they formerly had a large village but were cut off in a great measure by the Small pox Some years ago. So we Camped[2] here and dryed our baggage which got wet last night, &C the Musquetoes verry troublesome indeed.—

1. The Omaha village they had visited on August 13, 1804, just north of Homer, Dakota County, Nebraska.

2. In either Woodbury County, Iowa, or Dakota County, Nebraska. Ordway fails to mention that some of the party visited Floyd's grave this day and covered it again after it had been opened by some Indians.

Friday 5th Sept. 1806. a fair morning. we were routed at day light by the Musquetoes. we Set out and procd. on verry well without making any delay. we having made 75 miles this day and Camped[1] on a Sand beach to git as much out of the Musquetoes as possable.—

1. In Monona County, Iowa, a few miles south of Onawa.

Saturday 6th Sept. 1806. a fair morning. we Set out eairly and proceeded on about noon Saw a large flock of pillicans Some of the hunters killed three of them Shortly after we met a batteaux manned with 12 frenchman a canoe in compy this keel Boat belonged to Mr. Shoetoe[1] of St. Louis and is under charge of a frenchman and are going up to the yanktons at a wintering house below white stone river they gave us a little whiskey. I traded for a hat and Shirt by giveing them beaver Skins. our officers purswaded them not to trade with the Tetons nation we delayed about 2 hours and procd. on. Some of the hunters Stayed back to hunt and did not join us this evening. Camped.—[2]

1. René Auguste Chouteau. The possible identity of the leader of the boat party is discussed in Clark's entry for this day.

2. In either Harrison County, Iowa, or Burt or Washington County, Nebraska, between the Little Sioux and Soldier rivers.

Sunday 7th Sept. 1806. a pleasant morning. the party Set out eairly leaving me with my canoe to wait for the [hunters] we waited untill abt. 10 A. M. then hearing a blunderbuss fired a head as a Signal that the hunters were a head. So we Set out and followed on the wind So high that we could Scarsely proced. about 2 oClock P. M. we overtook the party who had halted to hunt as the wind was So high. the Hunters killed 4 Elk and caught three large catfish which was fat. towards evening the wind abated So that we procd. on untill after Sunset and Camped[1] on a sand beach. the Musquetoes not So troublesome as they have been for a long time past.

1. In either Harrison County, Iowa, or Washington County, Nebraska, near Blair, Nebraska.

Monday 8th Sept. 1806. a fair morning. we Set out eairly and procd. on verry well Gibson killed a deer from his canoe. the logs & Sawyers are pleanty in this part of the Missourie we having made 58[1] miles this day Camped[2] 12 miles above R. Platte

1. Clark says seventy-eight.
2. At the White Catfish camp of July 22–27, 1804, near the Mills-Pottawattamie county line, in Iowa.

Tuesday 9th Sept. 1806. a fair morning. we Set out eairly and procd. on. Soon passed the mouth of River platte and procd. on verry well all day without making any delay. having made 74[1] miles this day. Camped[2] on South Side opposite bald pated prarie the musquetoes Scarse &C.

1. Clark has it seventy-three.
2. In either Nemaha County, Nebraska, or Atchison County, Missouri, northeast of Peru, Nebraska, depending on the course of the Missouri River at the time. The bald-pated prairie was first noted on July 16, 1804.

Wednesday 10th Sept. 1806. a fair morning. we Set out as usal, & procd. on verry well one of the hunters killed a rackoon Saw a number of Turkeys about 3 P. M. we met four frenchmen[1] with a canoe loaded with goods going up trading. they gave us a dram we then procd. on untill evening and Camped[2] on an Island.

1. Clark gives one man's name as Alexander "La fass" but later spells it "la frost."
2. About four miles above the mouth of the Big Nemaha River, in either Richardson County, Nebraska, or Holt County, Missouri.

Thursday 11th Sept 1806. A Showery morning. we Set out and procd. on verry well untill about 11 A. M. we then halted to hunt a Short time.

found pappaws[1] and grapes in this bottom which is covred with cotten Honey Locus Seckamore timber &C. the rushes thick. Drewyer killed a large deer. we then procd. on. one of the hunters killed a deer from his canoe. at dusk we Camped[2] on a Sand beach on the N. Side.—

1. Pawpaw, *Asimina triloba* (L.) Dun.

2. On Nodaway Island in either Andrew or Buchanan County, Missouri. The island was first noted on July 8, 1804.

Friday 12th Sept. 1806. a foggy morning. we Set out as usal and procd. on about 9 A. M. we met 2 two canoes and 11 frenchman 1 of which was loaded with Mr. Shotoes goods from St. Louis the others going up trapping one of the men was along which accompanied us to the Mandans in 1804. he informed us that Mr. McLanen is but a Short distance a head below the hunters killed a bear we then procd on Soon met one of McLanens Hunters who gave us a fat buck he came on board, and we procd a Short distance and met Mr McLanen[1] with a large keel Boat which roed with 12 oars he was rejoiced to see us only two Englishmen beside Mr. McLanen the rest frenchman. Mr. Gravveleen & Mr Drewyong[2] was with him. this keel Boat was well loaded down with Marchandizes and is going up to the Marhars and yanktons to winter their. we mooved across the river and Camped[3] on N. S. 2 Small canoes Sent on a head to hunt. Mr. McLanen gave our officers wine and the party as much whiskey as we all could drink. Mr. McLanen informed us that the people in general in the united States were concerned about us as they had heard that we were all killed then again they heard that the Spanyards had us in the mines &C.[4] Mr. Gravveleen & Mr Drewyong had orders to make all enquiries for us. Mr. Gravveleen took a chief of the Rickarees[5] on to the Seat of government & he died their and Mr. Gravveleen has got the presents for his nation. Mr. Drewyong took Several Indians of the yanktons and Mahars down to St. Louis and as Capt. Stoddard was absent who had orders to Send all Indians on they were not Sent on and are now on their return. Mr. McLanen informed us that the Spanyards or Spain towards Mexico had broke out against the u. States and have killed a party of americans who went to See their country, and that all or a great number of troops had gone down to New orleans and up red river where a great number of Spaniards have gathred in a body for war. Some of our party exchanged robes &C. for Shirts. we had Small Showers of rain this evening, and we were treated in the best manner by this party.—

1. Robert McClellan, who was already known to the captains; see Clark's entry for this day.

2. Pierre Dorion, Sr.

3. At St. Michael's Prairie, Buchanan County, Missouri, near St. Joseph; it was first noticed on July 7, 1804.

4. Only Ordway reports this information on this date. Clark has something similar on September 17, 1806.

5. There is some confusion about the identity of this individual; see Clark's entry of October 9, 1804.

Saturday 13th Sept. 1806. a fair morning. Mr. McLanen Gave our party as much whiskey[1] as they would drink and gave our officers three bottles of wine and we took our leave of them and Soon after Sunrise we Set out and procd. on Soon overtook the hunters who killd. nothing the wind being high and as we were out of meat we detained along at different places to hunt and killed five deer, and Camped[2] having made but a Short distance this day.—

1. Clark says that each man received a dram.

2. In either Buchanan County, Missouri, or Doniphan County, Kansas.

Sunday 14th Sept. 1806. a fair morning. we Set as usal and procd. on Soon passed the old village of the Kansers.[1] Some of the hunters killd. Several deer from their Canoes about 3 oClock P. M. we discovred three keel Boats Sailing up the river. we put to Shore Spread our flags they Sailed up to us and halted with us a Short time they were tradors from St. Louis and frenchman but could Some of them Speak English. they are bound for the Mahars nations. they gave us ardent Spirits buiscuits and cheese &C. onion we then procd. on Gibson Shot an other deer from his canoe at dark we Camped[2] on N. Side.—

1. Probably the village of the Kansa, or Kaw, Indians, noted on July 2, 1804, near Ft. Leavenworth, northeast Leavenworth County, Kansas.

2. Near Leavenworth, Kansas.

Monday 15th Sept 1806. a fair morning. we Set off at eight and procd. on the wind a head as usal. our hunters shot a buck Elk from their canoe on the lower point of an Isld. and was fat. we took the meat on board and procd. on towards evening the hunters Shot a buck from their canoe. we have seen about 20 deer on the shores this day we Camped[1] at Sunset on N. Side an emence Site of pappaws & as the men were gathering them Saw a number of rattle Snakes and killed one of them and saved the skin.

1. The party passed the Kansas River this day and camped above the mouth of the Little Blue River on the opposite side in Clay County, Missouri.

Tuesday 16th Sept 1806. a fair morning. we procd. on as usal Soon met eight frenchman with a perogue loaded with marchandize and bound for the Panies Nation on River platte. about noon we met a keel Boat and 2 canoes the keel Boat belonged to Mr. Reubado of St Louis loaded with marchandize and bound for the Kanzas Nation of Indians. this boat was under the charge of Mr Reubados Son.[1] the 2 Canoes were going up trapping and hunting we delayed about an hour. their was about 20 frenchman in Company. our officers gave instructions to this trador after reading his passport directing them not to speak against the government of the United States to the Indians as his brothers did to the Zotoes last winter. we then procd. on the day verry warm indeed. about 3 P. M. we passd a hunting Camp of two frenchman they came out to us with their canoe to us they informed us that an american Boat was on their way coming up Some distance below this. we procd. on untill evening and Camped[2] on the N. Side. Saw a black bear which run a thicket of bushes.

1. Perhaps Joseph Robidoux, but several members of the Robidoux family were fur traders out of St. Louis. See Clark's entry of this day.
2. Between Carroll and Lafayette counties, Missouri, a few miles up the Missouri River from Waverly.

Wednesday 17th Sept. 1806. one of the men caught a large catfish last night which is juded to weigh a hundred weight. a fair morning. we Set out eairly and proceeded on verry well soon passd. riffle Isld. and a Short distance below at the petzaw Island[1] we passd through a verry bad part of the river which was filled So thick with logs Standing on end & Sawyers that we only found room to pass through. about 2 oClock P. M. we met a large Boat Commanded by one Capt. McLanen[2] loaded down with Marchandize about 15 hands & an Intrepter & Clark [clerk]. they are bound for the Spanish Country by way of River platte to the panies Indians & purchase horses and cross the Mountains leaving their goods on this Side and git the Spaniards to come and bring their silver & gold and trade it for goods as they are full of money and no goods among them of any account. and if Mr. McLanen has Success this voiage no doubt but that trade will be advantageous to the United States hereafter. we aired our baggage &C Several of our hunters Sent a head with 2 Small canoes to hunt. in the evening Mr. McLanen gave our party as much whiskey as they would drink and we Camped.[3] Mr. McLanen gave us a bag of Buiscuit &C.—

1. Clark does not name this island on either the outbound or inbound journeys and Ordway's designation is unclear. Clark does speak of the Missouri's turbulence at this point, which would be in the area of Malta Bend, Saline County, Missouri. See the captain's entry for this day and for June 15, 1804.

2. John McClallen or McClellan; see Clark's entry for this day.

3. They camped four miles above the mouth of Grand River on the south side of the Missouri River, according to Clark. That would put them in Saline County.

Thursday 18th Sept. 1806. a clear morning. we gave Mr. McLanen a kegg of corn. took our leave of him & his party and Set out early and proceeded on Soon passd. the Mouth of Grand river. Soon after we overtook our hunters they had killed nothing So we procd. on all day without detaining to hunt Saw a fiew Turkeys gathered Some pappaws which the party in general are fond of. in the evening we Camped[1] on an Island.—

1. Opposite the entrance of Lamine River (Ordway's "Mine River" of the next entry), which joins the Missouri in Cooper County, Missouri, a few miles above Booneville.

Friday 19th Sept. 1806. a fair morning. we Set out at light and procd. on Soon passed the mouth of Mine River. Saw a number of Turkeys but we being anxious to git down do not detain to hunt. gathered Some Pappaws which our party are fond of and are a kind of fruit which abound in these bottoms and are now ripe. in the afternoon one of the hunters killed a deer. late in the evening we arived at the Mouth of Osage River & Camped[1] having made 84 miles this day.

1. The mouth of the Osage River is at the Osage-Cole county line, Missouri. Clark has the party make seventy-two miles this day.

Saturday 20th Sept. 1806. as Several of the party have Sore eyes[1] & unable to work, our officers concluded to leave 2 Small canoes which was done as we had room for the men without them. we Set out eairly and proceeded on met a canoe & Several frenchman[2] going up this R. trapping. nearly Sunset we arived in site of St. Johns or Charette village[3] fired three rounds and was answered by Some boatsman who lay at this place & by the people of the village we Camped here here is 4 batteaux bound for the Mahars & other Indians our officers got 2 gallons of Whiskey for which they had to pay eight dollars an extorinatable [extortionate] price they got us some pork Beef and flour &C. the french people gave us Some milk &C &C.

1. Perhaps from infectious conjunctivitis or related to the diet of pawpaws, the handling of which can cause dermatitis. See Clark's entry of September 19, 1806.
2. The rather complicated discussion of the men's identities is discussed at Clark's entry for this day.
3. La Charette, Warren County, Missouri, since washed away by the Missouri.

Sunday 21st Sept. 1806. we Set out as at the usal time and procd. on passed the Scattering houses along the Shores. met a great number of Indians in canoes mooving up the River. the people of the Settlements were makeing inqueries of us & were Surprized to See us as they Said we had been given out for dead above a year ago. towards evening we arived at St. Charles fired three rounds and Camped at the lower end of the Town. the people of the Town gathered on the bank and could hardly believe that it was us for they had heard and had believed that we were all dead and were forgotton. the most of the paty got quarters in Town and refreshments. late in the evening hard rain commend. and continued hard during the night.

Monday 22nd Sept. 1806. the hard rain continued this morning untill about 11 Oclock A. M. at which time the party was collected and we Set out & procd. on towards evening we arived at Bell fountain[1] a Fort or cantonement on South Side which was built since we ascended the Missouri & a handsome place. we moovd. a short distance below and Camped, the Company of Artillery who lay at this fort fired 17 Rounds with the field peaces the most of our party was Quartered in the Canonment. Several flat Boats are built at this place. Some rain this evening. a number of these Soldiers are aquaintances of ours &C.

1. Fort Bellefontaine, Saint Louis County, Missouri, was established in 1805 by General James Wilkinson; it was the first United States fort west of the Mississippi.

Tuesday 23rd Sept. 1806.[1] a wet disagreeable morning. we Set out after breakfast and procd. on Soon arived at the Mouth of the Missourie entered the Mississippi River and landed at River deboise where we wintered in 1804. here we found a widdow woman who we left here & has a plantation under tollarable good way Since we have been on the Expedition we delayed a Short time and about 12 oClock we arived in Site of St. Louis fired three Rounds as we approached the Town and landed oppocit the center of the Town, the people gathred on the Shore and Huzzared three cheers. we unloaded the canoes and carried the baggage all up to a Store house in Town. drew out the canoes then the party all considerable much rejoiced that we have the Expedition Completed and now we look for boarding in Town and wait for our Settlement and then we entend to return to our native homes to See our parents once more as we have been So long from them.— finis.

1. The entry ends near the bottom of a page, then follows three blank pages, a table of "Estimated Distance" (reading back to front) across four pages, another blank page, and a final list of memoranda of two pages (also reading back to front), thus ending Ordway's third and final notebook of his journal of the expedition. The table of distances is similar to another one by Ordway found with his entry of October 10, 1804 (see also Clark's tables at the end of vols. 3 and 8 of this edition). The table reads as follows:

Estimated Distance in Miles from Mandans to Mo. of Missourie of remarkable places from one to the other.

	miles	
From Mandans to a old Ricara village	20	
Chiss cheter River	38—	58
Fish Creek	35	
Cannon ball R	5	
Wann na car ne R	13	
Stone Idle Creek	40	
To [Rictars?] village	18—	111
To We-ter-hoo—R	8	
Sar-war-nar-na R	25	
La-hoo-catte Isld.	37	
Chyannee River	43—	113
Teton River	47	
To Cedder Island	37	
To the big bend	23	
To the 3 Rivers of Souix pass	50	
White River	22	
Shannons Creek	7	
Island of Cedar	45	
Dome of Burrowing Squirrells	42	
Poncar River	20	
Quicurre R	8	
antient fortification	24	
Calumet Bluffs	18	
River Jacque	10	
white Stone R.	32	
Grand River de Souix	60	
Floyds River	3	
Mahars village	13	
war-car de Creek	48	
Little Rivr. Souix	55	
Soldiers River	44	
Council Bluffs	39	
Bowyers River	12	
Musquetoe Creek	28	
River Platte	10	
weeping water	32	
Blad pated Prarie	29	
Little nemahar	23	
Nesh-nah-ba-tone R.	8	
Big Ne-ma-har R	28	
wolf River	10	
Nodawa Rivr.	16	

	miles	
St. Michaels prarie	20	
Independence Creek	28	
old Kanzas village	28	
Little rivr. plate	30	
Kanzas River	10	
Blue water Rivr	9	
Coal Banks	10	
Hay cabin Creek	7	
Fire Prarie	12	
Eue berts Creek	14	
Tigers Creek & Isl.	15	
Little osage village	25	
Snake Creek	12	
Grand River	8—	225
2 Charitons Rivr.	22—	230
arrow prarie	14	
Mine River	8—	208
Good woman R	9	
Manitow River	9	
Salt River	10—	180
Split rock Creek	3	
Manitow Creek	9	
lead mine hill	9	
Cedar Creek & Isl.	10	
Morrow Creek	7	
Osage River	5—	137
Muddy River	19	
Gasconade R	15—	103
Shepperds C	19	
Chaurette village	15—	69
Cave Tavern	22	
Osage womans R	5	
Good mans C	9	
St. Charles	12—	21
To Mississippi or wood River—	21	

Ordway filled the final two pages of the notebook (reading backwards) with memoranda on Pacific Coast Indian trade. Due to wear and fading the material is barely legible. The following are words and phrases that are readable:

[Camped?] opposite to the Mouth of Quick Sand River 3rd day of April in the year 1806

A Memorandum of the best Indian trade on the Columbia River & on the Coast the Savages are more numerous about this plan than [*illegible*] Coast

Tobacco is valued the highest amongst them all   one of our party bought a Sea otter Skin for less than half a carrit &c

Blue beads white beads or green beads large fishing hooks for Sturgeon &c &c   large whole Buttons large needles &c

Brass rist bands trinkets of any kind large [*illegible*] of any kind Ear bobs &c

Files large or small Iron or Steel &c

Brass twisted wire [*illegible*] twegers &c

White linen or blue or red cloth

[Blankets?] Blue cloaths   Shirts of any kind

Muskets powder & led Balls &c.

Ther is many kinds of Morchandiz which they know nothing about nor know not the use of & will not buy   they have but little to trade of value   the Sea otter Scarce Some [Beaver?] and common otter Skins etc. dryed [Elk skins?]   Some Seal by giged by them [*illegible*] Skinning [*illegible*]

pelate pallow and [*illegible*] nations west Side of the [Rocky?] Mountains have horses with [*illegible*] for Sale   the goods [which?] they want for them is follows. Small light [*illegible*] mounted guns powder & balls, brass or copper kittles Small or middling Size knives Beeds blue & white   blue is Set the [first?] by all Indians in this [region?]   red cloath calicoes &c   Squaw axes tommahawks medl. awls Buttens tin cups & pans [*illegible*] of copper or brass trinkets or Combs   Silk linen lace or [twill?] white [*illegible*] of different kinds   Red paint needles Swords or big knives [*illegible*] of Iron & files of which they make arrow points to Suit themselves &c   war axes is in great demand as they purchase a fiew from the Indians on the Missourie.   [*illegible*] wide quality or binding but ribbens & tape is of no account among them but they will trade for anything that they know is of Service to them. I think twezers would be a fine thing as they pluck ther beards and ey brows all out [*several words illegible*]

Part 2: The Journal of Charles Floyd

Chapter Forty-Eight

Up the Missouri

May 14–August 18, 1804

A Journal[1] commenced at River Dubois— monday ⟨14th 180⟩ may 14th 1804 Showery day Capt Clark Set out at 3 oclock P m for the western expidition the party Consisted of 3 Sergeuntes and 38 working hands which maned the Batteaw and two Perogues we Sailed up the missouria 6 miles and encamped on the N. side of the River

1. Floyd's journal is a notebook of fifty-six numbered pages of text and eighteen unnumbered blank pages, covered in marbled boards, and 7½ by 5⅞ inches in size. It includes Floyd's due bills, his journal of the expedition with some writing by Clark within the entries, and then miscellaneous notes by Floyd. On the inside front cover of the journal, preceding this entry, is the following:

Recd. of Monsier Pier Shierker 5 Carrtts of tobacko at 3 s/o d per peece $ 2.50
Mayse Corn & Dolce Due .50

	ONail	2	Carrits	$1	dollr	P. Gass	G. for T.
Decemb	Newman	1	Do.	50	Cents	Jos. Field	G. for T.
8th	Shields	1	do.	50			
1803	Gibson	1	do	50			
				$2.50	Cents		

March 13 1804
Renued ouer Journey began our voyage much feteged after yester day worke

The persons mentioned above may be identified as follows: "Shierker" is probably Jean Pierre Chouteau; the remainder were members of the party, Hugh McNeal (perhaps), Gass,

John Newman, Joseph Field, Shields, and Gibson. "Carrits" are carrots, or rolls, of tobacco. The entry for March 13, 1804, cannot be expanded on since no journals for other members of the party exist for this date. It would appear that Floyd was on a trip with Clark during this time, yet on the back inside cover of this journal Floyd notes that he purchased the notebook on this date at River Dubois. See also Clark's entry of March 21, 1804, and the Weather Diary entry for March 19, 1804. Before the first page of Floyd's journal are the stubs of three sheets. On the reverse of the second sheet are the words: "Shore— mile the fam of the Hassas thare we ⟨luft⟩." On the obverse of the third sheet are these words: "our Dog + 2 miles I [lared?] ⟨on the in the⟩." Given the damage to the journal at this point, the transcription here is uncertain. Floyd's time, numbers, and distance vary from those of Clark and others for this day.

Tuesday may 15th 1804 Rainey mornig fair wind the Later part of the day Sailed som and encamped on the N. side Some Land Cleared the Soil verry Rich—

wensday may 16th 1804 Set out eriley this moring plesent arrived at St. Charles at 2 oclock P m one Gun Fired a Grait nomber of Friench people Came to see the Boat &c this place is an old French village & Roman Catholeck Some amerrican setled in the Countrey around.

Thursday may 17th 1804 a fair but Rainey Night

Friday may 18th 1804 we Lay at St Charles

Saturday may 19th 1804 a Rainey day Capt Lewis Joined us—

Sunday may 20th 1804 ⟨saved a number of the party went to St [Charles] and saw them [*illegible*] and S⟩ nothing worth Relating to day

monday 21st 1804 Left St Charles at 4 oclk. P m Showerey encamped on the N Side of the River

Tuesday may 22d 1804 Set out after a verry hard Rain and passed Bonnon Creek on the South Side of the River came 15 mi[les] encamped on the N. Side of the river at cliftes Some Indianes Came to See us wensday may the 23d 1804 we Set out at 6 oclock Am plesent day passed the wife of Osoge River three miles and half we pased the tavern or Cave a noted place on the South Side of the River 120 Long 20 feet in Debth 40 feet purpendickler on the South Side of the River high Cliftes one mile to a ⟨Crke⟩ Creek Called tavern Creek and encamped on the South Side of the River our armes and amunition Inspected

Thursday may 24th 1804 nothin Remarkable ⟨as we⟩ Nothing ocord this day encamped on South Side

Friday may 25th 1804 Set out and Came 4 miles passed a Creek Called Wood River on the South Side the Land is Good & handsom the Soil Rich & high Banks encamped at a French village Called St Johns this is the Last Setelment of whites on this River—

Saturday may 26th 1804 we Set out at 7 oclock A m 2 of our men[1] was Sent with the Horses by Land to meat us that night hard thunder and Rain this morning passed a creek Called otter Creek encamped on the N. Side

1. Drouillard and Shields.

Sunday may 27th 1804 pased ash Creek— on the South Side high Clifts on S Side arrived at the mouth of the Gasganade Rivber at 5 ock P. m on the South Side encamped on an Island oppeset the mouth of the River which is a handsom Situation high hiles on the Left Side the Bottom is of Good quallity &c. armes and ammunition Inspected—

monday may 28th 1804 rain Last night Severall men went out hunting &c. one of them Killed a Deer

Tuesday may 29th 1804 Rain Last night Set out at 5 ock P m ⟨[c]ame 3 miles encamped⟩ Came 3 miles pssed Deer Creek on the S. Side encamped all Night Jest above on the South Side on[e] man Lost hunting French men Left for him

Wednesday may ⟨30th 1804 wedneday Set out after a verry har rain Last night Rained all the with thunder and hail⟩ wedsday 30th 1804 Set out 7 ock after a very hard Rain and thunder it Rained During the Gratiest part of the day with hail passed one Creek on the South Side Called Rush Creek the Land is Low Bottom but Rich Soil 3 miles to River on the N Side Colled Littel muddy River the Land is Some what Like the Loer, it comes in opset an Isld 2 miles to River on the South Side Colled painter River[1] it Comes in opset to Isd. in the midel of the missoura encamped South side at the mouth—

1. Evidently Ordway's Panther Creek, which is probably Deer Creek, Osage County, Missouri.

thursday may 31th 1804 one perogue Loaded with Bare Skins and Beav and Deer Skins from the osoge village[1] one osoge woman with them our hunters went out and Kild one Deer we Lay By all this day on acount of the Wind the Land is Good but Broken it Rained and Cleard up nothing worth Relating to day

1. The village would probably have been at the Osage River in western Missouri. The Osage Indians are discussed at Clark's entry of this day.

Friday June 1t 1804 Set out come one mile past one River on the N Side called Big mudy River comes in opset the Louer pint of willow Island the Land is of Good quallity as aney I ever saw but Low two miles to Bear Creek on the South Side High Hill on the Loer Side it is about 30—yardes in weth at the mouth of ⟨water very Strong past Several Isld. Came 23 miles encamped at the mouth of the Gran Osage River the wind from the west the day Clear⟩ the day Clear wind from the west water strong Came 12 miles past several Islds encamped at [3? 4?] oclk at the mouth of the Grand osoge River

Saterday June 2d 1804 Lay By all this day for observations 4 men went out hunting Killed 4 Deer the day was Clear wind from the South the Land is of a Good quality High hiles on the S. Side a good Lick on the South S. Side it is about one mile and half from the mouth of the Gran osoge Dow the River a Butifull pint Betwen the two Rivers hills in the pints in about a mile Betwen the two the Second Bank is high at the mouth of this River in the pint a Butifull Isd. Jest Below the pint it Lays in the midel of the Rivers our hunters Return how had Ben with our horses 8 day and Say the country is as Good as aney they ever saw armes inspected all in Good order the missorea is 875 yardes wide osage River 397—yardes wide we fell a nomber of trees at the pint for the porpas of oberservations.

Sunday June 3d 1804 Set out at 4 oclock P. m the for part of the day Clear the Latter part Clouday with thunder and Rain wind from Est. Capt Lewis and G. Drureay[1] went hunting Kild one Deer & Grown hog 4 miles to River murrow on the South Saide it is about 30 yardes wide and High Cliftes on the Loer Side of it 3 hundrered yardes up the River Cliftes encamped at the mouth on the South Side ouer hunters Kild one Deer

1. Drouillard.

monday June 4th Set out the Clear morning 2 miles Byouer Stersman[1] Let the Boat Run under a lim and Broke our mast off 3 miles past a Creek on the South Side Called mast creek[2] ⟨on the S Side no name for it but I cal it Rich Land Creek at⟩ a Butifull a peas of Land as ever I saw walnut shoger tree ash and mulber trees[3] Level land on both sides. this Creek is Clear watter about 30 yardes wide one mile past a River on the N. Side called Sidder River[4] the Land is Level and good 4 miles past Creek Called Zon Cer on the S. Sid at the loer pint of Isld. on the same 3 miles to a pint on the N Sd Called Batue De charr[5] a prarie on the S Sid high Cliftes on the South Side ouer hunters Kild & Deer Strong water came 10 miles encamt on the South Side under the Cliftes ⟨Set out⟩

1. Perhaps Cruzatte or Labiche, probably the former, although Clark calls the man a sergeant.

2. Evidently Grays Creek, Cole County, Missouri.

3. Floyd's list of trees varies somewhat from the tree lists of Clark and Ordway. His trees are probably black walnut, the sugar tree may be either sugar maple, *Acer saccharum* Marsh., or silver maple, *A. saccaharinum* L., an unknown ash, and probably red mulberry.

4. Cedar Creek, near Cedar City, Callaway County.
5. See the rather complicated discussion of this term at Clark's entry for the day.

Tusday June 5th fair day pased Lead Creek on South Side of the River— Littel Good woman Creek on the N. Side Came 9 miles past the Creek of the Big Rock 15 yads wide at a 11 ⟨mil⟩ oClock we met 2 French in 2 conoes lashed together Loaded with peltry &c. they Came from 80 Leages up the Kensier River whare they wintered water Strong past Severall Isd. Came 15 miles encamped on the N. Side at the uper pint of Isd. the land is Good well timberd well waterd ouer hunters Kild one Deer

wensday June 6th 1804 Set out 6 oclock after ouer mast mended 4 miles past a Creek on the N Side Called Rock Creek on the Loer Side Blow Cliftes 3 miles past Sallin Creek ⟨Big Lick⟩ on the South Side ⟨Below⟩ Cliftes on the Loer Side water good the fore part of the day the Latter part Strong came 18 miles ouer hunters Kild one Deer encampet on the N Side ⟨the midel way of Isd.⟩

thursday 7th June 1804 Set out 5 oclock Came 2 miles past Som [s]prings Comes out of Clifte 2 miles past a Creerk on the N Side Called the River of the Big Devil one mile past a rock on the N. Side whare the pictures of the Devil and other things We Kild 3 Rattel Snakes at that Rock 5 miles to Creek on the N Side Called ⟨pon⟩ Good woman Creek Strong watter past severall Isd. George Druer [*X: George Drewyer or Druillard.*] [1] Kild one Bar⟨e⟩ encampet at the mouth the Land is Good well timberd, &c.

1. The interlined spellings of Drouillard's name and the underlining (not shown) of Floyd's "George Druer" were added in red ink by unknown hand.

Friday June 8th Set out erley this morning the day Clear wind from the west Came 5 miles past 2 Canoes Lasht to Gather Loaded with Bever Skins otter Skins from the Littel River [1] mean thay ar 30 day coming from that place 5 miles past the mouth of the Big River mine [2] it is about 100 and 50 yardes wide a butifull ⟨S⟩ River on the South Side the Land is Good first Rate Land well timberd this River is navagbl for Som hundreds miles aperintley water Strong past Several Isd. Came 10 miles ouer hunters Kild 5 Deer encamped on ⟨an⟩ the Loer pint of an Isd and on the South Side of the River

1. The traders were apparently coming from the Big Sioux River, which forms a boundary between Iowa and South Dakota.

2. Lamine River, at Booneville, Cooper County, Missouri.

Saturday June 9th 1804 Set out ⟨of⟩ after a verry hard Rain Last night the morning Clear wind from the Est Came 5 miles past the Prarice of arrows on the South Side half m. past the mouth of arrow Creek on the South Side this Creek is 8 yads wide this is a butifull Contry of Land the River at this place is 300 yads. wide the current Strong 3 mls past Black Bird Creek[1] on the N Side high Hills on the loer Side the Latter part of the day Couday with Rain maid 10 miles encampt on an Isd. in the middel of the River

1. Evidently Richland Creek, Howard County, Missouri.

Sunday June 10th 1804 we imbarked at the yousel ouer and proseded on our Jorney 5 miles past a Creek Called Deer Lick Creek on the N Side 10 yads wide the Land High ⟨Hel⟩ Delayed 1½ ouers three mls past the two Charlitons on the N. Side those Rivers mouth near togeathe the first 70 yads wide the Next 100 yads wide and navagable for Some Distance in the Cuntry halted and Capt Lewis Killed a Buck the Current is Strong a bout this place Came 12 miles past Severall Isd. ouer hunters Killed 3 Deer incamped on the South Side at a priara this priara is High well and well waterd &c. ⟨monday June 11th 1804 day Clear wind from the N W⟩ ouer hunters Kilded nothing ⟨2 Bare and two Deer⟩

monday June 11th 1804 Day Clear wind from the N. West Lay By all Day on account of the wind the Latter part of the day Clouday ouer hunters Kiled 2 Bar & 2 Deer

Tuesday June 12 1804 we Set out at the Usial ouer the day Clear wind from the west Came 4 miles past a Creek on the S. Side Called *Plumb Creek* about 20 yads wide the timber in this Bottoms is Cotten wood 2 miles when we met ⟨two⟩ 5 Cannoes from the ⟨Shoue Sue⟩ Soux nations Loaded with peltry and Greece thay have been 13 mounthes up the missorea River Delayed ½ day with the French, Bought Some tallow of them ouer hunters Did not Rettern Last night one French man hiard to go with us up the missorea who can Speak the Difernt [languages?] encamped on the N. Side the Land Good Bottom

wensday June 13th 1804 Set out at 6 oclock and Came 1½ miles past a Creek on the N. Side Calleded River missorea[1] Just above the Creek a Large Praria of Good Land on the N Side at this Praria antient Missourie Indianes had a village[2] at this place 300 of them were Killed by the Saukees[3] in former times[4] a fair day past the Grand River on the N. Side ⟨the⟩ Land is level on Both Sides a handsom Prarie on the Loer Side of it water Strong past Several Isd. Came 10 miles the Grand River is about 300 and 50 yads wide and Boates Can Go for Som hundreds of miles up it ouer hunters Killed yesterday and to day 1 Bar, 2 Deer encampted at the mouth of the Grand River on the N. Side of the River

1. Perhaps Palmer Creek, Chariton County, Missouri. Floyd's name, somewhat strange, is not used by others; Clark called it (with other streams at this point), "round bend Creeks."

2. The Missouri, or Missouria, Indians when first noticed in 1673 had a village at this place at the mouth of the Grand River.

3. Sauk Indians.

4. "Missourie Indianes" and the passage of "village at this place . . . in former times" was underlined in red by an unknown hand.

Thursday June 14th 1804. we Set out at the usuel ouer and proseded on our Jorney day Clear water Strong Came 3 miles ⟨past⟩ met 2 Conoes with 3 French men and one Negro [*X: Mallatto*] from the Poncye[1] Nations. they have ben up 3 years with the Indianes 2 of them is half preades of the poncas. past a Creek on the N. Side Called the Snake Creek it is about 25 yads wide a noted place whare Indianes ⟨Cross⟩ of Differnt nations to

Go to ware they Say that thar is hundreds of Snakes at this place ouer hunters killed one Deer encamped on the N Side of the River the Land is good about hear the Chief of the timber is Cotten wood.

1. Pawnee Indians.

Friday June 15th we Set out at 5 oclock ⟨of te⟩ after much Feteaged of yesterdays works pased a Creek on the South Side Calleded Indian Creek ⟨no⟩ it is about 15 yards wide Good Level Land ⟨eneo⟩ ouer hunters Killed 4 Bars and 3 Deer Strong water encampt on the N Side opset to antent old villag of Missures Indians[1] but the ⟨Indian village famley lived the ossage but the⟩ Saukies beng two trobelsom for them was forst to move and take protections under the Gran ossags[2] as they war Redused Small handsom a prarie as ever eney man saw the river is 3 miles wide hear

1. Gumbo Point site, Saline County, Missouri; see Clark's entries for this date and for June 13, 1804.
2. Grand, or Great, Osage Indians.

Saurday June 16th wes Set out ⟨of⟩ at 8 oclock day Clouday with rain nothing Remarkeble to Day water verry Srong past one place whare the water Roles over the Sand with grait fall and verry Dangeris for Boats to pass past Severall Isld. maid 10 miles ouer hunters Did not Return Last night encamped on the N Side of the River the Land is Good hear and well timberd

Sunday June 17th we Renued our Journey much fetegeued of yesterday's work Came one mil encamped for the purpos of maken ores for ouer Boat and make a rope for the pursos of towen on the North Side of the River ouer hunters Returnd and Killed on Bar one Deer and found a Stray Horse who had Been Lost for sometime nothing Remarkeble to day

Monday June 18th Clouday ⟨day N⟩ with Rain and Thunder and wind ⟨N. W⟩ from the Est the Land at this Bottom is Good Land the timbr is Cotten wood ouer hunters Killed one Bar 5 Deer nothing worth Relating

Tusday June 19th Set out at 8 oclock day Clouday wind from the Est Sailed past a Creek on the South Side Calleded tabor Creek it is about 40 yards wide and Clear water below High Hills Good Land well timberd past Several Isds Strong water Came 13 miles encamped on the South Side of the River ouer hunters Did not Return Last night

Wensday June 20th 1804 Set out ⟨as yousel late⟩ Clouday day Rain, Srong ⟨late⟩ water past Several Isd. Came 12 miles ouer Hunters Did not Return Last night encamped on an Isd in the middel of the River

Thursday June 21th Set out at 7 oclock Clear day past 2 Creeks on the South Side Callede *Deubau* Creeks they com in opset the middel of Isd ⟨at the opper pint of the Isd.⟩ the water at this Isd. is verry Strong the Land is Good and ⟨High⟩ well timberd on the South Side the Land high that on the N. is Low ⟨Bottom⟩ Land the timber is Cotton wood water Strong past Several Isd. Came 9 miles ouer hunters killed one Deer encamped on the South Side at the opper pint of isd. the Land is Low that on the N. is High Land.

Friday June 22d Set out at 7 oclock after a verry hard *Storm* thunder ⟨wind from the N. E.⟩ and Rain wind [*WC: from the West, proceeded on under a gentle Breeze from the N. W. passd*] ⟨from the N. E. past⟩ a Creek on the South Side Calleded the Littel Fire Creek it Comes in opset the middel of a Small Isd on the South Side Strong water Came 9 miles encamped on the Southe Side at a Prarie this Prarie is Called Fire on the N. Side Comes in a Creek Calleded the Big Fire Creek the Creek is about 50 yards wide and High Land

Saturday June 23rd a Small Brese from the N. W ⟨Set out day Clouday⟩ Set out at 5 oclock day Couday Came 3 miles Landed on acount of the wind from the N. W. armes and amunition ⟨examend⟩ enspcted all in Good order Capt Clark went hunting Did not Return Last night ⟨ouer Hunters Killed 2 Deer encamped on an Isld. Sunday June 24th Set out day Clear wind from⟩ [*WC: we continued on this Island all Day & night*] but Returnd erley in the morning Killed one Deer ouer Hunter Killed one

Bear 4 Deer. they encamped on an Isd on the N Side ⟨[*WC: we crossed a Sand bar where the water was So Short that we were obliged to Haul over the boat, Incamped on the L. Side below an Island*]⟩

Sunday June 24th 1804 Set out ⟨erley⟩ at 5 oclock A.m. wind from the N. E. Sailed Day Clear passed a Creek on the South Side Called Hay Creek it is about 40 yards wide Clear water Land High and Good well timberd Delayed 2 ouers to Dry some meat Capt. Lewis [*WC: & my self*] went hunting Kild one Deer [*WC: & a Turkey*] passed a Creek on the North Side Called Charriton Creek[1] it is about 30 yards wide passed a Creek on the Same Side Called the Creek of the Bad Rock[2] it is not far below the other it is about 15 yards wide the Land is High and well timberd ouer Hununters Killed 8 Deer water Good made 13 miles encamped on the South Side the Land is Good first Rate Land, [*WC: On this pt. of the River we observe feeding on the Banks & the adjasent ⟨Monday⟩ Praries— imince Hurds of Deer, Bear is also plenty in the bottoms.*]

1. Perhaps Rush Creek, Clay County, but its order with the next stream mentioned may be reversed.

2. Perhaps Big Shoal Creek, Clay County, but perhaps out of order with Floyd's previous stream; see Clark's entry for this day.

Monday June 25th we Set out at 8 oclock after the Fogue was Gon, [*WC: pass a Coal mine on the South Side above a Small Island, a Small Creek below which takes its name from the bank of Coal, and large Creek at about one Mile higher up the River on the Same Side Called (un batteur La benne River)*] [*X: passed several small Islands on the South Side. Some hard water, & camped on a small Island near the North Side Capt Lewis killed a Rabit, R. Fields a Deer this eving our Flanking party did not join us this evening (my hand is painfull)*]

[*X: Tuesday June 26th we set out early proceeded on passed a Island on the South Side, back of this Island a large Creek coms in call'd Blue Water Creek (River Le Bléue) The Hills or High lands on the River which we passed last evening & this morning on L. S. is higher than usial from 160, to 180 feet.*] Encampt at the mouth of the Kansas River in the pint it comes in ⟨oppeset⟩ on the Southe Side wensday June 27th ⟨Stayed hear⟩ Lay By all this day ⟨day Clouday⟩ ouer Hunters Killed 5 Deer

Thursday June 28the Lay By all that Day the Kansas River is 200 30¼ Yards wide at the mouth the Land is Good on Booth Sides of thes Rivers and well timberd well waterd

Friday June 29 Set out at Half past 4 oclock P. m. from the Kansas River proseeded on passed a run on the South Side, at the mouth of Kansas River armes and amunition enspected all in Good order encampt on the N. Side Late in the evning

Saturday June 30th 1804 Set our verry early this morning Saw a wolf on the Sind Bare passed the Littel River platte on the N. Side it is about 100 yards wide Clear water High Land on the Loer Side of it on this River it is Sayed that thare is a nomber of ⟨fowl⟩ falls on it fitting for mills the land is Rolling campt on the South Side the Land is Low that on the N is the Same.

Sunday July 1th 1804 Set out Clear day passed Small Creek on the South Side Called Biscuit C. High Land passed a Creek on the S. Side Called Frog Tree Creek[1] a Pond on the N S. Called the Same name Good water made 12½ miles Campt on an Isd. near the South Side ouer Flanken party Did not Join us Last evning.

1. Perhaps either Ninemile Creek or Fivemile Creek, Leavenworth County, Kansas.

Monday July 2d Set out verry early this morning passed on the Left of the Isd. parque &c High butifule Situation on the South Side the Land indifferent Lands a Creek Comes in on the ⟨So⟩ N Side called parkques Creek passed a creek on the N— Side called Turkey Creek High Landes came 10 miles campt on the N Side, ⟨on the South Side was a old French fort in former times the old Kansas village on the Back of this village in High Hills of Prarae Land T⟩ on the South Side was a old French fort[1] who had Setled hear to protect the Trade of this nation in the valley the Kansas Had a village between tow pints of High ⟨Lands⟩ Praria Land a Handsom Situation for a town

1. Fort de Cavagnial, or Cavagnolle, active from 1744 to 1764, about three miles north of Fort Leavenworth.

Tuesday July 3dth Set out verry erley this morning under a Jentel Breas from the South found a Stray Horse on the South Side Havg Had Ben Lost for Som time water verry Strong So Hard that we Could Hardley Stem it Came 10 miles Campt on the South Side the Land is verry mirey

Wensday July 4th 1804 Set out verry erley this morning passed the mouth of a Beyeu leading from a Lake on the N. Side this Lake is Large and was once the Bead of the River it reaches Parrelel ⟨with⟩ for Several miles Came to on the South Side to Dine rest a Short time a Snake Bit Jo. Fieldes on the Side of the foot which Sweled much apply Barks to [Cooverod?] passed a Creek on the South Side a bout 15 yards wide Coming out of an extensive Prarie as the Creek has no name and this Day is the 4th of July we name this Independance a Creek above this Creek the wood Land is about 200 yards Back of these wood is an extensive Praria open and High whigh may be Seen Six or Seven below saw Grat nomber of Goslins to day nearley Grown the Last mentioned prarie I call Jo. Fieldes Snake prarie Capt Lewis walked on Shore we camped at one of the Butifules Praries I ever Saw open and butifulley Divided with Hills and vallies all presenting themselves

Thursday July 5th 1804 Set out errley this morning Swam ouer Stray Horse a Cross the River to Join our other Horses prossed on for two miles under the Bank of the old Kansas village formaley Stood in 1724 the couse of the Indians moving from this place I cant ⟨tell⟩ Larn but natreley Concluded that war has reduced thair nation and Compelled them to Retir further in to the Plaines with a view of Defending themselves and to operserve their enemey and to Defende them Selves on Horse Back encampt on the South Side

Friday July 6th 1804 Set out prossed under a Jentell Brees from the South west the water wase So [s]trong that we Could Hardley ⟨Sewe⟩ Steem it, ⟨passed a Creek⟩ Came 12 miles encampt at the mouth of a Creek on the South Side of the River Called Whipperwill Creek it is 15 yards wide

Saturday July 7th Set out errley prosed along, passed Some Strong water on the South Side, which Compelled us to Draw up by the Cord Clear morning verry warm Strong water Came 10 miles Camt on the N. Side[1]

1. Clark and Ordway have the party on the opposite shore; either way, they were a little upstream of St. Joseph, Buchanan County, Missouri.

Sunday July 8th Set out at Sun Rise Rain Last night with wind from the E. passed some Good Land to day and High passed a Creek on the N. Side it Cam in Back of Islad it is a Bout 70 Yards wide Called Nadawa Creek the Land is Good and well timbrerd Camt on the N. Side

Monday July 9th 1804 Set out erley this morning prosed on passed a Small Creek on the South Side Called monter Creek High Land Rain to day Sailed the Gratist part of the day passed a prarie on the South Side whare Seveal French famileys had Setled and made Corn Some Years ago ⟨and Black Smith or Gun Smith⟩ Stayed two years[1] the Indians came Freckentley to See them and was verry frendley passed a Creek on the South Side Called wolf Creek it is about 60 yards wide the Land is Good water Strong made 10 miles encamt on the South Side Saw a fire on the N. Side thougt it was ⟨Indians⟩ ouer flanken partey Sent ouer perogue over for them and when they got over Saw no fire Seposed it to be Indians fired ouer Cannon for ouer men

1. Either Cruzatte or Labiche, but not Shields, the man usually called the blacksmith.

Tuesday July 10th Set out when we Could See, about us, when we Came to the place it was ouer men which had Left us two days ago, much feteged had Lay down and fell asleap passed a Small Creek on the South Side Called pape Creek it Comes through Bottom Land it is Called after a man who by drawning his Gun out of the Boat Shot him Self passed Som Strong water Campt on the north Side the Land is good

Wendesday July, 11th 1804. Set out errley this morning prosed on passed a Creek on the N. Side Called Tarcio Creek it Comes in Back of a Isd. on the N. Side Came to about 12 oclock P. m for the porpos of resting on[e] or two days the men is all Sick encamt on an Isd. on the Southe Side floos in Creek Called Granma ⟨maugh⟩ mohug Creek[1] it is about 100 yards wide the Land is good and well timberd High and well Waterd this ⟨R⟩ Creek Runs up and Heds near the River platt—

1. Big Nemaha River, Richardson County, Nebraska.

Thursday July 12th Som Hunters out on the No. Side those on the South Side not Return Last night ouer object in Delaying hear is to take Some observations and rest the men who are much fategeued, armes and amunition enspected all in Good order—

Friday July 13th Set out erley in the morning prosed on our Jorney passed a Creek on the N. Side Called the Big ⟨ne ma har⟩ Tarkuo River it is about 40 yads wide and verry mirey for Horses to Cross the Land is Low a verry hard Storm Last night from the N. E. which Lasted for about one ouer proseded with a Small Souer of Rain wind fare Sailed all day Came 20½ miles Camt on a Sand Bare in the midel of the River a Small Shouer of Rain

Saturday July 14th 1804 Set out at day Lite Came one mile and ½ Came a Dredfulle hard Storme from the South which Lasted for about one ouer and half which Cosed us to Jump out and hold hir She Shipt about 2 Barrels of water Came one mile the wind fare Sailed, passed a Creek on the N Side Called Neeshba Creek it is about 40 yards wide the Land is Low encamt on the Southe Side—

Sunday July 15th 1804 Set out at Six oclock A. m pased a Creek on the South⟨e⟩ Side Called Plumb Run water verry Strong passed a Creek on the South Side Called Nemahaw Creek it is about 30 yards wide the Land is High and Good. encamt on the South⟨e⟩ Side

Monday July 16th we Set out verry early and prossed on the Side of a Prarie the wind from the South Sailed ouer Boat Run on a Sawyer Sailed all day made 20 miles passed Sevrall Isd Camt on the North Side

Tuesday July 17th 1804 Lay by all this day for to kill Som fresh meat Capt Lewis & Go. Druger[1] went out Hunting Drugher Killed 3 Deer the Land is prarie Land the Blufs puts in about 2 miles from the River and all prarie Land betwen which Runs up and Down for Som distance ⟨to⟩ from 20 to 30 miles

1. Drouillard again.

⟨Thursda⟩ Wendesday July 18th 1804 we Set out at Sun Rise the day Clear wind fair Sailed the Side of the Prarie Hear we toed for about 5 or 6 miles the Elke Sine is [v]erry plenty Deer is not as plenty as it was below passed Som High Clifts on the South Side Which hase the apperence of ⟨ore⟩ Iron ore the Clay is Red passed a verry Strong pace of Water. Saw a Dog on the Bank Which we Sepose to be Indians had ben Lost this is the first Sine of Indians we have Saw Camptd on the South Side the Land is Low that on the N. Side is prarie Land

Thursday July 19th we Set out errly this morning prosed on passed a Run on the South Side Has no name we Called Cherry Run[1] the Land is High Cliefts and ⟨bore⟩ pore whare a Grate nomber of thos Cherres ⟨frute groe⟩ thay Gro on Low Bushes about as High as a mans hed Came 9 miles past Several Isd. water Strong Campt on the South Side on a Small willow Isd. near the South Side the Land on the N. is Low Land that on the South is High prarie Land

1. Floyd is the only person to apply this name to either North Table Creek or South Table Creek.

Friday July 20th Set out at 6 oclock proseded on passed he mouth of a Creek on the South Side Called Crys Creek it is about 35 yards wide it Comes in above Clifts oppset a willow Isd. at this Clift thare is a fine Spring on the top of this Hill is oppen prarie passed a Creek on the N. Side Called Piggen Creek[1] the Land is Low ⟨passed⟩ that on the South is High prarie Land passed Several Bad Sand Bares. Campt ⟨am⟩ on the South Side under a Large Hill

1. Not mentioned by the other enlisted men and crossed out in Clark's journal; it is Wabonsie Creek, Fremont County, Iowa.

Saturday July 21th 1804 Set out at 4 oclock a m prossed on ouer Jouney. Rain this morning wind fair Sailed passed the mouth of the Grait River Plate on the South Side it is much more Rappided than the missorea it is about ⟨3½ Three quarters of a mile⟩ [*X: from one mil to 3 miles*] wide the Sand Roles ⟨or⟩ out and formes Large Sand bares in the middel of the missorea up the Plate ⟨of⟩ about one mile the Hilles of Prarie Land about 2 days and half up the Plate 2 nations of Indians Lives vic The Souttoes the Ponney[1] this River is not navigable for Boats to Go up it passed a Creek Called the [*blank*] on the South Side it is about 20 yardes wide it Comes out of a Large Prarie Campt on the South Side

1. Oto and Pawnee Indians.

Sunday July 22d Set out verry erley this morning prossed on in Hopes to find Some wood Land near the mouth of this first mentained River but Could not we prossed on about 10 miles at Lenth found Som on Both Sides of the River encampt on the North Side

monday July 23d 1804 we Lay By for the porpos of Resting and take Som observations at this place and to Send for Som Indians Sent George Drougher and ouer ⟨entarp⟩ Bowsman[1] wo is aquainted with the nations nothing worth Relating to day

1. Cruzatte.

tuesday July 24th we mad Larg. and Long fags Staff and Histed it up Histed ouer Collars in the morning for the Reseptions of Indians who we expected Hear when the Rain and wind Came So that we wase forst to take it down Sent ⟨on⟩ Some of ouer men out to Hunt Some ore timber for us to make Some ores as the timber of that Coind is verry Carse up the River Continued Showery all day

Wendesday July 25th Continued Hear as the Capts is not Don there Riting ouer men Returnd whome we had Sent to the town and found non of them at Home but Seen Some fresh Sine of them.

⟨Thuresday July 27th we Set out at 12 oclock P. M prossed on under a Jentil Brees from the S. E. sited⟩ Thursday July 26th ouer men fineshed the oares nothing worth Relating except the wind was verry villant from the South Est—

Friday July 27th Swam ouer Horses over on to the South Side on acount of the travilen is beter Set out at 12 oclock P. m prossed on under a Jentell Brees from the South Este Sailed made 10 miles encamt on the South Side at Prarie

Satturday July 28th Set out verry erley this morning prossed on passed a Creek on the ⟨South⟩ North Side Called Beaver Creek[1] is about 20 yrds wide the Land is Low that on the South is Prarie Land Rain the fore part of the day the Latter part Clear with wind from the North Est. made 10 miles Campt on the N. Side the Land is Low that on the South is High prarie Land ouer flanken partey Came with one Indian thay found on the South Side

1. Probably the creek that Clark and others called Indian Knob Creek, apparently Pigeon Creek, Pottawattamie County, Iowa.

Sunday July 29th we Set out after we Dspashed the Indian and one of ouer men[1] with him to bring the Rest of his party the Reasen this man Gives of His being with So Small a party is that He Has not Got Horses to Go in the Large praries after the Buflows but Stayes about the Town and River to Hunte the Elke to Seporte ⟨His⟩ thare famileys passed the mouth of Boyers River on the N. Side it about 30 yards wide the Land is Low Bottom Land out from the River is High Hills Campt on the North Side at a prarie

1. La Liberté, who would abandon the expedition.

monday July 30th Set out verry erley this morning Cam 3 miles Sopt for the man whome we Had Sent with the Indian yesterday He has not Returnd Yet ⟨Campt⟩ Sent 2 men out Hunting Did not Return Last night Campt on the South Side at prarie

Tuesday July 31th 1804 we Lay By for to See the Indianes who we expect Hear to See ⟨us⟩ the Captains. I am verry Sick and Has ben for Somtime but have Recoverd my helth again The Indianes have not Come yet this place is Called Council Bluff 2 men went out on the 30th of July and Lost ouer horses

Wendesday august 1th 1804 Lay by all this day expecting the Indianes every ouer Sent George Draugher out to Hunt ouer Horses Sent one man[1] Down the River to whare we eat Diner on the 28th of July to See if aney Indianes ⟨were⟩ Had been thare He Returnd and Saw no Sigen of them

1. Gibson, according to Whitehouse.

Thursday auguste 2dth Ouer men ⟨hav⟩ hough we had Sent after ouer Horses Returnd With them and Killed one Elke. ⟨the Indian⟩ ouer men Killed 3 Deer to day the Indianes Came whare we had expected thay fired meney Guns when thay Came in Site of us and we ansered them withe the Cannon thay Came in about 2 hundred yardes of us Capt Lewis and Clark met them at Shakeing Handes we fired another Cannon— thare was ⟨Six⟩ 6 Chiefs and 7 men and one French man[1] with them who has Lived with them for som yeares and has a familey with them—

1. This man's identity is unknown, but possibilities are discussed at Clark's entry for this date.

Friday august 3dth the Council was held and all partes was agreed the Captens Give them meney presents thes is the ottoe and the Missouries The Missouries is a verry Small nathion the ottoes is a very Large nathion So thay Live in one village on the Plate River after the Council was over we took ouer Leave of them and embarked at 3 oclock P. m under Jentell Brees from the South Est. Sailed made 6 miles Campt on the South Side the Land Low, that on the N. prarie Land—

Satturday august 4th 1804 Set out erly this morning after the Rain was over it Rained Last night with wind and thunder from the N. W. it Lasted about an ouer prossed on the morning Clear passed a Creek on the South Side ⟨Colled⟩ as it has no name and the Council was Held below it about 7 miles we Call it Council Creek or Pond[1] this Creek Comes out of a Large Pond which Lays under the High prarie Hills the wood Land is not plenty hear ondley along the River Banks in places, passed Som bad Sand bares en[c]amt on the South Side a Large prarie that on the N. is prarie Land

1. Floyd was the only one to use this name for what is apparently Fish Creek, near Blair, Washington County, Nebraska.

Sunday august 5th Set out erley this morning Cam 2 miles when a verry hard Storm of wind and Rain from the North ⟨West⟩ Est it Lasted about 2 ouers and Cleard up I have Remarked that I have not heard much thunder in this Countrey Lightining is Common as in other Countreys a verry Large Snake was Killed to day Called the Bull Snake his Colure Somthing Like a Rattel Snake passed Severall Bad Sand bares made 16 miles Campt on the North Side at Som wood Land that on the South is woo Land

monday August 6th 1804 we Set out at a erley ouer this morning prossed on passed a Creek on the N. Side Called Soldiers Creek it Comes in Back of a Isld near the N. S. about 12 oclock Last night a villant Storm of wind and Rain from the N. W— Camt on the South Side the Land Low that on the N S. the Saim

Tuesday August 7th Set out at 6 oclock A. m prossed on day Clear wind from the North west— on the 4th of this month one of ouer men by the name of Moses B. Reed went Back to ouer Camp whare we had Left in the morning, to Git his Knife which he Had Left at the Camp ⟨bout⟩ the Boat went on and He Did not Return, ⟨pore⟩ that night nor the Next day nor Night, pon examining his nap-Sack we found that he had taken his ⟨Cal⟩ Cloas and all His powder and Balles, and had hid them out that night and had made that an excuse to Desarte from us with out aney Jest Case we never minded the Said man utill the 7th we Sent 4 men after him we expect he will make for the ottoe town as it is not mor than 2 days Jorney from whare he Run away from us ⟨made 16 miles⟩ Water Good made 16 miles Campd. on the ⟨South⟩ North Sid at Some Wood Land

Wendesday Augt. 8th 1804 Set out this morning at the usele time day Clear wind from the N. W. prossed on passed the mouth of the Littel Soue River on the N. Side it is about 80 yards wide this River is navigable for Boates to Go up it for Som Distance in the Cuntrey and Runes parelel with the Missourie 2 miles above on a Sand Bare Saw Grait ⟨qu⟩ Nomber of Pelicans Capt Clark went out on the South Side a ⟨and Jo Colline⟩ and ⟨one man the⟩ Jo Colines Killed on Elke water Bad mad 12 miles Campd. on the N. Side the Land is Low march Land that on the South is prarie Land

Thursday augt the 9th Set out at 7 oclocks a, m, ⟨we could see about us the⟩ after the fague was Gon which is verry thick in this Cuntrey Capt. Clark and my Self went out on the South side passed a verry Bad place in the River whare the water is verry Shellow mad 17 miles Campd. on the South Side at prarie

⟨Set out errley ouer this morning⟩ Friday augt the 10th Set out at errley ouer this morning prosed on passed a bad Sand bare which is verry Shallow made 23 miles Camped. on a sand bare on the N. Side the Land on the S. S. is High Hilley Land

Satturday august 11th 1804 Set out after a verry hard Storm this morning of wind and Rain continued untill 9 oclock A m. and Cleard up prosed on passed *a high Bluff*[1] whare the Kinge of the Mahas Died *about 4 yeares ago*[2] the Hill on which he is berred is about 300 feet High the nathion Goes 2 or 3 times a year to Cryes over him Capt Lewis and Clark went up on the Hill to See ⟨him⟩ the Grave thay histed a flage on his Grave as ⟨present⟩ noner [honor] for him which will pleas the Indianes, passed the mouth of a Creek on the South Side Called Waie Con Di Peeche or the Grait Sperit is Bad[3] whare this Chief ⟨Didd⟩ died and about 300 Hundred of his men with the Small pox this Chiefs name was *the Black Bird*[4] made 15 miles Camped on the North Side

1. These words are underscored in red ink.
2. These words are underscored in red ink.
3. Blackbird Creek, Thurston County, southeast of Macy. Floyd repeats "the Grait Sperit is Bad" in the left-hand margin.
4. These words are underscored in red ink.

Sunday august 12th 1804 Set out at the usel time prosed on under a Jentel Bres from North Est Sailed day Clear passed Red Seeder Bluffs on the South Side ⟨this the first Seeder we have Seen Sence we Left the S⟩ made 16 miles Camped on a Sand bare in the middel of the River

monday august 13th Set out verry erley this morning prosed on under a Jentel Brees from the South Est— Sailed ⟨day C⟩ morning Clouday about 10 ock, it Cleared up we aRived at the Mahas village about 2 oclock P. m Sent Som of ouer men to Se if aney of the natives was at Home thay Returnd found none of them at Home

Tuesday august 14th Lay by for ouer men How we had Sent after the Desarter on the 7th thes Indians ⟨onley live at this village⟩ has not Live at the town Sence the Smallpoks was So bad abut 4 years ago thay Burnt thare town and onley live about it in the winter and in the Spring Go all of them in the praries ⟨of⟩ after the Buflow and dos not Return untill the fall to meet the french traders thay Rase no Corn nor aney thing excep Som times thay

Rase Som Corn and then the Ottoe nation Comes and Cuts it Down while thay are in the praries

Wendesday august 15th Capt. Clark and 10 of his men and my Self went to the Mahas Creek[1] a fishen and Caut 300 and 17 fish of Difernt Coindes ouer men has not Returnd yet

1. Possibly Omaha Creek, Dakota County, Nebraska (identified as Pigeon Creek and incorrectly as in Thurston County in notes for Clark's entry).

Thursday august 16th Capt Lewis and 12 of his men went to the Creek a fishen Caut 709 fish Differnt Coindes

Friday august 17th Continued Hear for ouer men thay did not Return Last night

Satturday augt 18th[1] ouer men Returnd and Brot with them the man and Brot with them ⟨3⟩ the *Grand Chief* of the *ottoes*[2] and 2 Loer ones and 6 youers of thare nathion

1. This is the last daily entry in Floyd's journal; two days later he was dead. See the Introduction in this volume. Following this entry are eighteen blank pages, then a single page with the following:

the 22thd June
Charles Floyd
Winser ⟨1⟩ ⟨G.⟩ 22thd
R. Field ⟨2⟩ ⟨G.⟩ 22thd
J. Field ⟨3⟩ Gard for thompson 16th July
Newman 4
Gass ⟨5⟩ Gard for Thompson
mcNiel ⟨6⟩
thompson ⟨7⟩

And on the inside back cover is this material:

Chas. Floyd Baught at River Debaus 13th March 1804
Thomas M. Winn
Thomas M

Thamis Thomis
Thomas M. Winn
Elaxander Willard
George Shannon—
william Leboach
Lasuness
Pall—
Jos Whitehouse

These persons may be identified as: Windsor, Reubin Field, Joseph Field, Newman, Gass, McNeal, and Thompson, all members of the party. Thomas M. Winn is unknown, as is "Pall." Willard, Shannon, Labiche, La Jeunesse, and Whitehouse were also members of the party.

2. These words are underscored in red ink.

Sources Cited

Aoki, Haruo. *Nez Perce Dictionary*. University of California Publications in Linguistics No. 122. Berkeley, 1994.

Betts, Robert B. " 'The writingest explorers of their time': New Estimates of the Number of Words in the Published Journals of the Lewis and Clark Expedition." *We Proceeded On* 7 (August 1981): 4–9.

Chuinard, Eldon G. *Only One Man Died: The Medical Aspects of the Lewis and Clark Expedition*. Glendale, Calif.: Arthur H. Clark, 1979.

Clarke, Charles G. *The Men of the Lewis and Clark Expedition: A Biographical Roster of the Fifty-one Members and a Composite Diary of Their Activities from All Known Sources*. Glendale, Calif.: Arthur H. Clark, 1970.

Culin, Stewart. *Games of the North American Indians*. 1907. Reprint. 2 vols. Lincoln: University of Nebraska Press, 1992.

Cutright, Paul Russell. *A History of the Lewis and Clark Journals*. Norman: University of Oklahoma Press, 1976.

Moulton, Gary E., ed. *Atlas of the Lewis and Clark Expedition*. Lincoln: University of Nebraska Press, 1983.

Jackson, Donald, ed. *Letters of the Lewis and Clark Expedition with Related Documents, 1783–1854*. 2d ed. 2 vols. Urbana: University of Illinois Press, 1978.

Peebles, John J. "The Return of Lewis and Clark." *Idaho Yesterdays* 10 (Summer 1966): 16–27.

Quaife, Milo Milton, ed. *The Journals of Captain Meriwether Lewis and Sergeant John Ordway Kept on the Expedition of Western Exploration, 1803–1806*. Madison: State Historical Society of Wisconsin, 1916.

Ronda, James P. "Frazer's Razor: The Ethnohistory of a Common Object." *We Proceeded On* 7 (August 1981): 12–13.

Wheeler, Olin D. *The Trail of Lewis and Clark, 1804–1806*. 2 vols. New York: G. P. Putnam's Sons, 1904.

Index